Palgrave Studies in Nineteenth-Century Writing and Culture
General Editor: **Joseph Bristow**, Professor of English, UCLA

Editorial Advisory Board: **Hilary Fraser**, Birkbeck College, University of London; **Josephine McDonagh**, Kings College, London; **Yopie Prins**, University of Michigan; **Lindsay Smith**, University of Sussex; **Margaret D. Stetz**, University of Delaware; **Jenny Bourne Taylor**, University of Sussex

Palgrave Studies in Nineteenth-Century Writing and Culture is a new monograph series that aims to represent the most innovative research on literary works that were produced in the English-speaking world from the time of the Napoleonic Wars to the *fin de siècle*. Attentive to the historical continuities between 'Romantic' and 'Victorian', the series will feature studies that help scholarship to reassess the meaning of these terms during a century marked by diverse cultural, literary, and political movements. The main aim of the series is to look at the increasing influence of types of historicism on our understanding of literary forms and genres. It reflects the shift from critical theory to cultural history that has affected not only the period 1800–1900 but also every field within the discipline of English literature. All titles in the series seek to offer fresh critical perspectives and challenging readings of both canonical and non-canonical writings of this era.

Titles include:

Palgrave Studies in Nineteenth-Century Writing and Culture
Series Standing Order ISBN 978–0–333–97700–2 (hardback)
(*outside North America only*)

You can receive future titles in this series as they are published by placing a standing order. Please contact your bookseller or, in case of difficulty, write to us at the address below with your name and address, the title of the series and the ISBN quoted above.

Customer Services Department, Macmillan Distribution Ltd, Houndmills, Basingstoke, Hampshire RG21 6XS, England

---

Women in Journalism at the *Fin de Siècle*

Making a Name for Herself

Edited by

F. Elizabeth Gray
Senior Lecturer, Massey University, New Zealand

palgrave
macmillan

First published 2012 by
PALGRAVE MACMILLAN

Palgrave Macmillan in the UK is an imprint of Macmillan Publishers Limited,
registered in England, company number 785998, of Houndmills, Basingstoke,
Hampshire RG21 6XS.

Palgrave Macmillan in the US is a division of St Martin's Press LLC,
175 Fifth Avenue, New York, NY 10010.

Palgrave Macmillan is the global academic imprint of the above companies
and has companies and representatives throughout the world.

Palgrave® and Macmillan® are registered trademarks in the United States,
the United Kingdom, Europe and other countries.

ISBN 978–0–230–36171–3

This book is printed on paper suitable for recycling and made from fully
managed and sustained forest sources. Logging, pulping and manufacturing
processes are expected to conform to the environmental regulations of the
country of origin.

A catalogue record for this book is available from the British Library.

A catalog record for this book is available from the Library of Congress.

10 9 8 7 6 5 4 3 2 1
21 20 19 18 17 16 15 14 13 12

Printed and bound in Great Britain by
CPI Antony Rowe, Chippenham and Eastbourne

This book is dedicated to my mother, Pamela Anne Gray,
with love and gratitude:
you have helped light my way

Contents

Acknowledgements

First and foremost, the editor wishes to express her heartfelt appreciation to the contributors to this volume for their keen interest, their rigorous scholarship, and their comradely collaboration. It has been an unmitigated pleasure working with you on this project.

The editor would like to acknowledge the financial assistance provided by Massey University, New Zealand, in the form of a University Women's Award (2009–10), which helped in the preparation of this book. Thanks are also due to the School of Communication, Journalism and Marketing for teaching support while I was deeply engaged in the writing and editing process, and to Nicky McInnes in particular, for finding solutions to seemingly insoluble problems. Debbie Gamble's careful bibliographical work and eye for detail in the late stages of preparation of the manuscript were much appreciated. Hannah Benson's creativity and talent made an invaluable contribution to the volume's design.

Warm thanks are due to Drs Nikki Hessell, Ingrid Horrocks, and Sarah Ross, who read sections of this manuscript, were interested and supportive at every stage of the process, and offered kind, shrewd, invaluable advice. Thank you for being, as always, 'the better craftswomen'. Thank you to my parents, Murray and Pam Gray, and particularly to my mother, whose passionate interest in pioneering women has helped inspire me.

Thanks from my heart to my husband, Nigel Edgecombe, collaborator in all I do and my coauthor in the most joyous production of my life.

Notes on Contributors

Dr. Brenda Ayres is a full professor and member of the graduate faculty, and Assistant Honors Director at Liberty University in Lynchburg, Virginia, where she teaches nineteenth-century English literature. Her publications include over 100 articles plus the following books: *The Life and Works of Augusta Jane Evans Wilson*; *The Emperor's Old Groove: Decolonizing Disney's Magic Kingdom*; *Silent Voices: Forgotten Novels by Victorian Women Writers*; *Frances Trollope and the Novel of Social Change*; and *Dissenting Women in Dickens' Novels: The Subversion of Domestic Ideology*. Through Pickering and Chatto, she was the general editor for two four-volume series, *The Social Problem Novels of Frances Trollope* and *The Widow and Wedlock Novels of Frances Trollope*, as well as series editors for several of the novels in those series and for Jessie Fothergill's *Kith and Kin*.

Lee Anne Bache is a PhD candidate in English at Indiana University, Bloomington. Her research focuses on the British nineteenth century, particularly the novel and women's changing experiences of the object world. She has presented her work at conferences including BWWC, NAVSA, NACBS, and MLA.

Fionnuala Dillane teaches and researches nineteenth-century and contemporary literature at the School of English, Drama and Film, University College Dublin. She has published articles on George Eliot, nineteenth-century journalism and contemporary Irish poetry and provided 25 entries for the *Dictionary of Nineteenth-Century Journalism* (2008). She is editor, with Ronan Kelly, of *New Voices in Irish Criticism 4* (Dublin: Four Courts Press, 2003). Recent publications include: 'Re-reading George Eliot's "Natural History": Marian Evans, "The People" and the Periodical,' *Victorian Periodicals Review* 42, no. 3 (2009): 244–266. She is currently completing a monograph on George Eliot's work as an editor, journalist and serial fiction writer.

Terri Doughty teaches Victorian literature, children's literature, and fantasy at Vancouver Island University, British Columbia, Canada. She has edited *Selections from the Girl's Own Paper 1880–1907* (Broadview, 2004) and published book chapters on New Woman fiction, Victorian girls' adventure stories and emigration propaganda, and on children's and young adult fantasy literature. Her current research interests include Victorian girls' periodicals and New Girl fiction.

Alexis Easley is Associate Professor of English at the University of St. Thomas in St. Paul, Minnesota. Her first book, *First-Person Anonymous: Women Writers* *and Victorian Print Media*, was published in 2004. Her second book, *Literary Celebrity, Gender, and Victorian Authorship*, was published by Delaware UP in 2011. Easley's articles have appeared in *Victorian Poetry*, *Victorian Literature and Culture*, *Victorian Periodicals Review*, and other journals. Her work has also been published in book collections, including *Clio's Daughters: British Women Making History*, edited by Lynette Felber, and *Victorian Women Writers and the 'Woman Question'*, edited by Nicola Thompson.

Valerie Fehlbaum is a member of the English Department at the University of Geneva, where she specializes in the nineteenth century. She has also lectured at the University of Neuchatel, in Switzerland and tutored with the UK-based Open University. Her primary research interests are Victorian periodicals and *fin-de-siècle* literature. Her monograph on Ella Hepworth Dixon was published by Ashgate in 2005, and together with Gina O'Brien she has just edited a special edition of *Women's Writing* devoted to Ella Hepworth Dixon (2011). She is currently working on a project about women and urban space with colleagues in Spain and Greece.

F. Elizabeth Gray is a Senior Lecturer at Massey University, New Zealand, where she has taught nineteenth-century literature and writing since 2003. She is the author of *Christian and Lyric Tradition in Victorian Women's Poetry* (Routledge 2010) as well as a number of articles on nineteenth-century women's poetry and religious contexts. She is currently working on a new project on Alice Meynell and the *Pall Mall Gazette*.

Susan Hamilton is Professor of English at the University of Alberta, Canada. Her work focuses on Victorian and early twentieth-century feminist journalism, and the literature and cultural history of animal rights. Recent publications include: 'Reading and the Popular Critique of Science in the Victorian Anti-vivisection Press,' *Victorian Review* (2010); 'Women's Voices and Public Debate,' *Cambridge Companion to English Literature, 1830–1914* (2010); 'Marketing Antifeminism' in *Anti-Feminism and the Victorian Novel* (Cambria, 2009); and *Frances Power Cobbe and Victorian Feminism* (Palgrave Macmillan, 2006). She is also editor of *Animal Welfare and Anti-Vivisection, 1870–1910* (Routledge, 2004); *Criminals, Idiots, Women and Minors* (Broadview, 1995, 2nd edition, 2004); and (with Janice Schroeder) *Women's Education in Britain, 1840–1900* (Routledge, 2007).

Dorothy O. Helly is Professor Emerita of History and Women's Studies at Hunter College and the Graduate School at the City University of New York. Her field of research is Victorian imperialism and Victorian women. Her book *Making the Empire British: Flora Shaw and Her Times* is under contract with Manchester University Press. Her other publications include three books, *Gendered Domains: Rethinking the Public and Private in Women's History* (1992); *Women's Realities, Women's Choices: An Introduction to Women's Studies*

(1985, 1995, and 2005); and *Livingstone's Legacy: Horace Waller and Victorian Mythmaking* (1987). Among her many articles are four on Flora Shaw.

Linda K. Hughes, Addie Levy Professor of Literature at Texas Christian University, Fort Worth, Texas, is the author most recently of *Graham R.: Rosamund Marriott Watson, Woman of Letters* (Ohio University Press, 2005) and *The Cambridge Introduction to Victorian Poetry* (Cambridge University Press, 2010). She is currently completing, with Sharon M. Harris (University of Connecticut), a three-volume anthology of feminist writing from Sappho to the present. She has begun a new project on Victorian women writers and Germany in the context of female cosmopolitanism, study abroad, and a transnational women's literary tradition.

Kimberly Morse Jones is a Visiting Assistant Professor of Art History at Sweet Briar College in Virginia, United States specializing in late nineteenth-century British art. She is particularly interested in the role of criticism in the production of the visual arts. She is currently writing a book on Elizabeth Robins Pennell.

Michelle Tusan is an Associate Professor of History at the University of Nevada Las Vegas where she teaches British, gender, and imperial history. She is the author of *Women Making News: Gender and Journalism in Modern Britain* (2005). Her forthcoming book, *Smryna's Ashes: Humanitarianism, Genocide and the Birth of the Middle East*, will be published in the Berkeley Series in British History with the University of California Press, in 2012.

1

Introduction

F. Elizabeth Gray
Massey University, New Zealand

'I should much like to know what the *Pall Mall* means to pay me for the weekly articles. I shall not growl at £1 10s.; but £2 would make me very happy.'

(Alice Meynell)[1]

'For every hundred persons who listen to the priest, the journalist ... speaks to a thousand; and while the words of the one are often heard merely as a formality, those of the other ... may effectively influence the thoughts and consciences and actions of thousands in the near future. Shallow, indeed, would be the mind which undervalued the power of the journalist, or underrated the seriousness of his vocation.'

(Florence Fenwick-Miller)[2]

'... it was the fundamentally heterogeneous form of the Victorian periodical, its multiple and mostly anonymous authorship, its imperative of diversity, that provided a very particular space, both fluid and dynamic, in which women could negotiate a writing identity or writing identities.'[3]

As the nineteenth century drew to a close, women became increasingly numerous and prominent in British journalism, promoting themselves as never before, and capitalizing in new ways on the changing conditions of journalism. Ella Hepworth Dixon, in addition to making a living as a journalist, published many well-received short stories and novels that featured female journalists as protagonists. Sarah Tooley and Hulda Friederichs published interviews with some of the best-known celebrities of the day (including Frances Hodgson Burnett, William Morris, and Princess May), in the process granting their own names broad circulation. Flora Shaw sent to the *Times* investigative articles from African and Australian colonies that had the entire British Commonwealth talking.

Much of the ground-breaking work of these women, and even many of their names, have been unjustly forgotten. This volume has several aims. In part, its goal is straightforwardly recuperative – to bring back to critical attention the work and careers of a number of women tremendously significant in their own day but largely forgotten today. It aims to demonstrate the range and the quality of women's journalism in Britain at the *fin de siècle*, and also to examine how the cultural currents of the unique time period contributed to significant revisionings of feminine and journalistic roles. And it aims to reveal how the periodical press itself, in its ubiquity and its multivocality, contributed to women's various literary and identity constructions. The work of women journalists at the turn of the twentieth century furthers our understanding of the intersection of gender, canonicity, and the formation of cultural 'standards'; of women writers' strategic commodification of self and of style; and of the complex relationship between fame and literary style. The essays in this book offer fresh insights into women's contributions to these questions at the *fin de siècle*, and into the ways the periodical press itself enabled, generated, constrained, and shaped what women wrote.

A century after these female journalists blazed new trails in a period of transforming cultural, gender, and economic paradigms, women writers' negotiations with name and fame still resonate. The same questions posed then are relevant now: what is literary fame? What does it mean, particularly, for a woman? How might the transformations in journalism be used to women's advantage? Can one achieve literary fame in a contested, even borderline literary field like journalism? What was the status of journalism, particularly when produced by women? How might women writers manipulate both their writing and their publicity to secure both fame and financial success? Might their strategies be perceived to be 'selling out'? Martin Conboy suggests that the constraints limiting nineteenth-century women journalists linger into the twenty-first century: 'despite apparent advances, women continue mainly in the glamorous ghettoes of journalism as opposed to the serious areas of news journalism'.[4] While Chambers, Steiner and Fleming agree the '"real" work of "hard" news' is still the near-exclusive domain of male journalists,[5] this volume offers strong evidence to suggest that *fin-de-siècle* women effected certain strategic transformations of journalism and journalistic discourse that left a significant legacy for women writers who followed.

Women in Journalism at the Fin de Siècle draws on the particular areas of expertise of an array of leading scholars, who train a close focus on individual women writers but also on the turbulent period and industry in which those women worked and which they helped shape. Reflecting the dazzling volume and variety of the Victorian periodical press, the essays treat women's engagements with a wide array of periodical titles and topics, including some of the most pressing debates of the day. These include colonial politics, labour conditions, cultural and literary debates, and aspects of the Woman Question including suffrage, childcare, and marriage law. By setting each woman journalist in context, each essay treats these journalists not as isolates or exceptions but as what they were, women writing within and helping change an industry and a society that was increasingly being read, challenged, and changed by other women. Contributors to this volume bring to bear critical perspectives emerging out of a variety of disciplines, ranging from literature, history, art history, media history, and cultural studies. The illuminating diversity of these various interdisciplinary approaches and methodologies allows a number of points of entry into a body of work that was itself profoundly diverse. In her work on Victorian periodicals, Andrea Broomfield has noted that no single author, and no single journal, reliably presents a truly unified set of attitudes or beliefs.[6] Titles had composite identities[7]; often, so did their female contributors, many of whom also had their own composite 'titles' or names. The exigencies of the Victorian marketplace added rich complexity to women's writings, and consideration of those exigencies and women's varied responses to them informs all essays in this volume.

Each essay focuses on one woman journalist, discussing the construction of a career rather than concentrating solely on an individual piece of work. While the essays adopt a variety of theoretical frameworks, the volume as a whole draws on Foucauldian concepts of contestible and multiply constructed authorial identity. Bourdieu's theorization of cultural capital also proves significant to discussions of women writers' strategic stylistic manoeuvres, and to analysis of women writers' commodification of themselves and of their names. As Marysa Demoor has noted, 'The name of the author and the identity of the author attached to that name had become the foremost marketing strategy by 1900'.[8] The point of commonality in approach amongst the various essays in this volume might be described as cultural neoformalism, as contributors variously consider formal and stylistic elements of each author's artistic and self-production, while setting them firmly into their social and cultural context. In this respect, my ambition for this volume echoes the aims sketched by Fraser, Green, and Johnston, who described the dual trajectories of *Gender in the Victorian Periodical* as supplying empirical analysis – in the sense that their material was solidly grounded in historical and cultural specificities – and also supplying textual analysis.[9] Fraser's, Green's, and Johnston's valuable and systematic synthesis of these two methodologies has been a significant influence on this volume; however, while their work ranges over the Victorian period as a whole, this volume trains its focus on the historical specificities of a particular cultural moment, the *fin de siècle*, which has been bounded for this volume by the years 1880 and 1910. Women in this period struck new directions, building on their Victorian inheritance in various and novel ways. Further, this volume, in distinction from Fraser's, Green's, and Johnston's work, focuses on a series of case studies, analysing the achievements of individual women within that cultural moment rather than treating broader themes across a range of periodicals. In this way, this volume responds to Sally Mitchell's call for a new wave of studies to focus on individual women writers of the 1890s, both novelists and non-fiction writers:

> We still need to identify, recover, and consider the political and social writing by those women, examining it not only for information and opinions but also as texts: rhetoric, tactics, effects, philosophy.[10]

Although the Research Society for Victorian Periodicals has worked steadily over the last 40 years to articulate the importance of Victorian periodicals to literary culture, to this point few of the many important female contributors to the periodical press have received serious critical attention. This volume goes a considerable way towards filling that critical gap, a gap becoming increasingly evident with the rise in academic interest in the history of journalism and women's journalism particularly. Many of the journalists discussed in this volume opened doors for a later generation of writers and reformers: Emilie Peacocke, who became editor of the women's page of the *Sunday Express* from 1918, responded sanguinely to the equivocal nature of this 'promotion,' writing that it called 'for a new appraisal as opportunities for women were opening on every front'.[11] These essays provide both a rich biographical and historical resource for those interested in women's contribution to British journalism, and a provocative critical argument for the significance of these women's writings to changing ideas around the roles of women, the construction of professional identity, and the formation of literary value.

Historical and cultural background

In Britain in the latter part of the nineteenth century, women were increasingly drawn to journalistic work. For a growing female population, nervously facing demographic and societal changes that increasingly required them to support themselves financially, journalism offered an appealing alternative to nursing or school-teaching (pay rates were comparable and, potentially at least, much better; conditions of work were often far preferable; and little if any training was required). In 1891, the English census recorded 660 women listing themselves as 'author, editor, journalist', up from only 15 in 1841.[12] By the 1890s, journalism as a profession for women was being actively promoted by a number of women's magazines and by writers both male and female. In 1893, for example, W. T. Stead penned hearty and encouraging advice in 'Young Women and Journalism' in *The*

Young Woman,[13] and in the same year Emily Crawford more soberly outlined the expectations of the industry in 'Journalism as a Profession for Women', in *Contemporary Review*.[14] In the bracing *Press Work for Women* (1904), Frances Low wrote a detailed, dispassionate, and immensely practical guide for young women seeking 'to become a bread-winner' in journalism, providing systematic advice on embarking on a career, preparing copy, and placing articles in the literary market.[15] During the period under investigation in this volume, the growing army of women journalists in Britain produced an enormous volume of material – not just collectively, but individually. It is hardly overstating the case to say they wrote on everything. Charlotte O'Conor Eccles, writing in *Blackwood's Edinburgh Magazine* in 1893 of her early journalistic experiences, sketched the phenomenal amount and range of writing tasks she undertook:

> A weekly newspaper offered me 30s a week for all my time from nine in the morning till six in the evening. I did a column of 'mems.' on current events; two columns of educational news; a number of sub-leaders; two Ladies' Letters; Answers to Correspondents; a 'Children's Corner,' most troublesome of all, as it involved competitions and prizes; corrected all the proofs; and had in my hands the selection of matter for the weekly, and for an educational paper. Quite enough to do I found it.[16]

This productive and swelling feminine cohort gave rise to considerable anxiety in Victorian Britain, on the part both of men who perceived their position and privilege in established professions under threat, and also of a number of women (in 1897 Janet Hogarth referred to the ranks of female journalists as 'the monstrous regiment of women'). Many Victorians, citing the physical, temporal, and moral pressures of the industry, were unsure women should write journalism. Some were unsure women *could* write (good) journalism. In an advice volume for female journalists published in 1898, Arnold Bennett wrote: 'Stated plainly, my first charge amounts to this: women-journalists are unreliable as a class.… Women enjoy a reputation for slipshod style. They have earned it.'[17] In 1904, Frances Low, herself a professional journalist and editor over many years, took a similarly poor view of the standard of contemporary women's journalism, bemoaning the decline 'from the standard for many years sustained in this country by Harriet Martineau, Frances Power Cobbe, Mrs. Lynn Linton, and others, down to its present low—one hopes lowest—level'.[18] Low felt that the very popularity of journalism as a money-earning option for women had led to the decline in the quality of women's journalistic writing:

> No doubt the explanation is partly to be found in the fact, that whereas fifty years ago the women journalists were picked members of their sex, possessing scholarship and culture, added to a high sense of responsibility,

today every semi-educated girl attracted by an easy mode of earning a small income, takes to journalism.[19]

So, what was the state of female journalism in Britain at the turn of the century? Was it as parlous as Bennett and Low suggest? While examples of slipshod style, ill-informed reviewing, and hasty and often cribbed copy abound, the essays in this volume suggest that women's journalism was also complex and intellectually acute, and allowed a number of enterprising women to seize some extraordinary possibilities.

Definitions and challenges

Part of the challenge in decoding what women were doing in late Victorian journalism lies in the fact that late Victorian journalism was so various in and of itself, and so subject to multiple interpretations. The term journalism itself could cover many genres and types of contributions. By the 1880s it had come to be most usually associated with newspaper reporting, which, despite the pioneering contributions of Emily Crawford and Flora Shaw, remained firmly coded as masculine. But writing 'journalism' could also encompass magazine writing, very often linked to fashion and frippery, and definitely perceived as feminine[20]; reviewing, which was perceived as demanding, intellectual, and closer to literature than other forms of journalism[21]; journalistic essay writing, which enjoyed a particular vogue in the 1890s; and specialist kinds of columnizing, such as pious scriptural reflections, domestic advice columns, and so on, which generally were perceived as very lowbrow, and very feminine. In the *Fortnightly Review* in 1897, Janet Hogarth offered a bleak description of the kinds of journalistic hackwork through which a woman might eke out a living, stating that the average woman writer

> will have to content herself with a kind of journalism, far enough removed from literature – with the chatty article, or the women's papers, with the *Forget-me-Nots*, the *Home Notes*, the *Nursery Chats*, and the hundred-and-one scrappy periodicals which have so successfully hit off the taste of the rising generation, that they bid fair to reduce England once again to a condition of illiteracy.[22]

The status of journalism – and the ways in which its various generic branches were accorded greater or lesser literary value – were closely and complexly linked to gender constructions and to the challenging and reshaping of these constructions as the century drew to its close. At the *fin de siècle*, questions of literary status and authenticity as they intersected with the journalistic industry and with gender were being freshly and pressingly articulated. Either explicitly or implicitly, every essay in this volume discusses the relationship of journalism to literature, and considers how these women writers defined their own journalistic project and its 'worth'.

Discussion of authorship and authority in the periodical press is also complicated by the competing and sometimes conflicting interests of the editorial presence. Dallas Liddle warns of the ongoing challenge, for scholars writing on Victorian periodicals, of 'theorizing, attributing, and assessing authorship, which in a periodical text is always both mediated by and opposed to editorship'.[23] An editor could provide a woman contributor with a megaphone or a gag; could market or conceal her name; could allow her free rein or maintain entire control of what (if any) of her material reached publication. Several contributors to this volume highlight the complex power relations operating between women journalists and their editors (see for example Lee Anne Bache's chapter on Eliza Lynn Linton and Dorothy O. Helly's chapter on Flora Shaw); other chapters consider the editorial responsibilities certain women assumed (see for example Michelle Tusan's chapter on Lady Isabella Somerset), and how such women sought to negotiate professional roles that often appeared oppositional.

The British fin de siècle

The *fin-de-siècle* period is of signal importance to the considerations in this volume. The 30-year span between 1880 and 1910 was a complex period in Britain, challenging to define although linking easily classifiable periods on either side (late Victorian on the one, and Modernist on the other).[24] Working within a transitional period, women writers were transitional figures, through their work contributing to the birth of a new journalistic era when technology, practice, convention, subject matter, and style were all in revolution. The 'New Journalism' tirelessly scrutinized and analysed itself, and the period was one of rapidly progressing professionalization, a time in which both male and female journalists sought to regulate the industry, advocate professional training and standards, and set up professional associations.[25]

The late-nineteenth-century British literary marketplace expanded at a dizzying rate. Demoor calls the last 25 years of the nineteenth century 'the zenith of the Victorian commodity culture',[26] noting the soaring publication and readership figures at the end of the century, and citing the *Daily Mail's* 500,000 strong readership. Periodical publishing was big business, and it was also increasingly self-conscious business. Responding to an ever-expanding gallery of readers courtesy of expanding literacy rates and increasingly affordable production technologies, publications proliferated, and women journalists found, through both necessity and design, canny ways of positioning themselves and their literary wares within this voracious and various marketplace. Elaine Showalter's *Sexual Anarchy: Gender and Culture at the Fin de Siècle* considers the various cultural boundaries that were disrupted or transgressed as the century came to a close[27]; the concept of an exclusive and privileged reading public was similarly exploded.

The changes taking place in regard to journalistic anonymity in the last decades of the nineteenth century had significant repercussions, perhaps most particularly for women journalists. From the 1860s, when attribution began rapidly overtaking anonymity as industry practice, authorial names, including assumed names and pseudonyms, provided new sources of capital; in an increasingly commodified journalistic market, women were able to trade as never before on their names. Anonymous publication had been, as Onslow, Easley, and Fraser, Green, and Johnston have separately discussed, extremely significant for women in journalism particularly in the central decades of the nineteenth century, operating complexly both as an aid and a hindrance.[28] Unsigned articles allowed women to enter debates of the day but also to enter the industry itself, giving access, protection, and conferring a degree of authority. Anonymity, however, also meant that women contributors to periodicals often received no 'credit' for their work – the male editor, named, gained the cultural capital. For example, Flora Shaw wrote as a colonial correspondent for the *Times*, submitting insightful reports from Africa and Australia, but her identity was hidden from management for years by the editor, Moberly Bell (see Helly's chapter in this volume). Although in some particular types of journalism (such as literary reviewing) anonymity persisted into the final years of the century (and continued to be vigorously debated[29]), Fraser, Green, and Johnston report that by 1899 'it was ... common practice to print a separate list of contributors as well as identifying the authors of each article in the index'.[30]

The move to identification and sometimes popularization of the individual reporter or journalist was related in important ways to the development of the New Journalism. Responding to the vast expansion of the mass reading public in the nineteenth century, this popularizing trend reflected commercial and democratizing impulses. The Education Act of 1870 had led to broadly expanded national literacy; with the mid-century abolition of the newspaper tax and paper duty, allied with technological advances in press production, that mass readership could be fed with cheaper and more rapidly produced newspapers, and titles proliferated to meet multiple new audiences. The New Journalism, in responding to new audiences, had a wide-ranging impact on journalism's style and content. Champions such as W. T. Stead promoted a new, chatty, personal tone at the expense of the old periphrastic and authoritarian style; new topics were introduced as worthy of discussion, meaning human interest stories competed vigorously with more erudite political discussions; and as Kimberly Morse Jones notes in her chapter on Elizabeth Pennell, the very appearance of periodicals changed, with the introduction of attention-grabbing mastheads and illustrations.

Because of its emphasis on personal engagement, New Journalism proved a juggernaut behind the abandonment of anonymity, emphatically promoting the identification of contributors, who themselves sometimes became celebrities. Detractors of the New Journalism complained of the vacuousness of its content and the infantilization of its style, Matthew Arnold observing in 1887, 'It has much to recommend it; it is full of ... sensation, sympathy, generous instincts; its one great fault is that it is *feather-brained*'.[31] While Arnold doesn't explicitly raise the spectre of the 'feminization' of the New Journalism, the terms he uses raise echoes of other, less delicately phrased critiques. In moving away from topics and practices that had traditionally privileged male writers, the New Journalism offered women journalists access, opportunity, scope, and valorization. For these very reasons, critics of the New Journalism deplored its increased feminization and its diminished quality, characteristics perceived to be indistinguishable.

Thus at the *fin de siècle* the British periodical industry was reconstituting and questioning itself, fully engaged in the period's debate over definitions of literary value. Fraser, Green, and Johnston note that by the end of the century, 'the split between popular and high-aesthetic culture began to be broken down by the mass production of the periodical press in all its forms'.[32] The periodical press was at the crux of tensions between categories of aesthetic and economic, art and commerce; it constantly asked itself what it was, what its value was, and what its status was. At the *fin de siècle*, journalism was changing, the marketplace was changing, and ideas of authorship, fame and influence were conceptualized in entirely new ways. All this contributed to irrevocable change in conceptions of womanhood. As the new century dawned, women's involvement in journalism helped educate female writers and readers as to their political, educational, employment, and domestic rights. The influential suffrage journal *Votes for Women* (1907–18), which at its peak boasted nearly 50,000 subscribers,[33] marched triumphantly down the road paved by late-nineteenth-century forerunners like the *Englishwoman's Review* and the *Woman's Signal*.

The rewards for women journalists

In examining women writers' strategic negotiations with the *fin-de-siècle* periodical press, the essays in this volume investigate women's motivations and their complex, often conflicted negotiations for money, influence, and identity. The pecuniary interest was often paramount, as Low recognized in her advice to the aspiring 'bread-winner' in *Press Work for Women*: Low painstakingly lays out the pay offered, per page, per column, and sometimes per word, by scores of individual British periodicals. For example, she reports that the *Daily Chronicle* paid from £1 per 1000 words; for short paragraphs of 200 to 250 words, a contributor could expect 1½ pence per line. As quoted in the epigraph above, the letters of Alice Meynell, whose unceasing journalistic labours helped support her growing family, reveal how closely she reviewed her accounts, and how significant was each shilling. As already mentioned, journalism could offer comparable or better rates of pay than nursing or teaching. However, such a source of income brought women, as well as financial freedom, certain kinds of identity disruption. Penny Boumelha has examined the problematic nexus at the *fin de siècle* of femininity, commercial involvement, and professionalism[34]: in terms of payment for creative work, Kathy Psomiades has pointed to the 'difficult and vexed relation between the categories of the aesthetic and the economic'.[35] Thus periodical publishing became the site of multiple, interlocking tensions between commerce, art, and gender.

Journalism offered women other opportunities to challenge ideological constraints on appropriate fields of involvement. Women writing journalism sought and found new sources of influence, voicing and shaping opinions on topics from women's suffrage to labour legislation to fine art. Fraser, Green, and Johnston have demonstrated the myriad ways in which the periodical press enabled marginalized groups to participate and intervene in mainstream debates, at a time when the ability of such groups to participate in public meetings or parliamentary or legal debate was severely constrained. As Florence Fenwick-Miller wrote in one of the epigraphs beginning this introduction, journalists enjoyed a pulpit before a congregation hundreds or even thousands times bigger than that within any church building. Fenwick-Miller herself wrote a column as 'Filomena', for example, which was syndicated nationwide; Eliza Lynn Linton's *Saturday Review* columns on 'The Girl of the Period' between 1866 and 1877 sparked widespread controversy, response, and imitation; and in the mid-1890s Londoners rushed each Friday to read and discuss Alice Meynell's 'Wares of Autolycus' column in the *Pall Mall Gazette*.[36]

While British women journalists sought both income and influence, of key importance to the critical chapters in this volume is the examination of women journalists' search for new sources of recognition and new forms of identity through their writing for periodicals. Subject formation, genre development, and variation in the tides of taste and style are all inextricably linked in the case of women writing journalism at the *fin de siècle*. Subjectivities were of course, contested, contingent, and plural; women writers could through their writing consciously and strategically occupy and create different subject positions. *Women in Journalism at the Fin de Siècle* extends the work begun in Demoor's 2004 *Marketing the Author*, a collection of essays that discussed how male and female writers between 1880 and 1930 'fashioned a writerly self'. The focus of this volume, in contrast, is trained specifically on women's relationship with journalistic fame (in Demoor's volume, contributors also consider novel, short story, and poetry writing), and it has a specific focus on gender's relationship to issues of authorship and authority.

For the women journalists examined in this volume, writing became in certain ways interchangeable with their authorial or stylistic signature.

However, a 'signature style' becomes increasingly problematic (and suggestive) for *fin-de-siècle* women writers who frequently adopted a multiplicity of publishing names. For example, Eliza Lynn Linton worked strenuously (though not always successfully) to differentiate authorial personae, as Bache discusses: E. Lynn Linton was a separate identity from Mrs. Lynn Linton, and separate again was the transgendered hero of Linton's (auto)biographical 'novel', *The Autobiography of Christopher Kirkland*. Poet and journalist Rosamund Marriott Watson underwent multiple identity permutations, as Linda Hughes writes: born Rosamund Ball, the writer abandoned the popularly recognized pen-name 'Graham R. Tomson' for 'Rosamund Marriott Watson' on her (second) elopement.[37] Edith Simcox, discussed by Brenda Ayres, published extensively under her own name and under the *nom de plume* H. Lawrenny, a masculinized persona whose polemical columns regularly received replies addressed to 'Mr. Lawrenny' (to Simcox's delight). Sometimes women journalists sought to capitalize upon potentially different reading audiences by adopting distinct personae; sometimes they sought deliberately to elide their own gender or marital status; the construction and presentation of a particular signature was always, as these essays attest, a political choice.

An identity as a journalist was itself continuously debated, and each chapter in this volume explicitly engages with the ways in which the individual woman writer defined her journalism and her role within a journalistic enterprise. Women's pursuit of name and fame in journalism cannot be considered separately from the contested definition of journalist in the period.[38] All the women treated in this volume were other things as well as journalists – Frances Power Cobbe, for example, created a name (or, a series of names) as suffragist, journalist, and anti-vivisection campaigner. In 1893 Henri de Blowitz defined a journalist as 'any man who lives exclusively by regularly writing in a regularly appearing journal; who is a part – not necessarily a fixture, but a normal part – of a regularly organized sheet, and who treats in one or more such sheets, living questions whatever their nature'.[39] More recently, Onslow has countered by adopting the turn-of-the-century definition of the Society of Women Journalists, which said of its Presidents and Vice-Presidents that 'all of them have occasionally been contributors to newspapers or magazines …'.[40] For the purposes of this volume, the following definition has determined inclusion: women who made regular rather than merely occasional contributions to periodicals; women for whom journalism was a primary professional pursuit, even if not the exclusive pursuit; and finally, women whose writing in periodicals achieved in their own day a degree of public recognition; that is, women who in this period had begun to 'make a name for themselves' in journalism.

The volume demonstrates the exceptional range and versatility of these pioneering women journalists. Some developed specializations (for example Flora Shaw's international reporting, Sarah Tooley's interviewing, and Elizabeth Pennell's art criticism), while many remained extraordinarily prolific generalists. Thus the chapters attend to the breadth of topics and approaches deployed by women journalists in Britain in the period, emphasizing the myriad ways in which women interacted with the periodical industry, in preference to adopting an exclusive gender focus. Many women writing journalism (and most of the authors treated here) were passionately interested in women's issues, suffrage, and/or other activist causes, and frequently used their writing to further these causes. Nonetheless, as Onslow has suggested, 'if we mine their [women journalists'] writings only for opinions on one question – however important – we are getting a very partial intellectual picture',[41] and this volume seeks to expand the 'intellectual picture' of women's journalistic contributions in the period. However, no examination of women's writing in this period can (or should) attempt to avoid women's issues entirely, and this volume reveals a variety of ways in which 'The Woman Question' animated women journalists. It further demonstrates how the periodical press both permitted expression of resistance to existing ideology and also reflected and reinforced that ideology.[42]

This volume does not include activists who made use of journalism for ideological ends but didn't consider themselves 'journalists', or those women writers whose primary field of writing was fiction which may have been serialized in periodicals. Suggestively, these distinctions are quite hard to draw as women at the *fin de siècle* often wrote and gained a degree of success in quite diverse genres. Sarah Grand, for example, gained financial success and some notoriety as a novelist but also wrote prolifically for periodicals. Jane Harrison, another example, was a classical scholar whose journalistic contributions helped develop that primary vocation. The original intention for this volume was to exclude editors and owners,[43] in order to concentrate on the particular relationship between a woman's writing and her reputation. However, reflecting the complex operations of women in journalism in the period, several chapters do consider the cases of women who balanced journalism with editorial work. Lady Isabella Somerset, for example, combined article writing on a number of social topics with her editorship of the *Woman's Signal*, Frances Low worked as a journalist and as editor of the *Queen*, and Friederichs edited the *Westminster Budget* for several years, in the mature stage of a journalistic career in which she was 'probably the best known woman interviewer of her day'.[44]

Contents of this volume

The volume follows a simple chronological organizational principle, meaning chapters appear in the order of the dates of the individual journalist; this has had the unexpected benefits of some truly provocative and suggestive juxtapositions. Thus the volume opens with Lee Anne Bache's chapter on leading professional woman writer and vehement antifeminist, Eliza Lynn Linton and follows with Susan Hamilton's chapter on the redoubtable feminist and animal rights campaigner, Frances Power Cobbe. Although the lives of both women were drawing to a close in the years of this volume's focus, both were tremendously significant figures for subsequent women journalists, though in markedly different ways. Linton was the first female salaried employee of a major newspaper, and as Bache discusses, Linton constructed an array of complex, interlocking professional and gender identities. Bache outlines Linton's journalistic achievements and legacy, discussing excerpts from Linton's *fin-de-siècle* periodical writings in the light of her complex autobiographical writings, the incomplete and posthumously published *My Literary Life* (1899), and most suggestively, the *Autobiography of Christopher Kirkland* (1885). Interviews of the aging Linton by younger women journalists, and Linton's own vexed views on the development of the industry through her long career, offer illuminating commentary on the state of journalism in Britain at the end of the century.

Hamilton takes a different approach in her consideration of Frances Power Cobbe's legacy. The widely revered Cobbe had made her name as a journalist earlier in the nineteenth century, and Hamilton explores how certain *fin-de-siècle* feminist periodicals (the *Englishwoman's Review*, the *Woman's Signal*, and the *Woman's Journal*) used the name of Frances Power Cobbe to intervene in the debate on women in the journalistic profession that continued so vigorously at the century's close. The chapter traces Cobbe's name and influence into the new century, arguing that her persona was used to show how women's journalism exemplified feminist claims for women's (professional) abilities, and also used in the service of an ongoing campaign to legitimize and valorize women's journalism. Hamilton suggests that Cobbe was portrayed as simultaneously non-representative and yet exemplary, and outlines the significance of this (exceptional) example to following generations.

In the third chapter, Brenda Ayres explores the production of gender indeterminacy in Edith Simcox's journalistic and novelistic writing. An activist for labour and women's causes, Simcox was also a factory owner, and she sought to balance 'literature and doctrine' in a life of activism. Simcox's lifelong passion for George Eliot led to debilitating frustration but also informed various textual gender negotiations that were paradoxically creatively enabling. Simcox's deployment of a masculine persona in her journalistic writing enabled a suggestive satirical and critical freedom, but one that she had difficulty sustaining. The chapter suggests ways that the periodical press helped Simcox 'harness' gender indeterminacy to create and manipulate different forms of identity.

A more stable and authoritarian – though highly complex – persona was produced in the review journalism of Alice Meynell, which is examined by F. Elizabeth Gray. Gray's chapter focuses specifically on Meynell's production of a particular reviewing voice, which refused the gendered reviewing conventions of the period, instead producing the measured critique of an equal.

In a long and various career, Meynell became famous for her contributions to the *Scots Observer* and the *Pall Mall Gazette*, was importuned by numerous editors, and was eventually predicted by an acerbic Max Beerbohm to 'become a sort of substitute for the English Sabbath'. Meynell produced herself through her review criticism as an arbiter of style, a significant literary authority, and a cultural phenomenon in her own right.

The case of women balancing journalism with editorship is closely examined by Michelle Tusan in her chapter on Lady Isabella Somerset, who used her journalistic writings and her editorship of the *Woman's Signal* (formerly the *Woman's Herald*) to argue for not only temperance but also education reform and women's rights. Somerset's production of a journalistic voice, argues Tusan, is inseparable from her identity as a humanitarian reformer. Somerset saw her many causes as related, as globally relevant, and as all centring on the enfranchisement and empowerment of women. Somerset's promotion of the cause of Armenian refugees found commonalities in the causes of women's oppression at home and abroad, and she championed an ideal of global sisterhood in which all women would have a voice.

Dorothy O. Helly writes on Flora Shaw, a trailblazer on several fronts. Shaw became a salaried reporter for that most sacrosanct masculinist institution, the *Times*; became Britain's highest paid woman journalist, earning £800 per annum; and through her reporting from the colonies, her imperialist views influenced political views at a national level. Shaw's development of journalistic identity and imperialist thought were inseparable processes, and she believed implicitly in journalism's role in influencing government policy. Helly's chapter traces the stages of Shaw's move from novel-writing to a politically engaged journalism; her extraordinary ability to prevail against gender prejudice in her profession; and the suggestive disequilibrium between her progressive example and her less progressive views on gender roles.

Kimberly Morse Jones writes on the American-born art critic Elizabeth Pennell and the writing strategies that significantly cost her recognition. While Pennell published widely in the British periodical press and her travel writing received international renown, in her art criticism she regularly obscured her own name (and her considerable acumen and expertise) to promote the radical ideologies of the 'New Art Criticism'. In particular, Pennell used her periodical writings to champion the polarizing genius of Whistler. Her ultimately successful efforts to promote Whistler's artistic reputation worked in many ways to marginalize Pennell's own critical achievements.

Fionnuala Dillane treats Hulda Friederichs, reputedly the first woman in Britain to be engaged on exactly the same terms of work and pay as male journalists. Dubbed by the *London Journal* a 'sister journalist, who stands almost at the head of our profession', Friederichs contributed significantly to the Interview phenomenon in the New Journalism of the 1880s and 1890s.

Diverging in suggestive ways from the popular pattern of the celebrity interview, Friederichs published in the *Pall Mall Gazette* a series of gripping interviews with workers at the fringes of society, foregrounding and problematizing the construction of class and gender. In her own retrospective account of her interviewing career, Friederichs highlighted both the constraints she faced as a woman journalist and the ways she overcame those constraints. Dillane argues that the pragmatic, urbane, highly successful Friederichs presented a rebuttal of the stereotyped New Woman.

A fascinating counterpoint to Friederichs is Sarah Tooley, also a proficient and prominent interviewer, who enjoyed great respect in her own lifetime but who is generally only remembered now in relation to the leading female figures she interviewed. Terri Doughty argues for Tooley's importance on several levels. Tooley consistently and explicitly promoted women's professionalism and professionalization. She also provided her own interesting and challenging model of professional journalism: the chapter discusses Tooley's complex views on gender roles and journalistic practice, and closely reads her strategic manoeuvring to control her own representation when interviewed herself. Doughty reads Tooley's work for its demonstration of how women's professional identities were constructed on both sides of the interview convention.

Valerie Fehlbaum examines the career of Ella Hepworth Dixon, who is primarily remembered today as a novelist, but who made a significant contribution to British journalism in a career that spanned several decades. Dixon championed women's entry into the profession through her example and her writing, and Fehlbaum examines how Dixon's views concerning journalism and women's roles are developed through her periodical contributions, novels, short stories, and even a play. Dixon manoeuvred strategically and complexly with anonymity and autobiography, negotiated adroitly with her various editors, and, although she admitted she never 'burned' for activism, she made a significant contribution to the cause of women's employment.

Linda K. Hughes contributes a chapter on R. Armytage/Graham R. Tomson/Rosamund Marriott Watson. The career of this multiply-named journalist and poet demonstrates pointedly how the uses of signature – in the manufacture of celebrity and commodity status, and also the formulation of critique – may change over time. The chapter begins by examining the intersection of poetry and journalism, suggesting this writer's journalistic career is only fully explicable when read through and alongside her poetry. Tomson's 'women's journalism' is then read as self-consciously demanding respect and also intervening critically in certain arguments about literary value. Tomson the reviewer's self-production and self-empowerment as a woman of letters, and her insistence on her own authority as poet-critic, offers an interesting complement to the volume's chapter on Meynell. Finally, the chapter briefly considers the writer's signed and unsigned work after she became Rosamund Marriott Watson, when neither signature nor anonymity offered previously enjoyed rewards.

The volume concludes with a chapter from Alexis Easley on Frances Low, today one of the lesser known writers in the volume, but a significant influence on other women journalists of her day. Easley outlines the conflict between Low's simultaneous championing of the domestic ideal and her active promotion of professional careers for women. The chapter focuses particularly on Low's writerly 'sleight of hand'; her writing and her construction of herself as a particular, professional, and expert writer appears central to her contradictory stance on the Woman Question. Despite her opposition to women's suffrage and her published opinion that a woman's rightful place was in the 'little kingdom' of home, Low established professional credentials as a cultural critic, art critic, and investigative reporter; she promoted women's employment and safe childcare; and she offered substantial assistance to young women seeking to enter the journalistic profession.

Conclusion

In 1857, Marian Evans wrote to her friend Charles Bray:

> You needn't observe any secrecy about *articles* of mine. It is an advantage (pecuniarily) to me that I should be known as the writer of the articles in the Westminster. And I am a very calculating person now—valuing approbation as representing guineas.[45]

At the *fin de siècle*, women journalists in Britain following Evans/Eliot's extraordinary example experienced similar, complex motivations. Their efforts to secure themselves income, influence, and recognition are not separable efforts or impulses. Though the women in this volume deployed an extraordinary range of strategies, forged distinctive paths, and created an array of unique identities, their goals had much in common: they balanced pragmatic aims – to make money – with loftier ambitions – to procure fame, and gain a name.

This volume is both needed and timely. In *Victorian Literature and Culture* in 2009 Sally Mitchell predicted that 'the scholarly use of Victorian journals may be reaching a point of transition', with the 'number, variety, breadth, and depth of recent studies' bespeaking a surge in critical interest.[46] The accessibility of primary sources is surging apace. At the end of 2010, Routledge's publication of the comprehensive four-volume *Female Journalists of the Fin de Siècle*, edited by Lorna Shelley, made a wide variety of fiction and non-fiction texts in facsimile form far more readily available to scholars and students.[47] The ever-growing accessibility of digitized periodical resources will surely further contribute to the nascent but dramatic increase of academic inquiry into this wealth of information, and to a similar expansion of periodical studies in the academic classroom. By bringing to light and critically examining a body of women's journalistic work that has been insufficiently studied, *Women in Journalism at the Fin de Siècle: Making a Name for Herself* makes a significant contribution to that expansion, reinserting into critical conversation the literary strategies and the multiply constructed 'names' of trailblazing female writers. The trailblazing women figures examined in this volume challenge Chambers', Steiner's, and Fleming's suggestion that twentieth-century women journalists 'had few role models to guide them'.[48] Vera Brittain, the feminist, pacifist and novelist, had a forerunner in the earlier generation's politically engaged and prolific Alice Meynell. Winifred Holtby, who wrote novels as well as broad-ranging journalism for the *Manchester Guardian* and the feminist journal *Time and Tide*, echoed the trade-unionist as well as literary interests of Edith Simcox. When Hilde Marchant chronicled the Battle of Britain for the *Daily Express* (and reportedly rose briefly to become one of the best-paid reporters in Britain[49]), Flora Shaw and Florence Dixie had ridden before her as correspondents from war zones.

The present volume does not pretend to be exhaustive: dozens more influential figures like Emily Crawford and Mary Frances Billington cry out for critical reappraisal. Much more work remains to be done to recover and examine the literary and cultural contribution of Victorian and late-Victorian women journalists, as well as editors. Nonetheless, the 12 women writers examined here offer suggestive insights: their careers at this culturally dynamic period helped shape the development of journalism in Britain, and study of their work is of continuing importance to studies of journalism today.

Notes

1. Viola Meynell, *Alice Meynell: A Memoir* (London: Jonathan Cape, 1929), 100.
2. Florence Fenwick-Miller, *Harriet Martineau* (London: W. H. Allen, 1884), 164–5.
3. Hilary Fraser, Stephanie Green, and Judith Johnston, *Gender and the Victorian Periodical* (Cambridge: Cambridge University Press, 2003), 44.
4. Martin Conboy, *Journalism in Britain: A Historical Introduction* (London: Sage, 2011), 79.
5. Deborah Chambers, Linda Steiner, and Carole Fleming, *Women and Journalism* (London and New York: Routledge, 2004), 230.
6. Andrea Broomfield, 'Eliza Lynn Linton, Sarah Grand and the Spectacle of the Victorian Woman Question,' *English Literature in Transition* 37 no. 4 (2004), 251–272.
7. Brake and Codell observe that 'A journal title promises a false unity, appearing to present, despite its many articles, topics, and illustrations, a unified policy, or set of beliefs, as if the journal itself were a single author' (Laurel Brake and Julie Codell, eds, *Encounters in the Victorian Press: Editors, Authors, Readers* (Basingstoke Hampshire: Palgrave Macmillan, 2005), 1).

8. Marysa Demoor, ed., *Marketing the Author: Authorial Personae, Narrative Selves and Self-Fashioning, 1880–1930* (Houndmills, Basingstoke: Palgrave Macmillan, 2004), 15.

9. Fraser, Green, and Johnston, *Gender*, 16.

10. Sally Mitchell, 'The New Woman's Work: Past, Present and Future,' *Nineteenth-Century Gender Studies* 3 no. 2 (2007), http://ncgsjournal.com/issue32/roundtable.htm [accessed 10 November 2011]

11. Anne Sebba, *Battling for News: The Rise of the Woman Reporter* (London: Hodder & Stoughton, 1994), 56.

12. Ellen Jordan, *The Women's Movement and Women's Employment in Nineteenth Century Britain* (London and New York: Routledge, 1999), 78–79.

13. W. T. Stead, 'Young Women and Journalism,' *The Young Woman* 1 (1893), 12–14.

14. Emily Crawford, 'Journalism as a Profession for Women,' *Contemporary Review* 64 (1893), 362–71.

15. Frances Low, *Press Work for Women* (London: L. Upcott Gill, 1904).

16. Charlotte O'Conor Eccles, 'The Experiences of a Woman Journalist,' *Blackwood's Edinburgh Magazine*, 153 (June 1893), 830–838. Reprinted in *Victorian Print Media: A Reader*. Eds Andrew King and John Plunkett, (Oxford: Oxford University Press, 2005), 330–334: 334.

17. Arnold Bennett, *Journalism for Women: A Practical Guide* (John Lane: London and New York, 1898), 6–7.

18. Low, *Press Work for Women*, 91.

19. Low, *Press Work for Women*, 91.

20. See Margaret Beetham, *A Magazine of Her Own? Domesticity and Desire in the Woman's Magazine, 1800–1914* (London: Routledge, 1996), 1–2; and Fraser, Green, and Johnston, *Gender*, 7.

21. John Oldcastle (a pseudonym for Wilfrid Meynell) wrote in *Journals and Journalism: With a Guide for Literary Beginners* (Field and Tuer: London, 1880), that while journalism was 'writing for newspapers,' literature was 'the writing of books, magazines, and reviews.' Quoted in Sally Mitchell, 'Ephemeral Journalism and its Uses: Lucie Cobbe Heaton Armstong (1851–1907),' *Victorian Periodicals Review* 42, no. 1 (2009), 81–92: 82.

22. Janet E. Hogarth, 'The Monstrous Regiment of Women,' *Fortnightly Review* 68 (1897), 926–936: 928.

23. Dallas Liddle, *The Dynamics of Genre: Journalism and the Practice of Literature in Mid-Victorian Britain* (Charlottesville, VA: University of Virginia Press, 2009), 3.

24. Raymond Williams argues that the Victorian period actually ended in the late 1870s or early 1880s, when 'socially, culturally, economically, politically, a new phase of our history began' (*The English Novel from Dickens to Lawrence*, (London: Hogarth Press, 1984), 121).

25. The Society of Women Journalists was founded in 1894 by Joseph S. Wood, editor of the *Gentlewoman*. By 1896 membership numbered over 200.

26. Demoor, *Marketing the Author*, 1.

27. Elaine Showalter, *Sexual Anarchy: Gender and Culture at the Fin de Siècle* (London: Bloomsbury, 1991).

28. See Barbara Onslow, *Women of the Press in Nineteenth-Century Britain* (Houndmills, Basingstoke: Palgrave Macmillan, 2000); Fraser, Green, and Johnston, *Gender*; and Alexis Easley, *First-Person Anonymous: Women Writers and Victorian Print Media, 1830–1870* (Aldershot: Ashgate, 2004).

29. For a detailed discussion of the ongoing debate over journalistic anonymity, and the relationship between anonymity and the growth of the idea of the celebrity

author, see Rachel Sagner Buurma's excellent 'Anonymity, Corporate Authority, and the Archive: The Production of Authorship in Late-Victorian England,' *Victorian Studies* 50, no. 1 (2007), 15–42, especially pp. 20–27.

30. Fraser, Green, and Johnstone, *Gender*, 41.
31. Matthew Arnold, 'Up to Easter,' *Nineteenth Century* 123 (May 1887), 629–643: 638, emphasis in the original.
32. Fraser, Green, and Johnston, *Gender*, 171.
33. Michelle Tusan, *Women Making News: Gender and Journalism in Modern Britain* (Urbana, IL: University of Illinois Press, 2005), 155.
34. Penny Boumelha, 'The Woman of Genius and the Woman of Grub Street: Figures of the Female Writer in British *Fin-de-siècle* Fiction,' *English Literature in Transition* 40, no. 2 (1997), 164–180.
35. Kathy Psomiades, *Beauty's Body: Femininity and Representation in British Aestheticism* (Stanford: Stanford University Press, 1997), 3.
36. Katharine Tynan Hinkson, *The Middle Years* (London: Constable & Co, 1916), 112.
37. For the definitive account of Marriott Watson's career, see Linda Hughes, *Graham R: Rosamund Marriott Watson, Woman of Letters* (Athens, OH: Ohio University Press, 2005).
38. For a detailed discussion of the debates over defining 'journalist', and the rhetoric about journalists' self-definitions, see Mark Hampton, 'Defining Journalism in Late-Nineteenth Century Britain,' *Critical Studies in Media Communication* 22, no. 2 (2005): 138–155.
39. Henri de Blowitz, 'Journalism as a Profession,' *Contemporary Review* 63 (January 1893), 37–46: 41.
40. Onslow, *Women of the Press*, 4. Onslow quotes from the *Seventh Annual Report of the SWJ, 1900–01*.
41. Onslow, *Women of the Press*, 3.
42. Recent years have seen the publication of a number of valuable works focussing more directly on late Victorian women writers' proto-feminism, including Tusan's *Women Making News* and Ann Heilmann's *New Woman Strategies: Sarah Grand, Olive Schreiner, Mona Caird* (Manchester: Manchester University Press, 2004). A very limited sample of significant treatments of individual writers' feminist self-positioning includes those of Ella Hepworth Dixon, in Valerie Fehlbaum's *Ella Hepworth Dixon: The Story of a Modern Woman* (Aldershot: Ashgate, 2005); Frances Power Cobbe, in Sally Mitchell's *Frances Power Cobbe: Victorian Feminist, Journalist, Reformer* (Charlottesville, VA: University of Virginia Press, 2004) and Susan Hamilton's *Frances Power Cobbe and Victorian Feminism* (Basingstoke, Hampshire: Palgrave Macmillan, 2006); and Florence Fenwick-Miller, in Rosemary VanArsdel's *Florence Fenwick-Miller: Victorian Feminist, Journalist, and Educator* (Aldershot: Ashgate, 2001). Fraser's, Green's, and Johnston's *Gender and the Victorian Periodical* (2003) offers essential reading on the issue of the periodical press's reinstatements and challenges to gender ideologies.
43. Margaret Beetham argues that although the periodical industry allowed increasing opportunities for women by the end of the century, women did not enjoy 'proportional editorial opportunities,' and the position of those women who did work as editors was anomalous (*A Magazine of Her Own*, 129–130).
44. Onslow, *Women of the Press*, 225.
45. George Eliot, *The George Eliot Letters*, ed. Gordon S. Haight, 9 vols. (New Haven: Yale University Press, 1954–55), 2:287; emphasis in the original.

46. Sally Mitchell, 'Victorian Journalism in Plenty,' *Victorian Literature and Culture* 37 (2009), 311–321: 311.
47. Lorna Shelley, ed., *Female Journalists of the Fin de Siècle*, 4 vols. (New York and London: Routledge, 2010).
48. Chambers, Steiner, and Fleming, *Women and Journalism*, 27.
49. Sebba, *Battling for News*, 160.

2
Making More than a Name: Eliza Lynn Linton and the Commodification of the Woman Journalist at the *Fin de Siècle*

Lee Anne Bache
Indiana University, Bloomington

> It [Linton's autobiography][1] was an outpour no one hears
> me make by word of mouth, a confession of sorrow, suffer-
> ing, trial, and determination not to be beaten, which few
> suspect as the underlying truth of my life.
>
> Eliza Lynn Linton to Miss Bird[2]

Those familiar with Eliza Lynn Linton (1822–98) as the vitriolic author of the 'Girl of the Period' essays will most likely find this description of her life and autobiography surprising – perhaps even as unsuspected as Linton believed it to be amongst her contemporary audience. Linton's self-identification as a downtrodden woman trying to withhold and mask her suffering is at odds with the shrill, abusive antifeminist with whom literary critics have struggled in their assessments of Linton as Britain's first salaried female journalist.[3] As critics of Linton have emphasized since the nineteenth century, Linton's published opinions often sought to 'impose restrictions where she had insisted upon freedom for herself',[4] demanding more self-restraint than she ever exhibited. The foundational feminist recovery work on Linton, largely biographical in methodology, has focused on just such inconsistencies, particularly between her boundary-breaking career and her advocacy for a conservative, separate spheres ideology.[5] It would be easy, then, to dismissively identify the surprising disparity between Linton's persona in print and her representation of the 'underlying truth' of her life as one of the many hypocrisies for which she has been censured both by her own contemporaries and by feminist literary critics. However, I argue that attending to, rather than dismissing, the structuring opposition of Linton's melodramatic self-presentation – the opposition between reticence and self-revelation, between the author's private self and the public's knowledge of her authorial persona – allows us critical insight into concerns endemic for women journalists at the *fin de siècle*. This chapter will demonstrate the critical value of reading these oppositions, which appear throughout Linton's published reflections on the profession and autobiographical works, as indicative of women journalists' creative responses to changes in publishing and marketing practices – particularly the decline of anonymous publication and the rise in marketing of the 'celebrity' author.

Scholars researching developments in the periodical industry of the mid- to late-nineteenth century have recently begun to examine Linton's style and how she both contributed to publishing innovations, such as the turn to an 'open platform' symposia format, and helped to shape the styles and strategies of younger journalists.[6] However, by avoiding the biographical slant of earlier feminist criticism, such critics have yet to consider Linton's careful construction of a marketable authorial persona (consisting of more than her rhetorical style). This chapter contributes to this new wave of critical work on Linton by arguing that, like her 'dynamic'[7] style, Linton's self-marketing is an entry point to examine women's responses to publishing innovations that focused on marketing individual journalists rather than on marketing a 'uniform, identifiable editorial stance'.[8] Indeed, Linton's career trajectory, transitioning from a prolific but unnamed author to an (almost equally prolific) signed celebrity, provides a compact illustration of the move away from anonymity as the dominant industry practice and of the resultant changes to the marketing not only of journalistic copy, but also of the journalist.[9] Linton's own self-marketing is most evident in pieces published in the last 20 years of her career, when she was both contributing to published debates on the state of journalism and capitalizing on her long career in the form of autobiographical reflections.

Within this underutilized archive of Linton's autobiographical works and later periodical pieces, I will particularly consider moments when Linton employs or advocates for restraint, anonymity, and other forms of personal or literary reserve. Such quiet self-restraint seems uncharacteristic, not only within Linton's very vocal career, but within the 'New Journalism' that 'existed by calling attention to itself'.[10] Following this trail of restraint in Linton's writing, I will argue that rather than being anomalous, it is a significant pattern that sheds light on Linton's use of journalistic techniques to market her authorial persona. This chapter will argue that faced with the growing interest in literary celebrities' private lives, Linton reimagined and repurposed strategies familiar from mid-century periodicals – particularly anonymity and pseudonymity – to create and control the 'private' authorial persona(s) she marketed to her audience. Furthermore, turning in my final section to pieces written by Linton's protégé, Beatrice Harraden, I will suggest that along with the example of creating a versatile, highly marketable style, Linton's model of how to create an equally profitable authorial persona should be considered among her legacies for the younger generation of women journalists who were coming to the fore in the 1880s and 1890s.

Interviews and Reflections: Commodifying a Half-Century Career at the *Fin de Siècle*

Recognizing that 'New Journalism' is a relatively baggy catch-all for the 'accumulation from the mid-century of formal, professional, technological, and commercial shifts' which had modernized journalism,[11] the term is nonetheless useful as shorthand for the changes in journalism to which Linton so passionately responded. Indeed, Linton explicitly positioned herself as a censor of 'the new journalism – all its sensationalism, all its rant, all its personality', calling it a 'cockatrice' that had made 'the virtues of the past ... the clots and fetters of the present'.[12] Furthermore, the term's inclusiveness facilitates my investigation of how formal, professional, and commercial innovations overlap in Linton's construction of her authorial persona. For example, it is nearly impossible to separate the professional and commercial implications of changes such as the rise of signature and the increased marketing of individual authors (as in the celebrity author interviews I discuss below), and I argue that both distinctly influence formal choices Linton made in her autobiographical work. However, before turning to the complex formal innovations of her autobiography, which I will address in the next section, I will frame my discussion by examining Linton's more direct responses to New Journalism in which she makes clear her sentiments regarding these changes.

As her continued dominance in the periodical press suggests, one of Linton's key responses to the changes of New Journalism was to exploit them to her advantage.[13] For example, while Linton's censuring of authorial signature will form a major thread of this chapter, this had not always been her position. During the phenomenal response to her 'Girl of the Period' essay (1868), Linton had struggled against the enforced anonymity that blocked her from receiving recognition for her most (in)famous works. Although acknowledging that she 'had to pay pretty smartly in private life, by those who knew [of her authorship], for what they termed a libel and an untruth',[14] Linton nonetheless responded to those 'who, trading on the enforced anonymity of the paper, took spurious credit to themselves for the authorship'[15] by claiming it herself. For example, upon witnessing another author tacitly accept credit for the essays Linton responded by stating: 'Lady _____ may have written the article, but I certainly received the cheque'.[16] After her authorship of the essays was officially acknowledged with the publication of *'The Girl of the Period,' and other Essays from the <u>Saturday Review</u>* (1883), Linton 'confess[ed] that, whether for praise or blame, [she was] glad to be able at last to assume the full responsibility' for her work.[17] Thereafter Linton increasingly produced signed works, and for the last 15 years of her career her writings consistently appeared with signature. She even received the further recognition of her by-line appearing in the table of contents for *Chambers's Journal of Popular Literature Science and*

Arts,[18] and being sought out for composite celebrity articles, such as *The New Review*'s 'Anonymity?, I and II' (1890) and 'The Tree of Knowledge' (1894). By the last 20 years of her career Linton had secured the recognition she had sought during its most turbulent period.

However, in spite of these benefits of name recognition, Linton forcefully and repeatedly criticized the turn to signature that granted a wider circle of women journalists the individual recognition (if not the celebrity) that she had achieved. Linton's criticism appears most explicitly in her (ironically) signed contribution to the *New Review*'s 'Anonymity?' debate, in which she argued that 'anonymity is "more modest as well as more forcible"' than the new practice of signature.[19] In reference to reviews, Linton insisted that anonymity prevented the 'sickly flattery' and attempts to 'curry favour with notabilities'[20] that were increasingly the norm in a literary and journalistic field that had taken 'Barnum's advice to all who have anything to sell' to heart and fully embraced 'self-advertisement'.[21] Although these criticisms certainly have a moralizing tone, maintaining authorial propriety was not the only reason Linton rejected signature. Linton also made it clear that the 'self-advertisement' implied by signature could be a fraught endeavour, particularly for women journalists as the increased personal exposure of New Journalism ineluctably brought women's gender to the fore of their literary personas in new ways. As Alexis Easley argues in *First-Person Anonymous: Women Writers and Victorian Print Media, 1830–70*:

> By requiring signature, editors made it increasingly difficult for women to engage in low-profile literary careers. While the celebrity associated with signed publication was attractive to many women who wanted to make names for themselves, it was a barrier to those who relied upon anonymity as a means of separating their private and public identities.[22]

Although Linton's work suggests she was a woman to whom celebrity was 'attractive', she also clearly valued the privacy and separation of personal and authorial personas that celebrity made increasingly difficult.

Indeed, the potential for being abused in public for private foibles, and in private for public assertions in the press, was a growing problem for women authors that Linton herself had experienced as particularly acute. Dating from the period of her failed marriage with William Linton (effectively separating in 1864; fully separating in 1867 with his remove to the United States), Linton had experienced considerable social abuse – which she considered an 'injustice' – even though no more could be said of her 'than that her marriage had been ill-considered and unsuccessful'.[23] This abuse was augmented by responses to her infamous antifeminist middles published by the *Saturday Review* from 1866–77, which she described as inspiring those whom she censured to give 'back blow for blow, sometimes hitting below the belt, with even a few odd scratchings thrown in'.[24] During this period Linton increasingly came under attack from readers who blurred the distinctions between her public authorial persona and her private person, as well as from fellow authors who responded violently in private to the ideology and rhetoric of her work. Looking back on her career after having attained popular success, Linton not only complained that she had 'paid pretty smartly in private life'[25] for her published opinions, but that in her experience it was 'more than likely that your personal intimate will "slate" you the most severely of all your critics'.[26] Increased exposure of the individual, 'private' author would only further collapse the public/private boundary and make maintaining a successful public authorial persona and private life even more difficult.

It is therefore not surprising that in 'Literature Then and Now' (1890), another reflective comparison of mid-century and *fin de siècle* journalism,[27] Linton explicitly attacks the growing interest in authors' personal lives, and particularly the expectation that those interests will be gratified in interviews. For Linton, such interviews are a violation of the boundary separating one's private self from one's authorial persona, and effectively force the subject to abandon self-respect and cater to an impertinent audience:

> So, too, it comes into the idea of fitness and general harmony that you should be asked to submit yourself to the inquisitorial acumen of a girl young enough to be your granddaughter. ... The girl is a good girl, a clever girl, a pretty girl, and one whose literary career you would willingly help. But a certain feeling of self-respect and dignity, as well as regard for that general fitness of things makes you decline. ... [Y]ou are asked to bare your soul, scarred and seamed and tear-stained as it is with sorrow and experience, to the gaze of a fresh young maid just entering life, who is to question you on such topics as she shall see fitting. Fancy any of the self-respecting men of the past generation receiving such a proposition![28]

However, this particular rant conveys more than a nostalgic wish for the privacy of the past delivered by a prominent member of the older generation of journalists. Linton's portrait of the young 'girl' interviewer and the 'self-respecting men' also recalls anxieties about the 'feminization' of the rapidly expanding popular press in the 1880s and 1890s.[29] The implicit gender hierarchy emphasizes that the changes to journalism that incorporated and recognized more women journalists also became a source of renewed censure of the feminizing and female elements of the press. Women like Linton were caught in a double bind due to their gender; they could arouse public displeasure because of their private failures to live up to the feminine ideal, and they could equally displease certain audiences by illustrating other 'feminine' traits – such as being 'featherbrained' and sensationalizing.[30]

In order to be successful, women journalists often had both to satisfy interest in the journalist by marketing their femininity as part of their literary personas, and to adapt their style to avoid censure as dangerously 'feminine'. Stylistically and rhetorically, Linton illustrated this balancing act by simultaneously performing as a mouthpiece for popular concerns about changes to the press and capitalizing on those changes when possible. On the one hand, Linton's style, resistant to debate and identifying with extremes, exemplifies the sensationalism which was censured as excessively feminine. On the other, Linton focused her own caustic censorship on similarly 'feminine' characteristics of the press, such as the increased use of sex as a way to garner readers' interest.[31] Linton essentially used her 'loud', sensational style to advocate for quiet restraint in order to appease nostalgic critics of the press. For example, asked, along with 13 other signed contributors to the 'The Tree of Knowledge' (1894), to comment on what is appropriate sexual education for young women, Linton spends 6 lines of her 12 line response excoriating any discussion of the issue at all:

> I deprecate the public discussion of the whole subject. I think it indecent and unnecessary. There are certain things which belong to the secret life of the home, and to drag these out into the light of day is a violation of all the sanctities, all the modesties of one's existence. ... It is to be deeply regretted that the subject has been started at all. It is wholly unfit for public discussion, and can do no kind of good.[32]

Linton continues to rely on her mid-century tactic of abusing and censoring change and impropriety, but the way that she packages such censorship for her audience has changed.

With the use of signature Linton could no longer use gender ambiguity to sell her reassuringly masculine, antifeminist rhetoric as an anonymous female journalist.[33] As the evidence above suggests, one tactic Linton used to revise her authorial persona was to instead market her nostalgic conservatism as womanly propriety. Indeed, her article for the *Forum*, 'Mrs. Grundy's Kingdom' (1890), implies an alignment between Linton's public authorial persona and this composite figure of Victorian feminine propriety and censorship. Linton begins her analysis of Mrs. Grundy with several pages deriding the 'tutelary deity of opposition and negation',[34] but ultimately defends her usefulness in maintaining a certain 'standard' and 'order'.[35] Highlighting several of her own conservative viewpoints[36] as a means of defending Mrs. Grundy's conservatism, Linton collapses a clear distinction between herself and her subject.[37] Examining Mrs. Grundy, Linton essentially rehearses the type of complaints launched at her own censorious works, and effectively rises to her own defence; she, like Mrs. Grundy, is a defender of 'standard[s]', a maintainer of 'order'. By feminizing her own conservatism Linton could capitalize on the long-term marketability of a role like Mrs. Grundy's. As Linton herself claimed, no matter what else changes, 'one thing goes on forever and one person is the true Immortal – the power of Mrs. Grundy never fails and Mrs. Grundy herself never dies'.[38] With proper construction of her style and authorial persona Linton could conclude her career as one iteration of this immortal.

Such tactics to construct appropriately feminine authors were not unique to Linton, and indeed her own attempts were expanded upon by other marketers of her authorial persona whose manoeuvrings suggest uneasiness with the divisions that remain visible between Linton's persona, her rhetoric, and the feminine ideal. For example, while Linton modified her rhetoric and style to better meet the demands of New Journalism, her 'private' persona underwent a more thorough reconstruction and repackaging when she agreed to participate in two celebrity interviews in 1893 and 1894 (only three years after her rant against the genre in 'Literature Then and Now'). Rather than portraying Linton as a Grundy-esque ideal of feminine censorship, interviewers Mrs. Alec Tweedie and Helen Black censored the more abrasive elements of Linton's career to make her a more sympathetic, more saleable interview for female audiences. As with the majority of such biographical interviews, the key to this reinvention was to focus on Mrs. Lynn Linton the domestic woman at home, stressing her 'womanliness' and presenting her as 'essentially feminine rather than professional'.[39] Mrs. Alec Tweedie's 'A Chat with Mrs. Lynn Linton' (1894) wittily captures this softening, feminizing project by drawing attention to a moment of humble domestic duties:

> Fancy an authoress of seventy-two darning table-napkins, which are not even her own, for the good housewife's respect for property in general and linen in particular! It is hardly the idea the world has of an authoress. Yet writers are perhaps more human, and often more domesticated than other people.[40]

Helen Black similarly highlights Linton's skilled needle work and feminine domestic arrangements in the opening interview of her collection *Notable Women Authors of the Day*.[41] Both Black and Tweedie stress that rather than the 'stern or severe' figure Linton's writing suggests, the Linton one meets in person 'is bubbling over with the milk of human kindness, and her chief desire is to be of use or help to some one'.[42] The writing and the woman are strictly separated and all but disassociated from one another as only the latter is stressed.

Nonetheless, as Tweedie's 'chat' repeatedly suggests, this is an uneasy re-packaging of the 'Prurient Prude' and the lead 'Saturday Reviler'.[43] The tender 'woman in the flesh' cannot quite cover over or obscure the 'severe, hard, and critical … one on paper whom the world knows',[44] and although relegating it to a discrete space, Tweedie cannot entirely ignore the 'masculine severity [which] is strictly in keeping with her [Linton's] authorship' that is displayed in Linton's writing room, which 'more resembles a man's than a woman's'.[45] While Black and Tweedie certainly catered to the feminizing of popular journalism, the uncomfortable tension between their representations of E. Lynn Linton's severe prose and Mrs. Lynn Linton's kindly darning[46] suggests that while making over the problematic journalist with a feminine stereotype made a more marketable 'private' persona, it could not actually reconcile the friction between public and private personas, between Linton's authorial persona and the ideal of private, feminine domesticity. This lingering tension begins to explain the more complex censoring and reinvention that Linton attempted in her most extensive and puzzling autobiographical work, *The Autobiography of Christopher Kirkland*, to which this chapter will now turn.

Autobiographical Puzzles

Prior to, and contemporaneous with, these responses to the changing expectations for women journalists at the *fin de siècle*, Linton prepared quite extensive personal and literary recollections for popular consumption. These include her rather personal review of Cross's biography of Eliot, 'George Eliot' (1895); her autobiographical reflection on Gad's Hill and Dickens, 'A Retrospect' (1886); her recollections of other 'literary friends' for the *Woman at Home* (1895 and 1896), which were collected posthumously as *My Literary Life* (1899); and perhaps most problematically, *The Autobiography of Christopher Kirkland* (1885). While Linton's reminiscences certainly involved personal details, such as memories of her childhood home and her affection for her 'father' Walter Savage Landor, the majority of these reflections were most prominently literary in nature. Like the responses to New Journalism and makeovers to her persona discussed above, these published reflections provided a means for Linton to capitalize on her long career in order to help it continue; recollecting her relationships with other literary lights, Linton was able to position herself more firmly within the sphere of literary fame. *Christopher Kirkland*, on the other hand, was an entirely different form of self-commodification. The fictionalized, transgendered *Autobiography of Christopher Kirkland* was published by Richard Bentley almost 15 years before Linton's death. *Christopher Kirkland* is therefore even more incomplete and potentially misleading than the average autobiography, but nonetheless profoundly valuable for considering the active, overt construction of Linton's public and authorial persona. Indeed, the theme of quiet self-restraint that marks the changes to Linton's journalistic rhetoric and style is embedded in the very form of her autobiography.

Advertised as a three-volume novel, *Christopher Kirkland* is so substantially and clearly autobiographical that reviewers immediately identified

Christopher's autobiography as a fictionalized account of Linton's own life story. The reviewer for *The Athenæum* stated:

> Mrs. Lynn Linton's new book is a puzzle. Outwardly it is a three-volume novel ... but its resemblance to a novel stops there. Christopher Kirkland sometimes stands for the writer herself ... but at other times he serves only as a conduit pipe for the author's views.[47]

Even in a period when journals often demanded anonymous publication, autobiographically inspired fiction was common, and many novelists and journalists wrote under pseudonyms, this 'puzzle' suggests that *Christopher Kirkland* defied attempts at a clear definition. It undertook a double act of literary crossing: crossing between genders (Linton elides into Christopher) and between genres (fiction blurs into autobiography). Ultimately, however it is defined, *Christopher Kirkland* can be viewed as Linton's attempt to commodify her problematic life and career for a resistant literary audience; an attempt akin in some ways to those undertaken by Black's and Tweedie's domesticating celebrity interviews. As such, this fictionalized autobiography reveals much about Linton's perception of her career and the problems of literary reputation for a female author best known for her ideologically 'masculine' and rhetorically extreme journalism. Spanning her entire life, from her childhood until the time of writing, *Christopher Kirkland* is anything but a coherent, unified text; included within the 'novel' are a retrospect on growing up in the 1820s and 1830s, an account of Linton's entry into journalism in the 1840s and 1850s, numerous memories of key thinkers and literary figures of the mid-century, and explanations of the development of Linton's views on a number of the most prominent questions of her age, including religion, science, and the Woman Question. While certainly fragmentary in form, together these elements create an intellectual *bildungsroman*, tracing the development of Linton as a thinker and writer over the course of the century. Due to its experimentation with form, *Christopher Kirkland* was undeniably an 'extreme exercise in literary transvestism'[48] even for its time, and this extremism, as reviewers predicted, cost Linton her usually positive popular response, and the novel 'miscarried ... enjoyed a lesser vogue than any of her three-volume novels, and never reached a second edition'.[49]

While Linton's reinvention of her authorial persona was less successful than models like Black's and Tweedie's, her attempt raises similar questions as to what is at stake when the end of anonymity, and the rise of the celebrity author, reveals and markets the author as well as the text. What, then, is the more marketable commodity – the image of the author as identifiable through her prose, or what Tweedie, in her conclusion, called the 'real author,' the 'true author'?[50] To return to the epigraph that began this chapter, this is the issue that underlies Linton's comments to her friend Miss Bird after *Christopher Kirkland*'s commercial failure:

> It [*Christopher Kirkland*] was an outpour no one hears me make by word of mouth, a confession of sorrow, suffering, trial, and determination not to be beaten, which few suspect as the underlying truth of my life.[51]

On the one hand, the book's failure suggests that if the 'real' author was increasingly more marketable than a particular authorial style, then that 'real' needed to be something other than Linton's exasperating puzzle – something readily accessible to an audience and meeting certain generic and social expectations. The 'real' Mrs. Lynn Linton needs to darn linens, not philosophize on the value of religion.

On the other hand, as I suggested in the introduction, the organizing opposition here is not only between the real and the perceived; equally important is the opposition between revelation and restraint. Linton's description suggests that *Christopher Kirkland*'s success for the author (in spite of market failure) lies in the ability to circumvent this opposition, to convey the unsuspected, 'underlying truth of [her] life' while keeping that truth separated from her authorial persona. Linton's truth is not simply uttered, made 'by word of mouth', but rather communicated through a multiply mediated print publication. As Linton explained in a letter to her publisher, Richard Bentley, 'she could not publish her autobiography "without some such veil as this of changed sex and personation" – it was, she said, "a screen which takes off the sting of boldness and self-exposure"'.[52] These metaphors of 'veil' and 'screen' suggest that Linton's transgendering as Christopher is a withholding, an obfuscation of Linton's autobiographical materials but not an impenetrable block to readers' understanding of Christopher's true origin. This is a veil meant to be lifted, a screen made to be removed. Shielding herself as Christopher, Linton arguably achieves a separation of public authorial persona and private individual, thereby mitigating scandal for her 'boldness and self-exposure' by placing upon her audience the burden of reuniting her private and public personas; they must remove the veil and discover the 'secret' she is only willing to convey partially.

Enacting the restraint, the withholding of the self, she so often advocated, Linton problematizes and endlessly refracts 'true identity' in her autobiography. Faced with the challenge of presenting her truth, of demonstrating to an audience the gap between her authorial persona and her lived self, Linton chooses the opposite tactic from Black and Tweedie. Rather than shielding her problematic authorial persona and rhetoric behind a genial, more accessible 'true', 'private' persona, Linton, in *Christopher Kirkland*, shields her personal, individual self behind the truth of her authorial career (her 'determination not to be beaten') and the development of her ideological stance. As such, Linton staunchly maintains her authorial agency, creating distance between private and public selves by rewriting her life story as the creative property of E. Lynn Linton the author, rather than the lived experience of the private individual, Mrs. Lynn Linton.[53] In this way, *Christopher Kirkland* bizarrely revises the traditional journalistic anonymity Linton both chafed under and publicly supported. While earlier in her career Linton struggled with the enforced anonymity that allowed others to accept credit for her most well-known work, by the period of *Christopher Kirkland*, when her position as a star journalist was firmly established, she could play with the tactics of pseudonymity and anonymity to generate critical interest in the narrative of her life while distancing herself from the personal censure and ridicule that she had previously experienced. Rejecting the sensationalized form of the 'avowed "Confession"', which Layard, her biographer, believed would have garnered more significant public interest,[54] Linton nonetheless created a new kind of authorial anonymity and gendered ambiguity which she relied upon to be as successful as that which had helped raise the 'Girl of the Period' to the status of cultural phenomena.[55]

Indeed, just as Linton's journalistic rhetoric and style had invited readers' assumptions that a man had authored the 'Girl of the Period' essays, Linton's masculinization of her autobiography allowed a new audience to appreciate her career and accomplishments without the complications of prejudice against female authors or feminine impropriety. In some sense then, *Christopher Kirkland*, although a triple-decker novel, is simultaneously a work of journalism. It is as much inspired in its form by Linton's journalistic skill as by her experience as a prolific novelist (its relationship to journalism is further emphasized by the essay-like quality of much of the text and its greater attention to Christopher's role as journalist than as novelist). *Christopher Kirkland* therefore suggests the continued utility of such traditional journalistic tools as pseudonymity, anonymity, and gender ambiguity for women's deliberate commodification of their writing and their authorial selves. While Linton's appropriation of these once mandated techniques failed in terms of *Christopher Kirkland*'s poor performance, they still offered profitable and powerful possibilities. Understanding the power of these authorial manipulations to make women 'at once creators and constructions, cultural agents and culturally produced texts',[56] Linton's authorial choices in her autobiography seem to form a bridge between more successful attempts: George Eliot's decision in the 1850s to 'reestabl[ish] gender complexity in her novels by maintaining her pseudonym',[57] and later, 'New Women' adopters of the tactic in the 1890s, such as Sarah Grand and George Egerton.[58]

While I am not suggesting that Sarah Grand's choice to use a pseudonym reveals indebtedness to Linton, there is evidence that among the other lessons and assistance Linton offered aspiring women writers was an improved understanding of their position in the literary market and the tactics they could use to navigate its complexities, particularly in relation to those gatekeepers, the editors of the periodical press. In February 1888, just three years after Linton published her own account of dealing with editors in *Christopher Kirkland*, Linton's most devoted pupil, Beatrice Harraden, published 'My Fatal Visit to an Editor' in *Belgravia*. A fictional first-person account of the misadventure of Selina Mayfield, a young woman writer for the press, the story declares its 'main object' to be to 'warn magazine-contributors against coming out of the personal obscurity in which they live' and making themselves known to their editors.[59] In other words, the story aimed to teach women seeking to publish in the periodical press the lesson of restraint advocated by Linton, whom Harraden called her own 'literary godmother'.[60] Selina's 'fatal visit' occurs when she decides to call in person upon an editor who had consistently responded favourably to her work. Once there Selina grew so nervous that she 'could not express [her]self in neat language, and [she] was conscious of stammering most barbarously',[61] a circumstance not helped by her 'abominable eyeglasses', 'which slipped off at least twelve times'.[62] Selina's boldness at approaching her editor, as well as her awkward shyness, cannot help but recall Linton herself, struggling with 'extreme nearsightedness',[63] suffering such 'extraordinary shrinking shyness' that she 'could not speak till [she] was past forty',[64] and yet still bold enough to face the 'awful presence'[65] of her first editor, Cook, as an untried applicant for a position with *The Morning Chronicle*.

For Selina, the result of her foray into the editor's office is a cold shoulder. He refuses to print any of her subsequent submissions; with her bumbling interview and unappealing person she had undone his fantasy of a 'fair, golden-haired damsel, with blue eyes and cheeks like the bloom on a peach, and a gentle manner to subdue even editors'.[66] This reflection also suggests Linton's inspiration; in *Christopher Kirkland*, Christopher asserts that his falling out with Cook was due to the 'power of a pretty woman' who interfered with their friendship, after which Christopher 'suddenly failed to please'.[67] Although Linton's account of the power of feminine attractions to affect an editor's view of a submission is inverted by Christopher's transgendering, both episodes affirm the complexity, and potential pitfalls, of gender's influence on publication. In what was still largely a man's profession, even at the *fin de siècle*, the physical presence of a female contributor, her womanliness or lack thereof, could not be discounted as part of the process of commodifying her self and her works. Selina learns her lesson well, and when she gains entrance as a contributor with a new journal she puts her new knowledge to work:

> The editor has never seen me, and although I hear that he has a great wish to become acquainted with me, I have hitherto refused to give him a personal interview, so that if he has an ideal of me, his ignorance may guard it whole. ... I think the great difficulty is, given a friend, to discover

the best means of keeping him faithful; and my experience has taught me that where editors are concerned, the theory of unveiled mystery should be put into practice.[68]

As Linton warned in 'A Retrospect', 'to call an editor your dear friend in your drawing-room is to insure [sic] unfavourable treatment in his journal'.[69] The gendering of both warnings against editors suggests that journalism at the *fin de siècle* was still very much a field in which women, in spite of increased numbers as contributors and expanded influence as a market share, had to carefully adapt to rules that were not designed for them. However, as suggested both by Linton's attempt to adapt gender ambiguity to her own benefit in *Christopher Kirkland* and by Selina's successful adaptation of authorial anonymity as a means of maintaining her mystery and interest, the ability to commodify one's gender (or the ambiguity of one's gender) could become a valuable tool for a woman working in a periodical press that increasingly marketed femininity.

At mid-century Linton capitalized on traditional journalistic anonymity to market her female-authored work to a male-dominated audience, even while she struggled with anonymity's circumscription of her popular reputation. Reflecting on her own career, the careers of her peers, and the impact of *fin-de-siècle* New Journalism, Linton reveals that the abandonment of anonymity, and her own rise to celebrity status, did little to alleviate this tension. Rather, Linton continued to be concerned with the friction between her private person and public persona, and with the creation of a public persona as marketable as her journalistic style. These concerns suggest continuity between the difficulties faced by women journalists at the mid-century and those faced by the growing number of female journalists at the *fin de siècle*. However, Linton's efforts to create a marketable public persona (publishing conservative views on the rapidly developing New Journalism, participating in celebrity interviews, authoring *Christopher Kirkland*, and generally practicing and promoting restraint), also suggest that while female journalists may have encountered new iterations of the same old problems, they were also developing new ways to make traditional journalistic techniques like anonymity and pseudonymity benefit their careers. Such techniques could be used as tools to successfully negotiate the shifting public/private boundary experienced by the increasingly commodified *fin-de-siècle* journalist.

Notes

1. Linton is referencing *The Autobiography of Christopher Kirkland* (1885), which is her own transgendered autobiography published as a three-volume novel. I will discuss these bizarre formal decisions in the final section of the chapter.
2. George Somes Layard, *Mrs. Lynn Linton: Her Life, Letters, and Opinions* (London: Methuen & Co., 1901), vii.

3. For an account of the difficulties of recovering Linton see Valerie Sanders, 'Eliza Lynn Linton and the Canon,' in *Rebel of the Family,* ed. Deborah T. Meem (Orchard Park, NY: Broadview, 2002), 457–487.

4. Layard, *Mrs. Lynn Linton,* 139.

5. I am thinking here particularly of Elizabeth K. Helsinger, Robin Lauterbach Sheets, and William Veeder, *The Woman Question: Defining Voices, 1837–1883,* vol. 1 of *The Woman Question: Society and Literature in Britain and America, 1837–1883* (New York: Garland, 1983); Nancy Fix Anderson, *Woman Against Women in Victorian England: A Life of Eliza Lynn Linton* (Bloomington: Indiana Univ. Press, 1987); and Deborah T. Meem, 'Eliza Lynn Linton and the Rise of Lesbian Consciousness,' *Journal of the History of Sexuality* 7, no. 4 (1997), 537—60.

6. For this new attention to Linton in terms of the history and form of periodical publication see Andrea Broomfield, 'Much More than an Antifeminist: Eliza Lynn Linton's Contribution to the Rise of Victorian Popular Journalism,' *Victorian Literature and Culture* 29, no. 2 (2001), 267–83; Andrea Broomfield, 'Eliza Lynn Linton, Sarah Grand and the Spectacle of the Victorian Woman Question: Catch Phrases, Buzz Words and Sound Bites,' *English Literature in Translation 1880–1920* 47, no. 3 (2004), 251–72; Laurel Brake, 'Writing Women's History: "The Sex" Debates of 1889,' in *New Woman Hybridities: Femininity, Feminism, and International Consumer Culture, 1880–1930,* ed. Ann Heilmann and Margaret Beetham (London: Routledge, 2004), 51–73; Susan Hamilton, 'Marketing Antifeminism: Eliza Lynn Linton's "Wild Women" Series and the Possibilities of Periodical Signature,' in *Antifeminism and the Victorian Novel: Rereading Nineteenth-Century Women Writers,* ed. Tamara S. Wagner (Amherst, NY: Cambria, 2009), 37–55. All of these pieces share Broomfield's key critical assumption: 'Rather than continuing to focus on reasons for the contradictions between Linton's lifestyle and her prescriptions for other women, we should also pay attention to how her essays worked within journalism itself, how her pronouncements helped define new journalism' (2004: 261).

7. Hamilton, 'Marketing Antifeminism,' 44.

8. Hamilton, 'Marketing Antifeminism,' 41.

9. While this particular transition in Linton's career is underexamined, her life and career have often been studied as symptomatic of the period. For example, Vineta Colby called Linton 'a faithful register of the times in which she lived' (Vineta Colby, *The Singular Anomaly: Women Novelists of the Nineteenth Century* (New York: New York University Press, 1970), 22). Deborah Meem similarly described Linton's complicated life and career as a 'mirror of the inconsistencies of the Victorian Age' (1997: 537).

10. Stephen Koss, *The Rise and Fall of the Political Press in Britain,* vol. 1 (London: Hamish Hamilton, 1981), 343.

11. Kate Campbell, 'W. E. Gladstone, W. T. Stead, Matthew Arnold and a New Journalism: Cultural Politics in the 1880s,' *Victorian Periodicals Review* 36 (Spring 2003), 20–40: 20.

12. Eliza Lynn Linton, 'Literature Then and Now,' *Fortnightly Review* 53 (Apr. 1890), 517–31: 520.

13. As Barbara Onslow notes, by the end of her career and life Linton was 'noticed as a major journalist and author in articles highlighting men and women of the day and one [sic] of the first women members elected to the governing council of the Society of Authors' (Barbara Onslow, *Women of the Press in the Nineteenth Century* (New York: St. Martin's, 2000), 184).

14. Layard, *Her Life,* 144.

15. Layard, *Her Life*, 145.
16. Layard, *Her Life*, 145.
17. Layard, *Her Life*, 145. This battle for recognition continued even after Linton's death. Following the publication of his biography, *Mrs. Lynn Linton: Her Life, Letters, and Opinions* (1901), George Somes Layard found it necessary to respond to accusations he overstated Linton's authorship of the *Saturday Review* articles, including one still insisting that the 'Girl of the Period' article was 'from the pen of a clergyman still living' (Layard, 'Mrs. Lynn Linton and the Girl of the Period,' *Saturday Review* 91 (June 1901), 771).
18. See, for example, vol. 67, 1890, in which Linton's is the only name thus listed.
19. Tighe Hopkins, 'Anonymity? II,' *The New Review* 2 (Mar. 1890), 265–76: 268. Hopkins, the compiler/author of the articles, called Linton an 'uncompromising opponent of the signature' (268).
20. Hopkins, 'Anonymity? II,' 268.
21. Linton, 'Literature Then and Now,' 526.
22. Alexis Easley, *First-Person Anonymous: Women Writers and Victorian Print Media, 1830–70* (Burlington, VT: Ashgate, 2004), 5.
23. Layard, *Her Life*, 134.
24. Layard, *Her Life*, 137.
25. Layard, *Her Life*, 144.
26. Eliza Lynn Linton, 'A Retrospect,' *Fortnightly Review* 45 (1886), 614–29: 624.
27. While Linton begins this article with a discussion of classic 'literature' which we might distinguish from journalism, she quickly shifts to a rant against New Journalism (and the changing publishing, writing, and reading practices it represents) as it affected everything from writing letters to writing books to the periodical press.
28. Linton, 'Literature Then and Now,' 525.
29. Margaret Beetham, *A Magazine of Her Own?: Domesticity and Desire in the Woman's Magazine, 1800–1914* (New York: Routledge, 1996), 123–26.
30. Beetham, *A Magazine of Her Own*, 126.
31. Beetham, *A Magazine of Her Own*, 124–25.
32. 'Tree of Knowledge,' *New Review* 10 (June 1894), 675–90: 682.
33. Broomfield, 'More Than an Antifeminist,' 276.
34. Eliza Lynn Linton, 'Mrs. Grundy's Kingdom,' *Forum* 8 (Feb. 1890), 697–704: 697.
35. Lynn Linton, 'Mrs. Grundy's Kingdom,' 701–2.
36. For example, Linton references Mrs. Grundy's disapproval of the 'feminine cigar' (704), and would publish her own attack on smoking women three years later in 'A Counter-Blast,' *English Illustrated Magazine* 121 (Oct. 1893), 85–89, a response to the pro-smoking campaign of Lady Colin Campbell.
37. The alignment between Linton and Mrs. Grundy is not entirely new. In response to 'The Girl of the Period,' *Tomahawk* published a cartoon captioned '"The Girl of the Period" or, Painted by a Prurient Prude' that depicted the still-unknown author of the essay as a very Grundy-esque figure. See Helsinger, Sheets and Veeder, vol. 1, figure 5.
38. Linton, 'Mrs. Grundy's Kingdom,' 697.
39. Beetham, *A Magazine of Her Own*, 128–29.
40. Ethel Brilliana Tweedie, 'A Chat with Mrs. Lynn Linton', *Temple Bar* 102 (July 1894), 355–64: 362.
41. Helen C. Black, *Notable Women Authors of the Day* (1893; reprint, Freeport, NY: Books for Libraries Press, 1972), particularly 8.

42. Black, *Notable Women Authors* 9.
43. Helsinger, Sheets and Veeder, *The Woman Question*, fig. 5.
44. Tweedie, 'A Chat,' 355.
45. Tweedie, 'A Chat,' 364.
46. I am using the distinction between E. Lynn Linton (her most common authorial signature) and Mrs. Lynn Linton to more easily distinguish between Linton's public and private personas. See note 53 for further discussion of this distinction in relation to *Christopher Kirkland*.
47. 'Literature Reviews,' *The Athenæum Journal* 3013 (25 July 1885): 105.
48. Hilary Fraser, Stephanie Green, and Judith Johnston, *Gender and the Victorian Periodical* (New York: Cambridge University Press, 2003), 28.
49. Layard, *Her Life*, vii.
50. Tweedie, 'A Chat,' 364.
51. Layard, *Her Life*, vii.
52. Nancy Fix Anderson, 'Autobiographical Fantasies of a Female Anti-Feminist: Eliza Lynn Linton as Christopher Kirkland and Theodora Desanges,' *Dickens Studies Annual: Essays on Victorian Fiction* 14 (1985), 287–301: 290.
53. It is interesting to note that while *Christopher Kirkland* is packaged for sale as the work of 'Mrs. Lynn Linton,' her dedication to Edward Barrington de Fonblanque is signed E. Lynn Linton. While at one level this implies a certain interchangeability between E. Lynn Linton and Mrs. Lynn Linton for the reading public, it also suggests a decision on Linton's part to maintain a distinction between her own authorial signature and the persona with which both the literary and journalistic publishing system (in the form, most clearly, of the interviews discussed above) attempted to commodify her. This seems to be an extension of her decision to maintain her own first initial and maiden name in her signature in a period when it would have been common to sign herself as 'Mrs. William Linton'.
54. Layard, *Her Life*, vii.
55. See Helsinger, Sheets, and Veeder, *The Woman Question*, 112–125 for examples of the offspring of Linton's cultural juggernaut.
56. Easley, *First Person Anonymous*, 7.
57. Easley, *First Person Anonymous*, 11.
58. Margaret Beetham, 'Periodicals and the New Media: Women and Imagined Communities,' *Women's Studies International Forum* 29 (June 2006), 231–40.
59. Beatrice Harraden, 'My Fatal Visit to an Editor,' *Belgravia* 64 (Feb. 1888), 82–91: 82.
60. Beatrice Harraden, 'Mrs. Lynn Linton,' *The Bookman: a Review of Books and Life* 8 (Sept. 1898), 16–17: 16.
61. Harraden, 'My Fatal Visit,' 86.
62. Harraden, 'My Fatal Visit,' 90.
63. Anderson, *Woman Against Women*, 8.
64. Tweedie, 'A Chat,' 357.
65. Eliza Lynn Linton, *The Autobiography of Christopher Kirkland* (London: Richard Bentley and Son, 1885), 1: 266.
66. Harraden, 'My Fatal Visit,' 89.
67. Linton, *The Autobiography of Christopher Kirkland*, 2: 142.
68. Harraden, 'My Fatal Visit,' 91.
69. Linton, 'A Retrospect,' 624.

3
'Her usual daring style': Feminist New Journalism, Pioneering Women, and Traces of Frances Power Cobbe

Susan Hamilton
University of Alberta

In 1903, the feminist periodical *Womanhood* reprinted a memorial, organized by the *Central Committee for Women's Suffrage*, and one of many sent to Frances Power Cobbe on the occasion of her 80th birthday. By that date, Cobbe's journalism career had spanned four decades and many shifts in the journalistic landscape, from 1861 when she first published a periodical piece, through to the late 1890s when her journalism appeared irregularly. Her early periodical and newspaper writing in the 1860s on women's education, suffrage, property rights, and domestic violence circulated in newspaper leaders and established periodical titles operating on the 'debate in serial form' model. Her work from about 1875, in contrast, increasingly focused on antivivisection and the immorality of a purportedly materialistic medical science, and was circulated through letters to newspaper editors, pamphlets, books, and pressure-group periodical titles, as well as established periodicals. The signatories to Cobbe's memorial offered congratulations,

> recalling with deep gratitude how much you have contributed to inspire and uplift the hearts of toilers in the cause of the advancement of women, not only by your personal work or by your writings, but also by the cheering example of your whole life.[1]

Among the many names attached to the memorial, *Womanhood* highlighted the names of 22 prominent feminists, including Millicent Fawcett, Elizabeth Garrett, Jessie Boucherette, and Catherine Drew of the Institute of Journalists. Writing from temporary accommodations at Clifton, where she was about to deliver a talk on suffrage to a newly formed club for ladies, Cobbe's response to this public declaration of affection and respect is characteristically gracious and open-hearted. 'I have lived so long out of the world', she writes, '... that I might well have been forgotten by my old fellow-workers. To find myself remembered by them, and known familiarly by name to the younger generation, has cheered me to the heart'.[2]

The *Womanhood* article foregrounds two key issues: the importance of inter-generational recognition to Victorian feminists and the constitutive use of the press as a vehicle for circulating such recognition. Through the reprinted memorial, the journal draws readers' attention to the life work of a prominent Victorian journalist. The periodical editor's decision to draw attention to Catherine Drew's signature, affiliation and status as Vice-President of the Institute of Journalists amongst the highlighted names of prominent activist women in the period, further heightens the visibility of journalism to the periodical's readers. This chapter explores the meaning of journalism to Victorian feminism by tracing the cultural circulation of Frances Power Cobbe's name as a journalist and feminist reformer across generations and within selected communities of women journalists. It further examines the relations between such cultural circulation and the place and history of women journalists in the profession, at the height of the New Journalism, to contemporary assessments of Cobbe's power and successes as a pioneering journalist. Spurred by contemporary debates about women in journalism, feminist journals and journalists evoked Cobbe's name both to show that Cobbe exemplified feminist claims for women's professional abilities and to legitimize women's journalism.

As Chambers, Steiner, and Fleming have argued, the New Journalism produced three key changes for women: it increased women's entry into journalism as women were hired to interview and write stories about other women; it solidified 'women' as subject matter for journalistic treatment, since changing women's roles were seen to embody the social changes of the period and also proved the source of much social anxiety about that change; and its treatment of specific political issues, including women's suffrage, provided the popular press with an opportunity to confront the established press's 'documentary' style through sensationalist and 'human interest' treatments of those issues.[3] Fiction, memoirs, periodical essays, advice columns, employment advertisements, professional handbooks, reviews: the outpouring of texts tackling the place of women in journalism as subjects, reviewers, writers, and editors in this period was prodigious. Distinctive amongst producers and subjects of these texts, as Barbara Onslow has shown, women such as Frances Power Cobbe, Harriet Martineau, and Bessie Rayner Parkes (editor of *English Woman's Journal*), were 'icons in their own century'[4] for their careers. Examining feminist media traces of the late journalistic career of Frances Power Cobbe, particularly the reviews of her autobiography *The Life of Frances Power Cobbe, by Herself* (1894), is one of many possible routes by which to assess the ways in which, during this period of New Journalistic practices, women journalists circulated images of 'pioneering' women to explore, secure, and promote professional success. As we shall see, editors of feminist periodical and newspaper titles in this period actively used the name of Frances Power Cobbe – as a cross-title, subject for an article, and enticement to purchase materials – to convey the importance of feminist journalists and their writing to their readers.

The Institute of Journalists and the place of women journalists

In August 1894, at the Sixth Annual Conference of the British Institute of Journalists, Catherine Drew, one of the signatories to the Cobbe memorial and the only London woman delegate attending the Norwich conference, addressed the gathering on the subject of 'Women as Journalists'. The British Institute of Journalists was originally formed in 1884 as the National Association of Journalists, receiving its Royal Charter as a professional organization under the new name in 1886, and giving way to the National Union of Journalists in 1907. Catherine Drew was assistant editor of the *Irish Builder*, a highly successful trade magazine aimed at architects, civil engineers, surveyors, and builders,[5] and had written a women's interest column, titled 'Ladies' Letter', for the *Belfast News Letter* in the 1870s.[6] At the heart of Drew's address in 1894 is a desire to demonstrate that women contributed to the improvement and high status of the journalistic profession. This concern preoccupied various professional bodies of journalism, including the International Conference of the Press, which had met in Antwerp for the first time just one month before. Noting that the new President of the Institute of Journalists had closed the Antwerp conference by proclaiming that 'There is no more democratic body in the world than the Institute of Journalists of the United Kingdom. It rests on universal suffrage as its basis, it knows no distinction between man journalists and woman journalists',[7] Drew determines to explore for her audience the question of a woman journalist's ability 'to realize the ideal set before her, and live up to such a lofty conception of a journalist's aims and work'[8] as the Institute represented. The intent of Drew's address, in other words, is to put the question of women's status in journalism securely on the agenda of this professional organization and to answer the question in a way beneficial to women by drawing on examples of pioneering women, including Frances Power Cobbe.

Drew's focus on the profession's conception of journalists in her paper addresses a central tension in late-nineteenth-century journalism. As Mark Hampton has shown, from approximately the late 1880s through to the turn of the century, journalism experienced great professional and social insecurity, at the core of which lay 'the inherent tensions of a profession whose claims to status derived from control over an "open" public discourse, rather than arcane "professional" knowledge'.[9] Eschewing educational qualifications and entrance examinations as the only route to demonstrating and safeguarding 'professional' standards, the Institute of Journalists stressed ability and hard work as the guarantors of both individual success and the credibility of the journalistic public sphere.[10] The 'rigours of journalism', or what the contemporary *Gentleman's Magazine* in 1894 called 'the unfailing steadiness, the strictest temperance in the regulation of the daily life',[11] were promoted as individual competencies that were required in order to be successful in journalism. Those same rigours also increasingly served as testimony to the legitimacy and value of the work produced by journalists. Such an emphasis on personal competencies, however, also meant that the particular place of women journalists within this debate became more vexed.[12] On the one hand, an 'open profession' without strict educational requirements was, at least in theory, appealingly open to women; Drew's address reassuringly traces the increase of women in the profession, from a low of 15 women in the 1841 census to a high of 660 women in the English census of 1891, just three years before. On the other hand, the 'rigours of journalism' – the phrase is Hampton's – presented very different challenges. Punctuality, steadiness, as well as the ingenuity, independence, and quick wit central to journalists' self-representations, as Hampton has shown, were not readily identifiable with women journalists. Drew notes that the inclusion of women in the Institute of Journalists, which was boosted as evidence of the association's democracy by its new president in Antwerp, was considered by many to be a 'rash measure ... dangerous ... women would certainly prove themselves to be nuisances'.[13] In a period when one of the leading journalists of the day, *Times* foreign correspondent Henri de Blowitz, suggested that a great journalist needed to 'learn to box, to ride on horseback, and to use a revolver',[14] women journalists like Drew faced profoundly gendered opposition to their attempts to claim professional inclusion and status.

Aiming directly at the tense centre of the controversy, Drew's address offers a compendium of contemporary types of women journalists practicing in the broad field of journalism. If critics of women in journalism insisted that they were not sufficiently rigorous to be professional, Drew's request to her listeners to look closely at the work done by women constitutes a direct, if diplomatic, challenge. Her careful catalogue includes women 'contributors on literary, artistic, and scientific subjects, who work chiefly at home, sending out their contributions on well-digested subjects in cleverly constructed articles'; women 'doing office work, who are neither original thinkers, nor brilliant writers; but ... are accurate and painstaking, ... not the less journalists because they have to arrange, condense, and often re-write the work of others'; 'the sketcher [who cannot] be overlooked in these days of illustrated journalism. ... as yet the worst taught, and the most unmanageable quantity in the world of journalism'; '[t]he fiction writer ... [or] the associate type, [who] scarcely takes rank with the actual worker on newspapers'; and, the great majority of women journalists, the

> 'general practitioner' ... [with] an all-round knowledge ... of people and things, great and small, with a faculty for presenting topics in an attractive manner ... quick to observe, keen to appreciate, cautious to

accept statements, with a well-balanced sense of proportion, and a ready adaptation to circumstances.[15]

As these 'types' suggest, Drew responds to concerns about the potential danger and nuisances posed by women in journalism by pointing to women's accuracy and their capacity to synthesize or digest complex subjects. She is also determined to emphasize women journalists' intellectual qualifications for the profession, such as their keen observation and adaptability, their intellectual maturity and dependability, evident in both their caution and sense of proportion. Drew is also concerned to distinguish clearly between what she presents as 'journalism proper' and the work of other writers whose material might appear serially but whose 'associative' status importantly does not qualify them as journalists. The site of the workplace – the office – is key to Drew's definition of a journalist and to the catalogue of work performed by women journalists. Not all the journalistic work that Drew describes takes place in an office, that prize professional symbol. Yet her catalogue distinguishes between those who work at home and those who, however far afield their work takes them, return to the office to hone a phrase or file a story. Importantly too, in a period of concern about journalism's self-presentation and the particular dangers that women journalists appeared to embody, Drew's catalogue insists upon steadiness, balance, and adaptability. Interestingly, the effect of the catalogue is to de-mythologize one element in the profession's public image, the horse-back riding, gun-toting, adventuring journalist that Mark Hampton documents. In contrast to de Blowitz's valiant, hard-riding, masculine figure, Drew's woman journalist uses her feminine traits of keen observation, adaptability, and an abiding interest in people to work productively in her profession.

At the core of Drew's claim for the importance of women's journalism is her assertion of its commercial value. She insists on the need to include women journalists working on 'ladies papers' – the women whose interests she represents within the Institute – in the definition of 'journalist' then under contestation and debate. Drew emphasizes that such women journalists labour at the centre of a vast national communication network of indisputable economic clout. 'A whole army of women', Drew writes, under-scoring the national import of the undertaking,

> is engaged in this service of viewing, testing, and reporting on the novelties produced. On the verdict of the women journalists often depends the success, or the failure, of a venture on which a large sum of money has been expended. ... Ladies' papers, and the interests they serve, have become a great social and economic power.[16]

'Lady journalists' who work reviewing commercial products, from bonnets to new household appliances, might seem the embodiment of frivolity.

However, Drew's attention to the 'scientific' judgement and capacity to test, which domestic journalism demands, reassures the Institute of Journalists audience that women are not deficient professionals. Women journalists, by this account, cannot be shrugged off as 'nuisances' or excluded from the profession as 'dangerous'. Rather, the profession must embrace women. 'Gentlemen of the Institute', Drew urges,

> [i]t depends upon you what the woman journalist becomes in the future.
> ... She is in your hands, either to do honour to her profession or to cast a
> shadow over the whole profession. ...You have set us a standard, and the
> women I represent are prepared to accept it, and with all their powers to
> try and live up to it.[17]

If the new (male) president of the Institute of Journalists can claim, in front of an international audience, national distinction for his organization on the basis of its 'universal suffrage' for male and female journalists, Drew is equally concerned to claim the national import of women's journalism to the British economy for her national audience.

Within this argument, recognizing and building on the longer history of women's journalism is vital. Drew's address registers, and briefly memorializes, 'exceptional women, of which there were three brilliant examples, [who] contributed to the best leading journals of the day able reviews of scientific, philosophical and literary books, with essays on what is now known as sociology'.[18] The three exemplary women were Caroline Norton, Harriet Martineau, and Frances Power Cobbe. In Drew's account, Cobbe, Norton and Martineau fully realized the journalistic ideals promulgated by the Institute, although writing at a time 'when the professional writer was so small a factor in production'.[19] Drew's invocation of these names is brief, yet rhetorically central in her argument. They serve to mark the great shift that has taken place in journalism, and which Drew fears remains unacknowledged. In the past, she reminds her audience, 'the ordinary journalist woman gave her time to fashion magazines'.[20] In that world, women like Norton, Martineau, and Cobbe were few in number but nonetheless marked women's professional promise. Now, when 'the great majority of women journalists are" what in the medical profession would be known as "general practitioners"',[21] such exceptional women signal that the promise of women's journalism is closer to fulfilment.

In marking out exceptional women in this way, Drew here repeats the larger profession's rhetorical strategy in promulgating promising representations of the journalists. As already noted, Hampton's study of late-nineteenth-century journalists' memoirs demonstrates that it is the figure of the exceptional 'adventuring journalist' whose quick-thinking, adaptability, and courage safeguards the legitimacy of the 'open' profession, despite this figure representing a small minority of the overall work of journalists. Similarly, Drew turns to three women whose political advocacy journalism does not represent the bulk of women's work as journalists in order to demonstrate the legitimacy of women's work as general practitioners in the profession. Both Martineau and Cobbe worked as 'general practitioners' during their long careers, and all three were also prominent for their reform work (on child custody law; anti-slavery; suffrage and domestic violence). Precisely because of their exceptional status, they are the historical, and rhetorical, guarantee that the Institute of Journalists' gamble on women will pay out.

Adding significance to Drew's remarks is the *Englishwoman's Review*'s decision to reprint and recirculate them to its broader readership, using its recurring 'Record of Events' section, in its 15 October 1894 number to assert women journalists' progress and achievements in England. By bringing Drew's address to its readership, the feminist monthly periodical insists that the recirculation of what might seem a narrowly professional event – a paper delivered at an annual conference – holds broader, national interest. Importantly, in framing Drew's paper, the feminist periodical highlights nationalism, pointing both to the international Antwerp conference and the Norwich conference as 'proof of the equal position which our English journalists are ready to accord to the women members of their profession'.[22] The periodical frame for Drew's paper repeats, in other words, her emphasis on the national and political import of the status of women journalists. The periodical notes that Antwerp had invited one of only two women delegates (both English and both from the Institute) to read a paper on the position of English women in journalism, 'which was received with every mark of attention and approval', and highlights the Norwich conference, which 'renewed its expression of confidence' in women by approving Catherine Drew as delegate, and inviting her to read the paper that the *Englishwoman's Review* here strategically reprints for its readers.[23] The reprint, including its framing apparatus, operates at multiple levels in the *Review*. It embodies women's journalistic professionalism by providing an accurate story for its readers. It documents an event (a paper read by a woman at an important national conference) that represents women's increasing prominence in a profession. It emphasizes the place of journalism in women's rights campaigns both as a mechanism for (re)circulation and as a central measure of women's entry into the public sphere. It also memorializes three women pioneers, thereby promoting intergenerational knowledge for its readers. Finally, it registers the importance to this feminist periodical of an English professional organization's recognition of women journalists on an international stage. For the journalists putting together the *Review*, as for Catherine Drew, the place of women in journalism, their historic as well as contemporary achievements, are well worth documenting and promoting.

Feminist Traces of Frances Power Cobbe

Cobbe makes a fleeting appearance in Drew's address, yet her example anchors and makes real the promise of women journalists that Drew offers her Institute colleagues as reassurance for their support of women in the profession. In 1894, as Catherine Drew exults, Frances Power Cobbe 'still lives' and should be claimed 'as one of our honorary and most honoured members' of the Institute of Journalists.[24] Significantly, as the *Englishwoman's Review* readers were reminded of Cobbe's symbolic importance to the credibility of women's journalism, the *Review* was in the midst of preparing its review of her most recent publication. In 1894, Cobbe published *The Life of Frances Power Cobbe, by Herself,* a work that would receive extensive notice in the periodical and newspaper press, including feminist titles such as the *Woman's Journal, Woman's Signal,* and the *Englishwoman's Review.*[25]

The Victorian feminist journalist Frances Power Cobbe was one of a handful of women who made a steady living writing for the established press in that period. She was involved in the national women's suffrage campaign; she argued for women's increased educational and employment opportunities; and she was a vocal critic of both the institution and legal construction of marriage. She worked to improve education for 'ragged' or homeless children and the condition of workhouses. She was instrumental in the passage of the 1878 Matrimonial Causes Act, which made domestic violence grounds for legal separation. She also agitated on behalf of, and helped to write, the 1876 Cruelty to Animals Act, which sought to limit the use of live animals in scientific experiments. She was one of the best-known feminist thinkers of her day. As a historian of Victorian feminisms, Barbara Caine, has suggested, Cobbe's 'ideas were probably better known than those of almost any other feminist' in the period.[26]

The *Englishwoman's Review* publishes its account of Cobbe's two-volume *Life* at the head of its 'Reviews' department in the January number of 1895. Like most of the opening reviews in this section of the periodical, the three-page review of Cobbe's autobiography is lengthier than those which follow. It begins by drawing attention to Cobbe's personal charisma and her political activism as a 'frequent attendant at the Committee Meetings of the Women's Suffrage Society', where the reviewer 'well remembers the thrill of joy her entrance gave ... as if a radiant sunbeam had lighted the office'.[27] It opens, in other words, with Cobbe's suffrage and educational activism to remind its readers of Cobbe's political importance and by emphasizing the character – the sunny nature and committed habits of attendance – of the writer. As we shall see, the *Englishwoman's Review*'s accent on Cobbe's good nature reflects an important strategy by which feminist periodicals conveyed women's professional accomplishments as journalists.

Offering fairly substantial extracts, comprising about one third of the coverage overall, the review is clear about the particular interest such a book holds for its readers. '[C]ontemporary workers' on the many social and political campaigns which the *Englishwoman's Review* supported will find the book 'profoundly interesting', the writer suggests.[28] Similarly, since women's education was a long standing subject of interest in the pages of the *Review*, the chapter on Cobbe's school life

> will be read with special interest now, as a picture of the education pro-
> vided ... at the period when ideas about women's education had pretty
> well touched that lowest depth from which they have been gradually
> rising nearly ever since.[29]

Here, states the review, Cobbe's life illustrates the impact of the feminist push to improve and open up access to women's education, brought vividly before readers by an accomplished writer. But it is 'her life as a journalist ... the fact that Miss Cobbe was the first woman to come and work day by day in the office of a newspaper, [that] gives that part of her life special claim for attention in these pages',[30] and thus receives a substantial portion of the reviewer's attention. Cobbe's work on the London daily *Echo*, where she was on staff from 1868–1875 writing three leaders a week, is singled out for readers and proffered as evidence that, in Cobbe's own quoted words, '"a woman may be relied on as a journalist no less than a man"'.[31] As in its attention to Drew's Institute of Journalists address three months earlier, the *Englishwoman's Review* is eager to point to women's journalism as a sign of women's entry into the professional world of work. In a period of professional disquiet about the role of women in journalism, the review of Cobbe's *Life* is a strategic location in which to demonstrate the strength women have shown in this position. Interestingly, in this review, as in Drew's address, the distinction between long-recognized women writers whose labour is compatible with domesticity – the 'associate type, [who] scarcely takes rank with the actual worker on newspapers'[32] – and actual professional women journalists is critical. Here, the *Englishwoman's Review* enters explicitly into the debate that the Institute of Journalists explores at its conference. Once more, the fact that Cobbe's journalism at the *Echo* was predominantly activist – and so unlike the bulk of journalism undertaken by either male or female journalists – does not compromise its symbolic importance for the *Englishwoman's Review*. Drew had pointed confidently to Norton, Martineau, and Cobbe as exceptional women journalists who nonetheless represent what women are capable of achieving professionally. So too here, the *Englishwoman's Review* points to Cobbe's success as a journalist, working 'day by day in the office', as a rare, and prestigious, mark of women's new professional accomplishments. Hers is a working life well up to the challenge of the 'rigours of journalism'.

Other periodical titles similarly found Cobbe's *Life* worth noticing, and used their review departments to show how women's journalism more broadly exemplified their feminist claims for women's professional abilities. The American weekly feminist newspaper edited by Lucy Stone, *Woman's Journal*, whose masthead reads 'A Weekly Newspaper published every Saturday in Boston, devoted to the interests of Woman – to her educational, industrial, legal and political Equality, and especially in her right of Suffrage', ran a short piece on 3 November 1894. Its 'Literary Notices' department was a recurring element in the newspaper, giving brief synopses of books ranging from poetry to political treatises to art books. Cobbe's *Life* is recommended as a 'delightful book for reading aloud', and the 'cheerful spirit'[33] of its accounts of life as a single woman reformer, as a journalist, and as an antivivisection activist, receives a warm reception. Though the *Woman's Journal* is not in this issue overtly invested in the debate over the place of women in journalism, the notice's emphasis on Cobbe's cheerfulness and approachability helps to present an image of successful women's journalism. Here, the *Woman's Journal*, like the *Englishwoman's Review*, reproduces Cobbe's own self-representation in her *Life* as a successful, good-humoured feminist journalist whose accomplishments spoke more fully to women's overall professional abilities. As in the explicit debate over women's place in journalism, it is Cobbe's cheeriness and sunny disposition that is presented with particular approbation, yoking women's professional abilities and success to certain feminine character traits.

Though there is no extensive treatment of Cobbe's journalism in this review, which occupies about one quarter of what, overall, is a small two-column department of the paper, her importance as an exemplary woman is materially embodied both in the newspaper's ongoing attention to her writing and in the print presentation of her name. The *Woman's Journal* had maintained good journalistic relations with Cobbe over many decades. Just three months into its print run, it had printed her 'private' letter to the editor Lucy Stone, written as one journalist to another, recommending its 'calm and moderate tone'[34] to readers. The *Woman's Journal* continued to print letters to the editor from Cobbe on a variety of political issues such as domestic violence and suffrage activism, including an 1879 letter of 'testimony' about English women's municipal suffrage.[35] It also regularly recommended a small leaflet, *A Duty of Women*, as part of its Woman Suffrage Leaflets series made available to readers through its back pages for a small sum.[36] The title presumably refers to Cobbe's *The Duties of Women*, a book based on a lecture series she had presented in 1881.[37] The *Woman's Journal* would notice the *Life* again, four months after its initial review, in the form of a March 1895 letter to the editor from reader Hester M. Poole, which recounts Cobbe's position on women's suffrage, and notes the importance of her journalistic writing on a range of women's issues.[38] For all of these 'notices' of Cobbe – from the initial correspondence with Lucy Stone to this reader's letter recommending her *Life* – the *Woman's Journal* followed a seemingly established practice when recirculating material from Cobbe or printing materials that focused on her activities and writing. All of these notices receive a separate cross-title in mid-sized bolded and blocked capitals (in the instance of the letter, 'FRANCES POWER COBBE AND THE WOMAN QUESTION'), set mid-column to capture the reader's eye with this famous feminist name. The review of Cobbe's *Life*, brief as it is, seems secondary to the periodical's investment in graphically recording the continuing value of her name for readers.

The value and attraction of a review of Cobbe's *Life* to feminist periodicals is also evident in the *Woman's Signal*, which ran an extensive three-part review of *The Life of Frances Power Cobbe* in its 'Books Worth Reading' department. Originally published as the *Women's Penny Paper* (1888–90), edited by Henrietta Muller – becoming the *Woman's Herald* in 1891 through to 1893 – in 1894 the *Woman's Signal* had just become a predominantly temperance and philanthropic title edited by temperance leader, Lady Henry Somerset, that focused on women's lives and accomplishments. The 'Books Worth Reading' column was a big department in the *Woman's Signal*. But the coverage accorded Cobbe's *Life* was remarkable. Occupying an entire, three-columned page on three separate dates (15, 22, and 29 November 1894), the *Woman's Signal* devoted expansive and expensive print real estate to this review, offering lengthy excerpts and ensuring that the review was easily navigable, and highly visible, through extensive use of capitalized cross-titles that identified themes and critical events in Cobbe's autobiography. Written by Somerset herself, the review focuses equally on Cobbe's writing gifts, her 'burning, yet well balanced words', her perfection in the 'art of using the mother tongue', and her character, the 'healthy freshness of a mind'[39] revealed in this 'so cheery and wholesome a survey of life'.[40] Once more, a feminist periodical gestures to the larger debate surrounding women's place in journalism by reproducing Cobbe's self-representation as a balanced, healthy, articulate, and reasonable feminist. It is character – cheery, wholesome, and fresh – that underwrites Cobbe's rhetorical gifts and professional accomplishments. The bulk of the review is dedicated to substantial extracts illustrating Cobbe's range of celebrated acquaintances (a mix of political and literary figures), her thoughts on political and cultural concerns of her time such as religious heterodoxy and the Irish famine, and her adept ability at mixing 'practical housewifery, Greek and geometry'[41] and so proving 'instructive to those who believe all serious occupation incapacitates a woman for her daily duties'.[42]

More explicitly, the *Woman's Signal* wades into the decades-long debate on women's work, now sited explicitly in the debate on women's journalism, and chooses to intervene in that debate directly. The power and meaning of the weekly periodical's investment in a substantial three-week review is clear in its conclusion. Cobbe's exemplary life of professional work and accomplishment provides, the review argues in closing, an answer to the woman question—and the best answer possible. Ought woman to have a career? be independent of friends and fortune? live a spinster's life, and yet be free to make her influence broad and potent? Yes! a hundred times yes! answers Miss Cobbe; and none who have gone with her from the first chapter of the book to its last page will find in it a single reason for disagreeing with her.[43]

In the *Woman's Signal*, as in so many feminist journals in this period, Cobbe's *Life* seems almost purpose-made to assert and prove the connection between personal character and professional journalistic success. Again and again, in her description of her own professional career, Cobbe is careful to tie professional success with such personal attributes as dependability and commitment:

I made my way to my destination punctually; and, when there, I wrote my leader, and as many 'Notes' as were allotted to me, and thus proved, I hope, once for all, that a woman may be relied on as a journalist no less than a man. I do not think indeed, that very many masculine journalists could make the same boast of regularity as I have done.[44]

And throughout both volumes of her autobiography, Cobbe stresses the sunny humour and sense of personal good fortune that together yielded professional success:

Promptitude, clear and quick judgment as to what is, and is not, expedient and decorous to say; a ready memory well stored with illustrations and unworn quotations, a bright and strong style; and, if it can be attained, a playful (not saturnine) humour superadded,—all these qualities and attainments are called for in writing for a daily newspaper; and the practice of them cannot fail to sharpen their edge. To be in touch with the most striking events of the whole world, and enjoy the privilege of giving your opinion on them to 50,000 or 100,000 readers within a few hours, this struck me, when I first recognized that such was my business as a leader-writer, as something for which many prophets and preachers of old would have given a house full of silver and gold. And I was to be paid for accepting it![45]

The *Woman's Signal* returns to Cobbe's *Life* 14 months later in its 6 February 1896 number, when, with Florence Fenwick-Miller now sitting in the editor's chair, the weekly paper opens with a 'Character Sketch' based on the autobiography. The sketch is substantial. Spread out over four three-columned pages, it includes both a portrait of Cobbe and a reprint of her 1870 pamphlet on women's suffrage, 'Our Policy', which is presented undated and with nine cross-titles that did not appear in the original publication, but that are well suited to the print presentation of this weekly paper.[46] Once again, the combination of exceptional writing prowess and character is presented as politically – and journalistically – vital for the paper's readers. Cobbe provides evidence for feminist-identified readers that women do succeed in a highly competitive professional world. Cobbe's 'sunny and courageous disposition',[47] '[h]er powerful vitality, her strong, sympathetic magnetism, her eloquence of speech, her force of logic, and her perceptive powers', her 'gay good temper'[48] are foregrounded, and the importance of her journalism is stressed. The editor notes that, though Cobbe is author as well as journalist, it is clear that 'her most important literary work has been in journalism'.[49] Cobbe's work on the *Echo*, and later the *Standard*, is singled out, not least because a then 15-year-old Fenwick-Miller 'was able to appreciate those articles, not, of course, having any idea who was their author, sufficiently to cut one of them out and put it in a scrap-book, where I still have it'.[50] Once again, it is Cobbe's professional reliability as a journalist, 'never failing once to produce her copy at the time expected',[51] that serves to mark indelibly women's journalistic abilities and accomplishments.

In the mid-1890s, when changes in the practices and the organization of journalism as a profession created considerable instability, the representation of women journalists played a key role in women's negotiations of these professional opportunities. The presentation of a pioneering journalist like Frances Power Cobbe, an established figure yet one whose newly published autobiography brought her accomplishments freshly to the journalistic stage, offered one location where women journalists – as editors of periodicals and reviewers of books whose jobs required them to assemble an image of the contemporary scene – could control one representation of women's journalistic abilities. Though the documents examined here do not begin to exhaust the journalistic coverage of Cobbe in women's newspaper, magazine and periodical titles in this period, they nonetheless indicate the importance of the history of journalism to Victorian feminism. Through reviewing a writer whose political and cultural works balanced penetrating logic, hearty wit, and rhetorical eloquence, feminist journalists martialled a powerful figure in the debate about women's place in the profession.

When Cobbe died in 1904, readers were once more reminded of her work as a journalist and reformer, her professional prowess, and rhetorical eloquence, with extracts from her *Life* proving a staple of newspaper and periodical coverage. Two days after she died, the *New York Times* ran a quick obituary notice praising Frances Power Cobbe's journalism and her fearlessness in the pursuit of political goals.

> [S]he contributed articles to numerous magazines and weeklies, beginning in 1867, and was for seven years an editorial writer for The Echo of London. ... During this period of her career Miss Cobbe devoted her

principal attention to woman's suffrage, property rights for women, and vivisection. She was one of the foremost opponents of vivisection in England, and when her outspokenness on the subject closed to her the columns of the newspapers, she established a monthly magazine in which she handled it in her usual daring style.[52]

Though the notice incorrectly dates the start of Cobbe's journalistic career, and misrepresents her writing opportunities around vivisection, it rightly focuses on the combination of rhetorical, analytical, and political acumen undergirding her reforming politics: her famed courage, her outspokenness as a political journalist, and the 'daring style' of her journalism.

On the same day, the London *Echo* – Cobbe's employer for seven years and one that allowed her to prove that women were dependable professionals – also ran a substantial death notice. Occupying a full column on its back page, the announcement opened by marking Cobbe's journalism:

As a member of the staff her pen was incessantly active in connection with the leading questions of the day, which she dealt with in a bright, original, racy style that made her as effective as a journalist as she was on the platform.[53]

The notice memorializes the deep connection between Cobbe's journalism and her political activism. It recalls her workhouse reform essays, her women's rights advocacy, the antivivisection work for which she 'took up a pen "barbed with steel and fledged with fire,"'[54] as well as the 1901 donation of her books and personal library to start a town library in the Welsh town of Barmouth – all activities signposted for readers through the *Echo*'s bolded cross-titles. It ends with a brief bibliography of her writings, a considerable portion of which had found earliest expression in journalistic form. Though her political, reforming journalism was no longer – indeed never was – representative of the bulk of journalistic work that women and men undertook, the symbolic importance of such activist journalism to journalism's self-representation meant that Cobbe remained a name to reckon with.

Notes

1. 'Miss Frances Power Cobbe,' *Womanhood* 9, no. 51 (1903), 192.
2. 'Miss Frances Power Cobbe,' 192.
3. Deborah Chambers, Linda Steiner and Carole Fleming, *Women and Journalism* (London: Routledge, 2004), 21.
4. Barbara Onslow, *Women of the Press in Nineteenth Century Britain* (Basingstoke: Macmillan, 2000), 37.
5. Elizabeth Tilley, 'Trading in Knowledge: *The Irish Builder* and Nineteenth-Century Journalism', *Revue LISA/LISA e-journal* 3, no. 1 (2005). http://lisa.revues.org/index2602.html [accessed November 7 2011].

6. Chambers et al., *Women and Journalism*, 32.
7. 'Record of Events: The Institute of Journalists', *Englishwoman's Review* (15 October 1894), 245.
8. 'Record,' 244.
9. Mark Hampton, 'Defining Journalists in Late Nineteenth Century Britain,' *Critical Studies in Media Communication* 22, no. 2 (2005), 138.
10. Hampton, 'Defining Journalists,' 139.
11. Qtd in Hampton, 'Defining Journalists,' 146.
12. Lorna Shelley's 'Female Journalists and Journalism in Fin-de-Siecle Magazine Stories' (*Nineteenth Century Gender Studies* 5, no. 2 (Summer 2009) http://ncgs-journal.com/issue52/shelley.htm#return3 [accessed November 7 2011]) offers a persuasive analysis of the fictional representations of women journalists in the late 1890s, which testifies to the centrality of women in journalism's self-representation at this time. See also Sally Mitchell, 'Careers for Girls: Writing Trash,' *Victorian Periodicals Review* (Fall 1992), 109–113, on opportunities for women in journalism, and Howard Good, 'The Journalist in Fiction, 1890–1930', *Journalism Quarterly* (Summer 1985), 187–214, on fictional representations of journalists.
13. 'Record,' 246.
14. Hampton, 'Defining Journalists,' 147.
15. 'Record,' 248.
16. 'Record,' 249–50.
17. 'Record,' 250–51.
18. 'Record,' 247.
19. 'Record,' 247.
20. 'Record,' 247.
21. 'Record,' 247.
22. 'Record,' 244.
23. 'Record,' 244.
24. 'Record,' 247.
25. Frances Power Cobbe, *The Life of Frances Power Cobbe, by Herself*, 2 vols, (London: Richard Bentley, 1894).
26. Barbara Caine, *Victorian Feminists*, (Oxford: Oxford University Press, 1993), 104–5.
27. 'Reviews,' *Englishwoman's Review* 26, no. 2244 (15 January 1895), 59.
28. 'Reviews,' 60.
29. 'Reviews,' 60.
30. 'Reviews,' 61.
31. 'Reviews,' 62.
32. 'Record,' 248.
33. 'Literary Notices,' *Woman's Journal* 25, no. 44 (3 November 1894), 346.
34. 'Frances Power Cobbe,' *Woman's Journal* 1.13 (2 April 1870), 97.
35. See, for example, 'Testimony of Frances Power Cobbe: Municipal Woman Suffrage in England,' *Woman's Journal* 10, no. 11 (15 March 1879), 81; 'Frances Power Cobbe,' *Woman's Journal* 11, no. 10 (6 March 1880), 76; and 'A Letter from Frances Power Cobbe,' *Woman's Journal* 11, no. 14 (3 April 1880), 104.
36. 'Woman Suffrage Leaflets', *Woman's Journal* 25, no. 3 (15 September 1894), 295.
37. Frances Power Cobbe, *The Duties of Women: A Course of Lectures* (London: Williams and Norgate, 1881). Whether the pamphlet is based on this book or Cobbe provided a version edited for this series is unknown.

38. 'Frances Power Cobbe and the Woman Question,' Letter to the Editor, *Woman's Journal* 26, no. 11 (16 March 1895), 87.
39. 'Books Worth Reading: The Life of Frances Power Cobbe,' *Woman's Signal* 2, no. 46 (15 November 1894), 317.
40. 'Books Worth Reading: The Life of Frances Power Cobbe. Part III,' *Woman's Signal* 2, no. 48 (29 November 1894), 349.
41. 'Books Worth Reading,' 317.
42. 'Books Worth Reading: The Life of Frances Power Cobbe. Part II,' *Woman's Signal* 2, no. 47 (22 November 1894), 333.
43. 'Books Worth Reading. Part III,' 349.
44. Cobbe, *Life*, 60.
45. Cobbe, *Life*, 67.
46. Frances Power Cobbe, *Our Policy: An Address to Women Concerning the Suffrage* (London: London National Society for Women's Suffrage, 1870), 8 pages.
47. 'Character Sketch,' *Woman's Signal* 5, no. 110 (6 February 1896), 81.
48. 'Character Sketch,' 83.
49. 'Character Sketch,' 82.
50. 'Character Sketch,' 82.
51. 'Character Sketch,' 82.
52. 'Frances Power Cobbe Dead,' *New York Times* (6 April 1904), no page.
53. 'Death of Miss Cobbe,' *Echo* (6 April 1904), no page.
54. 'Death of Miss Cobbe,' no page.

4
Edith Simcox's Diptych: Sexuality and Textuality

Brenda Ayres
Liberty University

While the Victorians became very familiar with the name or at least the writings of Edith Simcox in the last three decades of the nineteenth century, most modern readers know her only in the context of her passionate devotion to George Eliot. Simcox's vigorous engagement in women's issues and labour activism, and her complex negotiations with gender representations, were significantly undertaken through the periodical press. The range of her interests, knowledge, languages, and logic confounded those contemporaries who held, as did fellow journalist W. R. Greg, that the 'cerebral organization of the female is far more delicate than that of man'.[1]

Like George Eliot and other women trying to earn a living from journalism, Simcox read and reviewed hundreds of books.[2] From 1860–1899, over 200 of her reviews, articles, and short stories appeared in *Academy*, *Fortnightly Review*, *Fraser's*, *Contemporary Review*, *Nineteenth Century*, *Portfolio*, *Longman's*, *Macmillan's*, *North British Review*, *Saint Paul's*, *Co-Operative News*, *Labour Tribune*, *London Times*, *To-Day*, *Manchester Guardian*, and *Women's Union Journal*. Regardless of genre, she wrote always with the mind to have 'a social bearing', a mission she set for herself and stipulated in her journal.[3] Late in her career when wrestling with some vignettes that would eventually be collected in her book *Episodes in the Lives of Men, Women, and Lovers* (1882), Simcox reminded herself to strike a balance between 'literature and doctrine'.[4] By 'doctrine', she meant political 'truth and righteousness'[5] towards women in regard to suffrage, equal opportunities in education and vocation, fair wages, decent working conditions, and the amelioration of prevailing patriarchal attitudes.

Even if an article by Simcox did not explicitly mention women's rights, her own knowledge, erudite expression, philosophical depth, and lucidity of thought confirmed that a woman possessed intellectual aptitude and extensive interest. The recognized literary authority Edmund Gosse said that she 'wrote ingeniously and learnedly'. [6] Charles J. Robinson, vicar and historian, extolled Simcox as a 'thoughtful and able writer upon the ethical problems which most concern the present generation'.[7] This was high praise indeed at a moment when biologist George J. Romanes was advancing the argument that because women's brains weigh five ounces less than men's, women were intellectually inferior.[8] This hypothesis, stated as fact, appeared in his article, 'The Mental Differences Between Men and Women' in *Nineteenth Century* (1887); Simcox speedily published a polemic rebuttal, 'The Capacity of Women' in the same magazine.[9]

Besides using the press to challenge misconceptions about women, Simcox travelled the United Kingdom and the continent, speaking and attending meetings to fight for better working conditions for women. Along with Emma Smith Paterson (1848–1886), she started the Women's Protective and Provident League in 1874, and they were the first women delegates to the Trade Union Congress that met in Glasgow in 1875.

The periodical press also catalysed and shaped Simcox's labour activism. In 1875 she read a small paragraph in the *Echo* about a public meeting to form a trade union for women employed in bookbinding. After that, she determined to begin a cooperative shirtmaking company with her friend Mary Hamilton that would hire only women and ensure decent working conditions and fair salaries. Thus came into existence Hamilton and Company in Soho, where for the next nine years Simcox would run day-to-day operations. She claimed that she learned how to manage a company from reading *Warehousemen and Drapers Trade Journal* and *Sewing Machine Gazette*.[10] Eschewing totalitarian management, she invited employees to share their ideas and needs regarding the improvement of both the company and their personal satisfaction. While this was not always a pleasant process of negotiation, it was revolutionary to invite employees to influence policy-making decisions, even if some days Simcox was settling disputes over a woman taking another's seat, or over a thoughtless worker impregnating the oven in the communal kitchen with the smell of onions.[11]

Besides the cooperative, Simcox 'worked tirelessly to promote the establishment of trade unions and supported not only shirtmakers but tailoresses and tailors, nailmakers, bookmakers, minders and metallurgists, tenants and lodgers, and hammermen',[12] advocating trade unionization for both men and women. Realizing, however, that most people – especially women – were handicapped from pursuing more lucrative and stimulating employment because of lack of education,[13] Simcox spent many years fighting for increased educational availability and expanded curricula. In 1879 she was elected by a large majority to serve as the Westminster representative to the London School board.[14] For three years she travelled throughout her district, visiting schools, writing reports, and constantly urging reform. In 'Women's Work, Women's Wages' (1879), she pressed for 100% literacy among children.[15] When reviewing *Personal Recollections of Mary Somerville*, Simcox emphasized that the famous female mathematician was self-taught, having received only a village education in 'truly feminine accomplishments—painting, music, needlework'.[16] Somerville told her own daughter, who would later write her biography: 'I was annoyed that my turn for reading was so much disapproved of, and thought it unjust that women should have been given a desire for knowledge if it were wrong to acquire it.'[17] Sir David Brewster, who reviewed Somerville's first book, *The Mechanism of the Heavens*, admired her scientific knowledge: 'acquired with comparative ease, and possessed with unobtrusive simplicity, all our prejudices against such female acquirements vanish'.[18] Simcox responds to this assumption of 'comparative ease' by pointing out that Somerville was 51 by the time she could write her book, and 89 when she published *Molecular and Microscopic Science* and was awarded the Victoria Medal of the Royal Geographical Society. That same year (1869), Somerville wrote that she had made a mistake in not devoting more of her life to Mathematics.[19] Simcox laments the loss of discoveries to humanity because this woman could not develop her potential earlier than she did.[20] In another article Simcox muses similarly on the unfortunate cost to religion and psychology when brilliant women are preoccupied with 'grinding corn' and 'looking after the maids'.[21]

In a witty review of a novel by Elizabeth Rachel Chapman, *A Comtist Lover, and Other Studies*, Simcox refers to Comte's perception of women as goddesses and his concession that there might be those females 'with a turn for "active life," and, therefore, better fitted to bear a hand with the administrative machine than to play the goddess in a domestic circle'.[22] Simcox agrees that we should all 'worship something' and that it is no bad thing for men to worship women, but what or whom are women to worship? Comte advised women to refrain from 'practical pursuits' and 'active life' however, as not to injure their 'delicacy of feeling', which, in Simcox's ironic paraphrase, 'is their mission to cultivate and preserve'. In her review, Simcox offers her own satirical advice: to preserve women's 'delicacy of feeling', men should take over their work, like 'scrub[bing] the floors'.[23]

Simcox herself was not exempt from domestic duties, in that she took care of her mother and sometimes her brothers most of her adult life, and Simcox did not oppose the institution of marriage itself: 'given a man who is adorably lovable and marriage is the natural climax of celestial bliss'.[24] Yet she resented the pressure upon women to be wives, when not all women were born to be wife or mother, or 'a housekeeper, teacher, and a nurse'.[25] Why, she queried, should 'Woman' mean the same thing as 'wife, or a sister of charity'?[26] While discussing two biographies of Dorothy (Dora) Pattison and Mary Carpenter, who made themselves useful to the world and not just within the confines of a small domestic circle, Simcox makes this assessment:

> Clearly it is more important that the Bristol ragamuffins should be reclaimed, and the goals of Bombay and Montreal reformed, than that one more Nonconformist minister should have an exemplary wife; it is more important that many as are sick or sorry in Staffordshire should

have Dora for their sister, than that she should be happy (if she could) in brightening a single home.[27]

In this article, Simcox questions why women, who are so varied in talent and temperament, should be forced into only one role or a 'common destiny'.[28]

Simcox never married even though her adored mentor, George Eliot, asked her time and time again to consider doing so, most likely to deflect the excessive ardour Simcox directed to Eliot that was disconcerting, uninvited, and emphatically unrequited.[29] Simcox once declared in her journal: 'I have never wished to be married in the abstract, and I would most decidedly much rather not be married to any Dick or Tom in the concrete.'[30] '*Was it my fault,*' she reminisced about her 'standing difficulty' – to wit, the love that she had for Eliot that transgressed socially acceptable bounds –

> that I didn't wish to be married in general and that no one in particular wished to marry me? ... If there had been a chance of devoting my life to Her, there would have been no question—right or wrong I could no more have helped myself than the spring tide can help rising.[31]

Although Simcox had been publishing journalism for three years before she met Eliot, and her political activism and accomplishments in reform had already secured her a place in the history books, Simcox seemed to lose a sense of her own achievement by dwelling in the shadow of the great novelist. Of all of Eliot's 'spiritual daughters',[32] Simcox was the most ardent, demonstrative, vocal, and obsessed. In a 1996 anthology of prose by Victorian women, Laurie Zierer suggests that it is only because of Simcox's connection with Eliot that she has not fallen into obscurity.[33] Her name does appear in every Eliot biography, which has memorialized her, but merely as historical footnote and anecdote in the retelling of Eliot's life. More recently, Wikipedia and other websites have designated her as the 'lesbian' who was in love with George Eliot. Unfortunately these references have reduced Simcox's *raison d'être* to her feelings for Eliot and thus militate against an assessment of her own achievements. Alison Valtin agrees with the need for a broader assessment and credits Emma Paterson and Edith Simcox as 'a primary force of the British women's labour movement', writing that because of Simcox's 'considerable influence on British attitudes regarding labor, her career—especially her writing—deserves a second look'.[34] Fortunately, three of Simcox's articles, 'Autobiographies', 'Women's Work and Women's Wages', and 'The Capacity of Women' have been reprinted in Broomfield's and Mitchell's anthology of *Prose by Victorian Women*,[35] but Simcox herself participated in the diminution of her critical regard. For example, she actually thought to withdraw the sale of her book *Natural Law: An Essay in Ethics* simply because Eliot, after having received a copy of it, had nothing more positive to say about it than 'nothing ... jarred on her reading the book.'

Eliot's opinion meant everything to Simcox; her own self-regard was shaped by Eliot's regard.[36]

Constance Fulmer, who is largely responsible for returning Simcox to the limelight in the past decade, asserts that it is time to recognize Edith Simcox for her own accomplishments.[37] However, as Gillian Beer has remarked, for Fulmer and Barfield to title Simcox's autobiography *A Monument to the Memory of George Eliot* actually perpetuates the obscurity of Simcox's accomplishments. If not for the recent publication of *Autobiography of a Shirtmaker*, Beer conjectures that Simcox would 'have vanished utterly'.[38] What is sadly lacking still is an awareness and appreciation of Simcox's literary works and how they complicate for the better our understanding of the struggle that women endured to find a voice of their own, only to realize, as did Simcox, it would never be one voice for all women, nor would it be one voice for each woman. Simcox was a polyglot in more ways than one. She commanded language – diction, syntax, tone, logic, metaphor, even silence – to say with precision what arose out of a multifaceted personality and mind that resisted gender bifurcation.

Early Life and Writing

Simcox's first publication appeared in October 1869: a 108-page, 71-source annotated bibliography of contemporary literature for the *North British Review*, published anonymously.[39] The range of topics is staggering: history, linguistics, physical science, dictionaries, religion, geography, art, sociology, biographies, politics, education, literature, philosophy, and agriculture. Many of the books were in French or German (Simcox could also translate Greek, Dutch, Italian, and Spanish). Despite receiving only a simple village school education for girls – although admittedly with a French governess[40] – Simcox's reading appetite was voracious and her range extensive.

She was born into a London family of intellectuals and writers on 21 August 1844, the youngest of three children and the only daughter. Very close to her older brother George Augustus, who never married, Edith was guided by him in books to read and encouraged to write, publish, and engage in political activism. The father, George Price Simcox, earned a good living from being a Kidderminster carpet maker,[41] by which he could afford to send his sons to Oxford, where both became fellows of Queen's College.[42]

Augustus and Edith became good friends with Charles Appleton, who was, like Augustus, an Oxford don, and who began the *Academy* in 1869. The target market for this journal was intellectual. Intending for it to be more 'academic' and 'scientific' than the *Athenaeum*, Appleton hoped that its style and contents would usher in an intellectual revival.[43]

In its first issue, Simcox (under the pseudonym of H. Lawrenny) published a review of Edmond François Valentin About's 1869 French-language novel, *Ahmed le Fellah*. Her bibliography for the *North British Review*, appearing in the same month, was published anonymously. The *Academy* would carry 77 articles penned by Simcox, more than in any other journal.[44] *Academy* reviewers were considered the best in the business, and of them, many recognized H. Lawrenny/E. J. Simcox to be the best.[45] As a corollary of that stature, Simcox reviewed the most renowned writers of her times, including Charles Dickens, George Eliot, Robert Browning, Charles Reade, Charles Lamb, and Benjamin Disraeli, plus famous composers, artists, politicians, and economists.

No information in her biographies, autobiography, articles, or extant letters explains why Simcox assumed the *nom de plume*. Lawrenny is a parish in Martletwy, in the county of Pembrokeshire in the southwest of Wales. It began as an ancient church prior to 1124[46] and has been a part of the county of Pembroke ever since, and in the hands of the Owens family. The manor of Lawrenny belonged to the Barlows but joined to the Owens through a marriage in 1714. Simcox did travel extensively through the United Kingdom and with her appreciation for history and language, conceivably learned about Lawrenny. The pseudonym's first initial, 'H,' might stand for Hugh,[47] who was the last of the Lawrenny Barlows, and more significantly was the name of the sixth and last baronet in the direct line. He died at the age of 26, unmarried,[48] the age and state of Simcox herself when she adopted the name in 1869. 'Lawrenny' derives from the Welsh *llawr*, which means 'floor or bottom'.[49] 'Enny' may come from 'eni' which translated means 'born' and is usually paired with 'born from' a certain place. Therefore, 'Lawrenny' could mean a place of birth at the bottom lands formed on the peninsula between Garron Pill and Creswell Estuary. The name is fitting, whether Simcox realized it or not, because she was very much like a peninsula herself, situated between and surrounded by social signifiers that elided her own gender identity.

Gender Indeterminacy: Lawrenny and Simcox

To Simcox's great delight, most critics referred to her, when responding to her articles, as Mr. Lawrenny. In her journal she indicated that she usually signed her letters as E. J. Simcox on purpose to get 'mistered'.[50] Adopting a masculine persona in her writing allowed Simcox to explore occasionally biting satire and suggestive, albeit subterranean, critique.

Exploiting the likely perception of a masculine byline (Lawrenny), Simcox published 'Custom and Sex' for the expressed purpose of saving 'us' (that is, men) from 'another year of agitation', because Jacob Bright was at that time introducing another bill for the enfranchisement of women. With typical humour, s/he identifies the problem to be 'agitation' and not the issue of suffrage itself. S/he opens in characteristic fashion with a clincher that excels in skill, universal premise, and diplomacy: 'While political questions are rarely or never settled by the natural action of logical force, it is unreasonable to expect that social problems should be more fortunate.'[51] In explaining, Lawrenny waxes elegant with metaphor:

> Both parties were doubtless aware of the fact; the rambling arguments of the opponents of the bill gathered cogency from the compact force of tradition behind them, and the advocates of innovation were compelled, like the victims of some enchantments, to blunt their swords upon the armour of phantom adversaries, whom they seem to slay, but who are revived again, after every battle, by the magic touch of the mighty witch, whom friends call Habit, and enemies Prejudice.[52]

The diction is ironically charged with references to idealistic notions of medievalism and chivalry. Victorian readers surely drew associations with John Ruskin's highly publicized lectures in Manchester (ironically the city that would become the centre for the campaign for women's suffrage) when he posited as 'eternal truth' that 'the soul's armour is never well set to the heart unless a woman's hand has braced it; and it is only when she braces it loosely that the honour of manhood fails'.[53] Lawrenny describes medieval idealism as 'make-believe'[54] and 'Habit' as something with deep roots but no bloom and no beauty.[55] To continue to argue that women's historically subordinate position is best for everyone is like arguing, s/he says, that we should go about without clothes and eat raw roots as they did in the Garden of Eden, which probably would not be either acceptable or agreeable in London or New York.[56]

This is followed by a puzzling assertion that in the past, a woman was 'happy', 'serene', and 'pretty' a 'contented fraction of a harmonious whole. Her course in life was traced out for her by opinion, which she shared, and custom, which was her own second nature.'[57] Readers could not know if Lawrenny was being sincere or sarcastic. S/he ends the description of an ideal woman of an ideal past with the words, 'she didn't lecture on the rights of women',[58] again as if the problem had nothing to do with women's rights but had everything to do with women agitators. Most unwitting readers were unaware that the writer was one of the most resolute agitators at the end of the century.

Another avowal Lawrenny can make convincingly, under the reader's presumption that the author's gender is male, is that the women's movement 'did not originate with women, but the alterations in their position brought about by material and external causes', such as '[c]ompetition, over-population, free-trade, radicalism, education, the poor laws, infidelity'.[59] Thus s/he uses 'masculine' jargon and theories of Malthus and Darwin that would have been abuzz in gentlemen's clubs, to say that equality for women is a natural social progression of evolution, brought on, not by women's rebellion, but by men's own invention.[60]

By projecting a male persona Lawrenny further attempts to allay a common masculine anxiety that if women were afforded public opportunities, they would transform into Amazonian fighting machines. But then as if to deliberately inflame masculine neurosis, s/he submits that there are many women who are physically stronger than men. Then, perhaps concerned at striking too great a blow to the male ego, Lawrenny resorts to traditional stereotypes and cutting satire by reasoning that the 'natural instinct of the female sex' is to heal instead of maim and that women will always oppose 'the prospect of slaughtering our fellow-creatures'.[61]

The gender politics of the Lawrenny persona become problematic again when s/he retreats from fighting for women by clarifying that s/he wants jobs only for the 'old Maids', and then for only a time between their education and inevitable marriage.[62] Lawrenny revises her stand a month later in a response to a complaint made in the *Pall Mall Gazette* about 'Custom and Sex' by reminding the reader that many women are not mothers, and those that do care for infants, may still be employed in later years. Besides, married women should not be inactive, and they were not. Pointedly, Lawrenny does not remember anyone expressing concern about the detriment to children because mothers were employed dancing or playing croquet, or, in the case of the poor, washing and cleaning houses.[63]

Exploiting rhetoric that was familiar to men from their discourse on Darwinism, and specifically social Darwinism, and striking chords of English nationalism, Lawrenny contends that only 'barbarous or semi-civilised races determined as rough-and-ready division of labour between warriors, priests, women, and slaves'.[64] Liberty and equality, not only for women but for all of the classes, is an inevitability, as sure as is progress, and will prove to be best not for only one class and one gender, but for all. Not once does Lawrenny advocate the rights of women; instead s/he argues what is right and best for all mankind, from a duplicitous male perspective.

Besides Simcox's agility in arguing through idiom familiar to masculinized discourse, her persona's generic wit must have garnered her respect as a journalist regardless of her sex, as this excerpt from 'Custom and Sex' illustrates:

> Girls are to try to get married, but without husband hunting; they are to aim at fascinating the men they meet, but without flirting; and public opinion has very prudently refrained from attempting to fix the line which separates, in each case, legitimate enterprise from unlawful speculation.[65]

H. Lawrenny would be listed as the author of thirty articles over only four years, ending with a review of a book in French by Michel Lévy. Simcox signed that review 'H. Lawrenny' but also added her own name in parenthesis.[66] The review was published only two months after Simcox had met George Eliot while working on a review of *Middlemarch*.[67] Simcox's need to be recognized and to promote her own merits as a woman writer thereafter became not only a political issue but also a personal angst that intensified exponentially with her relationship with Eliot. Thus the first time Simcox completely and permanently severed herself from the masculine or neutral name of Lawrenny was when she signed 'Edith Simcox' in June 1873 to a 21-page contemplation, 'On the Influence of John Stuart Mill's Writing', written in memorial of Mill's death, and quite appropriate for the man who urged women to have a literature of their own that does not imitate men's.[68]

Episodes and 'A Diptych': Simcox's Fiction

Under the name of 'Edith Simcox,' her fiction is densely packed with sexual indeterminacy, especially her books: *Natural Law: An Essay in Ethics* (1877), *Episodes in the Lives of Men, Women, and Lovers* (1882), and *Primitive Civilizations or, Outlines of the History of Ownership in Archaic Communities* (1894).[69] After publishing *Episodes*, Simcox wrote in her diary that she was Arnold, she was Reuben, she stood confessed as Eieiaio – all male characters in her book, which caused her to recall that when she was a child, she had dreamt that somehow she would be proven a boy after all.[70] In these male connections she seems to be aware of the animus within herself. But she admits that she also identifies with the widowed wife in 'The Shadow of Death' (in *Episodes*), who still feels afresh the loss of her 'twin soul' and the 'passionate friendship' of her mate.[71] For Simcox, this story is about the pain of 'nine years of struggling endurance',[72] which echoes the length of time that she has known and desired Eliot.

Arguably, any woman who did not conform to Victorian norms and who, as Daniel Brown cleverly put it, infiltrated the world of men through the Trojan horse of journalism,[73] either had to be very self-assured or very confused about her own gender identity. Although many reviewers judged works based on their assumed knowledge of the author's gender – and were often wrong, as Elaine Showalter delightfully notes in *A Literature of Their Own*[74] – one reviewer for the *Athenaeum* clearly knew that Simcox was the author of a short story titled 'A Diptych' [75] and attacked her solely for her gender. This short story was the third of twelve stories collected in *Episodes in the Lives of Men, Women, and Lovers*, ten of which were relayed through a male, first person point of view. The reviewer acknowledged the writer as that philosopher of moral science and representative to the School Board; and she was a mere woman who attempted 'to write about love in a quasi-scientific way', only to exceed being sentimental by being 'gushing'.[76] Yet the reviewer gives no proof of this, cites no passage, and identifies no characters or scenes or details to support the sweeping condemnation. The review's major concern with 'A Diptych' is that it was written by a woman attempting to portray a man in love, and the reviewer seems to think it folly that a female writer could 'approach any likelihood' of a realistic portrayal, for reasons 'so obvious that there is no need to dilate on them'.[77] Thus the story is summarily dismissed on the grounds of the reviewer's own gender assumptions.

The reality about *Episodes* is that it was fiction ahead of its time. It attempted to accomplish what Simcox attributed to *Middlemarch*, that is, to offer

> a fresh standard for the guidance and imitation of futurity ... an epoch in the history of fiction in so far as the incidents are taken from the inner life, as the action is developed by the direct influence of mind and character on character, as the material circumstances of the outer world are made subordinate and accessory to the artistic presentation of a definite passage of mental experiences.[78]

The stories in *Episodes* are proto-Modern, perhaps even proto-Laurentian in their raw exposure of vulnerable human interiority, as well as the narrative joust of psychological combat between men and women in love. A few years later, Simcox would vent in her journal her frustration that women were rarely forthright about their

> intimate natural feeling about men.... Historically, psychologically, intellectually—and it may be admitted from pure carnal curiosity too I should like to know how many women there are who have honestly no story to tell, how many have some other story than the one which alone is supposed to count and how many of those who think it worth while to dissect themselves are in a position to tell all they know of the result.[79]

Telling those 'other' stories is what Simcox attempted to do in *Episodes*, but as Bodenheimer observes, 'her story line becomes unclear'.[80] The result may be atypically Victorian, even beyond subversions of conventional plots found in *fin-de-siècle* fiction by women, but it is not atypical of what would follow in Modernist literature, such as the impossibility of knowing and presenting reality other than through a kaleidoscope, as exemplified in the works of James Joyce, as well as digging into the past and bringing it forth in instalments, which Virginia Woolf called the 'tunnelling process'.[81]

'A Diptych' is a good example. Sir Alfred Osborne is studying a diptych, that is, a tablet of two pictures. The story line is convoluted, beginning with the statement from the male narrator, Arthur, that the diptych was his 'wife's last birthday present'. Was it a birthday present from him to her or vice versa? Or is the 'present' referring to the portrait of the present wife that Osborne is going to paint, or has he already painted it and it now hangs above the diptych? Pieces of the story, when put together, indicate that Arthur has been married twice and has been in love thrice – so which wife gave or received the birthday present? These details are deliberately obscured because the present of the diptych, regardless of giver, is a gift to all the characters because of its message. The certain details, however, are these: Wife #2 is an artist who painted on the left Wife #1, named – significantly – Edith, the same as the story's author. Represented on the right is one of the most beautiful women in the world, a famous opera singer named Eleanora.

The plot, when reassembled, unfolds as follows. Arthur originally married Edith, but just a fortnight after the wedding, she learns that Arthur is religiously apostate (as was Simcox), and shortly after that, they separate. Off to Italy to heal his broken heart, Arthur is introduced to a woman whose physical features are very similar to Edith's. This Eleanora listens to his sad story, and unlike the very demure, feminine Edith, presents herself as gruff, assertive, and aggressive. She philosophizes about love and marriage in abstruse metaphors. She bemoans that there is a great gulf between men and women, that it is rare that they cross that gulf to help each other, and even rarer that they can do it for a lifetime of marriage. The unlikelihood of men and women of arriving at a deep understanding of each other and closeness is the gist of a metaphor Eleanora uses: 'Many put to sea who dare not cross the ocean, but I think it is not for those who spend their lives in sight of land to speak of the glory and loveliness of the deep.'[82] Simcox's theory seems to be that people (not necessarily just man and wife) desire to have intimacy but because they dare not go beyond the strictures of traditional gender moorings, they will never know a depth of relationship otherwise possible. Since Eleanora makes it clear that Arthur is incapable of reaching this intimacy with her, she represents unattainable love; she is too lofty, esoteric, philosophical, and asexual. Edith represents lost love, which is unsustainable through changing seasons and is erratically emotional and feminine.

Sir Alfred Osborne did paint a portrait of the current wife with a pose that moderates between the two extremes represented by Edith and Eleonora. Concurrently as the gazer gazes at her, she gazes 'fully into his' eyes, with 'neither sadness nor complaint, but the repose of unchanging, confident tenderness. She does not seek, or call, or banish; she makes welcome her secure possession.'[83] Simcox suggestively inverts the androcentricity that predominates in the Pygmalion myth and in Robert Browning's 'My Last Duchess' (1842) and 'Andrea del Sarto' (1855), in which men possess women through art. Following Christina Rossetti's 'In an Artist's Studio' (1856), which criticizes man's objectification of woman and creation of her identity to satisfy his own selfish needs, 'A Diptych' suggests that Simcox's ideal woman strikes a balance between the dyads, or else she embodies an pansexuality that hovers above and defies gender bifurcation. Regardless, she is the one doing the possessing. Her gaze possesses the gazer, and she is in possession of his everlasting love.

The psychological dynamics of the last paragraph, predating Lacan's theories on the Gaze, are complex: Arthur does not show the paintings to just anyone, so in that sense, he is in possession of these women's identity as they are on display, but only when he chooses to exhibit them. When he conceals them, he suppresses the work his wife did in interpreting the two former loves. She is objectified herself, having been painted by Sir Alfred for Arthur. When Arthur does unveil the paintings, he studies the gaze of the viewers, to see if they see the love that resides in the painted woman's eyes, all the while the women in the paintings are gazing at him and them. The text refuses to reinforce traditional gender attributes.

It is no wonder that of all Simcox's works, *Episodes* has such convoluted gender implications. She herself knew that the stories were to have an autobiographical element, but she had to disguise that element, writing: 'I should not like my own people to guess quite how much autobiography there might be in it', and admitting to herself that she 'always meant just the opposite of what [she] seemed to say'.[84] Simcox asked her brothers to read some of these vignettes,[85] and Augustus' response was that they had a 'great force and distinction', but were also 'queer', with doubts to 'what people will make of them'.[86] Simcox was deliberately abstruse, but at the same time, deliberate in emitting her own sexual frustrations.

Simcox saw life as a perpetual struggle, sexuality as a complicated conundrum, and depression as her constant, unwanted companion. Keith McKenzie, the only scholar to have written a book-length biography of Simcox (though she shares the biography's title with Eliot), has theorized that all but two of the stories in *Episodes* are palimpsests for Simcox's suppressed love for Eliot, and that they express a 'masculine love' for her.[87] Rosemarie Bodenheimer has identified the lack of coherency in the stories that comprise *Episodes*, assessing them as revealing not a flaw of the writer, but a flaw in life.[88]

Simcox's 'actual' autobiography was a journal she kept from 1876–1900. Much of it is written with painstaking care to grammar, detail, and clarity, as if she meant for it to be published, and she also gave it a title: *Autobiography of a Shirtmaker*. However, as Onslow points out, Simcox did not in fact publish it,[89] and Gillian Beer claims that Simcox kept it 'under lock and key'.[90] It contains much sensitive and distressing material. Besides the humiliation and devastating effects to her self-esteem due to her unreciprocated sexual love for Eliot, Simcox's very last entry on 29 January 1900 bespeaks a woman weary of causes, pessimistic yet still purposeful. Simcox hoped to recover her health, was still driven to write, and still passionately expressed her love for Eliot, even though Marian Evans Cross had died two decades earlier: 'When I was in bed I cried remembering how I had written to her from Egypt after 3 months away ... I rank her above my other love in perfection for all human relations.'[91]

From in-depth analysis of *Autobiography of a Shirtmaker*, Constance Fulmer and Margaret Barfield conclude that Simcox 'thoroughly enjoyed her own androgyny.'[92] If so, it seems also to have perplexed and tormented her, as well as filled her with self-loathing. One example is in January 1878 when Eliot was to go abroad for her health. In her diary, concerning other matters, Simcox confesses:

> The worst is that I don't care—about that or anything else—: it is possible to me to stay away from her [(Eliot)]; I am not actively unhappy; I laugh off my mother's protestations of concern; the days kill themselves somehow. It is in cold blood and with a kind of unconcern that I despise and condemn myself.[93]

Simcox longed for death, which finally came on 15 September 1901. She had made prior arrangements to be cremated and her ashes buried in her mother's grave, wishing that her own name not be added to the grave marker.[94] Nine years earlier when Simcox visited Eliot's grave, she imagined her own epitaph to read 'Here lies the body of E.J.S. &c, whose heart's desire lives wherever the name and memory of George Eliot is beloved.'[95]

Simcox's life resembled her diptych. On the left was Edith Simcox, the woman – whatever that meant – whose love for humanity compelled her to invest her entire life in improving the world for others. On the right was H. Lawrenny, a persona of indeterminate gender whose love for another woman condemned her to *Weltschmerz* or world weariness.[96] A representation of these two personae might appear Picassoan or Cubist, with parts of them scattered here and there, but never integrated in one coherent piece.

Researching nineteenth-century female journalists who wanted to make a name for themselves, Alexis Easley has postulated that they were always 'first-person anonymous', despite their efforts to the contrary.[97] Simcox was perhaps especially anonymous to herself. Carving out her own identity was a Sisyphean task, but her written legacy reflects her efforts in carving out the right for women to make a name for themselves and contest gender binaries and essentialism.

Notes

1. Of course this quote comes from the notorious article first published in 1862, 'Why Are Women Redundant?' in which Greg tries to solve the problem of what to do with the one-and-a-half million adult women in Great Britain who are unmarried. He argues with absolute certainty that what is essential to 'woman's being' is that, in italics, '*they are supported by, and, they minister to men*' (William Rathbone Greg, 'Why Are Women Redundant?' 1862 (London: Trübner, 1869), 32 and 26, respectively). I found no comment by Simcox made on this article, but I do think it hilarious and poetic justice that she would later review one of Greg's books, *Rocks Ahead; or, the Warnings of Cassandra* (1874) in the *Academy*, as well as two books by his son Percy (*The Devil's Advocate* and *Without God*).

2. Although many women were remunerated for them, reviews required extensive reading of books, drew very little pay, and were often published anonymously, giving no credit to the reviewer. Nevertheless, George Eliot read 166 books in 2 years (Kathryn Hughes, *George Eliot: The Last Victorian* (New York: Cooper Square Press, 2001), 167), and Geraldine Jewsbury reviewed over 2,300 books between 1850 and 1880 (Barbara Onslow, *Women of the Press in Nineteenth-Century Britain* (London: Macmillan, 2000), 70). Many women journalists averaged £2 a week when it took £4 to live (Onslow 38). Simcox hoped for at least £50 a year from her writing but apparently did not get it (*Autobiography of a Shirtmaker: Edith Simcox's A Monument to the Memory of George Eliot*, eds Constance M. Fulmer and Margaret Barfield (New York: Garland, 1998), 22 Feb 1880: 116). The chapter, 'How It Pays' in *How to Write for the Press* gives specifics about salaries (An Editor, *How to Write for the Press: A Practical Handbook for Beginners in Journalism* (London: Horace Cox, 1899), 112–18).

3. Simcox, *Autobiography*, 4 Dec 1878: 118. This and subsequent citations from Simcox's journal refer to its publication as *Autobiography of a Shirtmaker*, published in *Edith Simcox's A Monument to George Eliot* (1998).

4. Simcox, *Autobiography*, 10 June 1880: 125. See *Episodes in the Lives of Men, Women, and Lovers* (London: Trübner, 1882 and Boston: Osgood, 1882).

5. Onslow, 76.

6. Edmund Gosse, 'George Eliot,' in *Aspects and Impressions* (London: Cassell, 1922), 1–16: 1. In a voluminous literary career, Gosse's works include *Seventeenth Century Studies* (1883), *A History of Eighteenth Century Literature* (1889), *The Jacobean Poets* (1894), *History of Modern English Literature* (1897), and *English Literature: An Illustrated Record*, vols. 3 and 4 (1903). He also wrote biographies on Thomas Gray (1884), William Congreve (1888), John Donne (1899), Jeremy Taylor (1904), and Sir Thomas Browne (1905).

7. Charles J. Robinson, Review of *Episodes in the Lives of Men, Women, and Lovers* by Edith Simcox, *Academy*, 521 (Apr. 29, 1882), 296–7: 296.

8. George J. Romanes, 'The Mental Differences Between Men and Women,' *Nineteenth Century* (May 1887), 654–72.

9. Edith Simcox, 'The Capacity of Women,' *Nineteenth Century* 127, (Sept. 1887), 391–403.

10. Edith Simcox, 'Eight Years of Co-Operative Shirtmaking,' *Nineteenth Century* 15 (June 1884), 1037–54: 1040.

11. Simcox, 'Eight Years,' 1043.

12. Constance Fulmer and Margaret E. Barfield, introduction to *A Monument to the Memory of George Eliot: Edith J. Simcox's Autobiography of a Shirtmaker* (New York: Garland, 1998), xii.

13. Simcox, 'Capacity.'

14. Constance Fulmer, 'Edith Simcox: Feminist Critic and Reformer.' *Victorian Review* 31, no. 1 (Spring 1998), 105–21: 109.

15. The Editor [Edith Simcox], 'Women's Work and Women's Wages,' *London Times* 13, no. 11 (Nov. 1885), 539–47. In 1880, Parliament passed the Education Act that made school compulsory for children up to the age of 10. In 1918, school became compulsory for children up to the age of 14.

16. Keith A. McKenzie, *Edith Simcox and George Eliot* (Oxford: Oxford University Press, 1961), 18.

17. Quoted in Edith Simcox, 'New Books,' *Fortnightly Review* 15, no. 85 (Jan. 1874), 109–20: 111.

18. Quoted in Simcox, 'New Books,' 109.
19. Simcox, 'New Books,' 113.
20. Simcox, 'New Books,' 114–15.
21. Simcox, 'Capacity,' 393.
22. Edith Simcox, 'Review of *A Comtist Lover, and Other Studies*, by Elizabeth Rachel Chapman,' *Academy* 760 (27 Nov. 1886), 357–59: 358.
23. Simcox, 'Review of *A Comtist Lover*,' 358.
24. Simcox, *Autobiography*, Oct. 17, 1887: 236.
25. This was part of the response Simcox (writing as Lawrenny) made in the *Examiner* (3349, Apr. 6, 1872: 351) to a complaint in the *Pall Mall Gazette* about her article, 'Custom and Sex.' See H. Lawrenny, 'Custom and Sex,' *Fortnightly Review* 17, no. 63, New Series, 1 (Mar. 1, 1872), 310–22.
26. Lawrenny, 'Custom,' 321–2.
27. Edith Simcox, 'Ideals of Feminine Usefulness,' *Fortnightly Review* 21, no. 161, (May 1880), 656–71: 665. The first of the two biographies is *Sister Dora* (1880) by Margaret Lonsdale about Dorothy Pattison who, within and without the Sisterhood of the Good Samaritans, tended tirelessly to the sick and dying poor. The other is *The Life and Work of Mary Carpenter* by J. Estlin Carpenter (1879). Mary Carpenter taught poor children in the United Kingdom and women in India.
28. Simcox, 'Ideals,' 665–6.
29. Ruby Redinger speculates that the reason Eliot married was to 'evade the lesbian advances of Edith Simcox'. See *George Eliot: The Emergent Self* (New York: Knopf, 1975), 479–80.
30. Simcox, *Autobiography*, 17 Oct 1887: 236.
31. Simcox, *Autobiography*, 23 Sept 1881: 164.
32. These included Elma Stuart, who was buried next to George Eliot in Highgate, Barbara Smith Bodichon (a leading feminist and suffragist who created the *English Women's Journal*), Bessie Rayner Parkes Belloc (another leading feminist and suffragist as well as journalist), Maria Bury Congreve (Mrs. Richard Congreve, wife to the leading proponent of Comte's positivism), Georgina Burne-Jones (wife to Pre-Raphaelite painter Edward Burne-Jones), Mrs. Mark Pattison later Lady Emily Dilke (feminist, art historian, and trade unionist), and Alice Helps (daughter to writer Sir Arthur Helps, who was an old friend of Lewes). Martha Vicinus posits that Eliot had an 'insatiable need for unstinting love and praise from women', which is why she had such an intimate circle of female friends when she isolated herself from others (*Intimate Friends: Women Who Loved Women, 1778–1928* (Chicago: University of Chicago Press, 2004), 125). Rosemarie Bodenheimer also theorizes that Lewes encouraged this 'inner circle' to mitigate bouts of depression that often afflicted her, in *The Real Life of Mary Ann Evans: George Eliot, Her Letters and Fiction* (Ithaca: Cornell University Press, 1994), 242–3.
33. Laurie Zierer, 'Edith Jemima Simcox' in *Prose by Victorian Women: An Anthology*. Eds. Andrea Broomfield and Sally Mitchell (New York and London: Garland, 1996), 523–5: 524.
34. Alison Valtin, 'Clementina Black' in *Prose by Victorian Women: An Anthology*. Eds. Andrea Broomfield and Sally Mitchell (New York and London: Garland, 1996), 599–601: 601.
35. Andrea Broomfield and Sally Mitchell, eds. *Prose by Victorian Women: An Anthology* (New York and London: Garland, 1996). See [Edith Simcox], 'Autobiographies.' *North British Review* 51 (Jan. 1870), 383–414. See also notes 9 and 15 above.

36. Simcox, *Autobiography*, 9 and 17 Nov 1877: 4–7. See also Edith Simcox, *Natural Law: An Essay in Ethics* (London: Trübner, 1877).
37. Preface, ix. Besides co-editing Simcox's *Autobiography of a Shirtmaker*, Fulmer wrote 'Edith Simcox: Feminist Critic and Reformer' published in the *Victorian Review* (see note 14 above); 'A Nineteenth-Century "Womanist" on Gender Issues: Edith Simcox in Her *Autobiography of a Shirtmaker*' in *Nineteenth-Century Prose* 26, no. 2 (Fall 1999), 110–126; and 'Edith Simcox' in *Nineteenth-Century British Women Writers, A Bio-Bibliographical Critical Sourcebook*, ed. Abigail Burnham Bloom (Westport, CT: Greenwood Press, 2000), 367–69. In addition, Fulmer and Margaret E. Barfield created a website on Simcox, and Fulmer has presented on her at numerous conferences. See *Edith Jemima Simcox: Victorian Scholar and Reformer: 1844–1901*, http://faculty.pepperdine.edu/cfulmer/simcox/ [accessed 8 November 2011].
38. Gillian Beer, 'Knowing a Life: Edith Simcox—Sat est vixisse?' in *Knowing the Past: Victorian Literature and Culture*. Ed. Suzy Anger (Ithaca: Cornell University Press, 2001), 252–66: 253–4.
39. [Edith Simcox], 'Contemporary Literature,' *North British Review* 51, no. 101 (Oct. 1869), 196–304.
40. Simcox, *Autobiography*, 17 Oct, 1887: 234.
41. W. Robertson Nicoll, 'George Augustus Simcox,' in *A Bookman's Letters*, 4th edn. (London: Hodder & Stoughton, 1908), 105–13: 108.
42. Augustus wrote reviews for the *Academy*, *Manchester Guardian*, and *Fortnightly Review*, and he contributed articles to *Argosy*, *Nation*, *Expositor*, and *Bookman*. He taught his sister how to 'penny a lining', that is, earn a salary – albeit dismally meagre – from editing articles. He published several scholarly books and translated several classics from Latin. Augustus disappeared at the age of 64 while on a walking tour of Northern Ireland; his body was never found. The middle sibling, William Henry, took orders and became rector of a college with a living at Weyhill. Besides publishing articles on theology, he wrote a biography on Barnabe Barnes, famous for his Elizabeth sonnets.
43. Nicoll, 106.
44. Simcox published in *Academy* under both H. Lawrenny and E. J. Simcox, from its inception on 9 October 1869 to her review of *A Thousand Years of the Tartars* on 28 September 1895. See H. Lawrenny, Review of *Ahmed le Fellah* by Edmond About, *Academy* 1 (9 Oct 1869), 6–7. See also: H. Lawrenny, Review of *A Thousand Years of the Tartar* by E. H. Parker *Academy* 1221 (28 Sept 1895), 239–40.
45. John Sutherland, '*The Academy*' in *The Stanford Companion to Victorian Fiction* (Stanford: University of Stanford Press, 1989), 6.
46. Heather James, 'The Geography of the Cult of St David: A Study of Dedication Patterns in the Medieval Diocese' in *St David of Wales: Cult, Church and Nation*, ed. J. Wyn Evans and Jonathan M. Wooding (Suffolk: Boydell Press, 2007), 41–83: 63.
47. However, in an advertisement in the *Athenaeum* for a review on *Beaumarchais*, the reviewer is listed as 'Henry Lawrenny' and does refer to Edith Simcox, but this is the only incident where 'Henry' is used and therefore cannot be conclusive; it may not have originated with Simcox. See Review of *Théâtre Complet de Beaumarchais* by G. D'Heylli and F. de Marescot, *Academy* 11 (11 June 1870), 223–4. Also: *Athenaeum*, 2224 (11 June 1870), 759.
48. Henry Owen, *Old Pembroke Families in the Ancient County Palatine of Pembroke* (London: Charles J. Clark, 1902), 108–113.

49. George Owen, *The Description of Penbrokshire*, 1603, ed. and notes by Henry Owen, 1892 (London: Bedford Press, 1897), issue 1, part 2, 293, note 6.
50. Simcox, *Autobiography*, 13 Jan 1878: 20.
51. Lawrenny, 'Custom,' 310.
52. Lawrenny, 'Custom,' 310.
53. John Ruskin, 'Of Queen's Gardens,' *Sesame and Lilies: Two Lectures Delivered at Manchester in 1864* (London: Smith, Elder & Co., 1865), 88.
54. Lawrenny, 'Custom,' 311.
55. Lawrenny, 'Custom,' 310.
56. Lawrenny, 'Custom,' 313.
57. Lawrenny, 'Custom,' 311.
58. Lawrenny, 'Custom,' 312–13.
59. Lawrenny, 'Custom,' 312–13.
60. In another few years Simcox published 'The Capacity of Women' under her own name and openly mocked men for historically deriding women for their rebellion ever since Eve ate the forbidden fruit.
61. Lawrenny, 'Custom,' 316.
62. Lawrenny, 'Custom,' 319.
63. Lawrenny, Response to 'Custom,' 351.
64. Lawrenny, 'Custom,' 310.
65. Lawrenny, 'Custom,' 314.
66. Review of *Madame Recamier et les Amis de sa Jeunesse* by Michel Lévy, *Academy* 4, no. 67 (Mar. 1, 1873), 81–82.
67. Eliot sent a note to Simcox to call on 13 December 1872. See Gordon S. Haight, ed. *The George Eliot Letters*, 13 vols. (New Haven: Yale University Press, 1978), vol. 9, 206, n. 4. Also see H. Lawrenny, Review of *Middlemarch* by George Eliot. *Academy* 4, no. 63 (1 Jan. 1873), 1–4.
68. Edith Simcox, 'On the Influence of John Stuart Mill's Writings,' *Contemporary Review* 22 (June 1873), 297–318. See John Stuart Mill, *The Subjection of Women* (London: Longman's, 1869). However, Simcox would continue to publish some of her works anonymously, even as late as 'Rural Roads,' in *Macmillan's Magazine* 52, no. 3 (Sept. 11, 1885), 371–93.
69. Edith Simcox, *Primitive Civilizations, or Outline of the History of Ownership in Archaic Communities* (London: Swan Sonnenschein, 1894). Her last publication, 'The Native Australian Family,' appeared a few months before her death and was published under her name, in *Nineteenth Century* 45, no. 269 (July 1899), 41–65.
70. Simcox, *Autobiography*, 30 Apr 1882: 185.
71. Simcox, *Episodes*, 256.
72. Simcox, *Autobiography*, 30 Apr 1882: 185.
73. Daniel Brown and Hilary Fraser, eds, *English Prose of the Nineteenth Century* (London: Longman, 1997), 21.
74. Elaine Showalter, *A Literature of Their Own: British Women Novelists from Brontë to Lessing* (Princeton: Princeton University Press, 1977), 66–99.
75. The first 'episode' appeared in the June 1881 issue of *Fraser's*, with four more to follow ('A Diptych' was published in July; 'Midsummer Noon,' August; 'Love and Friendship,' October; and 'At Anchor,' November). In April 1882 Trübner (as well as James R. Osgood in Boston) published the four stories with eight more in *Episodes in the Lives of Men, Women, and Lovers*, a title that Simcox chose. See Edith Simcox, 'A Diptych,' *Fraser's Magazine* 619 (July 1881), 42–56; 'Midsummer Moon,' *Fraser's Magazine* 620 (Aug. 1881), 204–11; 'Love and Friendship,' *Fraser's*

Magazine 622 (Oct. 1881), 448–61; and 'At Anchor,' *Fraser's Magazine* 623 (Nov. 1881), 624–29.

76. Edith Simcox, 'Traits and Travesties, Social and Political,' [Review of *Episodes* by Edith Simcox], *Athenaeum* 2850 (June 10, 1882), 725–6.
77. Simcox, 'Traits and Travesties,' 725.
78. Lawrenny, Review of *Middlemarch*, 1.
79. Simcox, *Autobiography*, 17 Oct. 1887, 233.
80. Rosemaire Bodenheimer, 'Autobiography in Fragments: The Elusive Life of Edith Simcox,' *Victorian Studies* 44, no. 3 (Spring 2002), 399–433, *Literature Resource Center*, accessed Sept. 22, 2010, par. 42.
81. Woolf, Virginia, *The Diary of Virginia Woolf*, 5 vols. (London: Hogarth Press, 1978). Vol 2, 1920–1924, Ed. Anne Olivier Bell, 292.
82. Simcox, 'A Diptych,' 54–5.
83. Simcox, 'A Diptych,' 56.
84. Simcox, *Autobiography*, 26 Feb 1880: 116.
85. Simcox, *Autobiography*, 28 Mar 1880: 119.
86. Simcox, *Autobiography*, 5 June 1880: 124.
87. McKenzie, 66.
88. Bodenheimer, 'Fragment,' par. 34.
89. Onslow, 19.
90. Beer, 252.
91. Simcox, *Autobiography*, 280.
92. Fulmer and Barfield, introduction, xvi.
93. Simcox, *Autobiography*, 13 Jan 1878: 20–21.
94. McKenzie, 138–9.
95. Simcox, *Autobiography*, 4 June 1882: 186.
96. Simcox, *Autobiography*, 17 Oct 1887: 239.
97. Alexis Easley, *First Person Anonymous: Women Writers and Victorian Print Media, 1830–70* (Aldershot: Ashgate, 2004), 2.

5

Alice Meynell, Literary Reviewing, and the Cultivation of Scorn

F. Elizabeth Gray
Massey University, New Zealand

> [Ruskin] is very glad I am engaged, but very sorry I am going to be a Reviewer as it is a profession impossible to follow with honour unless I were an *archangel* 'and he will not go beyond angel even for me'. ... [He] ends by wishing me a happy marriage 'and a better trade'
>
> > (letter from Alice Thompson to Wilfrid Meynell)[1]

> Her scorn, when it is roused, is lightly phrased, her wit glances, her irony is invisible, though it slays; and if she admires she withholds exclamations. Intemperateness, redundancy, the *ampoulé* and pretentious, are discarded by her, nor may her heroes be guilty
>
> > (George Meredith).[2]

> ... I read her praise, while, sweet,
> She smiles in contemplation
> > Of her fame and her small feet. (Coventry Patmore)[3]

Arnold Bennett, editor of the late-nineteenth-century periodical *Woman*, produced in 1898 *Journalism for Women*, an advice volume that contained as much spleen as guidance.

> Unlike doctors who are women, of the dwellers in Fleet Street there are not two sexes, but two species—journalists and women-journalists—and the one is as far removed organically from the other as dog from cat.[4]

Women journalists, claims Bennett, enjoy a well-earned reputation for irresponsibility and slip-shod style. 'Not ten per cent of them can be relied upon to satisfy even the most ordinary tests in spelling, grammar, and punctuation.'[5] They lack training and they lack emotional restraint; they

71

are garrulous; they are shrill. Only one woman journalist escapes Bennett's scathing critique: 'Among modern writers, Mrs. Alice Meynell has a style unsurpassed in simplicity, fineness, and strength.'[6]

The writing career of the omni-capable journalist, essayist, and poet Alice Meynell spanned four decades. In these years she jointly edited two long-running periodicals, contributed journalism to over thirty more, published several books of poetry and several more books of essays, served as President of the Society for Women Journalists and on the Executive of the Catholic Women's Suffrage Society, was elected in 1914 to the Academic Committee of the Royal Society for Literature, and was twice nominated for Poet Laureate. She also bore eight children. Once disingenuously suggesting, 'I know nothing except literature',[7] Meynell helped chart new directions for review journalism and criticism at the *fin de siècle*. This chapter focuses on Meynell's periodical reviews and criticism and her production of a unique style and voice, with particular reference to her deployment of an elevated scorn. Her critical scorn offered arresting reevaluations of contemporary literary stars, helped Meynell navigate the difficulties of being both a critic and a woman, and also helped her produce her most famous literary creation: herself.

By the late nineteenth century, 'the review had become ubiquitous, in the daily press and magazine alike'.[8] While the pressure to churn out multiple reviews of lengthy tomes, in very tight timeframes, was bemoaned by many reviewers,[9] journalist Frances Low reported that in the latter part of the nineteenth century literary reviewing was regarded by many as 'the prize of the journalistic profession'.[10] Kimberly Jo Stern goes so far as to call the periodical review 'the genre responsible for defining literary standards, determining a writer's professional status, and translating popular literature into social commentary'.[11] This high valuation of Victorian reviewing requires some complication: as the century drew to a close, the very ubiquity of the review had somewhat diminished its cultural authority. The status of a review at the *fin de siècle* depended increasingly upon the periodical in which it appeared, and – when the review was signed – upon its author. Certain highly regarded reviewers took on a recognized literary power,[12] substantially shaping public opinion. Unsurprisingly, the role and the associated literary power of a respected reviewer were deeply gendered (Waller identifies Andrew Lang, Edmund Gosse, and George Saintsbury as 'the lords of the reviewing world before the Great War').[13] In 1863, an article in the *Saturday Review* suggested reviewing could not come naturally to women writers, for 'no one expects balanced and cold criticism from them'. According to the (anonymous) critic, women invariably 'pour out their whole souls in loving rapture, and think every decent bit of poetry or prose sublime, beautiful, and thrilling'. Therefore, in order to write balanced and unemotional criticism, a woman 'has to judge and write as a man'.[14] Marysa Demoor, one of relatively few scholars to have focused on women's reviewing in the Victorian period,[15] agrees that to gain regard female reviewers sometimes attempted to elide their femininity, suggesting 'that female critics gained [a] powerful place in the legitimate discourse about the work of art or any other publication they had been assigned, at the expense of concealing or even losing their gender when they wrote reviews'.[16] Relatively few women aspired thus, however; examples of that denigrated female reviewing style abounded, inscribing femininity in terms of swooning 'loving rapture.' Blanche Leppington's review of *Amiel's Journal* in *Contemporary Review* offers an illustration:

> From beginning to end, the book does not contain an unkind word. The pages are as warm with human gentleness as a little nest from which the mother-bird has only just lifted her warm wings. Besides, there are other joys. There is the rapture of imaginative sympathy ... There is the exquisite sensibility to the sun, the seasons, the weather, the way this autumn leaf is coloured ... .[17]

The restraint of emotion, it is important to note, was not necessarily a common feature of Victorian reviewing. Women reviewers assumed primary blame for swooning, but both men and women often 'slashed'. In charting the genre conventions of Victorian review journalism, Dallas Liddle explores contemporary methods for constructing and wielding discursive authority[18] and discusses the (dis)honourable history of 'slashing', of which even Marian Evans quite self-consciously took part.[19] Slashing involved intemperate, highly opinionated, often highly picturesque criticism, producing what Macauley called 'a bold dashing scene-painting manner'.[20] The following extract from the *Quarterly Review* illustrates the general tone:

> The edition of [Bolingbroke's] works by Mallet is, if we except the type and paper, one of the worst editions of an English author that ever issued from the press. It is frequently disfigured by misprints; it swarms with errors in punctuation; its text, as a very cursory collation with the original manuscripts will suffice to show, is not always to be depended on. It was hurried into the world with indecent haste ... .[21]

In a stately 1890 review of Ibsen, the *Saturday Review* trenchantly dismissed the two reviewing extremes of swooning and slashing as 'the shrieks of silly admiration and the objurgations of incensed prejudice'.[22] Slashing may have offered an entertaining means of procuring readership, but it didn't necessarily produce 'regard' or a high reputation as a reviewer. And while accusations of immoderate criticism, superficiality, and puffery were regularly levelled at Victorian reviewers irrespective of gender, women reviewers were particularly vulnerable to claims that the 'shrieks' of their innate emotionality were inimical to disinterested, balanced, and liberal criticism. Critical regard, for a woman reviewer, was hard to secure.

Multiple pressures thus bore down on Victorian literary reviewers. In addition to time and financial pressures, they had to negotiate a delicate balance between expressing their individual views on the literary work, and meeting the consumer's expectation of entertainment and provocation. Reviewers had also to negotiate the institutional voice of any particular publication, and its dictates concerning the rhetorical 'flavour' of the review. Demoor suggests that, at least to readers of anonymous periodical reviews, 'the person behind the review was inconsequential, [as] his or her individuality had to disappear behind the ideological uniform of the periodical in question'.[23] The question remains as to whether and where the Victorian reviewer's voice might actually be found. If, as Dillane says, the writer's conscious strategies militate against reading a review's stated opinions as articulations of a writer's creed,[24] could and can a reader ever take the critic at his – or her – word? What is left when rapturous emotion and vituperative slashing is factored out of the *fin-de-siècle* literary review? How could a reviewer negotiate the many opposing pressures of the journalistic marketplace, and create a voice of his or her own?

This clamorous context helps illuminate the groundbreaking nature of Alice Meynell's review criticism, at the *fin de siècle*, of well-known writers, including Tennyson, Elizabeth Barrett Browning, and Coventry Patmore. As adumbrated in her letter from Ruskin, Mrs. Meynell began writing reviews early in her journalistic career, when she and her husband Wilfrid wrote under ceaseless financial pressure to support their growing family. One of Meynell's earliest contributions to the periodical press, in 1876, was a six-part review of *Daniel Deronda* in *The Tablet*; in other early examples, she reviewed Harriet Martineau's *Autobiography* for *Yorick* in 1877, and Mary Wollstonecraft's *Letters to Imlay* in the *Spectator* in 1879. However, as her career progressed, Meynell's periodical reviewing assumed more diverse and fluid forms. She regularly and systematically reused and revised her critical writings upon authors and individual works, in expanded 'review articles', as passages within occasional essays on divergent topics, and in critical introductions to various volumes.[25] In her regular contributions to the *Pall Mall Gazette* in the late 1890s, Meynell published alongside purely occasional essays a large number of reviews and columns of literary criticism, some treating just-published works, and some retrospective reappraisals of contemporary or earlier writers. In the early years of the twentieth century she produced a series of introductions for Blackie's Red Letter Library series of authors' collected or selected works, but she continued to the end of her life to write reviews for *Saturday Review, Fortnightly Review, Poetry Review, Dublin Review, North American Review*, and others. In her capable and broad-ranging reviewing, Meynell neither slashed nor swooned; instead, she wielded an idiosyncratic and scalpel-like scorn.

After the death of Tennyson, Coventry Patmore wrote to the *Saturday Review* suggesting Alice Meynell as Poet Laureate.[26] Meynell critically appraised Tennyson's work on a number of occasions, and in 1910 she published 'Some Thoughts of a Reader of Tennyson' in *Dublin Review*. The review article opens by pointing out that Tennyson was first heralded as a great poet, but 50 years on, critics competed to disparage him. Meynell hails him as 'the nineteenth century master',[27] and, praising him for remaining completely free from French influence, as 'this most English of modern poets'.[28] But she produces a carefully even-handed critique. Tennyson's dramas, she states, are not high art. She distinguishes between his style (great) and his manner (which she styles pretty, insipid, 'too dainty ... nearly a trick').[29] While she criticizes Tennyson's occasional laxity, Meynell defends the apparent ease of his verse against the expectations of contemporary taste that values overt complexity in poetry. She argues Tennyson's lyrical ease is masterful but at the same time dangerous, as it lulls him away from precise, hard thought. Thus, although she praises Tennyson's themes: 'The religious question that arises upon experience of death has never been asked with more sincerity and attention than by him',[30] Meynell criticizes Tennyson for only posing the great question of human destiny, and never closing with it. Meynell also expresses the heterodox opinion that *In Memoriam* was not the high point of Tennyson's achievement. Several years earlier, in a 1904 introduction to the Red Letter Library edition of *In Memoriam*, she wrote, 'the song of loss and regret is affectionate and gentle—perhaps hardly more'.[31] In that critical introduction Meynell points to other great poems of loss, stating that though *In Memoriam* is sweet and grave, it is 'somewhat insignificant'.[32]

Meynell, in fact, offers a reevaluation of Tennyson as primarily a visionary poet of the English countryside: 'he was ... the poet of landscape, and this he is more dearly than pen can describe him.'[33] 'His own note of nature is what Tennyson contributes to our country's poetry; his chief—perhaps essentially his only—purely original addition to English letters.'[34] Meynell thus systematically distances herself from contemporary wisdom, discarding both the traditional points of praise of Tennyson's *oeuvre* and the contemporaneous fad for disparaging him. Her criticism is both opinionated and even-handed, is far from overawed, and sounds an entirely original note.

Meynell struck out in another deliberately polemical direction when she chose to exclude Thomas Gray's 'Elegy Written in a Country Churchyard' from her 1897 anthology *The Flower of the Mind*. In this volume, her self-stated aim was to collect solely the masterpieces of centuries of English poetry. The Victorians revered the 'Elegy' as a quintessentially English masterpiece (Hardy loved it, and borrowed from it the title of *Far From the Madding Crowd;* Edmund Gosse in his 'Modern English Literature' hailed it as the most characteristic single poem of the eighteenth century[35]). That Meynell chose to exclude it from her anthology was both extraordinary and extraordinarily tough-minded. The Introduction to the volume contains her careful but scything judgment of the Elegy.

> My labour has been ... to gather nothing that did not overpass a certain boundary-line of genius. Gray's Elegy, for instance, would rightly be placed at the head of everything below that mark. It is, in fact, so near to the work of genius as to be most directly, closely, and immediately rebuked by genius; it meets genius at close quarters and almost deserves that Shakespeare himself should defeat it. Mediocrity said its own true word in the Elegy:
>
> 'Full many a flower is born to blush unseen,
> And waste its sweetness on the desert air.'[36]

Meynell extended her critique of the 'Elegy' in a critical essay later published in the *Pall Mall Gazette* (21 April 1897): 'It is obvious and deliberate, but not quite a work of genius.'[37] She admits that the Elegy is beautiful, but not noble or stately.

> For the essence of the 'Elegy' is too ordinary for the state it seems to wear and for the beautiful and refined finish of its aspect ... . The heart of the poem is mediocrity—mediocrity at its best; and the world has not anything more widely loved.[38]

Viola Meynell reports 'the storm of discussion that met this opinion'.[39] The *Pall Mall Gazette*'s own review of Meynell's anthology began with purported perplexity, musing, 'The human mind is a bewildering thing', asking with exaggerated courtesy, 'Is Mrs. Meynell serious?', and closing by suggesting she had somewhat 'compromised her previously unique position as a serious and sure-footed critic of the gentler sex'.[40]

But the critical judgement for which Meynell became most notorious was that she passed on Edward Gibbon, author of the magisterial *The Decline and Fall of the Roman Empire*. The almost instantly infamous jibe at Gibbon appeared parenthetically in a 1900 critical volume on Ruskin. The volume was, on the whole, well received, but the attention of many fixed on the following passage:

> Ruskin, at this time and ever after, used 'which' where 'that' would be both more correct and less inelegant. He probably had the habit from him who did more than any other to disorganize the English language— that is, Gibbon.[41]

Meynell was strongly and widely rebuked for this condemnation of Gibbon. Wilfred Whitten, for example, wrote in the *Academy* regretting

Meynell's '*ukase* method of criticism' and 'the gentle, deaf autocracy of her mood'.[42] Meynell did not, however, back down. Her daughter was later to reflect on Meynell's critical stubbornness:

> If her opinions as a critic ... came in for severe criticism, she seemed only hardened in those opinions and inclined to flaunt them. She knew a great deal about yielding, but nothing about it in literary matters.[43]

In actual fact, Meynell had already flown her colours concerning Gibbon's style: 'A Corrupt Following' had appeared in the *Pall Mall Gazette* on 10 January 1900. Unyielding, Meynell later chose to republish that essay in her volume of collected essays, *Second Person Singular* (1921). Tartly and unapologetically championing grammatical and syntactic correctness, 'A Corrupt Following' primarily focuses on Gibbon's stylistic 'laxities' that have been seized and infelicitously copied. Meynell trenchantly catalogues those faults, declaring, 'the dregs of his style have encumbered the nation'.[44] In a critical essay on the Brontë sisters, first published in *Dublin Review*, 1911, Meynell censures Charlotte Brontë's literary style, again skewering 'the good custom of Gibbon's Latinity grown fatally popular'.[45] Meynell calls this custom 'an unscholarly Latin-English' full of wordiness, 'habitual metaphor', and 'strut.'[46]

However, even in her sharpest criticisms, Meynell deliberately set herself apart from the intemperate slashing tradition of reviewing, maintaining a balanced style of dispassionate coolness. Coventry Patmore suggested that she was in fact too good a critic to be capable of slashing, and that her characteristic tool was not a hatchet but a fine blade of diamond sharpness:

> The merits of Lowell and Oliver Wendell Holmes, and the vulgarity of Dickens and the caricaturists of fifty years ago, may afford very good subjects for ordinary critics, but diamond-dust and a razor-edge, though it may have the weight of a hatchet behind it, are quite unadapted for the working up of blocks of teak or sandstone.[47]

By her own definition, Meynell the reviewer expressed not the broad strokes of derision, but rather the fine distinction of elevated scorn. Meynell drew a tripartite division in her writing between derision, humour, and wit. Derision and humour she saw as a pair, respectively sneering and benignant forms of making merry. She called derision 'the unkindest mirth'[48]; that is, mirth at another's expense. Wit, Meynell defined as something else entirely:

> Humour and derision both make game, and make it of persons; while wit is rather amused with ideas and language. [...] Humour and derision watch the person, face to face or askance. Wit may stroll alone, in the light of its own smiles.[49]

Wit, then, is focused on language, and is deliberately elevated and elite. And in an occasional essay entitled 'Children in Burlesque' Meynell develops the idea of scorn as a form of wit predicated on an understanding of equality between the critic and the criticized:

> Between confessed unequals scorn is not even suggested. Its ... proclamation of inequality has no sting and no meaning where inequality is natural and manifest.[50]

What is more, Meynell believed that expressions of scorn should never be gleeful or vituperative: in a delicately phrased critique of Patmore's occasional 'intemperate scorn', Meynell writes that superiority should 'bear itself with ... its proper, signal, and peculiar grace—reluctance'.[51] Applying Meynell's taxonomy to her own reviewing, it is clear both that she refuses derision and slashing in favour of the rarefied commentary of wit, and that her passages of scorn indicate her claim to an equal standing with those she criticizes. Thus Meynell can express (reluctant) scorn for aspects of the work of Tennyson and Gibbon because she allows them no more stylistic laxity than she demonstrably allows herself; as a writer, she admits no 'natural or manifest inequality'.

The sharpness of Meynell's scorn needs particular analysis in regard to women writers, including Harriet Martineau, Miss Mitford, and Elizabeth Barrett Browning. Even Jane Austen was not exempt: in 'The Classic Novelist' (first published in *Pall Mall Gazette* on 16 February 1894) Meynell wrote, 'Miss Austen's art is not of the highest quality; it is of an admirable secondary quality', and she reproached Austen for a 'lack of tenderness and of spirit'.[52] Meynell's critiques of these fellow female writers may be analysed as a differentiation strategy, helping Meynell negotiate the perceived qualitative and stylistic shortcomings of her own gender. Approving herself by means of the critical standards and measures she outlines, Meynell accords herself double recognition as a creative artist and as a discerning literary authority.

In 'A Woman of Masculine Understanding' (first published in *Pall Mall Gazette* on 11 October 1895), Meynell disapproves of Harriet Martineau's 'plodding' prose style, her 'commonplaces' and 'persevering instructiveness',[53] and her sense of her own importance. Despite Martineau's significance as an early nineteenth-century woman of letters and forerunner for writers like Meynell herself, Meynell withholds no apposite criticism, and steadfastly refuses to gush. In a similarly cool critical consideration of Ouida, in 'Oblivion' (first published *Pall Mall Gazette* 16 August 1895), Meynell expresses her own

> regret to find an author of talent mistress of all the habits of mediocrity. Ouida says a thing, and then says it over again from the beginning,

exactly as a cook does. She owns easily a rich vocabulary, but she makes it commoner than she knows. She never approaches pathos even from a distance, though she seems to publish and to scatter its secret words.[54]

Of Miss Mitford's incredibly popular novel *Our Village*, Meynell writes simply: 'it is, in truth, a merely unoffending book, wholly without wit'.[55]

Meynell wrote at much more length, and with much more consideration, on Elizabeth Barrett Browning, who, half a century before Meynell, had also been touted for the laureateship. In an 1896 critical introduction to *Prometheus Bound and Other Poems*, Meynell expresses high praise for the *Sonnets from the Portugese*: 'With the higher workmanship goes closer thinking. Every sonnet of the series has a subject fit for it, a thought with a close.'[56] She calls Browning's sonnets among the very best in the language, but Meynell makes very clear the distinction she draws between Browning's 'high' workmanship and 'close' thinking, on the one hand, and her more rash and slapdash productions, on the other. Browning wrote (according to Meynell), 'a very *banal* literature of romance',[57] full of stuffed characters. In an earlier periodical review, Meynell calls 'Lady Geraldine's Courtship' 'the only nearly worthless piece she [EBB] ever wrote'.[58] Meynell consistently criticizes Browning's unrestrained emotionality. While allowing that important social consequences came through the publication of 'The Cry of the Children' and stating 'Mrs. Browning's morality was positive',[59] Meynell insists on pointing out that 'her poetry was almost always violent'.[60] She critiques Browning's 'strained attitude … [which] is so tense at times as to become defiant', particularly in *Aurora Leigh*[61]: 'The care of public affairs takes, in her verse, a teaching, announcing, denouncing, judicially excited tone.'[62] Meynell's criticism here encompasses Browning's politics as well as style; in Meynell's literary criticism, questions of aesthetics are inseparable from questions of morality.

In 1884, Meynell published in *Merry England* a review article entitled 'Poetesses'.[63] The putative subject of the review was Eric Robertson's recently published anthology *English Poetesses*, but Meynell seized the opportunity not only to critically assess the volume (and to comment acerbically on Robertson's choices), but also to expound her own particular arguments. The review opens by making a forceful case for 'giv[ing] up the division of poets by sex'.[64] Meynell proceeds to give a full, assured, and liberal outline of the history of women's poetry in England, and in so doing constructs a proto-feminist argument about the exclusion of women from literature's canons. Meynell readily admits to the difference in quality of men's and women's writing, but she insists on the cultural and social production of that inequality.

'Printing women,' as Aurora Leigh with a momentary bitterness calls her sisters, will evidently multiply; and as time goes on, and the education of the sexes grows more alike, there must needs be an obliteration of the differences which have justified, if they have justified, the word Poetess.[65]

While praising the courage of such literary pioneers as Katherine Philips and Aphra Behn, Meynell refuses to flatter all the writers whom Robertson has included in his volume:

> Nothing ... could warrant the admission of Lady Mary [Wortley Montague] into a company of poetesses. When he resolved that sex should be the boundary of his subject, the author no doubt congratulated himself upon the manageable size of his little field. But if every plant of a little field has to be collected, the harvest is ranker than if a mile of country were lightly searched for roses.[66]

Meynell offers a two-fold critique in this review. She criticizes Robertson's editorial laziness in terms of both inclusions and exclusions, and also his unwillingness to apply a uniformly strict standard of literary merit. This failure Meynell sees as patronising, and she resolutely refuses to apply this double standard herself. She then offers her own evaluation of the poetry of the women represented in Robertson's volume, offering a more contextualized critique, and in several passages consciously and thought-fully flying in the face of contemporary opinion.

> Mrs. Hemans['] mediocrity and sweetness gained for her that popular enthusiasm which is far oftener given to reward such apparently unexciting merits than to crown either great worth or showy worthlessness. [...] The populace does not simply like—it loves—respectable talent; loves it with unexpected emotion and excitement. The political *personnel* of our present day offers an instance of this kind of *bourgeois* feeling raised by a name which we dare not write for fear of enthusiastic indignation. Mrs. Hemans took the hearts of the overwhelming majority. Her sadness was pleasing—it never hurt a reader by penetrating between soul and spirit, as the sadness of high sincerity has pierced. Her work was thus all the more fit for schools and for the learning by children.[67]

As well as fine scorn, Meynell expresses high praise in this review. She acclaims Emily Brontë's genius, according her talent and originality great respect; Meynell also defends George Eliot's poetry against the 'somewhat harsh judgment' of the critics.[68] Certainly, very few contemporary critics would have concurred with Meynell's assessment that 'The close of "Jubal" is a passage so great and so poetic that to have written it should ratify [Eliot's] title to that name of poet which has rather glibly been denied her'.[69]

Thus, even while assuming equality with the period's most revered literary figures, Meynell's criticism may also be seen to seek to differentiate herself from her contemporaries, perhaps most pointedly from her female contemporaries. Whether she champions them (Emily Brontë, Christina Rossetti), defends them (George Eliot, Jean Ingelow), or critiques them (Ouida, Elizabeth Barrett Browning), Meynell insists on the reviewer's privilege of *distinction*, never wavering from authoritarianism into slavishness. Meynell's construction of her own literary status refuses any form of feminine literary lineage, rather building on a systematic stylistic and critical self-differentiation from female forerunners and contemporaries. Meynell helped create a name and a distinctive voice as a literary critic by very consciously lacerating precisely those stylistic qualities culturally perceived (and denigrated) as feminine. 'Women and Words' (a critical essay published in *Merry England* in 1886) argues that critical acclaim has quite understandably passed over women's writing. 'In England it is undeniably the case that the grammarians would think as readily of entrusting the nursery as the boudoir with the purity of the national tongue.'[70] Linguistic laziness and lack of restraint are sternly rebuked: 'Why are [English] women, nationally dainty in dress and perfect in person, such very slatterns in speech?'[71] Similar critiques of women's writing appear throughout Meynell's reviewing and literary criticism, and her critical rejection of undisciplined style exists in a mutually constitutive relationship with her own signature style, consciously regulated, emotionally reserved, and elevatedly scornful.

Meynell did, of course, also offer critical praise, although it never gushes, and it regularly swims against the tide of popular taste. Already mentioned is her praise of Emily Brontë's poetry, which Meynell recognized enjoyed little contemporary appreciation:

> Emily Brontë's genius, her great and lonely intellect, that force of hers in which there is none of the tensity of secret weakness, but an intensity that never falters; her solemnity, her solitary courage, her direct contemplation of essential evil, and the more than human liberty which she claims for her own great and melancholy heart—these have made her dear to no public.[72]

Meynell also greatly valued the poetry of the seventeenth century, and in this respect she was markedly ahead of her time (the metaphysical poets being 'rediscovered' by T. S. Eliot in the 1920s). She wrote glowing critical appraisals of Crashaw, Marvell, and Henry Vaughan, among others.

However, Meynell's highest and most distinctive praise – again in the face of prevailing opinion – was reserved for the poetry of Coventry Patmore, which she viewed as supreme genius. In 1891, she reviewed 'Mr. Coventry Patmore's Odes' in the *National Observer* (reprinting this review in her first collection, *The Rhythm of Life*), and she went on to publish several further reviews of his poetry, including those in the *Weekly Register* and in *Outlook*. Meynell uses the highest possible terms of approbation, calling Patmore 'the capturer of an art so quick and close that it is the voice less of a poet than of the very Muse',[73] and acclaiming the 'transcendent simplicity' of his art: 'there is nothing in the world more costly'.[74] She compares *The Unknown Eros* to the biblical Song of Songs, writing: 'The art that utters an intellectual action so courageous, an emotion so authentic, as that of Mr. Coventry Patmore's poetry, cannot be otherwise than consummate.'[75] In recognizing few shared her judgement of Patmore's poetry, Meynell chooses to recast the critical neglect of the Odes as a sign of their splendour and rarity:

> Whatever criticism may learn in time to come, *The Unknown Eros* will hardly then have many readers, and will no doubt still keep the accidental loneliness that surrounds it now by reason of the indifference of the majority; but its essential loneliness is its own quality.[76]

Meynell responded personally when Edmund Gosse published a book on Patmore which Meynell felt deliberately undervalued the *Odes to Eros*, penning Gosse a reproving letter: 'You write in a tepid spirit. ... You do not give expression to the homage of your heart.'[77] Although Meynell withdrew from her very close friendship with Patmore before his death in 1896, her praise of his supreme artistry never wavered.

Meynell offers one of the most explicit commentaries on her own literary ambitions when she takes up the topic of literary criticism itself, reflecting on its nature as a literary endeavour with the potential for its own lasting merit.

> For every one who has undertaken to write on the work of other men knows well how the act of homage more than all other appreciative acts tests and tries the critical style; sets the critic's words as it were against the sky, forlorn, conspicuous; exposes his platitudes; accuses him with the extremity of rigour, or excuses him with the last delicacy; approves his fastidiousness, secures to him a success honestly come by, without noise; or else leaves him uncomforted in his own prose—a dull writer making all the commonplaces more common, and aware that his reader holds them cheap.[78]

Meynell 'tested and tried' her own critical style by scrupulously avoiding those qualities she frequently stated she abhorred: superfluity, exaggeration, false emotions, laxity, and extravagant metaphors. In consciously differentiating her style from a particular gendered reviewing mode, and in reviewing as an equal rather than a swooner or a slasher, Meynell didn't try to turn herself into a man; rather, she turned herself into Alice Meynell.

In closing, I argue that Meynell's self-production as Alice Meynell, distinctive literary reviewer and distinguished creative artist, was mediated in complex and conscious ways by the periodical press itself. In *Becoming a Woman of*

Letters, Linda Peterson offers a thoughtful assessment of Meynell's career trajectory, focusing closely on Meynell's self-consciously performed 'shift from journalism to literature'.[79] I suggest, however, that Meynell worked out her literary identity and authority largely *within* and *by means of* her reviewing journalism. In the essay 'The Honours of Mortality', first published in *Pall Mall Gazette* on 29 September 1893 (and reprinted in the collection *The Colour of Life* in 1896), Meynell mused on two interlocking topics: the ephemeral nature of periodical production, and the production and duration of fame. This essay is so brief, but so dense, it should be quoted in full.

> The brilliant talent which has quite lately and quite suddenly arisen, to devote itself to the use of the day or of the week, in illustrated papers—the enormous production of art in black and white—is assuredly a confession that the Honours of Mortality are worth working for. Fifty years ago, men worked for the honours of immortality; these were the commonplace of their ambition; they declined to attend to the beauty of things of use that were destined to be broken and worn out, and they looked forward to surviving themselves by painting bad pictures; so that what to do with their bad pictures in addition to our own has become the problem of the nation and of the householder alike. To-day men have begun to learn that their sons will be grateful to them for few bequests. Art consents at last to work upon the tissue and the china that are doomed to the natural and necessary end—destruction; and art shows a most dignified alacrity to do her best, daily, for the 'process,' and for oblivion.
>
> Doubtless this abandonment of hopes so large at once and so cheap costs the artist something; nay, it implies an acceptance of the inevitable that is not less than heroic. And the reward has been in the singular and manifest increase of vitality in this work which is done for so short a life. Fittingly indeed does life reward the acceptance of death, inasmuch as to die is to have been alive. There is a real circulation of blood—quick use, brief beauty, abolition, recreation. The honour of the day is for ever [sic] the honour of that day. It goes into the treasury of things that are honestly and completely ended and done with. And when can so happy a thing be said of a lifeless oil-painting? Who of the wise would hesitate? To be honourable for one day—one named and dated day, separate from all other days of the ages—or to be for an unlimited time tedious?[80]

In what might be read as both a critique and a defence of consumer culture, Meynell both gently mocks the pretensions of poor quality rubbish (which becomes nothing more than a vaguely embarrassing societal encumbrance) and maintains the value and integrity of what she terms the 'enormous production of art in black and white', in daily or weekly 'illustrated papers'. She sincerely heralds the stature or 'honour' of art that recognizes and embraces the contingency and contextual nature of its own production. She issues no apology for periodical writing – quite the contrary, she praises the 'brilliant talent' lately arisen, and suggests that the very brilliance of that talent is fostered by the temporal constraints of the periodical genre.

'The Honours of Mortality', which specifically considers the relation of honour to critical regard, and to the terms (and term) of critical regard, may be read as a self-reflexive and revealing manifesto. The publication, *within* a periodical, of a discussion of fame in the context of ephemeral journalism, illuminates Meynell's views of the context in which she wrote, and of her own role within that context. Meynell used her journalistic career in complex ways to secure for herself 'honours' of both the ephemeral and lasting variety. As already mentioned, and as richly demonstrated by the material quoted in this chapter, Meynell undertook regular, strategic reworkings and republications of her journalistic writings, effectively harnessing journalism's ephemeral nature to the production of a more long-lasting regard. 'The Honours of Mortality' was initially published in a periodical, on 'one named and dated day' in 1893 – but in 1896, Meynell republished it in a volume, from henceforth available 'for an unlimited time'. By re-forming her own words for other periodical assignments, or by securing them a longer term of life by collecting and preserving them in book form, Meynell continued to interrogate definitions of art and the terms of value attached to literary genres. Meynell reveals an awareness of the character of the periodical press itself – and the opportunities it provided – that is inextricably connected to the fundamental question of her self-construction as a distinctive voice, as a name ('Alice Meynell'), and as a writer of 'immortal fame'.

In 'Honours of Mortality', Meynell explicitly considers the standards by which literary value is judged, and issues her own decree as to the according of status. This chapter has demonstrated that any assessment of Meynell's reviewing entails assessing her idiosyncratic and conscious assumption of the reviewing role. As Pierre Bourdieu has written in *The Field of Cultural Production*:

> All critics declare not only their judgment of the work but also their claim to the right to talk about it and judge it. In short, they take part in a struggle for the monopoly of legitimate discourse about the work of art, and consequently in the production of the value of the work of art.[81]

Meynell engaged deliberately and intimately in the 'production of the value of the work of art'. As a reviewer, Meynell's professional role was quite literally that of an arbiter of regard: she passed judgement and helped formed the judgements of others. By means of the periodical review, particularly, and of many years of building her own critical regard through this genre, Meynell quite consciously produced her critical and stylistic autocracy. Early in her journalistic career, Meynell worked assiduously for little recognition and little remuneration; Peterson has appositely referred to this period as Meynell's 'apprenticeship'.[82] For a number of years, for example, Meynell and her husband Wilfrid both contributed paragraphs to the anonymous 'Office Window' in the *Daily Chronicle*, but while Wilfrid's columns passed unedited to the printer and he received special terms of payment, Alice's initially were evaluated and edited, and she received only the common pay rate. From the very start of her career, Alice was deeply aware of the authoritative as well as the financial power of a regarded name. In 1885, in a column in *Merry England*, she wrote: 'As to judicial authority, most men, we fancy, would rather be judged by a judge than by a jury, and would rather have an anthology gathered for them by an autocrat than by a conjectural plebiscite.'[83] Meynell steadily built her own credentials as an autocrat, and by the last decade of the nineteenth century those credentials – embodied within the name 'Alice Meynell' – had become widely recognized.

Increasingly from 1889, when she began publishing essays in Henley's highly regarded *Scots Observer*, and particularly after 1893, when her volume of collected essays *The Rhythm of Life* appeared to great notices, Meynell's name was made. In the mid-1890s Meynell's authorship of the Friday 'Wares of Autolycus' column in the *Pall Mall Gazette* was an open secret, and contemporaries rushed to read Meynell's latest pronouncements.[84] Editors had such respect for her work, and for the market she commanded, that they eagerly sought anything she cared to contribute: Henley urged Meynell to send whatever she could,[85] and her contributions were solicited for the *Saturday Review*, the *Spectator*, the *Illustrated London News*, and *The Yellow Book*, among many others.

Hand in hand with the public appetite for her name had grown the reverence for her judgement as a reviewer and critic. In 1895, Meynell's essay on Eleonora Duse was hailed by George Meredith in the *Illustrated London News* as 'the high-water mark of literary criticism of our time'.[86] In 1896, Edmund Chambers suggested in *The Bookman* that '[Mrs. Meynell] is perhaps the first woman to make her way to the higher levels of criticism'.[87] Chambers wrote, '[she] has the choicer equipment of a critic, the comprehensive experience of life and letters, the acute vision, the easy control of an exquisite medium',[88] and he grouped her with 'the absolute critics, the two or three who interpret to an age'.[89] Meynell's immense popular and critical regard is also attested to by Max Beerbohm's typically satirical barb, in the same year: 'who made Mrs. Meynell a ruler over us? [...] in a few years, Mrs. Meynell will have become a sort of substitute for the English Sabbath.'[90]

Demoor's work on *Athenaeum* reviews briefly considers how reviews functioned as 'advertisements'. In her reviews, Meynell sought in part to advertise herself, producing a unique voice in terms of critical opinions and style. Her judgements never swooned nor fawned, but critiqued all writers with equanimity: as her obituary in the *Times* was to read after her death in 1922, 'She was not carried away by the admiration of the great, nor did she withhold from smaller writers that felicitous sympathy which is more than mere praise.'[91] Nor did Meynell intemperately slash: her critiques and expressions of fine scorn were built on an assumption of equal standing; she measured herself by the same standards as her subjects. The arbiter of style, Meynell came to be labelled by *The World* its 'Grammarian in Chief'.[92] Ultimately, Meynell's autocratic judgements and highly cultivated scorn enabled her to build her own regard, constructing herself into a revered literary authority as well as creative artist. This chapter has suggested that Alice Meynell both created and was created by her own brand of literary reviewing. Influencing the ways reviews were written and received, Meynell made a significant contribution to the contemporary debate over definitions of literary value and worked simultaneously to establish and preserve her own name. In creating a distinctive voice, Meynell created a distinguished name.

Notes

1. Quoted in June Badeni, *The Slender Tree: A Life of Alice Meynell* (Padstow, Cornwall: Tabb House, 1981), 65. Emphasis in the original.
2. George Meredith, 'Mrs. Meynell's Two Books of Essays,' *The National Review* 27, no. 162 (August 1896), 762–770: 763.
3. Coventry Patmore, *Seven Unpublished Poems by Coventry Patmore to Alice Meynell* (London: Pelican Press, 1922), 8.
4. Arnold Bennett, *Journalism for Women: A Practical Guide* (London and New York: John Lane, 1898), 5.
5. Bennett, *Journalism*, 8.
6. Bennett, *Journalism*, 18.
7. Letter to Miss Stephens, 1905, M23 Burns Library, Boston College.
8. Philip Waller, *Writers, Readers, and Reputations: Literary Life in Britain 1870–1918* (Oxford: Oxford University Press, 2006), 117.
9. Wilfrid Meynell reported in 1880 that 'a long book review in a literary weekly, which required reading several volumes, would earn £2 at the very most' (*Journals and Journalism: With a Guide for Literary Beginners*, quoted in Sally Mitchell, 'Ephemeral Journalism and its Uses: Lucie Cobbe Heaton Armstrong 1851–1907,' *Victorian Periodicals Review* 42, no. 1 (2009), 81–92: 82).
10. Frances Low, *Press Work for Women: A Text Book for the Young Woman Journalist* (London: L. Upcott Gill, 1904), 12.
11. Kimberly Jo Stern, *The Victorian Sibyl: Women Reviewers and the Reinvention of Critical Tradition* (Unpublished PhD dissertation, Princeton, 2005), 1. Lewis Roberts, in contrast, suggests that anonymous reviewing was largely unrewarded and not accorded respect as literary writing – only part of the apparatus *surrounding* literary writing (see "The Production of a Female Hand: Professional Writing and the Career of Geraldine Jewsbury,' *Women's Writing* 12, no. 3 (2005), 399–418: 413).
12. Waller, *Writers, Readers, and Reputations*, 117.
13. Waller, *Writers, Readers, and Reputations*, 155. Meynell was personally acquainted with all three.

14. 'Authoresses.' *Saturday Review* 16 (10 October 1863), 483–484: 484. I am indebted for this quote to Elizabeth Mansfield, 'Articulating Authority: Emilia Dilke's Early Essays and Reviews,' *Victorian Periodicals Review* 31, no. 1 (1998), 75–86.
15. In 1998 *Victorian Periodicals Review* produced a special issue on the subject of Victorian Women Editors and Critics (31, no. 1). Within the issue Eileen Curran examined Mary Margaret Busk's reviewing, Barbara Onslow examined Mrs. Oliphant's art and society criticism, and Elizabeth Mansfield looked at the early reviewing of Emilia Dilke. Since that time there have been regrettably few scholarly treatments specific to women's reviewing: see Monica Fryckstedt, Fionnuala Dillane, and Kimberly Jo Stern. Most recently, Joanne Wilkes has examined the critical reviews of eight nineteenth-century women, with a particular focus on the critical reception of Austen, Charlotte Brontë, and Eliot (Joanne Wilkes, *Women Reviewing Women in Nineteenth-Century Britain* (Aldershot: Ashgate, 2010)).
16. Marysa Demoor, *Their Fair Share: Women, Power and Criticism in the* Athenaeum *from Millicent Garett Fawcett to Katherine Mansfield, 1870–1920* (Aldershot: Ashgate, 2000), 8.
17. Blanche Leppington, 'Review of *Amiel's Journal*,' *Contemporary Review* 47, no. 279 (March 1885), 334–352: 338–339.
18. Dallas Liddle, *The Dynamics of Genre: Journalism and the Practice of Literature in Mid-Victorian Britain* (Charlottesville and London: University of Virginia Press, 2009), 104.
19. Liddle calls 'Worldliness and Other-Worldliness: The Poet Young' (*Westminster Review* January 1857) George Eliot's most severe 'slashing' article (her most well known is certainly 'Silly Novels by Lady Novelists' (October 1856)). For a fuller discussion of Marian Evans' reviewing, see Fionnuala Dillane, 'Re-Reading George Eliot's "Natural History": Marian Evans, "the People," and the Periodical,' *Victorian Periodicals Review* 42, no. 3 (2009): 244–66.
20. Dillane, 'Re-reading George Eliot,' 252. Monica Fryckstedt quotes an anonymous 1863 pamphlet called *The 'Athenaeum' Exposed*, which decried the slashing reviewer thus: 'he indulges at once, by rude attacks and abuse, his own peculiar tastes and vulgar appetite for slander ... with the true spirit of a literary garrotter, he takes a mean advantage of the darkness of "anonymous" to publish what he would not dare to put his name to' (Monica Fryckstedt, 'Geraldine Jewsbury's *Athenaeum* Reviews: A Mirror of Mid-Victorian Attitudes to Fiction,' *Victorian Periodicals Review* 23, no. 1 (1990), 13–25: 25).
21. 'Review of The Works of the Late Right Honourable Henry St. John, Lord Viscount Bolingbroke by David Mallet,' *Quarterly Review* 149 (Jan–April 1880), 2–47: 2.
22. 'Ibsen's Plays,' *Saturday Review* 69 (Jan 4 1890), 15–16: 15.
23. Demoor, *Their Fair Share*, 12. Demoor suggests that women's contribution to the critical reception of the late Victorian period has not been fully recognized partially because the policy of anonymity persisted longer in reviewing than in other branches of periodical writing. 'Anonymity of reviews was a policy which many editors preferred to maintain until after the First World War even though the success of periodicals publishing signed reviews, such as the *Fortnightly Review* and the *Cornhill Magazine*, was a powerful incentive to change the policy' (*Their Fair Share*, 14).
24. Demoor, *Their Fair Share*, 246.
25. Seeley notes how Meynell blurred the boundaries between the familiar and the polemical essay; this was particularly the case in those essays which contained

review and literary critical material (Tracy Seeley, 'Alice Meynell, Essayist: Taking Life "Greatly to Heart",' *Women's Studies* 27 (1998), 105–130: 113).

26. Viola Meynell, *Alice Meynell: A Memoir* (London: Jonathan Cape, 1929), 120. Meynell was suggested again, with considerable public support, following Alfred Austin's death. *T. P.'s Weekly* ran a poll in 1913 in which Meynell came second only to Kipling; Robert Bridges, of course, was eventually named Laureate.

27. Alice Meynell, 'Some Thoughts of a Reader of Tennyson,' *Dublin Review* (Jan–March 1910). Reprinted in *Hearts of Controversy* (London: Burns & Oates, 1917), 1–22: 4.

28. Alice Meynell, 'Some Thoughts,' 12.

29. Alice Meynell, 'Some Thoughts,' 2.

30. Alice Meynell, 'Some Thoughts,' 15.

31. Alice Meynell, *'In Memoriam,'* Introduction to *In Memoriam* (Red Letter Library, Blackie & Co., 1904). Reprinted in *The Wares of Autolycus: Selected Literary Essays of Alice Meynell*, Chosen and Introduced by P. M. Fraser (London, New York, and Toronto: Oxford University Press, 1965), 150–154: 150.

32. Alice Meynell, *'In Memoriam,'* 151.

33. Alice Meynell, 'Some Thoughts,' 19.

34. Alice Meynell, *'In Memoriam,'* 153.

35. As quoted in the *Aberdeen Weekly Journal*, 1 Dec 1897.

36. Alice Meynell, *The Flower of the Mind: A Choice Among the Best Poems* (London: Grant Richards, 1897), vii–viii.

37. Alice Meynell, 'Elegy Written in a Country Churchyard,' *Pall Mall Gazette* (21 April 1897); reprinted in *The Wares of Autolycus*, 28–31: 29.

38. Alice Meynell, 'Elegy,' 29.

39. Viola Meynell, *Alice Meynell*, 158.

40. 'Preferences of an Eclectic,' *Pall Mall Gazette* (12 November 1897), 4.

41. Alice Meynell, *John Ruskin* (Edinburgh and London: Blackwood, 1900), 17.

42. Quoted in Badeni, *The Slender Tree*, 149.

43. Viola Meynell, *Alice Meynell*, 209.

44. Alice Meynell, 'A Corrupt Following,' *Pall Mall Gazette* (10 January 1900); reprinted in *Prose and Poetry*, by Alice Meynell, with biography and critical introduction by Vita Sackville-West (London: Jonathan Cape, 1947), 176–180: 177–78.

45. Alice Meynell, 'Charlotte and Emily Brontë,' *Dublin Review* (July–Sep 1911); reprinted in *Hearts of Controversy*, 77–99: 84.

46. Alice Meynell, 'A Corrupt Following,' 177.

47. Coventry Patmore, 'Mrs. Meynell, Poet and Essayist,' *The Fortnightly Review* 58 (1 Dec 1892), 761–766: 766. Vita Sackville-West uses a different but related metaphor: 'Her strength lay, not in violent onslaughts, but in the flexible tendons of the fencer's wrist' (Vita Sackville-West, 'Introduction,' *Prose and Poetry* (London: Jonathan Cape, 1947), 7–26: 18).

48. Alice Meynell, 'The English Women-Humorists,' *North American Review* (June 1905), 857–72; reprinted in *The Wares of Autolycus*, 111–126: 111.

49. Alice Meynell, 'The English Women-Humorists,' 111.

50. Alice Meynell, 'Children in Burlesque,' *The Children* (London and New York: John Lane, 1896), 69–71: 69.

51. Alice Meynell, 'Mr. Coventry Patmore's Odes,' *National Observer* (25 July 1891); reprinted in *The Rhythm of Life* (London: John Lane, 1896), 89–96: 94.

52. Alice Meynell, 'The Classic Novelist,' *Pall Mall Gazette* (16 February 1894); reprinted in *The Second Person Singular* (Oxford: Oxford University Press, 1921), 62–67: 64–65; 66.
53. Alice Meynell, 'A Woman of Masculine Understanding,' *Pall Mall Gazette* (11 October 1895); reprinted in *The Wares of Autolycus*, 8–12: 10.
54. Alice Meynell, 'Oblivion,' *Pall Mall Gazette* (16 August 1895); reprinted in *The Wares of Autolycus*, 5–8: 6.
55. Alice Meynell, 'Miss Mitford,' *Pall Mall Gazette* (23 February 1898); reprinted in *The Wares of Autolycus*, 82–85: 82.
56. Alice Meynell, 'Introduction,' *Prometheus Bound and Other Poems by Elizabeth Barrett Browning* (London: Ward, Lock and Bowden Ltd., 1896), xiv.
57. Alice Meynell, 'Introduction,' *Prometheus Bound*, vi.
58. Alice Meynell, 'Poetesses,' *Merry England* 2:11 (March 1884), 290–302: 298.
59. Alice Meynell, 'Introduction,' vii.
60. Alice Meynell, 'Introduction,' vii.
61. Alice Meynell, 'Introduction,' ix.
62. Alice Meynell, 'Introduction,' xii.
63. *Merry England* was a shilling monthly Alice and Wilfrid Meynell co-edited between 1883 and 1895.
64. Alice Meynell, 'Poetesses,' 291.
65. Alice Meynell, 'Poetesses,' 302.
66. Alice Meynell, 'Poetesses,' 294.
67. Alice Meynell, 'Poetesses,' 295–96, italics in original.
68. Alice Meynell, 'Poetesses,' 300.
69. Alice Meynell, 'Poetesses,' 301.
70. Alice Meynell, 'Women and Words,' *Merry England* (March 1886), 301–305: 303.
71. Alice Meynell, 'Women and Words,' 304.
72. Alice Meynell, 'Poetesses,' 300.
73. Alice Meynell, 'Mr. Coventry Patmore's Odes,' 96.
74. Alice Meynell, 'Mr. Coventry Patmore's Odes,' 89.
75. Alice Meynell, 'Mr. Coventry Patmore's Odes,' 93.
76. Alice Meynell, 'Mr. Coventry Patmore's Odes,' 94.
77. Quoted in Badeni, *The Slender Tree*, 177.
78. Alice Meynell, 'Alexander Smith,' *Pall Mall Gazette* (12 January 1898); reprinted in *The Wares of Autolycus*, 78–81: 78.
79. Linda Peterson, *Becoming a Woman of Letters: Myths of Authorship and Facts of the Victorian Market* (Princeton: Princeton University Press, 2009), 178.
80. Alice Meynell, 'The Honours of Mortality,' *Pall Mall Gazette* (29 Sep 1893); reprinted in *The Colour of Life* (London: John Lane, 1896), 30–31.
81. Pierre Bourdieu, *The Field of Cultural Production: Essays on Art and Literature* (New York: Columbia Univ. Press, 1993), 36.
82. Peterson, *Becoming a Woman*, 175.
83. Anne Kimball Tuell, *Mrs. Meynell and her Literary Generation* (New York: E. P. Dutton, 1925), 186.
84. Katharine Tynan Hinkson, *The Middle Years* (London: Constable & Co., 1916), 112. From April 1896, Meynell began writing the Wednesday column. Wilfrid Whitten wrote of the youthful keenness of himself and his friends to pick up the latest *National Observer*: 'How we shouted and wrote each other notes about Mrs. Meynell's "Rejection"…' quoted Viola Meynell, *Alice Meynell*, 74.

85. Viola Meynell, *Alice Meynell*, 73.
86. George Meredith, *The Letters of George Meredith to Alice Meynell: With Annotations Thereto, 1896–1907* (London: Nonesuch Press, 1923), 8.
87. Edmund Chambers, 'Mrs. Meynell,' *The Bookman* 3.6 (August 1896), 516–19: 516.
88. Chambers, 'Mrs. Meynell,' 519.
89. Chambers, 'Mrs. Meynell,' 519.
90. Max Beerbohm, 'Mrs. Meynell's Cowslip Wine,' *Tomorrow* (September 1896), 162.
91. 'Alice Meynell,' *The Times* (28 November 1922), 15.
92. Tuell, *Mrs. Meynell*, 135.

6
Humanitarian Journalism: The Career of Lady Isabella Somerset

Michelle Tusan
University of Nevada Las Vegas

'The life of English village children stands always in our minds in painful contrast to the pent-up dreary life of the child born and bred in our crowded cities. With special pity do we think of those little ones who go forth from our workhouses and workhouse schools with so little that is bright to help them on the weary journey of life with all its uphill struggles. For the sake of such as these I seek your indulgence for my little work.'[1]

So began Lady Isabella Somerset's preface to *Our Village Life*, a colour-illustrated book of poetry for children published to raise money to support her home for workhouse girls. Writing for Somerset, a woman of wealth and privilege, did not offer the means to earn a living or achieve literary fame. Rather, she made a name for herself in print for the 'sake of such as these', a literary voice that increasingly came to define her own subjectivity as a writer, editor, and political activist.

This chapter explores the humanitarian journalism of Lady Isabella Somerset.[2] Best known as editor of the *Woman's Signal* in the early 1890s, her career as a writer spanned a period that witnessed the growth of women-led reform campaigns. Somerset made a profession of social advocacy during a time when humanitarianism was serious business particularly for women.[3] Temperance, suffrage, and human rights campaigns on behalf of oppressed minorities in the Near East earned her a reputation as a social crusader who championed women's causes. Somerset's activist programme found commonalities in the causes of women's oppression at home and abroad, casting the problem of drunkenness, prostitution, a disenfranchised female electorate, and women living under a despotic state in the Ottoman Empire all as symptoms of a distressed humanity. She connected these distinct causes by forging an identity as a voice for the voiceless through her journalism. An independent income, a mouthpiece in the form of the *Woman's Signal*, and a network of influential supporters placed her at the centre of an emerging culture of women-led human rights advocacy that shaped her understanding of self and the meaning of literary notoriety.

Somerset used her role as a patron of social and humanitarian causes to build a reputation as a serious journalist and advocate. Her literary identity was thus intertwined with her role as social activist. The chapter begins by briefly placing Somerset's career as journalist, essayist, and advocate in the larger context of the Victorian humanitarian movement. I then compare her humanitarian journalism in the advocacy and mainstream presses. Finally, I take a look at one of her lesser known campaigns on behalf of Christian minorities persecuted in the Ottoman Empire. Here Somerset's journalism takes centre stage in the columns, opinion pieces, and charitable appeals that she wrote for the *Woman's Signal*. The network that she forged in her various campaigns reveals a web of supporters that included readers in England, the United States, and throughout the British Empire. Somerset's work appeared at an important intersection in the literary marketplace where the need to create a sustainable business model for her advocacy journal the *Signal* met the demands of a well-informed constituency of readers who wanted journalism with a higher purpose.

Balancing these demands at the dawn of the New Journalism offered new possibilities and pitfalls for the humanitarian journalist. How Somerset negotiated these demands as a writer reveals as much about the changing profession of journalism as it does about the status of the woman writer. Remembered today primarily for her feminism, Somerset's journalism reveals how concerns over women's rights found articulation in a broader commitment to human rights. In the pages of the press she fashioned an identity as a humanitarian and social advocate that burnished her reputation among contemporaries as a formidable literary crusader.

The development and expansion of women's presence in journalism in Britain coincided with a rapidly changing periodical market. New journalistic practices and technical innovations developed during the 1870s and 1880s translated into dramatic structural changes for the periodical press during the 1890s.[4] Developed first in America, 'Yellow Journalism', as it came to be referred to by its critics, thrived on the publishing of sensational narratives of heroism, scandal, and, in the case of the Spanish–American war, political propaganda. Photographs replaced less sophisticated woodcuts as bold headlines competed for readers' attention. Most notable was the wide application of advanced mechanical printing techniques in printing shops in the latter years of the century that made it possible to print periodicals cheaply and quickly.[5] Advertisers utilized this new medium as a space to hawk their wares as the periodical became a site of economic exchange. This new journalistic license to print dramatic stories as news, along with new printing techniques and applications, ultimately transformed newspapers and periodicals into commodities with widespread appeal that individuals of all classes and incomes could afford to purchase.[6]

Advocacy journalists like Somerset were quick to exploit the changes ushered in by the New Journalism. During this period, women journalists embraced a new professionalism. Women could expect payment for contributions to periodicals, could consider journalism a means of earning a livelihood, and began to list 'journalist' as a primary occupation. Women editors, though still small in number when compared to their male counterparts, managed news staff, solicited advertisers, and appealed to shareholders for support. As a journalist and an editor, Somerset offered lively and sometimes sensational coverage of advocacy issues, using these new opportunities and techniques to raise awareness for her causes and ultimately make a name for herself as a humanitarian journalist.

Understanding how women journalists such as Somerset fashioned a writerly self in the midst of these changes requires examining both the stories they told and why they told them.[7] Somerset's biographer Olwen Niessen claims Somerset as part of the 'pantheon of women reformers' of this period. Somerset's 'humanitarian spirit' in this reading came out of her quiet rebellion against her cloistered childhood and attempts to get over a failed marriage.[8] Although these experiences certainly played an important role in shaping Somerset's sense of self, her identity as a social reformer took clearest shape through the act of writing stories about the dispossessed. As Kali Israel suggests, biography is as much about the events of a life as the stories told about an individual.[9] The story of a life is also about the narratives individuals craft about the society that they inhabit. In the case of Somerset, her journalism fashioned a world made better by women's activism. The journalist had a higher purpose in this reading and it was this purpose, rather than literary fame, financial success, or political notoriety that defined the gendered humanitarian self in the late nineteenth century.

The Emergence of the Humanitarian Journalist

'The woman with an ideal ought to make a niche for herself in journalism.'[10]

Lady Somerset, who by the mid-1890s had already made a name for herself as a humanitarian journalist, must have been pleased to publish Ashwell's call for the woman journalist to take a stand. Born Lady Isabella Caroline Somers-Cocks (1851–1921) in London on 3 August 1851, she was eldest of the three daughters of the third Earl Somers. She grew up in the palatial setting of Eastnor Castle, a Norman-revival-style castle in Herefordshire. Here she lived a sheltered childhood governed by the rituals of aristocratic country life. The education of Lady Isabella consisted of a 'dull' but rigorous study of languages and English literature. Her mother, Virginia, unimaginative and overly attentive, lorded over her daughter making sure not to introduce the wrong kind of reading, which included romantic literature and political writing. Though keen to keep her mother happy, in quiet rebellion Lady Isabella would occasionally read what she liked, including J.S. Mill's *Essay on Liberty*, and embarked on unauthorized visits to family living off of the estate grounds.[11] In 1872 she married Lord Henry Richard Charles Somerset (1849–1932), second son of the eighth Duke of Beaufort, a decision she soon came to regret. Accusations of spousal cruelty and Lord Henry's homosexual proclivities led to the 'almost unheard of step' of Lady Isabella separating from him in 1878.[12] In 1883, the death of her beloved father left her with a sizable inheritance and the new responsibility of caring for her only son, Henry, and managing the family's finances, properties in Surrey, Gloucestershire, and London and tenants on the Eastnor Estate.[13]

By her early 30s Somerset thus found herself in a peculiar position for a privileged Victorian woman. Free from the demands of an ill-fated marriage and wealthy by even aristocratic standards she nevertheless faced a life full of new responsibilities. Her unorthodox roles as single mother and landlord soon came to include a fledging commitment to social reform. By the mid-1880s she had started a temperance organization for her own tenants and began to seek speaking engagements at local temperance meetings. She travelled over 15,000 miles giving lectures over a period of several years, speaking to working class and middle class audiences with a commitment and energy that she later brought to her work for women's suffrage.[14] Somerset had an independent streak, a product of her own rebellion against a sheltered upbringing and her new-found financial independence, which sometimes led to clashes with other women reformers. Somerset's support for women's suffrage during her tenure as president of the British Women's Temperance Association (BWTA), starting in 1890, led to tensions with the member of the organization who believed her stance unnecessarily politicized the organization.[15] Later, Somerset's stance on the Contagious Diseases Acts unleashed a firestorm and led to conflicts with leaders like Josephine Butler.

The obligations of public life both sustained and exhausted Somerset. By the early 1890s she had discovered journalism as an ideal vehicle for her own brand of social advocacy that continued until she resigned from official work with national and international temperance organizations in the early twentieth century. Journalism allowed Somerset to follow her own path throughout the 1890s when she began regularly to write for the women's advocacy press and periodicals, including most notably the *North American Review*. By 1903 her writing for the press all but ceased as she chose to dedicate her time to the Colony for Women Inebriates at Duxhurst in Regate, Surrey that she had founded in 1896.[16] Writing for the press freed Somerset from the pressures of speaking in public and being apart from her young son, whom she was determined to keep away from the influence of his disgraced father. Journalism also offered her the opportunity to join a growing community of humanitarian women journalists which included American temperance reformer Frances Willard. In October 1891, accompanied by her teenage son, Somerset travelled to America to attend the World Women's Christian Temperance Union (WCTU) conference. The trip lasted six months during which time she met Willard and came to admire the success of the temperance movement's publishing arm in America. Somerset apprenticed at the *Union Signal* newspaper offices (the organ of the WCTU) alongside her new friend Willard, and later served as a temporary editor of the paper hoping that she could replicate this work in Britain. During her time at the WCTU, Somerset helped establish a new 'press department' that improved the profile and work of the *Union Signal* and *National Bulletin*, both important organs of the American temperance movement.[17] Once returned to England, Somerset continued to travel and give public lectures during the 1890s while cultivating an identity as an advocacy journalist. These activities came to define her particular brand of humanitarian politics.

Writing for the press allowed Somerset to diversify her commitments while maintaining her public identity as temperance advocate and her private identity as aristocratic landowner and mother. In this task she found inspiration in her growing friendship with Willard. Beyond the business side of political advocacy, to which Willard introduced her during her visit to the US, Willard also helped Somerset understand the profession of journalism for women as linked to a higher cause. As Somerset wrote in the introduction to Anna Gordon's biography of Willard:

> But to no special cause did Frances Willard belong; her life was the property of humanity, and I believe that there was not a single cry that could rise from the world, not a single wrong that could be redressed, not a 'wail of weakness' of any kind that did not find an immediate echo in her heart, that did not call her to rise and go forth in that chivalric strength and gentleness which, [in] the battle of life, have clad her as with a holy panoply.[18]

Closer to home, journalists like Francis Power Cobbe embodied the ideal of the humanitarian journalist that Somerset sought to emulate. In 1895 the *Woman's Signal* cast Cobbe as the archetypal humanitarian advocate: 'She has done valiant service in the various "causes" which embrace the uncared for of both the human and the animal species, but others have done the same, and many even more than she in these directions'. What set Cobbe apart from these other advocates was her willingness 'to think for herself'.[19] Offering her the distinction of 'The Oldest New Woman', this article approvingly cast Cobbe as a principled, independently-minded pioneer for social justice.

Cobbe herself had long believed that women had a special claim to status as humanitarian journalists. Writing on 'Journalism as a Profession for

Women', Cobbe made the case for the special status of the woman journalist based on a gendered notion of humanity:

> For the good of the community at large, which would be advanced by a larger infusion of womanly conscientiousness, tenderness and purity of feeling into the morning and evening draughts of literature – and for the sake of our sex, which would thus obtain ready utterance for its aspirations and a career of great honour and influence opened to many of its members – I should rejoice exceedingly in the introduction of two or three women on the staff of every newspaper in the kingdom.[20]

Cobbe believed that the salutary effect of women's presence in the newsroom would extend to what today would be called the feminization of the news: a combination of empathy and human interest reporting that resulted in a more purpose-filled journalism. Somerset took such calls to heart. Through her advocacy work she crafted a professional identity for herself as woman journalist who served a higher moral cause.

Somerset and the Mainstream Press

Somerset's journalism spanned the spectrum from political advocacy to mainstream reviews and appeared in an array of newspapers published in Britain and the United States. These included the *Contemporary Review*, the *North American Review*, the *New Review*, the *Woman's Journal*, the *Iowa Woman's Standard*, the *Women's Tribune*, *American Magazine*, and the *London Times*. She also edited and wrote for the *Woman's Signal* and *Woman's Signal Budget*. A survey of her writing for these periodicals reveals the evolution of Somerset's own brand of humanitarian journalism. Active throughout the 1890s, she used the press to advocate on behalf of temperance reform, education, and the Woman Question.

Her writing for the *North American Review* in particular cast Somerset in a leading role as a humanitarian advocate. A periodical widely read in Britain and America during the late nineteenth century, it provided Somerset with an ideal venue to craft a transatlantic identity as a reformer. The 'Story of Our Farm' told of her rehabilitation centre in the Surrey hills, the Colony for Women Inebriates, Duxhurst. This 'farm colony,' funded by Somerset and contributions from the BWTA and World WCTU, 'is not a village where family life is lived, but rather one where it is rebuilt'. Somerset extolled her method of treatment for women alcoholics and their children as a work of 'restoration that must be accomplished physically and morally'.[21] Work in the garden and workshop where women wove at looms and produced linens and embroidery, coupled with round the clock supervision, contributed to Somerset's vision of rehabilitation. 'None can be saved as masses, only as individuals', she declared.[22] Such a capital intensive project for Somerset represented more than curing alcoholism. The stories of the women and children from her farm colony also offered a moral vision of showing those she cared for 'the possibility of another life and an ideal which they may live up to'.[23]

These stories of redemption had their complement in a larger humanitarian political ethos with which Somerset strongly identified, taking on a role as both a patron and guiding light. She dedicated her work with the World Women's Christian Temperance Union to waging a 'holy war' against alcoholism. In an address to the organization published in the journal *Lend A Hand* in 1892, she remarked 'I deeply feel, my comrades that we must come into closer touch as toilers for humanity'. Temperance work, she concluded, should be done for one reason: 'the profit of humanity'.[24] That same year, Somerset compared the vice districts of New York and London in another piece for the *North American Review* showing the level of 'demoralization' that results from access to drink. 'Let a man or woman give up the public house, and within three months his or her whole environment will have changed; in six he or she will have forever left the slum where hitherto he or she lived contentedly.'[25]

Such easy solutions would nevertheless need a boost from legislation that limited the access of the poor to alcohol at home. 'Practical Temperance Legislation', which Somerset published in the *Contemporary Review*, offered a series of concrete suggestions to fix the situation in England in 15 pages of argumentative prose that ranged from limiting the number of public house, to the direct veto, to a proposal by which individual constituencies could vote to 'suppress the liquor traffic', to outright prohibition. This direct political advocacy certainly would not seem surprising from a woman so invested in the work of the temperance movement. Somerset, however, sets out to make more than a 'practical' case for temperance reform. She concluded with a call to others to join her cause as citizens of the 'great army of reform'.[26] 'We are possessed with the belief that what touches one member of the community touches all', she proclaimed, 'it has permeated every phase of our national life'.[27] The temperance cause in Somerset's vision relied as much on individual action as it did on legislative victories. Somerset's narrative cast her as a central actor in this drama, a leader of a moral and political cause that would force England to live up to its 'great responsibility' to those who suffer most from alcoholism's effects: women and children.

This identity as patron/reformer found its clearest expression in Somerset's writing in the press about her dear friend Frances Willard. The death of Willard in 1898 had a profound effect on Somerset. In the same year, while serving as the acting president of the World Women's Christian Temperance Union, Somerset wrote a loving tribute to her American friend's global vision. In it she used Willard's life to articulate the humanitarian ideal that had motivated and inspired her own work. 'Frances Willard felt that a woman owed it to all other women to live as bravely, as helpfully and as grandly as she could', wrote Somerset.[28] Willard's own words put this vision of an activist life in perspective. Calling for a 'universal brotherhood' rooted in a Judeo-Christian ethic of service Willard, according to Somerset, looked forward to the day when 'all men's weal shall be each man's care'.[29] For Somerset this vision relied necessarily on the work of women like herself.

The *North American Review* again provided Somerset with a venue to fashion an identity as a womanly feminist reformer. Feminism, for Somerset, remained deeply connected with a highly gendered sense of duty that came from her own sense of class privilege and a Victorian understanding of woman's role as 'the sad priestess of humanity'.[30] 'What has changed woman's outlook so that she now desires that of which her grandmother did not dream?' Somerset asked her readers in 'The Renaissance of Women'.[31] The answer came from a rapidly industrializing world that demanded women adapt to changing circumstance. The four walls of the 'home' have opened up to the wider world requiring woman to 'take her place with man in framing laws that affect the well-being of those … who now dwell outside in that larger family circle that we call a nation'.[32] Somerset seems to have drawn upon her early clandestine reading of Mill in formulating this notion of a woman's expanding role. In a passage that could have come directly out of *On Liberty* she asserted, 'to deprive a government of the keen moral sense that is native to women as a class is to rob the nation of a strong support by which it would undoubtedly benefit'.[33]

Somerset, however, wore her liberalism uncomfortably. Influenced by the paternalism of her class and her own gendered subjectivity, she understood the role of women as participants in this community as an obligation: 'true philanthropy means the dealing with cause and not effect, searching out the root of evil and attaching it at all risks; not pulling down the leaves from poisoned boughs in the leisure moments of a summer's day'.[34] The 'renaissance' of woman would correct the 'moral patchwork' of women's reform work. Somerset concluded: 'the nation will be wisest and best that preserves the sanctity of womanhood and the influence of mothers'.[35] Humanitarian journalism opened up a space for Somerset to square the circle where an activist feminist self met more traditional understandings of women's community service as philanthropic duty and even *noblesse oblige*.

Somerset's views on education reflected a similar humanitarian ethos, no doubt reinforced by her own experiences in the schoolroom. 'The truest education is that which most adequately prepares the young for those duties which are likely to be called upon to fulfil in later years', wrote Somerset in a roundtable debate on education published in the *New Review* in June 1894, 'but none are so important as those which pertain to their relations to humanity'.[36] Her faith in this particular brand of women's education would be nothing short of transformative as it would welcome women's participation in the wider world instead of confining them to a life of dependency. 'Nagging women', Somerset believed, were a symptom of the current state of a stifling, cloistered domesticity imposed on middle- and upper-class women. Appealing to 'all sensible men and women, all philanthropists and reformers', Somerset proposed as a cure to the problem of the nagging wife that society let 'the education, occupations and aspirations of men and women become more and more allied'.[37] Here Somerset offered a portrait of an activist, womanly self that transcends the strictures of domesticity by embracing an equality rooted in the metaphor of home as nation.

The pursuit of literary fame in the mainstream press meant for many *fin-de-siècle* writers wealth or elevated social status. Somerset's ambition lay elsewhere. Somerset built a writerly identity as a reformer with a universalist sensibility that stemmed from her work in England and America. She crafted a highly gendered persona as a humanitarian reformer through her writing in the press about her own reform projects, the temperance and women's movements, and education. Literary fame in this way represented for Somerset an emblem of a new model of internationally focussed humanitarian womanhood. Advocacy journalism provided her with the ideal venue to present this vision of self. In the feminist press this meant inventing a newspaper that mirrored her particular vision of the womanly humanitarian reformer.

Somerset's Journalism and the Advocacy Press

Somerset took on the role of editor with the same reforming zeal that characterized her journalism, putting her own money on the line, and seeking a broader and longer-lasting promotion of her causes. Purchasing the controlling interest in the *Woman's Herald* in 1892, Somerset looked to establish a forum for women reformers. As she declared:

> The women's cause is one, whether it be Franchise, Temperance, Peace, Education, Sanitation, or whatever else it may be, the time has gone by for dealing with it piecemeal. The *Woman's Herald* will endeavour to familiarize its readers with the wider outlook, and treat every question from a standpoint common to all those who are labouring for one cause.[38]

Her London-based paper would serve as an 'organ for women who whether by necessity or choice were taking part in the growing public duties open to them'.[39] By December of 1893, she transformed the *Herald* into a penny paper renamed the *Woman's Signal*, 'Flashing its light from "humanity's capital"'.[40]

Editing a journal helped facilitate Somerset's social advocacy programme, an essential element of her sense of herself as a journalist. Examining

Somerset's history with the *Woman's Signal* reveals how writing for the press served as more than a vehicle to promote her own views. Rather, she sought to secure her status as a model of woman's activism connected to Victorian print-based advocacy culture. Setting up a journal in the late nineteenth century was expensive and required a steady infusion of capital to keep it going.[41] Despite her sizable fortune, Somerset did not want to start from scratch. Rather, she drew upon the experience of other women's advocacy writers in setting up her vision of a journalism that served a higher moral cause. Somerset understood her job as editor as a way for her to craft an identity as an author who would leave a mark on humanitarian journalism for years after the end of her editorship.

The origins of Somerset's *Woman's Signal* started with the story of another woman journalist, Henrietta Muller. Muller started the *Women's Penny Paper* in 1888 as a general interest feminist newspaper. In the winter of 1890 she changed the name of the paper to the *Woman's Herald*, 'in deference to the wishes of many friends and subscribers', claiming that the paper had made its primary 'aim to herald in the New Womanhood'.[42] 'Our new name', remarked Muller, 'is thought to be more consistent with the high place which the *Women's Penny Paper* has taken'.[43] Muller now pitched social advocacy as the main purpose of the paper:

> Our policy will be in the future, as it has been in the past, to reflect truth-fully and accurately every phase of woman's work and thought ... and to promote her development in any and every direction which she herself believes to be right.[44]

As the motto on the new masthead of the *Herald* read, 'Speak unto the People that they go Forward'. Muller's concept of what she called the 'New Womanhood' was intended as a call to action.

Two years later ill health led to her retirement from journalism and she sold her entire interest to Somerset and the newly formed 'Women's Herald Co'.[45] Vowing to continue Muller's mission, Somerset looked for new ways to extend the paper's influence. She also worked to make it more accessible through the later publication of a cheaper sister paper, the *Woman's Signal Budget* (1894–1895).[46]

Somerset's *Herald* encouraged women to act politically. First, she affiliated the paper with the Liberal Party: 'As it is the aim of the Liberal women to educate their sisters in politics, they need an organ such as the *Herald* to embody their views.'[47] However, the lack of support from the Liberal Party for Somerset's causes led her to quickly tire of mainstream politics. Somerset's journalism came to take a more universalist approach, and she appealed to 'all the most distinguished women' to help her with her project. In 1893 she also hired a subeditor, Edwin Stout, who was the current assistant editor of the *Review of Reviews* and had served on the *Pall Mall*

Gazette. Although Stout was employed for less than a year on the *Herald*, together he and Somerset introduced techniques adapted from the New Journalism that included artistically rendered mastheads depicting images of saintly political women, a new triple-column format, and increased space for advertising.[48]

Somerset's editorship increasingly emphasized politics and humanitarian advocacy as going hand in hand. Proclaiming God on her side, Somerset changed the name of the paper to the *Woman's Signal* in 1894. As she declared:

> The *Woman's Signal* will go into battle. Its mission will be to rally the multitude of earnest women who feel that they are responsible for the use of all the energy and influence which highest Power has given them, and who believe also that they will have to account, not only for any whom they may have caused to perish, but for those also whom they might have saved. Thus we shall seek to define and defend the place of woman in political life, to direct and enforce her influence among the great army of workers.[49]

Under Somerset's influence, along with that of her new assistant editor, Annie Holdsworth,[50] the *Signal* grew to a large penny paper that printed between 20 and 30 9×12 1/2 triple-column pages each week. Somerset's vision of the paper as a beacon of morality superseded concerns with profitability.[51] 'We shall preach, not parties, but principles; not expediency, but purity of motive and purity of practice', claimed the editor.[52] Somerset aligned the paper with the BWTA and soon temperance news and editorials that lambasted the English people as a 'nation of drunkards' filled its pages.

Moralizing journalism, however, did not pay. After a year and a half of disastrously falling circulation rates, it looked like the *Signal* would fail. Somerset was forced to consider how her brand of humanitarian journalism would survive in an increasingly competitive periodical market. Tired of subsidizing the paper and writing most of its copy, she resigned the editorship of the *Signal* in October 1895, turning it over to friend and well-known journalist, Florence Fenwick-Miller, who had contributed to the paper since its beginnings as the *Women's Penny Paper*.[53] Fenwick-Miller made the paper into a broad-based publication while drawing upon a humanitarian narrative that had animated Somerset, appealing to readers to follow Somerset's example as one who 'worked for what she thought was right'.[54] Long after she resigned her editorship, Somerset continued to influence the *Signal* and shape its mission by continuing to write for the paper. Her contributions included, most notably, her human rights campaign on behalf of persecuted Ottoman Christian minorities during the mid-1890s.

Somerset's Eastern Question

Somerset's work on behalf of a small group of foreign refugees living in the Ottoman Empire marked an important chapter in self-fashioning an identity as a humanitarian journalist. Advocacy on behalf of the Armenians appeared as a steady theme in her journalism throughout the 1890s. Lady Somerset introduced her readers to the Armenian cause not long after taking over the *Woman's Herald* in 1892. In this campaign she advocated on behalf of Armenian victims of Turkish atrocities as part of the Eastern Question.

One of the most talked about foreign policy questions of the day, the Eastern Question had at its heart the problem of what Britain should do to ameliorate the plight of the minority Christian population living as second class citizens under Ottoman rule. The question of Britain's responsibility for its 'fellow Christians' in the Ottoman Empire animated writers in the mainstream, advocacy, and feminist press. In the case of the Armenians, Somerset found a cause with broad appeal in feminist circles. In November of 1890 the *Women's Penny Paper* published the following announcement:

> It is intended shortly to start a Women's Vigilance Association in London for the purpose of calling attention to the condition of the women in Armenia. All round the country of Armenia dwell the Kurds and other hostile tribes who are in the habit of swooping down upon bridal parties and carrying off the women to sell as slaves to the Turks. These facts are brought to the attention of English women by a series of addresses and meetings ... We intend from time to time to publish authenticated statements concerning the carrying away of Armenian women.[55]

Women's papers including *Our Sisters* and *Shafts* published reviews of books on the Near East and biographical sketches. A biography of Madame Thoumaian in the *Woman's Herald*, for example, dubbed her 'A Heroine from Armenia'.[56] This Swiss woman's campaigns on behalf of Armenian causes made her a familiar figure in feminist reform circles and a regular participant in debates over the Eastern Question.[57]

The slaughter of an estimated 200,000 Armenians in the mid-1890s during the so-called Abdul Hamid massacres offered Somerset an opportunity to more clearly cast the Eastern Question as a women's issue and a human rights concern. Somerset led the agitation against the massacres, using the *Woman's Signal* to sound the alarm. In a report of her address at the annual meeting of the British Women's Temperance Association she argued:

> The Turkish Empire has been kept alive by treaties which have been broken again and again and yet in a great crisis when our fellow Christians cry to us in their death agony, we as a country are powerless to move and

are obliged to acknowledge that we are impotent to save the people we agreed to defend.[58]

Coverage of the Women's National Liberal Association included a similar line of argument claiming that 'the sufferings of the Armenians appealed to the sympathies of all' present at the meeting.[59] Lead articles contained references to 'the persecuted Armenian' and appealed to readers to heed 'the bitter cry of Armenia'. News briefs referred to the 'attacks on Armenians in the very heart of the Turkish government's rule' while describing the rule of Sultan Hamid.[60]

Somerset, a liberal committed to the Gladstonian line on the Eastern Question, understood England's affinities with Armenians in terms of both religion and gender. 'The situation in Armenia does not seem to improve', Somerset lamented in September of 1895,

> As our readers know, Russia and France have withdrawn from the Conference of the Great Powers, and have left England to work out Armenia's salvation alone, or else to leave the unspeakable Turk to exterminate a people who have been Christian since Christianity was.[61]

Gladstone's 85th birthday celebration provided Somerset with opportunity to make the case for 'A Call to Action' in her columns. The story of Mrs. Bedros, who escaped the Sassun massacre and sat next to Somerset at the birthday celebration, was told by a missionary after dinner. Somerset related to readers in graphic detail the murder of Mrs. Bedros' three month old baby and her two aunts by Turkish soldiers. The 26 year old Bedros was saved by remarkable circumstance, according to Somerset: when coins that her husband had fastened to her belt fell along the ground, she escaped to the woods while the soldiers picked up the gold and quarrelled over the money.[62]

Somerset's dramatic retelling of the story echoed W.T. Stead's Bulgarian Atrocities narrative almost 20 years earlier, when Ottoman troops slaughtered Bulgarian Christians on the eve of the 1878 Russo–Turkish war.[63] Outrages of rape, violence, and greed figured prominently in the story as retold by Somerset, who spoke for Mrs. Bedros through her missionary patron interpreter. 'The Christian womanhood of England as presented by the *Woman's Signal* can be depended on to demand that the extermination of these people shall be stopped.'[64] Britain's moral responsibility for Armenia, in this representation of the events of the massacres, found expression in the protection of womanly virtue. Somerset's moral outrage was strengthened by her status as a woman. Unlike Stead and his depictions of outrages against Bulgarian virgins, Somerset, as a woman, held a more authentic position of ownership over such narratives of injustice. She represented to her audience an authentic voice of sympathy and thus added moral weight to her call for action.

Somerset's self-fashioned identity as a journalist reformer drew upon gendered notions of British justice that had broad resonance to her reading public. 'We should be callous indeed, if our sympathy remained unmoved by the fearful crimes in the Turkish dominions', wrote Somerset in response to a letter from the 'Armenian Women of Constantinople' in *Shafts*.[65] *Our Sisters* published reports of the massacres in Diarbekir describing events like the mass murder of 'the defenceless crowd of men, women and children' gathered in a church set fire to by Kurds who lived in the hills surrounding the village. The poem 'Deserted Armenia' followed this appeal:

A Nation's History! How shall it be writ?
With tears of blood- in a sealed book of shame.
For when the weak and persecuted call her name
The mighty heart of England – slept![66]

Here the language of 'sisterhood' connected readers with the cause of Armenia in an intimate way. *Shafts* published a letter addressed to Somerset from the Armenian women of Constantinople, signed 'Your Suffering Sisters', that described the massacres in that city in 1895. Somerset's response to the letter concluded with a specific call to English womanhood: 'Will English women be deaf to the voices that call to them in the hour of their supreme agony? Will they not rise to demand that such steps be taken at all hazards as will secure the rescue of this tortured people?'[67]

Somerset's call to forge a sisterhood with Armenian women resonated with readers. Following Somerset's lead in linking the condition of all women, one *Signal* correspondent suggested in a letter entitled 'Our Sisters in Armenia' that the franchise for women in England would result in real change for Armenian women.[68] Somerset's growing disillusionment with the Liberal Party due to its lack of commitment to either votes for women or the Armenian cause most likely influenced her decision to turn to an extra-parliamentary approach. The occasion of the 'national protest against the Armenian atrocities' held at St. James' Hall in the spring of 1895 gave Somerset the opportunity to make her case in a public forum. Like the national meetings to protest the Bulgarian Atrocities held by Gladstone at the same venue in December 1876, a list of distinguished speakers spoke to a massive crowd on the need for intervention.[69]

Somerset's authority in a group made up entirely of distinguished male speakers relied on the claim that she represented the voice of the womanhood of England and Armenia. Her speech 'touched a new note' according to one report, 'pointed as it was by the presence of "the child-mother" to whom she alluded with a touching pathos'. The retelling of the story of Mrs. Bedros, who stood on the stage next to her husband, moved the crowd to cheer Somerset's call to intervene on behalf of the martyred Christians of Sasson who, she claimed, 'died that the untrammelled beneficent, consecrated life of England's purest womanhood might slowly come to women in their own beautiful and pleasant land'.[70] This language of mutual sacrifice contained within it the seeds of redemption. For Somerset, helping Armenian women was inextricably linked to the elevation of English womanhood.

In 1896, Somerset launched the idea for the Armenian Rescue Fund. The *Signal*, now under the editorship of Florence Fenwick-Miller, created the '*Woman's Signal* Armenian Refugee Fund' distributed through Lady Somerset. Donations ranged from £100 to one shilling and totalled in one week alone in October 1896 over £240. Prayer meetings, British Women's Temperance Union Branches, Congregational church members, individuals, and anonymous donors (including 'An English Sister') contributed to the fund, whose purpose was 'not only to cover and feed these suffering ones, but to see that they have homes and work'.[71] Potential donors were assured of the worthiness of the 600 refugees helped by the fund: 'Let it be remembered that they do not drink, that they are devout and earnest, exceedingly docile and kind and remarkably quick-minded'.[72] (Despite these credentials refugees would be resettled in Marseilles, not London.) The fund eventually came to serve the destitute Armenians still living in Eastern Anatolia. Somerset claimed in March 1897 that she had raised enough money to support a three year programme to educate and care for orphans in Van. To Fenwick-Miller and the readers of the *Signal* she offered her thanks. The money collected from readers served as 'eloquent proof of the worth of your paper which has gathered round it the best hearts of the womanhood of England'.[73]

Somerset's journalism made her humanitarian relief work on behalf of Armenian refugees possible. Under her influence the BWTA took a position on the Armenian issue and pressured the Salisbury government to act in the winter and spring of 1896. Somerset undertook this lobbying on behalf of the refugees in part because stalled diplomacy with the Ottoman government on the Eastern Question meant that the £2,000 she had collected from donors in Britain and the United States was not being used to fund resettlement of women and children who survived the massacres. Somerset worked with the *Daily News* correspondent who helped break the story in London and received international praise for her efforts on behalf of refugees from the massacres at a resettlement camp in Marseilles, when attempts to resettle them in the United States failed. This hands-on approach to social problems was made possible by her humanitarian journalism. The *Women's Signal* Fund accepted donations until March 1897 applying £500 to support a group of orphans for a year.[74] The Fund continued to support orphans in Van for another three years. In this small way, Somerset's humanitarian journalism put into practice a universalist brand of activism that had come to animate an outward-looking *fin-de-siècle* Victorian feminist movement.

Conclusion

The humanitarian feminism that dominated Somerset's journalism was self-consciously cultivated by a woman who understood her unconventional place in Victorian society in terms both of a life of privilege and her own dispossession. Somerset in her writing argued for the essential dignity of dispossessed communities that included alcoholics, women, and refugees. Humanitarian activism offered her a broad platform from which she could then launch more specific critiques. Though the success of Somerset's individual campaigns was uneven, at best it did open up new possibilities for women, aristocratic and otherwise, to channel prescribed roles as philanthropists into more overtly political identities.

Being Lady Somerset also made it possible to seek a particular kind of literary fame. She resisted allowing her privilege as a wealthy, titled single female aristocrat to fully define her literary persona. Obligations to her only son and the tenants on the Eastnor estate bound her to her community in a way that belied the easy conventions of life as a wife, mother, woman, and aristocrat. After her separation from her husband and death of her father she had to reinvent herself within the bounds of her new responsibilities. By the time of her death in April 1921 at age 69 Somerset had secured an identity that conformed to her understanding of personal service and humanitarian activism.

Notes

1. Lady Henry Somerset, *Our Village Life* (Sampson Low and Co: London, 1884), Preface, n.p.
2. Known in her lifetime as both Lady Henry Somerset and Lady Isabella Somerset, I follow Ian Tyrrell's usage in the *DNB* employing the latter title in this chapter.
3. See F. K. Prochaska, *Women and Philanthropy in Nineteenth-Century England* (Oxford: Clarendon Press, 1980); see also Michelle Tusan, 'The Business of Relief Work: A Victorian Quaker in Constantinople and her Circle,' *Victorian Studies* 51 no. 4 (Summer 2009), 633–661.
4. See Lucy Brown, *Victorian News and Newspapers* (Oxford: Clarendon, 1985), 9–15; Mark Hampton, *Visions of the Press, 1850–1950* (Urbana: University of Illinois Press, 2004), 36–39; and Aled Jones, *Powers of the Press* (Hants, UK: Scolar, 1996), 144.
5. New typesetting machines such as the monotype and linotype played a major role in this transformation of the industry during the last decades of the nineteenth century. See Richard E. Huss, *The Development of Printers' Mechanical Typesetting Methods, 1822–1925* (Charlottesville: University of Virginia Press, 1973), 3–24.
6. See R.A. Scott-James, 'The Crisis in London Journalism,' *English Review* (April 1912), 85–98; Sydney Brooks, 'The American Yellow Press,' *Living Age* (January 13, 1912); Michael Emery and Edwin Emery, eds., 'The New Journalism,' in *The Press and America* (Boston: Allyn and Bacon 2000), 171–209.
7. Marysa Demoor, ed., *Marketing the Author* (Houndmills, Basingstoke: Palgrave Macmillan, 2004), 13.

8. Olwen Claire Niessen, *Aristocracy, Temperance and Social Reform* (Online: Tauris Academic Studies, 2007), 8.
9. Kali Israel, *Names and Stories: Emilia Dilke and Victorian Culture* (Oxford: Oxford University Press, 2002), 13.
10. Frances Ashwell, 'One Phase of Journalism,' *Woman's Signal* (12 Sept. 1895), 171–172.
11. Niessen, *Aristocracy*, 70.
12. 'Obituary: Lord Henry Somerset,' *Times* (11 October 1932), 16.
13. Ian Tyrrell, 'Lady Isabella Caroline Somerset,' *Dictionary of National Biography* (Oxford: Oxford University Press, 2004), 594–595.
14. Niessen, *Aristocracy*, 70–71.
15. Niessen, *Aristocracy*, 77–79.
16. The last article by Lady Somerset that I have been able to locate, 'At the Back of the Hills,' *North American Review* 201 (January/June 1915), 727–729, was written in 1915 and told the story of her village's attempt to come to grips with losing one of their own in wartime combat.
17. *National Bulletin* was to serve as a conduit for temperance news and started publication on 5 November 1890. A year later it had a circulation of 4,000 copies weekly (Niessen, *Aristocracy*, 80–87).
18. Lady Isabella Somerset, 'Introduction,' *The Life of Frances E. Willard*, Anna Adams Gordon (Evanston, Illinois: National Woman's Christian Temperance Union, 1914), ix–xii: x.
19. M.B.W., 'The Oldest New Woman,' *Woman's Signal* (7 February 1895), 85.
20. Frances Power Cobbe, 'Journalism as a Profession for Women,' *Women's Penny Paper* (3 November 1888), 5.
21. Lady Isabella Somerset, 'The Story of Our Farm,' *North American Review* 175, no. 5 (November 1902), 691–700: 692–694.
22. Lady Isabella Somerset, 'The Story of Our Farm,' 696.
23. Lady Isabella Somerset, 'The Story of Our Farm,' 700.
24. Lady Isabella Somerset, 'A Personal Word From Lady Henry Somerset,' *Lend a Hand* 9, no. 4 (October 1892), 264–266: 266.
25. Lady Isabella Somerset, 'The Darker Side,' *North American Review* 154, no. 1 (Jan. 1892), 64–68: 67.
26. Lady Isabella Somerset, 'Practical Temperance Legislation,' *Contemporary Review* 76 (October 1899), 512–527: 527.
27. Lady Isabella Somerset, 'Practical Temperance Legislation,' 527.
28. Lady Isabella Somerset, 'Frances Elizabeth Willard,' *North American Review* 166, no. 4 (April 1898), 429–436: 436.
29. Lady Isabella Somerset, 'Frances Elizabeth Willard,' 436.
30. Somerset appropriates this phrase from Lecky, claiming that the Middle Ages took 'a far more logical view' of women's duty to the community through service and philanthropic work (Lady Isabella Somerset, 'Renaissance of Women,' *North American Review* 159 (July/Dec 1894), 490–497: 495–496).
31. Lady Isabella Somerset, 'Renaissance of Women,' 490.
32. Lady Isabella Somerset, 'Renaissance of Women,' 491.
33. Lady Isabella Somerset, 'Renaissance of Women,' 492.
34. Lady Isabella Somerset, 'Renaissance of Women,' 493.
35. Lady Isabella Somerset, 'Renaissance of Women,' 497.
36. Lady Isabella Somerset, 'The Tree of Knowledge,' *New Review* 10 (June 1894), 675–690: 683.

37. Lady Isabella Somerset, 'Nagging Women: A Reply to Dr. Edson,' *North American Review* 160 (Jan/Jun 1895), 311–312: 312.
38. Lady Isabella Somerset, 'Our Policy,' *Woman's Herald* (3 February 1893), 1.
39. Lady Isabella Somerset, 'Our Policy,' 1.
40. Rosemary VanArsdel, *Florence Fenwick-Miller* (Aldershot, UK: Ashgate, 2001), 183.
41. Michelle Tusan, *Women Making News: Gender and Journalism in Modern Britain,* (Urbana: University of Illinois Press, 2005), 123–27.
42. Henrietta Muller, 'Change of Name,' *Women's Penny Paper* (29 November 1890), 1.
43. Muller, 'Change of Name,' 1.
44. Muller, 'Change of Name,' 1.
45. Rosemary VanArsdel, 'Mrs. Florence Fenwick-Miller and *The Woman's Signal,* 1895–1899,' *Victorian Periodicals Review* (Fall 1982), 107–118: 117.
46. To further the cause of temperance, Somerset started the *Woman's Signal Budget* as a supplement to the *Woman's Signal* in July of 1894. This monthly penny paper mainly focused on the happenings of the British Women's Temperance Association and provided propaganda for the temperance campaign. Somerset's hope was not that the *Budget* would replace the *Signal*, but 'that the *Budget* shall go where goes the *Signal*' (*Woman's Signal Budget* (July, 1894), 1).
47. Anon., 'The Woman's Herald: A Liberal Paper', *Woman's Herald* (30 April 1892), 1.
48. Somerset employed Stout, an already established professional in the field, primarily to give the paper a more credible image as a newspaper, a task that she believed he had fulfilled. As she stated after his departure in December of 1893, 'The name of Edwin Stout is no longer openly associated with out paper; but all the qualities he pressed into its service, and by which he won for it a place among the best journals of the day – these are still with us for our help and direction, given generously now as aforetime'. (Lady Henry Somerset, 'Ring in the New,' *Woman's Signal* (December 28, 1893), 2.) Men's roles in women's advocacy journalism after 1890 often functioned to lend women's newspapers a professionalism that moved them away from the fringe and closer to the mainstream journalistic establishment.
49. Lady Isabella Somerset, 'Ring Out the Old,' *Woman's Herald* (21 December 1893), 2.
50. Little is known of writer Annie E. Holdsworth. For information see an interview conducted with her in the *Woman's Signal* (20 June 1895).
51. The paper contributed to the steady decline of her fortunes. See Niessen, *Aristocracy*, 153; VanArsdel, 'Miller,' 109.
52. Somerset, 'Ring Out the Old,' 2.
53. Florence Fenwick-Miller (1854–1935) had been involved in politics and journalism since her youth. In 1876 she was elected to the London School Board and served three year terms. She was a regular contributor to newspapers and magazines and was a columnist for the *Illustrated London News* from 1886–1918. In addition to editing the *Signal* she also edited an English language journal circulated in the colonies called *Outward Bound*. Fenwick-Miller was actively involved in international women's organizations and served as treasurer of the International Woman's Suffrage Committee, Washington, DC. She was also a delegate and speaker at the International Congress of Women in Chicago 1893 (VanArsdel, 'Miller,' 117, fn. 3).
54. VanArsdel, 'Miller,' 110.
55. 'The Condition of Armenian Women,' *Women's Penny Paper* (15 November 1890), 57.

56. Lady Isabella Somerset, 'Editorial,' *Woman's Herald* (10 August 1893), 392.
57. See for example Lucy Thoumaian, 'Letter to the Editor,' *Woman's Signal* (6 June 1895), 416–417.
58. Lady Isabella Somerset, 'Annual Address,' *Woman's Signal* (25 June 1896), 405.
59. 'Report of Women's National Liberal Association Meeting,' *Woman's Signal* (21 May 1896), 331.
60. Lady Isabella Somerset, 'Editorial,' *Woman's Signal* (22 April 1895), 121; Lady Isabella Somerset, 'Lead Editorial,' *Woman's Signal* (29 Aug 1895), 487; Lady Isabella Somerset, 'Foreign Troubles,' *Woman's Signal* (10 October 1895), 232.
61. Lady Isabella Somerset, *Woman's Signal* (26 Sept 1895), 201.
62. 'Armenians at Hawarden: Mr Gladstone and the Refugees,' *Woman's Signal* (25 April 1895), 264–265.
63. Richard Shannon, *Gladstone and the Bulgarian Agitation* (London; Thomas Nelson, 1963), 49–50.
64. 'Armenians,' 264–265.
65. Lady Isabella Somerset, 'A Cry from Armenia,' Response to a Letter from Armenian Women of Constantinople to Lady Henry Somerset, *Shafts* 3 no. 9 (1895), 132.
66. A. Bradshaw, 'Deserted Armenia,' *Our Sisters* 2, no. 14 (1897), 52.
67. Somerset, 'A Cry,' 132.
68. 'Letters to the Editor,' *Woman's Signal* (27 February 1896), 189.
69. 'Eastern Question Conference,' *Illustrated London News* (16 Dec. 1876), 577.
70. 'Armenian Atrocities,' *Woman's Signal* (9 May 1895), 302.
71. 'Lady Henry Somerset's Efforts for the Armenian Refugees,' *Woman's Signal* (15 October 1896), 246.
72. 'Lady Henry Somerset's Efforts,' 246.
73. 'Lady Henry Somerset's Letter of Thanks,' *Woman's Signal* (18 March 1897), 172.
74. Niessen, *Aristocracy*, 163–166.

7
Flora Shaw and the *Times*: Becoming a Journalist, Advocating Empire[1]

Dorothy O. Helly
City University of New York (Emerita)

> 'She is a fine, handsome, bright, upstanding young woman, as clever as they make them, capable of any immense amount of work, as hard as nails and talking like a *Times* leader all the time. ... She is imbued with the modern form of public imperialism. It is her religion.'[2]

The woman described is Flora Shaw, colonial editor of the *Times* of London. The words are those of the African traveller Mary Kingsley, whose sharp-edged remarks reflect the fact that she held Shaw responsible for the newspaper ignoring her books about West Africa. How did Flora Shaw come to hold such an elevated position in the world of British journalism in the 1890s? She grew up appreciating the military and political contributions to the British nation made by her Anglo-Irish forbears. She also understood from that tradition that if an upper-middle-class daughter wished to realize her ambition to become a writer, she would have to negotiate the conventional expectations of her family and class. Shaw's mother's death and her father's remarriage, when she was 19, provided her with her first opportunity to strike out on her own. She left home for an extended visit with her mother's relatives in France. This proved to be the first of a lifetime of choices based on the principle that if one pushed resolutely at the outer boundaries of what was possible, the next set of choices would be wider. Shaw's background shaped her adult values in important ways. Shaw learned to use both her class position and her gender to open doors. She was willing, and eager, to do the intellectual work and take the necessary risks to achieve success. Learning to become an effective journalist led to her commitment to Imperial expansion, which in turn led to world-wide fame. Her vision of journalism as active politics helped shape the public perception of the British Empire and influence British imperial policies.

Born in 1852, Flora Shaw grew up in a military family in Woolwich, the site of the Royal Military Academy. Both her great-grandfather and grandfather, baronets in Ireland, served in the Imperial parliament. A younger son, her father chose a military career, retiring as a major general. Her French mother, born on Mauritius, married George Shaw, accompanied him to England and bore him 14 children over a period of 20 years. When she died in 1871, Flora was 18 and took charge of 8 younger siblings until her father remarried the following year. The Shaw children spent summers on their grandfather's estate in Dublin. From him, Shaw learned that if one was born a 'gentleman', one had a natural responsibility for those who were less privileged. The more cautionary lesson she learned from her mother was that an early marriage could lead to unending domestic duties, leaving no time for any other ambition.

And Flora Shaw was ambitious. From an early age she taught her younger siblings, spinning stories and dreaming of becoming a writer. As a high-spirited girl, both charming and intelligent, her ambitions attracted a succession of valuable male mentors. John Ruskin, who lectured at Woolwich, met her just before she turned 17 and was entranced. He encouraged her education, allowing her to buy books and charge them to his account at his London bookstore.[3] He supported her desire to become a writer by urging her to write down the stories she told. When she was 24, in 1877, she published *Castle Blair*, about an unconventional family of Anglo-Irish children caught up in the struggles of landlords and tenants. Ruskin gave it enthusiastic public praise. His words, 'the best description of a noble child ... that I ever read; and nearly the best description of the next best thing—a noble dog', became a standard encomium for advertising the book in Britain, and in the USA, where it was promptly republished.[4] In 1883 Ruskin invited Shaw to visit him at Brantwood, his Lake District home. There she met Charles Eliot Norton, the American literary and art critic, with whom she began a lifetime correspondence.

Another valuable mentor was Colonel Charles Brackenbury, a family friend and a cousin by marriage who wrote on military subjects for the *Times*. After her year in France, Shaw no longer wished to live at home. As a proper upper-middle-class single young woman, however, it was out of the question to work for wages. Colonel Brackenbury and his wife welcomed Shaw to live with them, manage their large household, and teach their children. This arrangement gave her enough time and space to practice her craft. By 1881, Shaw's career as a writer was launched and she was listed by the Census as a 'visitor' and 'authoress novelist'.

At the Brackenburys' dinner table Shaw met the novelist George Meredith, an old friend of Colonel Brackenbury. They would become neighbours in 1883, when Shaw left the Brackenburys for a 'room of her own' in a cottage in Abinger, Surrey. By this time she had written three novels aimed at younger readers. Her experiences in southern France and living with the Brackenburys at the Royal Gunpowder Factory in Waltham Abbey became the backgrounds for her second and third novels.[5] She had learned from Ruskin how to observe the world in minute detail: people and places, objects and their settings. In her novels, essays, and journalism, she would use her ability to describe a scene swiftly and focus in on its significant aspects. When Meredith introduced her to his circle of literary friends, he described her as someone 'to know whom is to look through an Eyelet on the promised Land.... She is Irish and French, that's why. Quite ... delightful to talk with ...'.[6]

Her next mentor, W.T. Stead, entered her life in 1886 when her fourth and fifth novels failed to provide her with sufficient income to live on. Meredith introduced her, suggesting that Shaw try earning money from journalism, as he had done some years before.[7] Stead, the editor of the *Pall Mall Gazette*, was making his name as a new kind of audacious journalist, exposing sex-trafficking of very young girls and writing about journalism as a form of politics. Nearer her own age than Shaw's earlier mentors, Stead opened up the world of journalism to Shaw, promising to publish anything of political interest she found in her travels and giving her a variety of assignments when she was in England. Their relationship shifted gradually from a mentoring one to that of colleagues in the profession of journalism.[8] When Shaw wintered in Cairo in 1888–1889, Stead commissioned her to report regularly as a 'Special Correspondent'. When he left the *Pall Mall Gazette* to publish the monthly *Review of Reviews*, he asked her to review the major French periodicals. Shaw did not always agree with the positions Stead espoused. She no longer wrote for him after 1891, but they became serious antagonists only in the last years of the 1890s over the question of British policy in South Africa.

Shaw's first newspaper story appeared on the front page of the *Pall Mall Gazette* in June 1887, when she was 34, under the by-line, 'A Lady's Interview with the Captive Chief'. The by-line suggests Stead did not yet take her seriously as a journalist, but he recognized the newsworthy nature of the story. Zebehr Pasha, a Sudanese merchant believed to be a notorious slave trader, had been exiled to Gibraltar in 1885 by the British authorities in Egypt.[9] The previous year, when General Gordon suggested that once the Sudan was evacuated by its Egyptian rulers, Zebehr should become its Governor, Stead had led the opposition against Zebehr in the *Pall Mall Gazette*. Shaw's interview allowed the merchant to defend himself. He denied trading in slaves, claiming his aims were always to keep the peace by discouraging slave trading in the region and to bring in 'civilization' by promoting long-distance trade in local resources. He had bought slaves, but only in order to train them as soldiers; he had never sold them himself. Shaw laid out his defence in a longer, three-part version of the interview in the *Contemporary Review* that fall.[10] Shaw and Zebehr both believed that his release later in 1887 was a direct result of her interview. From the beginning, therefore, like Stead, Shaw was convinced that journalism could provide a writer who had a cause with a powerful political voice.

Shaw worked steadily thereafter writing freelance journalism for the *Pall Mall Gazette*, the *Manchester Guardian*, and Stead's new *Review of Reviews*.

By late May 1890 she began to write for the *Times*, inaugurating a fortnightly 'Colonies' column for them in November. By this time Shaw's journalistic identity had become inextricably interwoven with her thoughts about and commitment to British imperialism. As a novelist, Flora Shaw was not a committed imperialist; quite the contrary. Despite growing up in the British military world, she did not think the use of arms constituted the first or best resolution of conflict. Learning from Ruskin, the young Shaw viewed the expansion of the British Empire as the result of the spread of 'civilization' by Britons to 'empty' or 'savage' lands. Shaw's core values, depicted in her novels, featured boys who understood the honour and responsibilities of being born a 'gentleman' as well as clever girls who loved independence and 'adventure'. The message that privilege meant both responsibility and courage would also inform the conception of empire she came to champion in her journalism at the end of the 1880s.

At the beginning of that decade, Shaw was still exploring these values in her own life. Between 1881 and 1883, swept up in Ellis Hopkins' idea of 'rescuing' young women from turning to a life of prostitution, Shaw worked in the slums of London's East End with Mary Steer. After two years she gave up her rescue work, concluding that only a national solution, like government-sponsored emigration, could root out such endemic problems.[11] Later, when she became an advocate of empire and travelled to Australia, she called for involving young women in the emigration process, but by then her appeal involved cultivated middle-class women, not the urban poor.[12]

Shaw was aware that the British government in the early 1880s, a time of domestic agricultural depression, would not soon be subsidizing emigration efforts for the poor. However, it had found the funds for an expeditionary force to quell a nationalist uprising in Egypt in order to safeguard its investment in the Suez Canal. In the last novel she wrote, *Colonel Cheswick's Campaign* (1886), a British expedition to teach the Egyptians 'a lesson' provides an ever-present background to the action. Her protagonist, a strong-willed, capable young woman, has a beloved military father whose campaign at home is to ensure that his daughter married another soldier, the man he believes to be the best choice for her. What it means to be a soldier and whether or not it is important to fight for a cause are explored in the dialogue. When her father is called away to do military duty, the daughter admonishes him sternly: 'your sense as a man forces you to admit that the Egyptians have a grievance—as a soldier you want to go and kill them for it'.[13]

This acerbic comment about the unjust use of military force was not an isolated one. Shaw sounded it again in a letter from Gibraltar written late in 1886:

> ... our guns stand row on row with muzzles threatening Spain.... English bugles bray between the cactuses. English soldiers swarm ... we sound the

war note as though we were still in the heart of the middle-ages. They tell me ... that English prestige depends upon her Eastern Empire, her Eastern Empire upon such possessions as Gibraltar.... Our true Eastern Empire is the civilization which we have spread and that depends on other forces than the force of cannon. Fancy how the Spaniards must hate us![14]

During that winter on Gibraltar, while interviewing Zebehr Pasha, Shaw also visited Morocco, continuing to search for stories that Stead might publish. She was aware of increasing tensions between European powers, especially France and Spain, over their influence in Morocco. Specifically, she was aware of the privileges Europeans had obtained to protect their own citizens and the Moroccans with whom they traded from the penalties of Moroccan laws concerning crime, taxes, and debts. She investigated claims that this power was being abused and was often for sale, interviewing the European consuls in Tangier about their use of these extra-territorial privileges. She came away with the sense that the British ought to help redress what she saw as wrongs against Moroccan sovereignty. Stead not only agreed to publish her story about Zebehr, but also a series of articles about the situation in Morocco in the fall of 1887, this time with the by-line, 'From an English Correspondent'.[15] When the *Morning Post* published a series of letters about the growing urgency of the situation in 1889, Shaw used her knowledge of the situation to offer a political analysis, under her own name, in a Letter to the Editor:

> Sir.- If the deluge of blood in Morocco be indeed within measurable distance, as your Correspondent points out in the Letter you publish this morning, is this not an argument of urgency for cordial co-operation between the non-Mussulman powers within that empire?... if by a long course of provocation we have put ourselves in a position in which in the event of internal disorders, popular fury might with some show of justice ... be turned against us and the *protégés* we are pledged to support ... would it not be politic as well as just to withdraw from it before the dangerous crisis is reached?[16]

As in the case of the Egyptian uprising, Shaw sympathized with the Moroccans who resented European interference. She wanted European representatives in Morocco to act to avoid a conflict and find a peaceful solution to a threat looming in international relations. By 1889, Shaw's willingness to express her opinions about current events in her own name in published letters and journal articles is a measure of how far she had come in claiming a strong, confident journalist's voice.

Part of finding a strong journalistic voice was Shaw's new commitment to imperial politics. At the end of the 1880s, two critical experiences awakened in Shaw a new and powerful reframing of her position on empire, a position significantly shaped by her journalism. Arriving at Shepheard's Hotel in Cairo in 1888, accompanying elderly friends wintering in Egypt, Shaw was called upon with great fanfare by Zebehr Pasha, still grateful to her for his release.[17] With a letter of introduction from Stead, Shaw consulted the man who was in charge of British control over Egypt, the British consul-general, Sir Evelyn Baring. He offered to see her two or three times a week to keep her informed about British plans and activities. Although Baring, like other mentors, may have received her warmly in response to her class and gender, the promise of her journalism was of critical importance to him. For the British government to maintain their control over Egypt they needed a favourable public opinion at home; to achieve that, they needed a favourable press.

Baring plied Shaw with official papers, carefully pointing out what the British administration was attempting to do on behalf of the country and its inhabitants. According to Sir Evelyn, the British were aiding the Egyptian peasants by ending the *corveé* or labour tax, reorganizing Army conscription on a more equitable basis, developing new irrigation systems, putting an end to the legal status of slavery, and trying to find a solution to Egypt's staggering debt problem. He recommended she speak with the other British officials in charge of these activities.[18] She interviewed all the major French and Egyptian players in Cairo as well. Her ability to fill in the background of all she was investigating was helped by meeting the *Times* correspondent in Egypt, C.F. Moberly Bell. They immediately formed a strong and lasting friendship. Bell, a fierce advocate of Britain's 'civilizing mission' in Egypt, admired Shaw's work and they both enjoyed sparring over politics.[19] In Egypt, interviewing the men in leading positions and writing weekly news columns for the *Pall Mall Gazette*, Shaw was learning about imperialism and practical journalism.

When Shaw returned to London in the spring of 1889, she was still uncertain about her way forward. Writing for the *Pall Mall Gazette* in Egypt had earned her a total of £13 for nine weekly columns, and her expenses amounted to £12.10. 'That is a handsome result is it not', noted Shaw dryly, 'for two months of constant work'.[20] Despite the work she had done, she remained hesitant about laying claim to being a professional journalist. When Stead suggested she write a leader for the *Pall Mall Gazette*, she demurred: 'What a compliment! Write a leader and be mistaken for you! No alas not yet. You have taught me a great deal ... but you have not brought me on so far as that.' Similarly, returning a form he had sent her, she confessed: 'I leave the Profession blank because I have not the impertinence to call myself anything. A year hence I might perhaps know better.'[21] That prediction would come true.

Shaw's concern about earning a living from her writing remained paramount. The financial failure of her last novel in 1886 underlay that anxiety. Looking for other sources of income that year, she had sent Charles Eliot

Norton in America a short story, which he placed the *New Princeton Review*. This news came with a cheque whose amount impressed her. While considering her next step, she wrote a critical essay on Meredith's novels and sent it along to Norton, telling him that she was aware of a new interest in Meredith in the United States. To her immense satisfaction, it too was published in the *New Princeton Review* and brought her a cheque for £8.[22] During the next three years, as she explored journalism, she economized by spending the winter months accompanying elderly friends who sought health in warm spots around the Mediterranean. In addition to finding news stories for Stead, she made use of these visits to write a series of travel articles.[23] The period between late 1886 and late 1889, therefore, proved pivotal for Shaw's determination not only to find a way of making a living as a writer, but also to find a distinctive voice.

Influenced by the positive view of empire opened to her by Baring in Egypt, by June 1889 Shaw's imperialist ideas were taking shape. She wrote to Norton: 'The work in Cairo was different from anything that I have done before and I think I learnt something from it. I find myself taking certainly a more close and practical interest in public questions than I did before and I am glad of it.'[24] At this point, Stead introduced her to a charismatic figure whose intense imperialist convictions complemented her new thoughts about the positive benefits involved in the expansion of British power. Talks over the summer with Cecil Rhodes, a millionaire politician from South Africa, reinforced that new vision and helped shape the direction of her writing career. Emigrating from England to the Cape as a young man, he had become wealthy from mining investments. He now shared with Shaw his imperial dreams of how he proposed to use that wealth in the service of the British Empire. Rhodes was in London seeking a royal charter for his new South African Company, as a way of claiming British protection while exploiting the mineral rights granted to the company by local African chiefs. The region involved lay north of the Zambezi River, just beyond the Boer republics in South Africa. Rhodes' clearly stated *political* aim was to expand British imperial power over the entire southern portion of the continent. Shaw thought him 'a man of evident power' as he paced up and down the two rooms of her London lodgings, committing himself to 'render myself useful to my country'.[25] He spoke of a British Empire made up of self-governing colonies straddling the globe to bring law, order, and prosperity to all within its reach.

For Shaw, Rhodes's vision both captured her imagination and gave her pursuit of journalism a new sense of mission. She began to see journalism as a way of awakening public attention to what was the right course for the nation, not just to remedy grievances in Egypt or Morocco but to act positively around the world in the name of the British Empire. To actively encourage such policies would give her the opportunity to fulfil the concept of 'honour' she had imbibed from her grandfather. By means of this kind of journalism, she too might serve the empire. Stead had taught her that journalism could be an active form of politics. Shaw now saw it as a form of politics that she, as a woman, might successfully pursue.

Two articles Shaw wrote for the *Fortnightly Review* in the fall of 1889 reveal how her recent experiences had set her imagination on fire, providing her with a new lens through which to see the world. The first, 'Dry-Nursing the Colonies', is a dramatic announcement of her new position regarding empire. Her energies had been galvanized; from her references to current events, she had begun an intense study on what was happening in the colonies and in Africa. From the topics raised in the article, it is clear that Shaw was reading colonial newspapers and had sought out information at the Colonial Office. In energetic terms, she condemned the 'blunders' being made all around the world by 'Downing Street'. The phrase embraced every arm of policy-making at that location. On the one hand, she faulted the Colonial Office for interfering too much in decisions made by self-governing colonies, and on the other, she took the Foreign Office to task for not more strongly supporting the efforts of British agents trying to increase the influence of their nation in Africa. She laid down the gauntlet: 'Is our Imperial policy to be friendly or antagonistic to our Colonies?'[26]

Like Stead, Baring, and Rhodes, Shaw was convinced that a successful forward policy depended on arousing British public opinion. '[W]e shall have to enlarge our common conception of Imperialism', she announced, 'or be content to ... see our Colonies withdraw one after the other from an Empire grown too small for them'.[27] In such statements Shaw was, in fact, laying out her agenda for the next decade, and beyond. Her follow-up article, 'The British South Africa Company', hailed Rhodes's newly chartered company, which she predicted would spread 'civilization' to a new portion of southern Africa while increasing imperial wealth and trade.[28] An imperial enthusiast had been born. With a deep belief that the British 'race', a term she often used, was at its best characterized by the high-minded ideals she valued, she dedicated herself to work through journalism to expand its reach. A century later, looking back on the creation of Rhodesia (now Zimbabwe) Shaw's failure to give sufficient weight to the way the imposition of power carries with it the potential for ill as well as for good is apparent. But she was a new convert, certain that she had found the truth and eager to share it with the world.

As Shaw expressed it much later, 'I never thought of my work exactly as journalism, but rather as active politics without the fame'.[29] As a Victorian woman, she could not follow directly in the footsteps of her grandfather and great-grandfather and enter parliament. By her journalism, however, she might influence imperial politics and policy-makers. That became her goal. Almost immediately after writing these articles in the fall of 1889, she had an opportunity to put her new vision to work. The editor of the *Manchester Guardian*, C.P. Scott, who had agreed to publish a number of her letters from Egypt, now asked her to report from Brussels on the Anti-slavery Conference being convened there that November. This meeting of European powers was to reach agreements that would help close down the continued trade in slaves in eastern Africa.

Shaw found herself the only woman journalist at the conference. Undaunted, she brought to bear the knowledge she had acquired about the slave trade before arriving in Brussels. Once there, she honed her interviewing skills to tease out information from reluctant delegates. To the delegates she appeared as an elegantly dressed young woman, tall and slender with a poised bearing and clear blue eyes. Dressed in black silks with high necks and sleeves to the wrist, she conveyed a mixture of femininity and professional propriety marked by inner discipline and self-confidence. As she wrote to Stead, with whom she maintained a private correspondence, she judged by their silences what part of the agenda the delegates were currently engaged in debating behind closed doors. She wrote to Stead about her frustrations at the way the conference was going, especially as she became aware of the diplomatic games being played. In particular, she believed France was manoeuvring to ensure the weakening of any new regulation of the arms trade or any agreement which would allow their own vessels to be boarded in a search for slaves. Because she was now convinced that the press could and should play an important role in influencing policy, she wrote an editorial on the subject and asked Stead to publish it. Her experience at the conference had emboldened her to write her first leader. 'Should France Block the Way?' appeared in the *Pall Mall Gazette* December 10, 1889.[30]

Shaw also wrote indignantly to Stead that the journalist covering the conference for the *Times* seemed to care nothing at all about its outcome. She was unhappy that because the *Manchester Guardian* was an afternoon paper, her telegrams were not being picked up by the London morning papers. She declared she wished she could replace the *Times* correspondent herself, and half in jest asked Stead to help her.[31] To write for the *Times* was beginning to take shape for her as an explicit goal.

When Moberly Bell was recalled from Egypt in March 1890 to aid the manager of the *Times*, he immediately sought her out. Just as he had been her local informant in Cairo, so she was a local source of information for him in London. They discussed how to reinvigorate the newspaper's falling circulation.[32] Bell wrote Sir Robert Herbert, permanent undersecretary at the Colonial Office, for a recommendation for a possible 'colonial correspondent'. Shaw had regularly been consulting Herbert about colonial affairs since 1889. Bell then wrote her a formal letter, telling her that Herbert 'gave us your name', and asked her for a 'specimen column for next week'.[33] 'The Egyptian Debt' was published 29 May 1890. It was such a clear exposition of the complicated and tangled Egyptian financial situation that the editor and proprietor immediately assumed that it had been written by Moberly Bell himself. At this stage, Bell introduced Shaw to the editor, George Earle Buckle, but thought it better not to reveal her gender to the proprietor, John Walter, who had strong views about women journalists. Bell enthusiastically informed her, 'If you were a man you would be Colonial Editor of *The Times* to-morrow'.[34] Shaw discovered over the next two years that it was an important caveat, and only after she wrote her brilliant Letters from South Africa did John Walter learn the truth.

Shaw received two or three assignments for the *Times* in each of the next several months. In connection with one, she needed an introduction to General Joubert of the South African Republic (the Transvaal). She consulted the Agent-General of the Cape Colony in London, Sir Charles Mills, who had introduced Stead to Cecil Rhodes the previous year. Mills reported the incident to a friend at the Cape, his description making clear how Shaw had learned to approach important men to get an interview. She not only used her affiliation with the *Times* and her class position as a 'Lady', she also displayed an intellectual mastery of the situation she was writing about. According to Mills, General Joubert 'was delighted with her, and could not believe that a Lady should know so much, and ask such searching questions'. Mills described her as 'an exceedingly clever, fascinating lady', who 'has thoroughly studied and mastered South African politics'.[35]

Yet Shaw continued to find that real barriers existed between her and a salaried position on the *Times*. When she approached Moberly Bell on the subject at the end of 1891, he confessed that he would still find it difficult to convince the editor and proprietor to add a woman to their all-male staff. The *Manchester Guardian* was now offering to hire her, but not as a specialist on the colonies. Faced with this decision and stressed from overwork doing freelance reporting for three editors, Shaw collapsed with influenza. Contemporary medical wisdom ordered rest in a warm climate for those who could afford it. Bell convinced the editor of the *Times* that Shaw was just the person to send to the Cape as a Special Correspondent to write a series of letters on that colony and its energetic new premier, Cecil Rhodes.[36] Still convalescent, she sailed for South Africa in April 1892.

Shaw's series of six 'Letters from South Africa', the first published in mid-July 1892, attracted worldwide press attention and praise. While at the Cape less than a month, she had decided to investigate the diamond and gold mines in Kimberley and Johannesburg and to assess the commercial, agricultural, and political situation throughout the region. She called upon Cecil Rhodes and his Railway minister for advice; from them she received both transport aid and letters of introduction. In what was becoming her characteristic style, Shaw's letters first drew her readers in by describing the vast distances to be travelled in southern Africa. Gradually she shifted the reader's eye down to the ground, where they could find evidence of the changes taking place over time. Then she sketched in the people and places she observed and visited, giving graphic details and making comparison with objects and scenes familiar to them at home. Shaw not only provided careful descriptions of the workings of the mines she visited, but gave specific details about their geology, current financial situation, and attempts to solve labour needs. She also visited an innovative farm in the Transvaal and wrote glowingly of the agricultural potential of the land. Her overall message was clear: South Africa was a vast territory with enormous possibilities for the investment of capital in economic development.

The impact of Shaw's letters on the British political and literary scene was extraordinary. Shaw's sister Lulu wrote to her,

> The *World* this week quotes your opinions about the mining in a series of important articles lately appearing in the *Times*. They of course call you He. They can't imagine She is doing anything so good.[37]

The editor and proprietor of the *Times* were very impressed, both by the articles themselves and their tremendous reception. More importantly for Shaw, they were ready to agree that she would be an important addition to the staff of the newspaper.[38] Bell immediately wrote Shaw, '... never have I so often heard the term "Remarkable" applied so generally & by so many different sorts of people as to your letters'.[39] He delightedly described to a colleague the proprietor's reactions:

> He has a horror of females doing anything. He was struck by the first letter, but when he learned it was by a *Miss* Shaw it nearly killed him ... but the fourth bowled him over, and he got so far as 'most remarkable.' At about the sixth he began to lose his head, compared them to Wellington's dispatches (to him the Bible of all Literature) and now he revels in his apostasy....[40]

As a result, Miss Shaw, clearly an exception to her sex, was sent a year's contract and asked to report on the Australian colonies.

Shaw had taken a calculated gamble when she decided on her own initiative to travel out of Cape Town to report on the political situation and economic prospects of South Africa. Her goal was full time employment, but she was reluctant to join the *Manchester Guardian* as a generalist. She had to prove to the *Times* her value as a specialist on the colonies, so she made her plans quickly to avoid any instructions from Bell to stay put. It was a risk, but it paid off. By late August 1892, when she set sail for Australia, Bell was writing to Australian newspaper editors to introduce her and to alert them that on her return to Printing House Square, Flora Shaw would be in complete charge of colonial news.[41]

An important question in journalism is how ideological commitments affect how a story gets reported. Shaw consciously brought to her writing her class background, her values, and her enthusiasm for imperial expansion and colonial economic development. Her attitudes regarding class, gender, and race reflect the dominant attitudes that flourished in her contemporary world, and on the *Times*. The 'Letter' she sent to the *Times* from Australia on the sugar industry in Queensland provides an example of how her class and racial attitudes could affect her journalism.[42]

Arriving in Brisbane, Queensland's capital, in late September 1892, Shaw stayed by invitation with the Governor. There she was aided by officials and businessmen to plan a tightly scheduled trip around the colony. Her first task was to investigate the controversy raging for some years about the use of Kanakas, South Pacific contract labour, in the sugar industry. These dark-skinned labourers did the hot, dirty, exhausting work of cutting the ripe sugar cane. In the previous year, the highly organized white labour unions in Australia had tested their strength by organizing a series of devastating strikes in the sheep and shipping industries. Organized labour was vociferously opposed to the importation of cheap, non-white labour, seeing it as a ploy to bring down wages. Sugar planters complained to Shaw that no white man would take the job at any wage. In the meantime, she sought to report on the current condition of the Kanakas, visiting the workers in the field and where they lived. She reported that the heavy meat diet allotted them was a regime which any English labourer would have treasured, and she observed some pleasant cottages with small children who happily ran to welcome home their parents at the end of the day.

Her observations led Shaw to inform the readers of the *Times* that the exploitation and abuse of Kanaka labour no longer existed, and that British investment in the sugar industry could expect good returns. She even predicted the plantation economy would replicate the traditional class system at home. Modern scholarship, however, makes clear that Shaw misread some elements of what she 'saw'. She had no way of knowing that the nutritional needs of these workers, based on a different way of life in Melanesia, were not being met. Her visit to the cottages of the few married couples in the labour force left invisible the actual predominantly male, dormitory-housed composition of the Kanaka work force. What Shaw thought representative was actually the exception, a fact that did not emerge from her quick visits. Possible continued abuse in the hiring and transporting of this labour was similarly beyond the scope of her journalism. Finally, the post-federation development of the sugar economy would shift from large plantations to small sugar farms and sugar mill cooperatives.[43] Shaw did not recognize the early signs of this development. Significantly, though she had misread the situation, her views resonated with the contemporary management and readers of the *Times*. Rather than conclude from this example that Shaw's journalism was regularly biased, however, it would be necessary to examine it, in all its complexities, over the next ten years of her professional life.[44] What is clear is that Shaw both reflected and sought to shape the public attitudes of her day.

By any number of measures, Shaw's journalistic success was extraordinary. As the colonial editor of the *Times*, Flora Shaw became the highest paid woman journalist of her day, earning an annual salary of £800. Once embarked on journalism, she began to move in the circles of other well-known writers. She was one of the first five women invited to join the Society of Authors in 1889.[45] She became acquainted with suffrage advocate Millicent Garrett Fawcett, dined with her sometime before she left for South Africa, and sent Fawcett a ticket to listen to her read a paper on 'Colonial Expansion' at the Royal Colonial Institute in November 1894.[46] In January that year Shaw, having returned to London six months before, became the first woman to address this all-male institution, speaking on the 'Australian Outlook'. This accomplishment made news. Reporting her remarks, the *Queen* and the *Gentlewoman* both emphasized Shaw's call for younger sisters to accompany brothers who were planning to emigrate to the colonies.[47]

Shaw was one of a 14-member committee of women in 1897 who planned a 'Women's Jubilee Dinner and Soirée' in honour of Queen Victoria's Diamond Jubilee. The committee included Fawcett and her sister the physician Elizabeth Garrett Anderson, Classics scholar Jane Harrison, African explorer Mary Kingsley, novelist Mrs. Humphry Ward, and society hostess and writer Lady Jeune. The dinner for 'One Hundred Professional Women' and an equal number of men of matching professions was held on 13 July. Just 11 days earlier Shaw had appeared for a second time to give testimony before a Parliamentary Select Committee examining the political scandal called the Jameson Raid in South Africa, a challenge she had carried off with success, though it added to her notoriety. The *Queen*, reporting on Shaw's presence on the Jubilee committee and at the dinner, called her 'a writer, a journalist, and a political thinker'.[48]

Shaw also joined the women's Writers' Club, founded in 1892, where she served at one time as 'chairman of committees'. Among the women who became members was Marie Belloc Lowndes, the daughter of one of the founders of the *Englishwoman's Journal*, a journalist and writer whom Shaw met when working for Stead on the *Pall Mall Gazette* and the *Review of Reviews*. Other members included Flora Annie Steel, who wrote novels set in colonial India, and Mary Cholmondeley, the author of *Red Pottage*, a novel that caused a sensation in the 1899 season. Cholmondeley became a good friend of Shaw's, as did Lady Jeune.[49]

While Shaw knew many leading women activists, her contribution to contemporary debates on gender is complex. The *Englishwoman's Review* noted in 1893 the republication of Shaw's *Letters from South Africa* by the

Macmillan Press, though the title page listed the author only as '*The Times* Special Correspondent'. Many people knew her identity, of course, but no by-lines were ever used in the *Times*. The *Englishwoman's Review*, explicitly citing Shaw's authorship, added an anecdote about her attributed to Sir Evelyn Baring. He had expressed his surprise when, 'having expounded to a journalist upon some "financial details", he found in print not some "loose ... generalization" but "an exposition of the case ... at once lucid, detailed, and absolutely correct"'.[50] Women's journals claimed Flora Shaw as a model of a successful professional woman. Her career exemplified the desire of feminist journals of the 1890s for women to speak out publicly about the burning issues of the day. In Shaw's case, however, it was not a voice raised 'regarding women's status', but a voice explaining important colonial and imperial issues, intent on rousing the public to a concern equal to her own.[51]

On a number of occasions Flora Shaw did express criticism of the gender system of her society, but she never took the next step of endorsing any collective attempt to change that system. If late-Victorian feminism may be defined as an awareness of the problems and barriers that women faced and a concern for that situation, Shaw might be labelled a feminist, but she would have rejected that label for herself. In 1908, asked by Sir Evelyn Baring, by then Lord Cromer, to sign a petition against parliamentary suffrage for women, she complied, agreeing that women were not yet ready for the right to decide on the fate of the empire. Yet, while still living with the Brackenburys in 1883, she wrote to Charles Eliot Norton about the need for time to develop a skill and the unending tasks usually expected of women in a household. She sounds much like Florence Nightingale in 'Cassandra':

> Sunday afternoon and all duties done. People staying in the house walked with and talked with, sick old ladies visited, tea dispensed in the drawing room.... Day after day in a household like this something arises which ... becomes mine because no one else is attending to it ... till the days are filled up and stronger more continuous lines of work & thought are pushed on one side. This is the woman's difficulty....[52]

On another occasion, on her way to Egypt in 1888, Shaw met an American man who expressed great distress to hear that she would be spending her days working as a journalist. Writing to Norton from Cairo, she reported on the encounter: 'What he thought so especially devilish is on the contrary a comfort to me. It is that every woman who does public work makes it easier for those who come after her to work in their turn.'[53] Shaw was clear; she supported women's efforts to earn a living and believed it honourable for them to do so. She worked hard at acquiring the writing skills that would earn her a living and was proud of the independence she gained by doing so.

After a very full and rewarding career as a journalist, Flora Shaw agreed to marry Sir Frederick Lugard, High Commissioner of Northern Nigeria. Before they married, the *Times* sent her one more time to report on the continuing war in South Africa. From Johannesburg in February 1902, she wrote to Lugard, reflecting on the gender differences encouraged by society. It echoed the same analysis she had made two decades before:

> From the cradle a boy is taught ... that he must infuse his individuality on his surroundings[,] that he must make his own decisions and go his own way[,] that he must have the courage to say No when other people want him to do things ... it is inevitable that he should learn to think himself a being of some serious importance. The girl on the contrary is from the beginning taught that the sweet and nice thing for her to do is to put herself and her tastes on one side and to hold herself at the disposal of anyone who wants her.... Inevitably in her case the habit grows of ... doing things just as well as may be convenient not as well as she could.[54]

Shaw's understanding of the barriers women had to overcome to achieve ambitious goals still stopped short of a commitment to seeking a political remedy. Instead, looking forward to her own marriage, she saw couples balancing each other's strengths and weaknesses.

The announcement of Shaw's marriage to Lugard in June 1902 provoked another woman journalist, writing for the *Lady's Pictorial*, to comment with enthusiasm on Shaw's successful career on the *Times*:

> Miss Shaw is as charming personally as she is gifted intellectually. One might write a great deal of her services to the Empire without being exhaustive. Nowadays we are all interested in the Colonies, and the Colonies in us. But it is no exaggeration to state that the development of this interest dates from the moment when Miss Shaw began to write so helpfully, hopefully and informatively about the Colonies in the columns of the *Times*.[55]

As the wife of a leading colonial administrator, Lady Lugard did not stop trying to influence public views about empire. When, however, she earned one of the first official Honours awarded British women, becoming a Dame Commander of the Order of the British Empire in 1918, it was for her contribution to Belgian Relief work during World War I.

As a journalist of empire, Flora Shaw earned worldwide acclaim. Her determination to earn her living as a writer shaped her career. After a decade writing novels, she needed to change direction, and experimented with literary and travel essays before focusing on journalism. To her writing about empire she brought her narrative and analytical skills. Week by week she followed the economic and political stories of the colonies, directing the public's attention to their significance. She negotiated the gender conventions of her day to establish a professional career and encouraged other women to develop their talents. Committed to the importance of empire, she came to agree with those who were concerned that women's suffrage might pose a threat to vital imperial policies. The last decade of the nineteenth century saw an increased public enthusiasm for empire. As a journalist, Shaw played a significant part in building that enthusiasm. However we evaluate, in hindsight, the nature and consequences of imperialism, we need to understand the ways in which journalism fostered it. Shaw's role on the *Times* in helping to shape public attitudes and imperial policies is a vital part of that history.

Notes

1. The author wishes to express gratitude for helpful suggestions to members of the Women Writing Women's Lives and the Columbia Women and Society seminars, and especially to the editor of this volume, F. Elizabeth Gray.
2. Mary Kingsley to John Holt, 20 February 1899, quoted in Katherine Frank, *A Voyager Out: The Life of Mary Kingsley* (Boston: Houghton Mifflin Company, 1986), 264.
3. E. Moberly Bell, *Flora Shaw (Lady Lugard D.B.E.)* (London: Constable, 1947), 20–23. Diaries cited by Bell are now lost.
4. John Ruskin, *Fors Clavigera: Letters to the Workmen and Labourers of Great Britain*, new edn., 4 vols. (London: George Allen, 1896), vol. 4, Letter 87, March 1878, 313–314.
5. Shaw's second and third novels were *Hector: A Story for Young People* (London: George Bell & Sons, 1882) and *Phyllis Browne* (Boston: Little, Brown and Company, 1883). Both were first serialized in *Aunt Judy's Magazine*. *Phyllis Browne* was published as a book only in the United States.
6. Bell, *Flora Shaw*, 39–44; George Meredith to Admiral Frederick A. Maxse, 24 June 1889, *The Letters of George Meredith*, ed. C.L. Cline, 3 vols., (Oxford: Clarendon Press, 1970), vol. 2, 1211.
7. Shaw's fourth novel was *A Sea Change* (London: George Routledge and Sons, 1885) and her fifth, *Colonel Cheswick's Campaign*, 3 vols. (London: Longmans, Green, and Co., 1886).
8. Bell, *Flora Shaw*, 78–79. Shaw's letters to Stead are in the Stead Papers, Churchill College, University of Cambridge [hereafter SPCC].
9. Abd al-Rahman Munir Zubayr Pasha 1830?–1912. Roger Owen, *Lord Cromer: Victorian Imperialist, Edwardian Proconsul* (Oxford: Oxford University Press, 2004), 196–200, 202, 212.
10. Flora L. Shaw, 'The Story of Zebehr Pasha, as told by himself, Parts I, II, and III,' *Contemporary Review*, 52 (September, October, and November, 1887), 333–349, 568–585, 658–682.
11. Bell, *Flora Shaw*, 33–38. Shaw used this experience in her novel *Phyllis Browne* and in a short story, 'Rose of Blackboy Alley – An East End Story,' *Sunday Magazine* (September–October 1883), 564–570, 597–603.

12. Flora L. Shaw, 'The Australian Outlook,' *Royal Colonial Institute* 25 (1893–94), 138–65.
13. Flora L. Shaw, *Colonel Cheswick's Campaign*, vol. 1, 31.
14. Flora Shaw to Charles Eliot Norton, Gibraltar, 12 December 1886, Papers of Charles Eliot Norton, Houghton Library, Harvard University [hereafter, NP].
15. Bell, *Flora Shaw*, 57–59. 'Consular Protection in Morocco,' *Pall Mall Gazette* (17 October 1887), 5; (25 October 1887), 2–3; (27 October 1887), 2–3; (31 October 1887), 2–3; (9 November 1887), 2; (1 December 1887), 2–3.
16. Flora L. Shaw, 'The Future of Morocco,' Letter to the Editor, the *Morning Post* (8 November 1889), 2.
17. Bell, *Flora Shaw*, 64–66. Shaw visited his palace outside the city and had an opportunity to meet his harem, but confessed in her diary that she was depressed by 'the dreary spectacle' of both.
18. Among the men Shaw interviewed was General Wingate, head of military intelligence. Shaw to Francis Wingate, Cairo, n.d., Wingate Papers, Sudan Archive, University of Durham [SAD 155/3/136].
19. Bell, *Flora Shaw*, 63–75; Owen, *Lord Cromer*, 74–78, 243–252.
20. Flora Shaw to Colonel Charles Brackenbury, March 10 [1889], Shaw Papers, Rhodes House Library, Oxford University. [Hereafter, SPRH].
21. Flora Shaw to William T. Stead, 12 June [1889], SPCC.
22. Shaw to Norton, 16 July and 13 November 1886, NP. 'An Episode, A story,' *New Princeton Review*, 2 (1887), 106–129; 'George Meredith,' *New Princeton Review*, 3 (1887–1888), 220–229.
23. 'Gibraltar,' *Sunday Magazine* (July 1887), 453–459; 'Under the Peak,' [Tenerife] *Good Words* 30:47 (October 1889), 665–670 and (November 1889), 742–747; 'Majorca, I,' *Sunday Magazine* 19 (May 1890), 302–308; and 'Majorca, II,' *Sunday Magazine* 19 (June 1890), 407–415.
24. Shaw to Norton, 11 June 1889, NP. She had written to him earlier from Cairo that the work she was doing 'involves being more or less in regular relations with the men who are making history ... and that is the interest of it'. Shaw to Norton, 22 February 1889, NP.
25. Bell, *Flora Shaw*, 80. Rhodes's exact phrase is in his 'Confession of Faith' of 1877, John Flint, *Cecil Rhodes* (Boston and Toronto: Little Brown & Company, 1974), Appendix, 248.
26. Flora L. Shaw, 'Dry-Nursing the Colonies,' *Fortnightly Review*, 46 n.s. (September 1889), 373.
27. Shaw, 'Dry-Nursing,' 373.
28. Flora L. Shaw, 'The British South Africa Company,' *Fortnightly Review*, 46 n.s. (November 1889), 662–68.
29. Flora L. Lugard to Frederick D. Lugard, 13 November 1904, Margery Perham Papers, Rhodes House Library, Oxford University, MP 309/1, ff. 24–25.
30. Shaw to Stead, 30 November and 9 December 1889, SPCC.
31. Shaw to Stead, no date, archived between 3 November and 9 December 1889, SPCC.
32. The newspaper had just lost a costly libel case brought by the Irish leader Charles Parnell. *The History of The Times: The Twentieth Century Test, 1884–1912* (New York: The Macmillan Company, 1947), 89, 112, 161–162. E.H.C. Moberly Bell, *The Life & Letters of C.F. Moberly Bell* (London: The Richards Press, 1927), 140, 156.

33. Bell to Herbert, 1 May 1890, Manager's Letter Book, *The Times* Record Office, London [hereafter MLB], Volume I/folio 135. Bell to Shaw, 23 May 1890, MLB 1/144.
34. Bell, *Flora Shaw*, 82.
35. Quoted in Phyllis Lewsen, *Selections from the Correspondence of John X. Merriman*, 4 vols. (Cape Town: Van Riebeck Society), vol. 2 (1963), 8.
36. Bell, *Flora Shaw*, 97–98, 100.
37. Louise (Lulu) Shaw to Flora Shaw, 11 August [1892], SPRH.
38. Bell, *Flora Shaw*, 119–120.
39. Moberly Bell to Shaw, 12 August 1892, MLB 5/57–58.
40. E.H.C. Moberly Bell, *Life & Letters*, 156–57.
41. Typical of these letters was Bell to Andrew Garron, 14 February 1892 [by placement, 1893], MLB.
42. 'Letters from Australia, II. The Sugar Industry in Queensland,' *The Times*, 7 January 1893.
43. Clive Moore, Jacqueline Leckie, Douglas Munro, eds., *Labour in the South Pacific* (Townsville: James Cook University of Queensland, 1990); Adrian Graves, *Cane and Labour: The Political Economy of the Queensland Sugar Industry, 1862–1906* (Edinburgh: Edinburgh University Press, 1993); Tom Brass, 'Contextualizing Sugar Production in Nineteenth-Century Queensland,' *Slavery and Abolition* 15, no.1 (April 1994), 100–117; and Patricia Mercer, *White Australia Defied: Pacific Islander Settlement in Northern Queensland* (Townsville: History Department, James Cook University, 1995).
44. This task is being undertaken by the author of this chapter.
45. The first five included 'Miss C.M. Yonge, Mrs. Linton, Mrs. Humphry Ward, Mrs. [sic] Flora Shaw, and Mrs. Ormerod', G.H. Thring, 'History of the Society of Authors,' British Library Mss. Add. 56868–69, f. 47. 'Miss Flora Shaw' was reported attending the annual dinner of the Society of Authors in July 1889, *Pall Mall Gazette* (4 July1889), 7a. Meredith may have recommended her.
46. F. Edmund Garrett to his cousin Agnes Garrett, 9 June 1897 in Gerald Shaw, *The Garrett Papers* (Cape Town: Van Riebeeck Society, 1984), 95. M.G. Fawcett to Shaw, 14 November 1894, SPRH.
47. 'The Future of Australia,' *The Queen: The Lady's Newspaper & Court Chronicle* (Saturday, 20 January 1894), 82; *The Gentlewoman* (20 January 1894), 76. Both the *Times* and the *Westminster Gazette* published glowing accounts on 10 January 1894.
48. *The Queen*, 102 (Saturday, 17 and 24 July 1897), 105 and 157.
49. *Young Woman* (March 1901), 201. By 1899 membership of the Women's Writer's Club numbered 300 women writers.
50. Quoted in Barbara Onslow, *Women of the Press in Nineteenth-Century Britain* (Houndmills, Basingstoke: Macmillan Press Ltd, 2000), 51–52.
51. Michelle Elizabeth Tusan, 'Inventing the New Woman: Print Culture and Identity Politics during the *Fin-de-Siècle*,' *Victorian Periodicals Review* 31, no. 2 (Summer 1998), 169–82: 173.
52. Shaw to Norton, 10 November 1883, NP.
53. Shaw to Norton, 22 February 1889, NP. There is still discussion of whether feminism in the second half of the nineteenth century consisted solely of a commitment to systematic campaigning for women's rights or also a 'sensitivity to [women's] needs, awareness of their problems and concern for their situation'.

Mary Maynard, 'Privilege and Patriarchy: Feminist Thought in the Nineteenth Century,' in *Sexuality & Subordination: Interdisciplinary Studies of Gender in the Nineteenth Century*, eds Susan Mendus and Jane Rendall (London and New York: Routledge, 1989), 222.

54. Shaw to Lugard, 25 January [1902] SPRH. The relationship between experience and knowledge, and whether the experience of being a woman in a patriarchal society itself leads inevitably to resistance to oppression is still being debated. See, for example, Joan W. Scott, 'The Evidence of Experience,' *Critical Inquiry* 17, no. 4 (summer 1991), esp. 786–87.

55. *Lady's Pictorial: A newspaper for the home* (18 March 1902), 316. The article was signed 'Miranda'.

8

'Making a name for Whistler': Elizabeth Robins Pennell as a New Art Critic

Kimberly Morse Jones
Sweet Briar College

Respected and revered in her day, Elizabeth Robins Pennell is today most commonly known for her biography of the artist James McNeill Whistler, cowritten with her husband Joseph, and for her writings on travel and food, published in both book and periodical format. She was also a prolific art critic, contributing numerous articles to many publications in Britain and the United States between 1883 and 1919. Pennell's art criticism, unlike her other writings, was largely anonymous. Adopting a variety of cryptic, gender-neutral pseudonyms allowed Pennell to engage in an intellectual, male-dominated discourse on art. In contrast to other female art critics who can be considered generalists, Pennell was amongst a new breed of professional art critics who possessed critical expertise. She strategically utilized her journalistic platform to encourage her readership to change their view of art, by considering form above content, thus becoming a significant advocate for what was deemed the 'New Art Criticism'. Her various 'signatures' gave her a voice, albeit disembodied, which when united with those of other New Art Critics disseminated a fledgling modernist agenda. Pennell's career in art criticism therefore revolved not around self-promotion, but rather around the promotion of a specific ideology. The primary beneficiary of Pennell's championing was Whistler. This chapter will examine Pennell's journalistic strategies within the wider context of women and art criticism at the *fin de siècle*, and the way in which these strategies promoted the principles of New Art Criticism, exemplified by Whistler, but denied Pennell herself due recognition.

The New Journalism

Elizabeth Robins, an American by birth, published her first art review on two exhibitions held in New York City in 1883 in the *American*, at the age of 28. She attended the show with her soon-to-be husband, the illustrator Joseph Pennell. Her stint at the newspaper was short-lived, as Robins, a neophyte, was freshly entering the world of art. In 1884 the two began collaborating on projects for the *Century*, with Joseph contributing illustrations and Elizabeth text. They married in 1884 and soon after set sail for England. This move would prove propitious for Pennell, because in England her career as an art critic began to take off.

The British press underwent radical change in the 1880s, in a series of transformations that came to be known as New Journalism. One of its primary objectives was to make newspapers, and the contents thereof, more accessible to the common man or woman. According to New Journalist W.T. Stead, editor of the *Pall Mall Gazette*, he and T.P. O'Connor of the *Star*, 'may fairly claim to have revolutionized English journalism. We broke the tradition and made journalism a living thing, palpitating with actuality, in touch with life at all points.'[1] They achieved this by making over the style of the newspaper, replacing the flowery, periphrastic language that had previously been employed with rhetoric that was 'unpedantic, nervous, flexible, [representative of the] good English of common life ... which men of education use in their talk and in their letters'.[2] Presentation style also changed in order to appear more reader-friendly by introducing cross-heads, shorter paragraphs, and larger, punchier headlines, and increasing the number of illustrations.

Another strategy employed by editors was to emphasize the individuality of the contributors by the adoption of 'signatures', albeit sometimes pseudonymous, thereby establishing an authorial voice. In an article on New Journalism published in the *New Review* in 1895, Evelyn March Phillipps observed:

> The writer comes more directly to the reader than of old; individualism is allowed full play; simplicity and truth encouraged; shibboleths are at a discount; charming essays and studies abound; and no pains are spared to secure excellence.[3]

A journalist writing for the *Saturday Review* made a similar observation, commenting on the 'authority' and 'impartiality' of contemporary journalists. Although the author recognized New Journalists' partisanship, he claimed their unfailing belief 'that frankness and honesty are the best policy' superseded it.[4]

Subsequently journalists, in particular critics, were in the position to educate and influence public opinion. An anonymous contributor wrote in the *Pall Mall Gazette*:

> [It is important that the critic] recognises the immense responsibilities attaching to his influence. He may be said to affect the destiny of generations unborn; it is his ennobling occupation to unmask hypocrisy, to penetrate the disguises of falsehood, to dissipate the tears of superstition, and to unravel the meshes of sophistry; to winnow the chaff from the wheat, and to detect the spurious coin that would debase the currency of

the mind. To be a standard-bearer of the truth, to be proudly privileged, as on vantage ground, to fight for freedom in the high places of the field, this surely is the vocation of the critic; whether literary, artistic or dramatic, for which inspiring task he will need to be endowed with the spirit of wisdom and of a sound mind.[5]

While the above quote undoubtedly hyperbolizes, the following more moderate assessment similarly acknowledges the cultural currency offered by the New Journalism:

The cheap newspaper and periodical cannot perhaps be defined strictly as educators. Yet for good or evil, and probably on the whole good, they are very powerful ones. [...] Notwithstanding the many sins and shortcomings of the newspaper press, the working man of today, with his broadsheet for a penny is by its aid a man of fuller information, better judgment and wider sympathies than the workman of thirty years back who had to content himself with gossip and rumour.[6]

Pennell entered this dynamic journalistic environment at the end of the 1880s. Admittedly, the *Star* first hired Joseph, whose predilection for evoking controversy was well known. Joseph replaced the incendiary criticism of George Bernard Shaw, who was too contentious even for the firebrand *Star*. Reeling from four separate lawsuits, the newspaper soon deemed Joseph, who was purported to have made 'all of London gasp', equally libellous. Subsequently O'Connor hired Pennell as Joseph's replacement, at Joseph's own recommendation. Indeed it is unlikely that the *Star* would have hired Pennell without her husband's nomination, as it was particularly difficult for women to secure a foothold in journalism. Charlotte O'Conor Eccles described her experience trying to launch her journalistic career in an anonymous article for *Blackwood's Edinburgh Magazine* in 1893:

One is horribly handicapped in being a woman. A man meets other men at his club; he can be out and about at all hours; he can insist without being thought bold and forward; he is not presumed to be capable of undertaking only a limited class of subjects, but is set to anything. Mr T.P. O'Connor, in one his clever articles, tells a would-be journalist that the first essential is to get taken on in an office in any capacity. 'Go as an office-boy, if need be,' he says – I quote from memory – 'but get into an office anyhow.' The immense difficulty a woman finds in getting into an office in any recognized capacity makes a journalistic beginning far harder for her than for a man. Where a man finds one obstacle, we find a dozen.[7]

As progressive as the *Star* strove to be in terms of politics and social reform, it did not serve as an organ for feminism, nor did it foster the intellectual lives of professional female journalists, who were generally relegated to columns dedicated to tittle-tattle. Positing 'washerwomen are as keen on society gossip as Duchesses', O'Connor was the first Victorian editor to resurrect the daily gossip column, which had been popular at the beginning of the century. He made his wife editor of the column, whose first line read 'Lady Colin Campbell is the only woman in London who has her feet manicured'.[8] The *Star*'s Woman's Column, which concentrated on the latest fashions, was no more cerebral. Indeed O'Connor and other New Journalists were chided for feminizing the press by elevating commonplace subjects at the expense of more hefty, 'masculine' subjects, such as politics.[9]

Because Pennell initially retained the same gender-neutral (although implied male) voice adopted by Joseph, it is difficult to determine precisely when her first article appeared in the *Star*. In all likelihood Pennell had assisted her husband from the very beginning, but the extent of her involvement gradually increased between 1890 and 1891, during which time attribution of the articles oscillated between 'ARTIST UNKNOWN' and 'A.U'. The pair probably collaborated on the articles produced during these years. It was not until 1892, at which point 'A.U.' received her own weekly column entitled 'Art and Artists', that an implied break in authorship appears. An article in November of that year signed 'NOT A.U.', presumably written by Joseph, indicates an oblique desire to distinguish between the two designations and voices. Although not as truculent as her predecessors, Pennell in her own restrained yet riveting manner proved to be a boon to the *Star*. The fact that Pennell continued to contribute to the newspaper up until 1908 reveals the value editors placed on her work.

Although assuming a *nom de plume* was common for both male and female critics in the nineteenth century, many women deemed it essential practice.[10] Adopting a *nom de plume* and ventriloquizing Joseph's authorial voice enabled Pennell to adopt a masculine guise, securing her a greater degree of freedom in which to voice her opinion. She once explained that a primary reason to adopt a policy of anonymity is to avoid being held accountable for the opinions set forth.[11] In a letter to the editor of the *Nation*, who had asked her to reconsider her stance on preserving her anonymity, Pennell explained, 'I have always liked best to remain anonymous in doing work of this kind – one has more freedom'.[12] This freedom was particularly important for Pennell, who capitalized upon her platform to espouse radical principles, particularly in her art criticism.

However, for women, other issues were also at play in the choice of anonymity or pseudonymity. For instance, women traditionally received a much harsher reception than men. According to Alexis Easley, women writers were often 'held accountable to confining definitions of "female authorship," which constrained their choice of subject matter and exposed their personal lives to public scrutiny'.[13] Retaining anonymity allowed women to maintain a low profile and to some extent evade censure. Pennell would have been particularly conscious of avoiding negative comment as she began contributing criticism to the London press shortly after the publication of her biography of Mary Wollstonecraft, which critics panned.

Unlike women journalists who advanced an overtly feminist agenda, Pennell did not 'need' to reveal her gender. Except for the signed article 'A Century of Women's Rights' in the *Fortnightly Review*, written to coincide with the release of a new edition of Wollstonecraft's *A Vindication of the Rights of Woman* (1792) in 1890, Pennell rarely spoke of gender in the press. Opining there 'should be no question of sex in art', gender did not feature in her criticism either.[14] Indeed she made no attempt to promote the work of female artists in her articles. Not until 1918, in one of her last articles published in the *Nation*, and one of the few signed articles for the publication, did Pennell comment explicitly on women's art. Unable to account for the lack of great women artists, she argued that thus far women had made no original contribution to the history of art.[15]

Throughout Pennell's long and prolific career, she adopted various pseudonyms, including: 'A.U.' for the *Star*; 'N.N.' (No Name) for the New York *Nation*; 'P.E.R.' (her initials jumbled up) for *Woman*, and 'Autolycus' (taken from her weekly contributions to the column 'Wares of Autolycus' published in the *Pall Mall Gazette*) for *Art Weekly*. Her articles for the *Daily Chronicle* are unsigned. While Pennell occasionally published signed art reviews, she did so only at the absolute insistence of the editor, such as that of the *Fortnightly Review*, who in keeping with the periodical's policy, dictated that all authors sign their contributions.

Victorian women writers had a tendency to avoid what Harriet Martineau in an 1839 article dubbed 'Literary Lionism', by which she criticized writers for seeking after fame rather than concentrating on their work.[16] Such egotism was particularly damaging to the cultivation of women's careers, Martineau posited. In 1892, Fitzroy Gardner, editor of the New Journalist penny paper *Woman*, also discouraged women from promoting themselves, in an article advising women on how to enter the field of journalism:

> The desire for self-advertisement on the part of women writers is generally a sign of weakness.[...] While one who is getting herself and her gowns (of somewhat imaginary smartness) into so-called 'society' paragraphs, and perhaps congratulations on work she has not written, the best work is being done and a better income made by another who sits down at home to read widely and wisely, and write brilliant anonymous articles.[17]

Pennell's own experience suggests an avoidance of lionization. Although Pennell roamed the streets alone carrying out research at the British Library or attending exhibitions, her career for the most part was comprised of hard work carried out within the confines of her home. She participated in social events, including the Thursday evening salons she and Joseph hosted in their home, attended by Oscar Wilde, George Moore, George Bernard Shaw, and many others. Pennell's direct involvement however appears to have been minimal, as she recorded her distraction at the impending weekly deadline for her Saturday cookery article for the *Pall Mall Gazette* and her 'sense of duty as hostess'.[18] Her memoirs lionize the personality and achievements of others, however, including William Henley to whom she devoted an astounding 25 pages. On one occasion, Pennell modestly recorded having been recognized at a social gathering as 'Mrs. Pennell of cycling fame'.[19] That she recorded the incident suggests it was not an everyday event.

Paradoxically, Pennell concurrently enjoyed a prolific career and popular regard as an author of a series of signed articles published in the American magazine the *Century*, recounting her and Joseph's journeys around Great Britain and Europe on bicycle. These articles, later published as books in the United States and England, were well received by critics on both sides of the Atlantic. These include: *A Canterbury Pilgrimage* (1885), *An Italian Pilgrimage* (1886), *Our Sentimental Journey through France and Italy* (1888), *Two Pilgrims' Progress* (1889), *Our Journey through the Hebrides* (1889), *Play in Provence* (1892), and *Over the Alps on a Bicycle* (1898). In contrast to her critical writing, Pennell actively promoted herself in these works; in the introduction to *Over the Alps on a Bicycle*, for which Pennell traversed 108 miles and crossed 10 of the highest Alpine peaks in 6 weeks, she stated her intent to publicize her achievement by 'immortalis[ing] the name and adventures of the first woman [to cross the Alps on bicycle]'.[20] This inconsistency was not uncommon for nineteenth-century women journalists, who quite often both revealed and concealed their gender identity in different platforms. Pennell's gender would have enhanced the intrepid nature of her cycling adventures, which appealed to a distinctly bourgeois audience.

The New Journalism benefited Pennell by allowing her to establish a strong authorial voice and by endowing her with a platform from which to disseminate her radical artistic convictions. Nonetheless, her practice of pseudonymity has posthumously obscured her work.[21] While men often published compilations of their criticism or exposed their identity in other public formats, women critics generally did not. This has made identifying Pennell and other women journalists from the late nineteenth century an often laborious task for scholars. But, as Meaghan Clarke has asserted, 'It is only by unravelling the variety of signatures that women published under that one is at all able to discern the considerable contribution women in fact made'.[22]

Professionalization of Art Criticism

Professionalization was a by-product of England's new industrial society, which gave rise to a job market wherein merit and expertise were highly valued.[23] Before the 1860s, when journalism began rapidly professionalizing, editors often employed 'artist-critics' (artists lacking literary experience) or 'literary critics' (writers lacking knowledge of art) to write press art criticism. The role of the art critic was strictly objective: to catalogue, record, and report. As long as art critics were satisfactorily literate, it was not considered essential for them to possess specific qualifications. Art critics, who usually remained anonymous, reported on art as they would any other subject and rarely formed opinions on the art under review. Kate Flint has described their capacity thus:

> The rôle of the critic was not to problematise acts of spectatorship; not to make his or her readers think about the relationship between the visible world and the world of imagination; not even, frequently, to educate them in looking carefully at the techniques and means of representation used in publicly displayed works. Rather, a commentary tended to be offered on the painting's contents: a commentary which often assumed an unquestioned continuity between the world represented and the world inhabited by the reader of criticism. Ironically, it was this refusal to take art *as* art, which united, at least at one level, those who otherwise were implacably at odds in their attitudes towards painting.[24]

Critics during the first half of the nineteenth century tended to adopt the first-person plural, creating impartiality and homogeneity, but as the century progressed, 'I' began to replace 'we', thereby fragmenting a publication's monolithic voice of authority.[25] As one journalist noted:

> The babel of tongues is healthier than the sound of the voice melodiously proclaiming prejudices as vital truths and getting them accepted as such.... But while we have now no critic who is Samson amongst his fellows, we have a greater number of capable critics than ever before.[26]

This 'babel of tongues' facilitated a multitude of what Laurel Brake and Julie F. Codell have coined 'encounters,' or:

> [...] any set of articles or letters to the editor in which the writer, whether journalist or reader, responds to a published article in a periodical, often as a reply to special topics or issues of the day, or other articles with which the respondent agrees or disagrees.[27]

According to Brake and Codell:

> The concept of encounters is important not only because it mediates periodicals' social function, but also because it offsets another tendency: a journal title promises a false unity, appearing to present, despite its

many articles, topics, and illustrations, a unified policy, or set of beliefs, as if the journal itself were a single author.[28]

Encounters therefore expose the fact that the periodical press did not construct and disseminate ideas, but rather provided a locus for discourse from which ideas generated. Essentially the Victorian press had transformed into a tumult of competing voices.

According to Elizabeth Prettejohn, from the middle of the nineteenth century onwards, two divergent value systems emerged in Victorian art criticism – generalist and professional.[29] Generalist art critics, who lacked training, continued in much the same vein as had art critics prior to 1860, by appealing to the layperson through use of sentiment and anecdote. They believed their foremost duty was not to educate, but rather to entertain. Like their predecessors, generalist art critics made no attempt to assess the merit of a work of art, but instead left assessment to the reader, who, having been conditioned to consider art in terms of entertainment, made judgements according to its sentimental value. In contrast, professional art critics adopted a more expert method, opting to focus strictly on its artistic qualities. As informed intermediaries, art critics after 1860 began to influence the formation of public opinion.

In 1892 M.H. Spielmann published a two-part article in the *Magazine of Art* offering insight into the opaque world of London press art critics. He explained that press art critics numbered approximately 300, and were comprised of both generalist and professional art critics. His tongue-and-cheek description of the latter follows:

> Let us watch the constantly increasing body of critics and writers, so heterogeneous in the individuals that compose it, and look at them as they stand critically before the pictures. [...] Here is one, a well-known and accomplished writer, a scholar, too, of polished taste – not a mere Press-man, as he would have you know – but one of a handful of serious art-critics and historians, with definite views and definite knowledge, and definite literary individuality.[30]

Spielmann went on to discuss various characteristics of professional art critics, including education and a background in art. While scores of female amateur journalists flooded the market, professionals like Pennell were few and far between. Indeed, Gardner asserted:

> [T]here are some thirty or so of women efficient, all-round journalists; about fifty more who write well on special subjects of which they have special knowledge, and perhaps a couple hundred who contribute occasional articles to the daily and weekly press, or are content with penning

descriptions of subscription balls, bazaars, and suburban and provincial festivities for ladies' fashion papers.[31]

The road to becoming a professional journalist for both women and men was neither straight nor narrow. In an article offering advice to women on how to enter the profession, Pennell admitted the difficulty of explaining exactly how one goes about that entry. During the nineteenth century no systematic program for training professional journalists existed, 'no body of doctrine, no series of fixed rules, apparently no possible method of instruction'.[32] Nonetheless Pennell, who used her platform to voice radical opinions, may certainly be counted within Spielmann's 'handful' of professional art critics. She based her judgements on expertise acquired from personal study, extensive travel, and exposure to prominent figures in the Victorian art and literary worlds. Interestingly, Pennell fenced with the identity of a professional art critic, frequently questioning her own qualifications. For instance on 14 February 1893 in the *Star* she referred to her 'poor critical faculties', writing in parentheses, 'I have no pretensions as a critic you will remember'.[33] In another article she wrote, 'Probably because it is not my usual role, I like occasionally to play the critic', after which she continued her critical analysis, summing it up with 'but I have played critic long enough'.[34] On another occasion, she commented, 'I wish for today at least that I were the art critic whom I have always taken pains to explain that I am not'.[35] Paradoxically these self-negating comments coexisted with bold gestures of bravado. In response to another critic, Pennell explained how she would go about defending her argument:

> I would begin with graceful persiflage, I would gradually and quietly plunge into philosophical depths whither the average man would never follow, and I would wind up with a few open-air touches just to show that, after all, I am human.[36]

One possible explanation for this conflicted attitude to a critical identity may lie in Pennell's admiration for Whistler, who abhorred critics, as evidenced by his lawsuit against John Ruskin for accusing the artist of 'flinging a pot of paint in the public's face' after viewing *Nocturne in Black and Gold: Falling Rocket* at the Grosvenor Gallery in 1877. Critics like Ruskin stood for everything Pennell and her artistic cohorts disliked about the Victorian art world; taking on the very same egotistic tone of critical authority from which she was trying to free art may have seemed to her hypocritical.

The same propensity for problematizing her own authoritative critical status is present in Pennell's writings on cookery, as Jamie Horrocks and Talia Schaffer have noted in their respective studies of Pennell's cookery articles.[37] First published anonymously in the *Pall Mall Gazette*, these articles were compiled into a book, *The Delights of Delicate Eating*, in 1896. Pennell repeatedly reminded readers that her only qualifications were a healthy appetite and love of food, and she had a habit of aborting recipes halfway through descriptions.[38] Employing aesthetic rhetoric in her discussions of food, Pennell described a meal as one would a painting. As a result Pennell shifted authority away from herself towards the readers, 'for when Pennell steps backward', observed Horrocks, 'she requires that her readers step forward in compensation, assuming the position of author and creator that Pennell vacated'.[39]

Unlike many of her male counterparts, Pennell did not publish a compilation of her art criticism. Such compilations were common practice among professional critics, to bolster their authority. Pennell's fellow New Art Critic George Moore published *Modern Painting* in 1893. D.S. MacColl, too, solidified his authority by publishing a survey of nineteenth-century art in 1902. While Pennell published a number of books outside the sphere of art criticism, her first published book regarding art did not appear until 1908, *The Life of James McNeill Whistler*. Although Pennell went to great lengths to stake her claim on being Whistler's authorized biographer, her primary objective lay in feting the artist rather than in establishing her own authority.

Indeed, while most other professional critics went to no great lengths to conceal their identities, and by writing press art criticism deliberately built their own professional reputations, it is possible that even some in Pennell's inner circle did not know that she penned radical art criticism. In 1897 artist and art critic Walter Sickert mistakenly identified 'A.U.' as Joseph Pennell.[40] And as late as 1911 Sickert attributed an article published in the New York *Nation* published by Pennell under 'N.N.' to her husband Joseph.[41] It is possible that Sickert knew perfectly well the true identity of 'A.U.' and 'N.N.' but did not find it important to distinguish between Joseph and Elizabeth because at this point their identities to both the public and those close to them were still conflated. It is also possible that Sickert, who wrote radical art criticism himself, simply did not want to acknowledge a woman within his radical circle. Nevertheless, Sickert's public refusal to recognize Pennell is suggestive.

The New Art Criticism

Of the many women art critics at the end of the nineteenth century in Britain, Pennell was unique in her espousal of radical art criticism. Indeed she advanced the most progressive ideas with regard to contemporary art in England. Pennell was one of a small band of newspaper art critics who came to be known as the New Art Critics, 'new' being a pejorative term at the time. The New Art Critics were a loosely knit group, never formally uniting, whose voices in concert championed the new painting as manifest in the work of Édouard Manet and Edgar Degas. In addition to Pennell, they included: Alfred Lys Baldry, D.S. MacColl, George Moore, Joseph Pennell, R.A.M. Stevenson, Frederick Wedmore, and Charles Whibley. Other than a commitment to 'art for art's sake', the New Art Critics had little else in common. Some were college educated, while others were not; some artists, while others *littérateurs*, and indeed some were both. They differed in nationality, age, and at times artistic allegiance. For instance, Moore, although an admirer of Whistler's work, criticized the artist in *Modern Painting*, and did not share Pennell's unwavering devotion to Whistler. Wedmore had an actual run-in with Whistler, immortalized in the artist's *Gentle Art of Making Enemies* (1890), which has cast him erroneously as a conservative art critic. Regardless of these differences, this small band of critics, less interested in touting their own positions of authority than a specific ideology, created a unified voice in the press that could not be ignored.

The New Art Critics received their name in the winter of 1893 as a result of a debate – or encounter, to borrow Brake's and Codell's term – that transpired in the press over Degas's *L'Absinthe* (1876), exhibited at the Grafton Gallery in London. The furore, according to Alfred Thornton, an art student in the 1890s, constituted 'the greatest aesthetic battle waged in England'.[42] *L'Absinthe* depicts a solitary woman in a bar slouching over a table topped with a glass of absinthe, which, although relatively normalized in Europe, served as an emblem of vileness and vulgarity in England.[43] Scholars have made much of the moral nature of the debate, but morality in fact had very little to do with it.[44] Critics did not initially find the painting rebarbative; in fact, the critic for *The Times* gave it a fairly judicious review commenting on how far public opinion had come since Degas's initial reception in England a decade earlier when critics castigated his work. Pennell, although conceding to the 'grim[ness] in its realism', esteemed *L'Absinthe* 'incomparable in its art'.[45] The catalyst for the debate that ensued was a comment made by fellow New Art Critic D.S. MacColl, who wrote the following in the *Spectator*:

But *L'Absinthe*, by Degas, is the inexhaustible picture, the one that draws you back and back again. It sets the standard by which too many of the would-be 'decorative' inventions in the exhibition are cruelly judged. [...] M. Degas understands his people absolutely; there is no false note of an imposed and blundering sentiment, but exactly as a man with a just eye and comprehending mind and power of speech could set up that scene for us in the fit words, whose mysterious relations of idea should affect us as beauty, so does this master of character, of form, of colour, watch till the *café* table-tops and the mirror and the water-bottle and the drinks and the features yield up to him their mysterious affecting note. The subject, if you like, was repulsive as you would have seen it, *before Degas made it his*. If it appears so still, you may make up your mind that the confusion and affliction from which you suffer are incurable.[46]

MacColl's pronouncement of *L'Absinthe*'s beauty bewildered conservative critics, who asked how a wretched picture like *L'Absinthe* could warrant such an accolade. Spender led the Philistine party in the *Westminster Gazette* arguing: 'the "new critics" are in possession of most of the weekly and several of the daily papers, and with one accord they tell us the same thing. These two sodden people are their ideal.'[47] MacColl retorted:

> For what is the New Art Criticism? It is simply the attempt to apply to current art the same standards which we apply to ancient art, to disengage from the enormous stream of picture-producers the one or two contemporary masters who are worthy to be named beside the ancients, the one or two promising talents that may some day deserve the same praise; to refuse steadfastly to confound the very good with the pretty bad, and to take mediocrity at its own estimate.[48]

Here MacColl succeeded in explaining the ultimate goal of the New Art Critics, but failed to clarify why he valued *L'Absinthe*, or in other words, neglected to outline the criteria by which he judged a work of art. Not satisfied, the artist W.B. Richmond intervened in the discussion, followed by myriad individuals, including fellow artists Walter Crane and Walter Sickert. The debate played itself out over the course of several weeks, during the course of which time the tenets of the New Art Criticism were fleshed out.

The New Art Criticism grew out of aestheticism, a philosophical approach also referred to as 'art for art's sake', which was introduced to England around 1868. Simply put, the aesthetic ideal pronounces that a work of art does not exist to tell a story nor to preach a sermon, but rather to be appreciated for it own inherent beauty stemming from the artist's manipulation of form, such as colour and composition. In England a primary proponent of aestheticism was Walter Pater, whose writings, particularly *Studies in the History of the Renaissance* (1873), had a profound influence on each of the New Art Critics. Pater promoted a search to find fixed points within the flux of the modern world. He believed that these fleeting moments characterize the modern world, the essence of which can be discerned by its appearance. A viewer should focus his attention on these moments, or impressions, which are transmuted through the senses. Pater encouraged the viewer to ask:

> What is this song or picture, this engaging personality presented in life or in a book, to *me*? What effect does it really produce on me? How is my nature modified by its presence, and under its influence?[49]

Pater supposed that the impression the viewer receives from a work of art does not result solely from its content, nor can it be discerned intellectually.

Rather it lies in the way in which the artist treats the subject. Pater's famous dictum 'All art constantly aspires to the condition of music' sets forth the idea that in music it is impossible to distinguish between matter and form, or more accurately form absorbs matter. To Pater, matter meant nothing without form. 'Form', he wrote, 'should become an end in itself, should penetrate every part of the matter: this is what all art constantly strives after'. He continued:

> Art, then, is thus striving to be independent of the mere intelligence, to become a matter of pure perception, to get rid of its responsibilities to its subject or material; the ideal examples of poetry and painting being those in which the constituent elements of the composition are so welded together, that the material or subject no longer strikes the intellect only; nor the form, the eye or the ear only; but form and matter, in their union or identity, present one single effect to the 'imaginative reasons', that complex faculty for which every thought and feeling is twin-born with its sensible analogue or symbol.[50]

Pater's ideas stood in stark contrast to the prevailing view of art during the mid-nineteenth century, as set forth by Ruskin. For the new middle class with little cultivation of taste, Ruskin provided a beacon to guide them in matters of art. He taught them that 'Painting, or art generally as such, with all its technicalities, difficulties, and particular ends, is nothing but a noble and expressive language'.[51] According to Ruskin, the purpose of art is to enlighten and exhort. He believed that art had an obligation to ameliorate society by depicting narrative and didactic scenes, and accordingly he measured the value of a work of art by the degree to which it achieves this. His theories, which value content above all else, instilled in the Victorian public a taste for pictures that appeal to the heart or intellect. Pater's views therefore challenged the Victorian public to view art differently.

Although Pennell's writings do not indicate that she and her husband knew Pater, evidence suggests that they may have made acquaintance with him. Soon after arriving in England in 1884, the Pennells began to frequent the home of the poet Mary Robinson, a place where artistic figures gathered weekly to socialize and exchange views on artistic matters. Pater, a neighbour of Robinson's, was a regular attendee around the same time as the Pennells. Pennell had long been familiar with Pater's ideas on art, having read his work in school when she was a child.[52] In this light, Pennell's self-negations as an art critic discussed earlier may be seen as a highly modernistic strategy offered in response to Pater's writings on subjective criticism. Pennell's deliberate attempts to downplay her own authority and lack of self-promotion as a critic therefore may have had as much to do with her modernist agenda, calling into question traditional authority and the acceptance of absolutes, as the other factors discussed above.

While we can only speculate that the Pennells knew Pater, their relationship with the American artist James McNeill Whistler, another champion of aestheticism in Britain, is well documented. In 1855, Whistler travelled to Paris where he was exposed to the idea of aestheticism; thereafter his work reflected his aim to produce paintings that were free of 'clap-trap', the word he used to describe all superfluous elements in painting. Whistler summed up his aesthetic beliefs in the 'Ten O' Clock Lecture' delivered in London, where he made his home after 1859, on 20 February 1885. Although the Pennells never recorded that they attended the lecture, they undoubtedly knew the principles promoted in it, for it was during this time that the couple became friendly with Whistler. Of course, the artist's reputation as a leading exponent of aestheticism was well established before his famous lecture: his lawsuit against Ruskin in 1878 had brought aestheticism and his own art into the spotlight. Pennell first heard about Whistler when she met Oscar Wilde at the home of her uncle Charles Godfrey Leland in Philadelphia, where Wilde expressed admiration for the artist's work. She had seen Whistler's *Arrangement in Grey and Black: Portrait of the Painter's Mother* exhibited at the Pennsylvania Academy in 1881 and *Symphony in White, No. 1: The White Girl* on display at the Metropolitan Museum of Art in New York. Upon the Pennells' arrival in London, Joseph quickly sought out Whistler in order to ask him to draw some sketches to accompany an article he and Elizabeth were writing. This marked the beginning of a long and consuming friendship for the couple.

'Whistler Whistler Whistler'

In an undated letter to the editor of the *Star*, the artist L.R. Deuchars noted Pennell's incessant references to Whistler:

> I am a great admirer of your paper and have much sympathy with its principles. But I write to make exception to the writing on Art and I often wonder why you the Editor do not deter dogma in the eternal preaching [of] Whistler Whistler Whistler.[53]

Deuchars, a contributor to the Royal Academy and an admirer of G.F. Watt's work, makes an undeniable point: Pennell drops Whistler's name in nearly all of her articles, even those pertaining to exhibitions that did not contain his work. Considering that Pennell contributed hundreds if not thousands of articles on art to myriad newspapers and periodicals over a 30-year period, this amounted to a very considerable endorsement.

It appears Pennell was aware that she and Joseph, who both wrote unsigned art criticism for the *Daily Chronicle*, pushed the limits when it came to promoting Whistler. In her journal she recorded a conversation she had with

Whistler just a few months before his death in 1903, wherein he asked why she had not mentioned his absence as President at the International Society of Painters, Sculptors, and Engravers dinner in her most recent article for the *Daily Chronicle*. She recorded:

> I didn't have the heart to tell him that Fisher [editor of the *Daily Chronicle*] had just complained that Joseph is forever dropping in the name of Whistler in his *Chronicle* article.[54]

Pennell's advocacy of Whistler was not a simple case of nepotism, but rather stemmed from the profound belief that Whistler constituted a modern 'Old Master', and that the onus was on her, in MacColl's words, to 'disengage from the enormous stream of picture-producers the one or two contemporary masters who are worthy to be named beside the ancients'.[55] Like other New Art Critics, Pennell abhorred the state of art in nineteenth-century Britain. She observed that the art most popular with the public, who applied Ruskin's criteria for judging art, was oftentimes of the poorest quality. Pennell explained:

> According to all appearances, pictures have never been as popular as they are just at present. We read with wonder of the crowds that followed Cimabue's Madonna through the streets of Florence; future genera-tions will record with envy the artistic tendency of the latter half of the nineteenth century, when the polite public found one of its chief amuse-ments in meeting at private views. Posterity will not know, as we do, that it was but a passing fad, and that half of the pictures which are the nominal attraction are not worth looking at.[56]

Only by applying a new standard, Pennell believed, could Whistler's work be appreciated and upheld for future generations as it deserved, and she dedicated herself to educating the public about his work.

Whistler, perhaps more than any other avant-garde artist in Britain during the latter half of the nineteenth century, needed a champion. Only after 1892, during the last decade of his life, did the artist's work begin to be generally praised in England. His carefully constructed image as the dandified, bohemian artist made him the brunt of much parody. Pennell expended a great deal of energy attempting to strip Whistler bare of this image with the hopes of exposing his greatness as an artist. In her biography of 1908, and later in *The Whistler Journal* (1921), *The Art of Whistler* (1928), and *Whistler the Friend* (1930), she vigorously defended him against charges of being a cantankerous lightweight. In the aftermath of Whistler's death Pennell, along with Whistler's colleagues at the International Society of Painters, Sculptors, and Engravers, was instrumental in organizing a memorial exhibition held at the Grafton Gallery in 1905. In her review for the *Star*, Pennell relished the triumph:

> Yes, it is a triumph, and a complete one: a triumph over the artless; for the artists—a handful—it is no triumph, but simply a vindication, for they knew it must come. And now it has come. But to have stuck the critics in this country in pillories and made them grin, to have fastened them with thumbscrews and made them screech with lying tongues, 'We always knew how great he was,' is some compensation for a year's hard work. [...] And those animals, the British critics and the British public, have been muzzled and silenced. Ignorantly and stupidly, and foolishly and blatantly, they laughed, and they grinned, and they sniggered, and they chortled, with the loud laugh that marks the vacant mind, at the French Impressionists for a month. Now their fun is over, and they are taking Whistler seriously. Not because they understand Whistler any more than they understood the Impressionists, but because he who, only a few years ago, was called a buffoon and a coxcomb has triumphed over all his enemies, and been proved not only the greatest artist of the nineteenth century, but in some ways the greatest artist who has ever lived.[57]

This 'triumph' notwithstanding, nothing Pennell did to promote Whistler came easy. She and Joseph faced opposition from Whistler's executrix, Rosalind Birnie Philip when they attempted to publish *The Life of James McNeill Whistler*. The Pennells, along with the publisher William Heinemann, took Philip to court in 1906 to fight for the right to publish Whistler's authorized biography, which cost them a great deal both financially and emotionally. Further, in 1911 both Elizabeth and Joseph played a central role in exposing the 'Greaves Affair', as the press deemed it. The pair fought for nearly two years to defend Whistler from charges of plagiarism made by a former pupil Walter Greaves and London art dealer William Merchant.

Pennell's most extraordinary gift to Whistler was a collection, of graphic art, papers, photographs, publications, and press clippings pertaining to Whistler, comprising some 96,000 items collected over the Pennells' lifetimes, which they donated to the Library of Congress in Washington D.C. in 1917. This included bills, notes, correspondence, and lawyers' briefs pertaining to the *Whistler v Ruskin* case, and later Whistler's correspondence with the artist Henri Fantin-Latour, all of which Pennell went to great lengths to procure. Herbert Putnam, a librarian at the Library of Congress at the time the Pennells bestowed the collection, remarked that Whistleriana 'has, as a record, a completeness probably unparalleled by that of any other artist or writer'.[58] In terms of a single repository, this probably remains true today.

In 1913 the Pennells coauthored in the *Bookman* an article entitled 'The Triumph of Whistler' wherein they seem reconciled to the fact that they had done all they could to fashion Whistler's legacy as the greatest artist of the nineteenth century.

We have written as strongly as we could and have nothing to take back - we have told the truth as we know it, and we stand by it. We shall never again see a man in whom we can believe with all our might and with all our hearts and with all our souls. We know that Whistler was the greatest artist of modern times, and the most interesting man of our time. We have made the world see this, and we have hastened his coming into his own. But without us or any writers, by his work alone he would have been acknowledged the great man he is. We have had the chance to show it – the chance of our lives – and we are proud of it. We have done our best. But we shall never have such a chance again, and we know his fame is too secure for any to prevail against it. He has triumphed.[59]

The Pennells' friend and confidant Edward Larocque Tinker commented retrospectively: 'The admiration and affection in which the Pennells held Whistler is seldom known in human relationships. They spent half their days in spreading his fame.'[60] While today Whistler's name is known worldwide and his *oeuvre* universally adored, Pennell and her contributions to periodical press have been all but ignored. This is most unfortunate, as Pennell, a key figure in the development and dissemination of the principles that underlay progressive late nineteenth-century British art, deserves attention and due appreciation in her own right.

Notes

1. Alan J. Lee, *The Origins of the Popular Press in Britain 1855–1914* (London: Croom Helm, 1976), 120.
2. Lee, *Origins*, 129–30.
3. Evelyn March Phillips, 'The New Journalism,' *The New Review* 13 (August 1895), 182–89: 188.
4. Laurel Brake, 'The Old Journalism and the New: Forms of Cultural Production in London in the 1880s,' in *Papers for the Millions The New Journalism in Britain, 1850s to 1914*, ed. Joel H. Wiener (New York: Greenwood Press, 1988), 1–24: 15.
5. John Stokes, *In the Nineties* (New York: Harvest Wheatsheaf, 1989), 182.
6. Lee, *Origins*, 27.
7. Anon [Charlotte O'Conor Eccles], 'The Experiences of a Woman Journalist,' *Blackwood's Edinburgh Magazine* (June 1893), 830–38: 831.
8. John Goodbody, '"The Star": Its Role in the New Journalism,' *Victorian Periodicals Review* 20 (Winter 1987), 141–50: 144.
9. Mark Hampton, *Visions of the Press in Britain, 1850–1950* (Urbana and Chicago: University of Illinois Press, 2004), 119–21.

10. Helene Roberts, 'Exhibition and Review: The Periodical Press and the Victorian Art Exhibition System' in *The Victorian Periodical Press: Samplings and Soundings*, eds Joanne Shattock and Michael Wolff (Leicester: Leicester University Press, 1982), 79–107: 83.

11. Elizabeth Robins Pennell, 'A Protest and What it Suggests,' Sidney Woodward Papers, Archives of American Art, Smithsonian Institution, Washington D.C.

12. Elizabeth Robins Pennell, Pennell-Whistler Collection, Special Collections, Library of Congress, Washington D.C, box 249.

13. Alexis Easley, *First Person Anonymous: Women Writers and Victorian Print Media, 1830–1870* (Aldershot, Hants, England: Ashgate, 2004), 1.

14. A.U. [Elizabeth Robins Pennell], 'Art and Artists,' *Star* (4 July 1892), 4.

15. Peter G. Meyer ed., *Brushes with History: Writing on Art from* The Nation (New York: Thunder's Mouth Press/Nation Books, 2001), 123.

16. Alexis Easley, 'Authorship, Gender and Power in Victorian Culture: Harriet Martineau and the Periodical Press,' *Nineteenth-Century Media and the Construction of Identities*, eds. Laurel Brake, Bill Bell, and David Finkelstein (Basingstoke, Hampshire: Palgrave, 2000), 137–77: 157.

17. The Editor [Fitzroy Gardner],'What Women May Do. – II,' *Woman* (30 March 1892), 4.

18. Elizabeth Robins Pennell, *Nights: Rome, Venice, in the Aesthetic Eighties: London, Paris, in the Fighting Nineties* (Philadelphia and London: J.B. Lippincott Company, 1916), 143.

19. John Waltman, *The Early London Journals of Elizabeth Robins Pennell* (University of Texas at Austin, PhD dissertation, 1976), 392.

20. Elizabeth Robins Pennell, *Over the Alps on a Bicycle* (London: T. Fisher Unwin, 1898), 11.

21. Barbara Onslow, *Women of the Press in Nineteenth-Century Britain* (London: St. Martin's Press, 2000), 61–2.

22. Meaghan Clarke, *Critical Voices: Women and Art Criticism in Britain* (Aldershot: Ashgate, 2005), 21.

23. See Harold Perkin, *The Rise of Professional Society: England since 1880* (London and New York: Routledge, 1989).

24. Kate Flint, *The Victorians and the Visual Imagination* (Cambridge: Cambridge University Press, 2000), 169.

25. Laurel Brake, *Subjugated Knowledges: Journalism, Gender and Literature in the Nineteenth Century* (New York: New York University Press, 1994), 60.

26. John Sandon, 'Certain Critics: An Estimate,' *Artist and Journal of Home Culture* 15 (1March 1894), 77–8: 77.

27. Laurel Brake and Julie Codell eds., *Encounters in the Victorian Press: Editors, Authors, Readers* (Basingstoke, Hampshire: Palgrave MacMillan, 2005), 1.

28. Brake and Codell, *Encounters*, 1.

29. Elizabeth Prettejohn, 'Aesthetic Value and the Professionalization of Victorian Art Criticism, 1837–78,' *Journal of Victorian Culture* 2 (Spring 1997), 71–94: 73.

30. Marion H. Spielmann, 'Press-Day and Critics II,' *Magazine of Art* (1892), 222–28: 222.

31. The Editor [Fitzroy Gardner], 'What Women May Do. – I,' *Woman* (23 March 1892), 3.

32. Onslow, *Women of the Press*, 32.

33. A.U., 'A Few February Shows,' *Star* (14 February 1893), 4.

34. A.U., 'Art and Artists,' *Star* (13 February 1893), 3.

35. A.U., 'Minor Art Exhibitions,' *Star* (11 February 1892), 4.

36. A.U., 'Art and Artists,' *Star* (July 4, 1892), 4.
37. See Jamie Horrocks, 'Camping in the Kitchen: Locating Culinary Authority in Elizabeth Robins Pennell's *Delights of Delicate Eating,' Nineteenth-Century Gender Studies*, Summer 2007 http://ncgsjournal.com/issue32/horrocks.htm [accessed 8 November 2011] and Talia Schaffer, 'The Importance of Being Greedy: Connoisseurship and Domesticity in the Writings of Elizabeth Robins Pennell,' *The Recipe Reader: Narratives, Contexts, Traditions*, eds Janet Floyd and Laurel Foster (Burlington, Vermont: Ashgate, 2003), 105–26.
38. Horrocks.
39. Horrocks.
40. Anna Gruetzner Robins, *Complete Writing of Walter Sickert* (Oxford: Oxford University Press, 2000), 134.
41. Robins, 282.
42. Alfred Thornton, *Diary of an Art Student in the 1890s* (London: Sir Isaac Pitman & Sons, Ltd., 1938), 22.
43. Jad Adam, *Hideous Absinthe: A History of the Devil in a Bottle* (Madison, Wisconsin: The University of Wisconsin Press, 2004), 55.
44. See Kimberly Morse Jones, 'The "Philistine" and the New Art Critic: A New Perspective on the *L'Absinthe* Debate of 1893,' *British Art Journal* 11 (Fall 2008), 50–61. For other analyses of the debate over Degas's *L'Absinthe* see Ronald Pickvance, '"L'Absinthe" in England,' *Apollo* 77 (May 1963), 395–98; Kate Flint, 'The "Philistine" and the New Art Critic: J.A. Spender and D.S. MacColl's Debate of 1893,' *Victorian Periodicals Review* 21 (Spring, 1988), 3–8; and Kate Flint, 'The Philistine and the New: J.A. Spender on Art and Morality,' in Joel Wiener ed., *Papers for the Millions*, 211–24.
45. A.U., 'The Grafton Gallery,' *Star* (23 February 1893), 4.
46. D.S.M. [D.S. MacColl], 'The Grafton Gallery,' *Spectator* (23 February 1893), 256.
47. The Philistine [John Alfred Spender], 'The New Art Criticism – A Philistine's Remonstrance,' *Westminster Gazette* 1 (9 March 1893), 1–2.
48. D.S.M., 'The Standard of the Philistine,' *Spectator* (18 March 1893), 357.
49. Walter Pater, *The Renaissance: Studies in Art and Poetry* (London: MacMillan and Co. Limited, 1904), viii.
50. Pater, *Renaissance*, 138.
51. John Ruskin, *Selections from the Writings of John Ruskin* (London: Smith, Elder and Co., 1863), 93.
52. Agnes Repplier, *Our Convent Days* (Boston and New York: Houghton Mifflin Company, 1905), vii.
53. Pennell–Whistler Collection, box 242, folder 3.
54. Joseph and Elizabeth R. Pennell Papers, Harry Ransom Center, University of Texas at Austin, diary entry dated 4 May 1903.
55. D.S.M., 'Standard,' 357.
56. P.E.R. [Elizabeth Robins Pennell], 'In the World of Art,' *Woman* (15 June 1892), 8.
57. A.U., 'Art and Artists,' *Star* (28 February 1905), 4.
58. Elizabeth Robins Pennell, *The Whistler Journal* (Philadelphia: J.B. Lippincott, 1921), vi.
59. Joseph Pennell, 'The Triumph of Whistler,' *Bookman* 36 (1913), 158–64: 163. Elizabeth's personal writings indicate that she too contributed to the article.
60. Edward Larocque, Tinker, *The Pennells* (London: n.p., 1951), 17.

9

'A fair field and no favour': Hulda Friederichs, the Interview, and the New Woman

Fionnuala Dillane
University College, Dublin

'I asked for nothing but "a fair field and no favour"', Hulda Friederichs once explained of her working life as a full-time staff journalist at the *Pall Mall Gazette*.[1] The Prussian-born Friederichs did seem to overcome the challenges of gender and national biases in her professional career: she was one of the first women journalists in Britain to be employed on the same terms and conditions as her male colleagues under W.T. Stead at the *Pall Mall Gazette* in the early 1880s, and from 1896, as editor of George Newnes' *Westminster Budget*, she was left 'entirely free' to dictate the content and form of that illustrated family weekly.[2] In what has been called a 'landmark appointment',[3] Friederichs capitalized fully on the opportunity to set the agenda of the *Budget* for almost nine years. Little is known of Friederichs' personal history, however: details of her Prussian origins and her education in Cologne are obscure and to this day she remains a marginal figure in accounts of *fin-de-siècle* literary history. If Friederichs' name is recognized at all it is usually because of her association with leading newspaper men: namely Newnes, whose biography she wrote in 1911, and Stead, for whom she worked at the *Pall Mall Gazette* (henceforth, *PMG*) from around the time of his early association with the paper in 1882. By the late 1880s she was the paper's 'chief interviewer'.[4] The *PMG* has secured its place in literary history for Stead's championing of reforming new journalism; not just for the controversial content Stead sought out for its pages but also for its innovative use of new journalistic forms. The paper's role in making the interview part of the mainstream popular press has been widely acknowledged.[5] Hulda Friederichs, his chief interviewer, has yet to be credited fully for her part in this popular and influential innovation.[6]

It is not entirely clear when Friederichs joined the *PMG* but her ascent through the ranks from personal assistant to leading journalist was swift. In her retrospective review of her career in 1893, 'Difficulties and Delights of Interviewing', Friederichs states that she has been perfecting her craft for 'nearly ten years'.[7] This would suggest that she began to work as an interviewer at the *PMG* from the mid-1880s. Friederichs left the *PMG* in

1892 with E.T. Cook, its then editor, to join Newnes' new liberal daily the *Westminster Gazette*.[8] Her reputation established, she continued to work as an interviewer for the *Gazette* and on a freelance basis for magazines oriented towards women readers such as *Young Woman* and *Woman at Home*.[9]

Friederichs' interests in women's rights, particularly the right to work and to education, that continuously surface in her journalism no doubt stemmed from her own experiences. Following her arrival in London from the Continent in the late 1870s or early 1880s she pursued English literature at a higher level through an outreach programme from the University of St Andrews that sought to increase women's participation in higher education.[10] Though never overtly political in her writing, Friederichs nonetheless provides us with an early journalistic embodiment of the New Woman that offers a conspicuous rebuttal of mainstream journalism's more typical lampooning of the New Woman figure. Sally Ledger has demonstrated how the 'New Woman' 'manifested herself in multifarious guises in fiction and the periodical press' through the last two decades of the nineteenth century.[11] Friederichs, who was to make a career for herself as a journalist paid on terms equal to her male colleagues, and later take on managerial roles for Newnes' publications, offers one articulation of the New Woman phenomena: the independent professional woman, rivalling male success, working on a very public stage. Ledger points out also, however, that the 'New Woman' was 'predominantly a journalistic phenomenon, a product of discourse', and most typically, a caricatured figure in the traditional press in its propaganda war against the perceived threat of this transgressive species.[12] Friederichs contributed significantly to these discursive battles. She adopts the multifarious guises that constitute the attentive interviewer: at once the amateur seeking insight and the expert asking subject-specific questions; the transgressor of class and gender boundaries in order to make her subject present to her readers. This chapter will focus on the early stages of Friederichs' career and on her own (later) published version of her role as chief interviewer at the *PMG*. It suggests that Friederichs used that increasingly dominant and popular mode of New Journalism, the interview, in a strategic way to make a career for herself in the overwhelmingly male-dominated newspaper environment that offered anything but a 'fair field', and that she deliberately rewrote her own career history after her successful *PMG* years in a calculated move to illustrate by example the ways that the willing worker can challenge the limits of gender expectations. In all, this New Woman's negotiation of New Journalism provided her with a platform that allowed her to carve a career so distinctive that, by the 1890s, the name Hulda Friederichs was synonymous with the Interview.[13]

The Interview and New Journalism

New Journalism is a capacious term that indicates a change in newspaper practices in Britain both at the level of content and of form. It refers to a range of technological advances in the newspaper industry that built on and contributed to the mass expansion of media and of audiences; it also signals a strategic shift in the tone of articles that led to the emergence of new narrative formats such as the embedded or undercover report and the interview. The interview exemplifies the combined features of New Journalism: in its layout it capitalized on advances in illustration techniques, often displaying sketches or, later, photographs, to personalize further the interview pieces; it commonly used headlines and cross-heads to break up the interview into neat parcels for easy consumption; and of course the content itself involves personal conversation, anecdotes, the cultivation of intimacy. In all these ways the interview embodies the 'human interest' focus of the New Journalism.

The emphasis on the personal aspect of New Journalism was central to W.T. Stead's vision of his role as writer and editor. In the second of his manifesto pieces 'The Future of Journalism' he makes it clear: 'everything depends upon the individual, the person. Impersonal journalism is effete. To influence men you must be a man, not a mock-uttering oracle.'[14] This type of personalized journalism, which should be distinguished from the personal interview that is ostensibly subject- rather than issue-focused, was used to influential effect by Stead, most famously in his embedded-reporter style investigations into child prostitution in the mid-1880s.[15] In comparison with the seismic effect such personalized reporting produced, resulting not only in Stead's celebrated prison term, but more importantly to changes in the law that raised the age of consent for girls from 13 to 16, the personalized interview pieces Friederichs composed for entertainment, information, and distraction seem, if not effete, then somewhat secondary in terms of political and cultural significance. However, I suggest that Friederichs' contributions to the development of the interview mode in the pages of the *PMG* are linked to the broader reforming agenda of the paper. In particular, her conversations with workers in the worlds of entertainment, fashion, and commercial industries signal an attempt to change ideas about what constitutes valid subject matter for an interview.

The late-nineteenth-century incarnation of the interview had evolved from Edmund Yates' overtly masculine and gossipy 'The Lounger at the Clubs', in the *Illustrated Times* from 1855, to encompass a more targeted attention to celebrities in the interests of securing a broader readership, including women readers. Yates' more influential 'Celebrities at Home' style interviews, popularized in his *World* from the mid-1870s, became a model for the interview mode. Adopted widely in periodicals and newspapers, it remains a central feature of various media to this day. Friederichs' interviewing, however, is often conspicuously different from this dominant 'celebrity at home' model. It is not centred on 'great names' but regularly attends instead to the men and women who are making (often unusual) careers for themselves within the leisure trades in particular (examples include the woman leader of a troupe of Russian musicians; a tattoo artist; and a seller of ornamental feathers for hats).[16] These trade/art subject pieces offer a deliberate blending of the categories of work and leisure and are related broadly to New Journalism's attempt to situate itself as a demotic form of both enlightenment and entertainment. Most typically, Friederichs interviews her subjects on site, such as her conversation with the keeper of books at the second reading room at the British Museum, or her interview with a daffodil grower in the fields of Tooting.[17] Friederichs did go on to interview more famous people for the *PMG*, but tellingly, her retrospective piece 'Difficulties and Delights of Interviewing' refers only very generally to this type of interview, suggesting in vague, somewhat clichéd terms that such 'eminent' artists are very different from the music hall performers and other 'trade' artists. Sounding (perhaps disingenuously) a little star-struck, she claims that she treasures the meetings with such sculptors, painters, poets, and musicians, and the friendships that often ensued, above all other work. Significantly, however, Friederichs does not focus on these famous names in this review of her career. They receive only a paragraph's notice in this long article, pointing, I suggest, to her keen awareness of the atypical and pioneering aspect of her work on less celebrated subjects.[18]

It is important to acknowledge that interviews with more famous figures did feature in Friederichs' later career: such celebrity interviews indicate just how established a figure she was by the mid-1890s.[19] Arguably, Friederichs' body of work for the *PMG* that week after week drew attention to ordinary artists and workers evolved from a pragmatic realization that she had to make something of the material accessible to her as she started out in her working life. Moreover, her account of how early stories came about suggests that the original focus on the ordinary rather than celebrated 'worker' was part of the broader *PMG* New Journalism agenda: interviews were assigned to her, and she understood the balance of news and entertainment, personal and representative, that was required. A professional press woman, Friederichs was naturally alert to different facets of the New Journalism that defined the late-nineteenth-century press. In her biography of Newnes she draws out the distinction between the two pioneering pressmen with whom she had worked most closely, Newnes and Stead. Newnes, she notes,

> was mainly concerned with giving the public a chance of filling their leisure hours with pleasant entertainment; Mr Stead was bent on supplying information of a more solid kind to the mass of busy mortals eager enough for knowledge and keenly interested in the topics of the day but unable to find time for reading of long review articles.[20]

Friederichs is referring to Stead's *Review of Reviews* in this context, but her own interviews in Stead's *PMG* are clearly pitched to this same busy reader seeking both information and distraction from a busy life. The considerable bulk of her interviews that focus on workers in various leisure trades lends itself entirely to this blending of education and entertainment: Friederichs does not shy away from incorporating into her pieces technical vocabulary that is work specific, but neither does she forget the thrill of transgression that is at the heart of the mode from the reader's perspective, as well as the writer's. The interview, embodying a particularized version of New Journalism's personal dimension, claims both subject (the interviewee) and writer (the interviewer) as part of its story. These features of the interview in its late-nineteenth-century incarnation are heightened when the interviewer is female: both the self-representation of the interviewer and the implicit contravention of class, space, and/or gender boundaries that form the substance of the interview take on more acute political and personal dimensions.

Friederichs played purposefully with the transgressive potential of the interview format in 'Difficulties and Delights of Interviewing', published shortly after her departure from the *PMG* in 1893. Her summary of her *PMG* pieces indicates how she manages middle-class expectations. Quite often, she starts out by playing up the challenges and restrictions enforced by the codes of a patriarchal public sphere and individual moral propriety, for instance, foregrounding her nervousness at the thought of entering a music hall late at night and without a male chaperon.[21] The interview, however, personal, intimate, and based on the premise that its purpose is to trespass for voyeuristic pleasure but also, crucially, with educative intent to help the reader to understand the 'other', provides an acceptable means by which Friederichs goes on to extend the dimensions of those separate spheres without alienating her predominantly middle-class audience. The structure of the interview offers, as it were, a type of sanctioned – but measured – slippage of space, class, or gender constraints.

Caution was necessary: even apart from the exceptional lesson of Stead's imprisonment, Friederichs' working environment, though increasingly accepting of women, was not easy. There appears a striking discrepancy between the ways that gender is made central to her retrospective analysis of her work but is elided in the actual interviews themselves, which took place from the mid-1880s to 1892. The *fin-de-siècle* press comprised clearly demarcated spaces for men and women readers and for men and women journalists. Although Friederichs worked with one of the more supportive of male editors in W.T. Stead, widely recognized for championing a number of women journalists and women's rights, she nonetheless had to deal with both resentment from colleagues (famously, her one-time colleague Robertson Scott nicknamed her 'La Friederichs' and 'The Prussian Governess'), and gossip about the particular favour shown to her by Stead. More generally, Friederichs had to make her way in a business where, as Margaret Stetz puts it simply, 'gender did matter':

> Women seemed to feel more acutely the social deprivation necessitated by the 'industrious' pursuit of a livelihood by the pen. Barred by the code of respectability which still weighed so heavily upon all women of the

middle classes, they could neither travel at night unchaperoned nor enter public establishments unescorted.[22]

In part, the types of interviews Friederichs carried out could be recognized as characteristic of the gendered division of subject matter typifying late-nineteenth-century journalism, where the ever-increasing number of women professionals was herded into appropriately gendered roles within individual publications to attract the ever-increasing number of women readers. Women would deal with fashion, the arts, women's advice columns, but not the more straightforward reporting of facts, political commentary pieces, business, or sport, especially not in a more masculine-oriented paper such as the *PMG*.

Friederichs' interviews, however, may be seen to be pitched to appeal to a more general readership and in themselves challenge the notion of dividing up the paper into parts specific to men and women. Her work often appeared on the front page, not sequestered away in any 'woman's corner'. Interviews were linked occasionally to main news stories that were running in the paper over some weeks and so were integrated seamlessly into the broader news agenda. For instance, the enormous interest in the discovery by the German Dr. Koch of a potential cure for consumption was reflected across the British press in the late 1890s. The *PMG* included articles on the subject on 15, 19, 21 and 22 November 1890. Friederichs contributed two interviews from Berlin to add to this coverage on 26 and 29 of November, both featuring on the front pages.[23] Even when not specifically adding to a main story line, quite often Friederichs' work is categorized in the 'news' rather than the 'arts' section of the paper. Further, through the device of authorial anonymity, and more particularly in the treatment of her material, Friederichs frames her work to appeal to curiosity and sympathy in ways that defy simple gendered categorization: one interview will provide the technical details to explain why guns jam on discharge; another will ask the reader to reflect on the damage done to women and children caught up in the male world of music hall entertainment.[24] At times, Friederichs' gender identity (though not her name) is made clear; at times her work appears unmarked by gender signifiers and suggestively neutral.

Part of this protean interview voice, is, of course, integral to the interview mode itself, and in particular, to its commercial reach. Whether focused on celebrities, exotic performers, or more ordinary workers, the interview, as Richard Salmon has argued more generally, is always also a compromised form: the intimacy it purports to offer is underscored by the transformation of the interviewed subjects into 'products to be circulated and consumed'.[25] As Salmon argues elsewhere, it is no coincidence that

at the very moment when the material base of the press made it harder to locate an individuated source of authorial value, the discourse of journalism should so insistently declare its personalized character.[26]

The engaged encounter the interview purports to recount, and the construction of the interviewing voice, are entirely informed by the distance between the subject-to-be-known and the increasingly unknown public. Sala and Yates, Dickens' 'Young Men', pioneers of the intimate turn in journalism at mid-century, were always conscious like Dickens himself of the performative aspect to their work. As P.D. Edwards reminds us, as a result, they cannot be taken at their word:

> In most of their writing, whether journalistic or confessedly fictional, Sala and Yates both tend to be intensely 'personal,' often seeming to shed more light on themselves than on their ostensible subjects. As a putative source of evidence about their characters and activities, however, it has to be treated with even more extreme caution than such 'textual' evidence generally requires.[27]

Not all *PMG* interviews foreground the voice of the interviewer. Following the type of interview that featured in the press from the 1830s or 1840s, some *PMG* interviews comprised unmediated reported speech of the subject presented in direct quotation without any sense of an intervening or interpreting voice. Celebrated interviews by correspondents for other journals that are subsequently repeated in the *PMG* take this unmediated form: in those examples, no space is given to the framing of the interview that becomes an important feature Friederichs' pieces from 1888–92 as she established her position as chief interviewer. The 'I' voice of Friederichs' interviews demands attentiveness to its strategic formation.[28] Alexis Easley has demonstrated the constructive ways that women journalists used the 'first person anonymous' mode up to the 1870s:

> To be a woman author in Victorian society was to be 'first-person anonymous,' that is, to both construct and subvert notions of individual authorial identity, manipulating the publishing conventions associated with various print media for personal and professional advantage.[29]

Friederichs tactically foregrounds her gender only once her career has been established, and then does so not as an apology but as a challenge. Her range of interviews, from her first outing to profile working class women on canal boats in the Midlands to her series of pieces on circus and music hall performers, offers fascinating subject matter. Looking back over ten years of her career in 'Difficulties and Delights of Interviewing', Friederichs consistently highlights interviews that proved particularly testing because of gender and class constraints. Her focus on the interviewer's own role in travelling to the margins of the socially acceptable is arresting. As represented in Friederichs' retrospective view, a self-conscious meta-narrative underscores each encounter so that a complex triangular interaction is constructed between the interviewee and the interviewer, the interviewee and the reader, and finally, crucially in this name-making competitive newspaper market, between the reader and the interviewer herself. Friederichs' account of her *PMG* career provides a meta-commentary on her own processes as an interviewer, typifying that other important aspect of New Journalism, as Stephen Koss has put it, that existed as a phenomenon by 'calling attention to itself'.[30] And importantly, this piece is signed: by 1893 Friederichs' name was recognized and representative of a by-now entrenched mode.

'Difficulties and Delights of Interviewing': Gender and Class

Friederichs' article 'Difficulties and Delights of Interviewing' is presented in the *English Illustrated Magazine* in 1893 as an important pronouncement on the art of the Interview. It offers the writer an opportunity to frame her career and it offers the reader insight into how this key figure of New Journalism, whose personal history remained so veiled, positioned her own work in the context of this transformative period. Throughout the piece Friederichs emphasizes her gender in a fashion manifestly different from the more circumspect, often gender-neutral tones of her actual *PMG* interviews. From the outset she attempts to demystify the privileged public sphere of a still predominantly masculine press by drawing an extended comparison between her work as an interviewer and the wide-eyed admiration of a recently-widowed woman, who, because she was 'never initiated into the mystery of the cheque book' by her now dead husband, transfers her dependence and awe to her cheque-writing son: 'It is quite wonderful how you do it', she exclaims.[31] Friederichs provides a blunt rebuttal, referring at once to the simple act of signing cheques and to her work as a journalist in a deliberate blurring of these masculine worlds of finance and public commentary: 'As a matter of fact it is not amazing at all.'[32] She goes on to provide some facts about her early career through a series of lively anecdotes, all of which emphasize different types of transgression of expected norms: she talks of her journey unchaperoned across Europe, which involved switching trains at midnight in the middle of nowhere; of waiting for transport from a small village full of men who seemed to have nothing to do but drink and smoke and watch her; of her hazardous tram trip with a drunk driver and even more inebriated conductor, all to make it to Haarlem to view the hyacinths in bloom. The chaotic adventures are pitched deliberately against the pastoral destination and the more stereotypical remarks (for a woman writer) about the beauty of fields of flowers. Her tone is never self-aggrandizing, however: this is not *braggadocio* in skirts; in fact, it is deliberately the opposite, humorously self-deprecating for the purpose of suggesting that gender barriers are there to be taken on and taken down by all.

Throughout this piece Friederichs characteristically first emphasizes her own limitations: as a woman who does not understand the first thing about guns being sent to interview an inventor of a new revolver; as a woman who thinks she is going to interview a leader of the Women's Liberation Federation ending up having to interview an authority on the Queensland slave labour issue when she knows little about this contentious topic; as a woman surrounded by men late at night in the male world of the music hall. Friederichs then turns all situations around to positive or instructive effect. Her 'colleagues' (she consistently uses this gender-neutral term) point her to the man in the *PMG* office who knows most about guns to provide her with enough basic reference points for a detailed interview. She gets a chance to read through a *PMG* article on the 'Kanaka question' prior to carrying out her interview with the Queensland expert. She turns the champagne and cigar-smoke atmosphere of her music hall experience into a surreal account of a journey across the West End with three foreigners, one a German giant, that ends in a grim exposition of the troubling relationship between child entertainers and their masters/fathers. The interviewer's initial ignorance or discomfort is part of a strategic ploy to stress her typicality so that her reader will not think her exceptional for a woman. Her humour, however, reveals her alertness to the potential scandal her work could provoke: her conversation with a tattoo artist about his profession concludes with his offer to 'ornament' her ears with 'tattooed black pearl' and her neck with tattooed jewels: 'I told him if the thing had to be done a skull and cross-bones on my forehead would probably be more effective in the long run.'[33] Friederichs' awareness that her work in the world of men constitutes for some a type of toxic leakage corroding the boundaries of distinct gendered spheres underlines her joking comment: the skull and crossbones brand seems more appropriate than feminine jewellery for such a woman, she implies with humour, and that humour, arguably, offers a double-edged strategy that at once raises and defuses the threat.

This interview, 'An English Tattooer', makes up part of the art/trade series that separated Friederichs' work from the dominant 'celebrity' model. She asks the tattooer about his customers, the price of tattoos, the instruments used in the trade, and also the 'processes of the art', including all the finer points of detail about colours and textures down to the glycerine used to keep the skin soft. She reports that the favourite designs of customers (after coats of arms and regimental crests) include a tiger stalking his prey, and, we are told, 'many people like to have a fox-hunt tattooed all down their back'.[34] The interview's dual focus, educating her readers about the skill of the tattooer's craft and titillating with the frivolity or occasional outrageousness of the consumers' desires, typifies Friederichs' *PMG* work. Her foregrounding of her own presence in the text signals another important stylistic characteristic that comes to feature more and more as she established her position as chief interviewer in the late 1880s. Friederichs' account of her visit to the tattoo studio in the basement of the Hammam Turkish Baths on Jermyn

Street repeatedly draws attention to her own sense of journeying into the unknown. The opening paragraph sets up her trepidation at the thought of 'willing victims ... operated upon', though she reassures her reader, with some irony, 'Victims, though, I must not call them for I was assured that by the use of cocaine which is injected under the skin, the operation causes not the slightest pain.'[35] In another gesture typical of these pieces, the 'opening out' to the unexpected undertaken by her lively, wide-ranging treatment of the topic is countered by the close of the interview, where Friederichs returns to safe middle-class middle ground with the interjection that she will not reveal all the extraordinary things that she saw in the tattoo artist's book of designs. 'I could only wonder', she explains, 'how people could be brought so to disfigure the fair skin that nature had given them.'[36] The turn back to modesty is necessary to keep her conventional middle-class reader 'on side'. But the tattoo artist, the respected worker, is yet given a right to reply: he explains his work could compete with the greatest Japanese masters of the form, 'in both respect of accuracy of design and general excellence of work'. Friederichs does not contest this assertion. She concludes: 'But in spite of this, and of the assurance that the operation was painless, I came away without a pattern on me.'[37]

This calculated repackaging for reassurance at the end of the interview offers an escape for the reader who wants to leave the interview unmarked by the transgressions recounted in the body of the text. The return to familiar territory is figured in the interviewer's repositioning of the *PMG* voice at the close of the interview outside of the scenes or situations described. No indication of the interviewer's gender is given throughout the interview, although, importantly, Friederichs draws attention to her gender in the retrospective account, telling us of the offer of a free earring and necklace tattoo. This revision of her own writing and repositioning of her writing self is illustrative of the strategic formation of identity in Friederichs' work, and follows a predictable pattern employed by many women journalists. While in the process of establishing her name amongst her colleagues and her peers she hides her gender from her readers. Her name established, she reconfigures her interview experiences foregrounding her gender, so that her readers (including her twenty-first-century readers) must acknowledge that for an interviewer, the body is always in the picture, if not always in the final text.

While treated in her retrospective account of her career, explicit attention to gender as part of the subject of the interview is rare in Friederichs' work for the *PMG*, though consideration of gender does appear in one of Friederichs' more bizarre interludes in unfamiliar territory: her account of her meeting in a music-hall late at night as she attempted to get an interview with a girl acrobat starring in a show at the West End's Trocadero.[38] The interviewer is identified from the outset as a woman (though she is not named) and a series of oppositions are established that include the exceptional presence of a woman in the overwhelmingly male environment of the music-hall.

The foreignness of the performers is emphasized for the domestic English reader. The controlling and assertive presence of the luxuriously-clothed father of the child acrobat (the self-styled 'Professor' Petrescu) is pitched pointedly against the reduced, drab conditions in which his wife and daughter live most of their days in an implied critique of Petrescu's exploitation of his family, and more broadly of the treatment of women and children in the music-hall business. This critique is sharpened by the most overt binary of the piece: the unspoken gulf between the middle-class reader (and interviewer) and the pretender-to-learning figure of the father, who is implicitly questioned throughout the piece for apparently ignoring the fact that he profits from the unnatural and difficult life he has forced on his daughter. His defence of the rigorous training methods to which she is subjected to make her a supple acrobat contains a garbled account of Darwinian evolution: we are like apes so it is in fact quite natural to develop our arms and legs as apes do. The interviewer's attack on his affected pretensions to knowledge is underscored by the use of inverted quote marks around his title, 'Professor', and repeatedly, by exposing his very partial grasp of French, as in a direct quote from an appointment letter the father sends to Friederichs: '"nous pouvon lavoire au Trocedaro Musiquehawll domain"[sic]'.[39] Clear lines of alignment are drawn between the interviewer and the wife and daughter (the woman and child open up to Friederichs once Petrescu has left them alone); between the wife and daughter and the reader through the interviewer's use of pathos (her extended description of the family's drab accommodation; the innocent babbling of the child); and between the interviewer and the reader against Petrescu by invoking the seemingly impenetrable barriers of class.

The gender of the interviewer herself is not the key defining feature of the oppositions in this piece in its original form, published in 1890. Gender takes on a central role, however, in Friederichs' revision of the original interview in her retrospective retelling three years later. Class divisions are not nearly as overtly emphasized, and in fact, the father's limited education is transformed into 'elegant French' as Friederichs foregrounds instead, and in much more vivid detail, her discomfort with her necessary intrusion into the almost all-male world of the music hall:

> At 9 pm ... I was for the first time in my life inside a music-hall, though as yet only in the vestibule. After a quarter of an hour of somewhat unpleasant waiting, the father of the little acrobat came, a jovial, black-eyed, middle-aged Pole. Of course, of course, I must come inside, he said in elegant French; why his *p'tite* was not going to perform till after ten. Would I take a cigarette? And what would I drink?
>
> Ye gods, here was a dilemma!
>
> There was not a lady in the body of the hall, only one or two in the boxes, and all the men smoked and laughed and sang the refrain of

whatever was sung on the stage. For a moment I thought I would give it up and go home. But then, after all, what did it matter?[40]

Friederichs tells us she battles through this collective male experience (arguably a thinly veiled analogy for the club-like world of nineteenth-century journalism), because she has spent her career asking for a 'fair field and no favour' in this business, and she will not return to work the next day having failed to secure her copy because she was a woman.

Conclusion: Hulda Friederichs and the New Woman

Friederichs' work at the *PMG* preceded the widespread use of the term, the New Woman.[41] Her public status and renown was secured after her hugely successful *PMG* career, and not least because she went on to run the *Westminster Budget*. That status is also indicated in the fact that Friederichs was numbered amongst the group of women called on to offer public pronouncements on various issues related to the woman question, in opinion pieces that sought to define the 'New Woman'. Friederichs offers typically controversial and unexpected responses to set pieces on why women do not get married, what women should or should not wear, and so on. With humour and with caustic irony, she implicitly undercuts the characterizations of the New Woman promulgated in the mainstream periodical press of the 1890s as summarized by Sally Ledger:

> Whilst a range of feminist views were expressed by those women who promoted the cause of the New Woman, her opponents condemned her with a lampooning stereotype. Simultaneously over-sexed and mannish, over-educated and asinine, the stereotype of the New Woman rapidly proliferated in the periodical press in the 1890s.[42]

Though measured and mostly neutral on gender issues in her interviews throughout the late 1880s for the *PMG*, in various opinion pieces Friederichs uses her new status as a now-representative voice or 'talking head' to confront gender stereotypes with lively, frank, often earthy responses to these 'New Woman' set pieces.[43] Stead's *Review of Reviews*, out of friendship, loyalty, or genuine amusement, regularly highlights Friederichs' comments in these surveys, quoting her views with approving glee as a welcome counter voice to the bland and limiting opinions of her fellow experts, who more typically maintain the traditional line of response. The 1903 *Young Man* symposium on what women admire in men, for instance, is flagged in the *Review*, as 'very striking' but for the wrong reasons:

> it is a series of confessions fit to make thorough-going advocates of equality between the sexes weep. ... When educated and enlightened

women confess that the chief ambition of their sex is to be in a state of adoring slavery under the dominance of man, the prospect of frank equality between man and woman seems very far removed.[44]

The *Review* reports that Friederichs alone of the 15 'noted women' who took part in the symposium bucks the trend with her 'startling confession' of what appeals to her in a man, citing Friederichs' pithy response: 'I have always had a great leaning towards the Shakespearian lines –

"Let me have men around that are fat
sleek-headed men, and such as sleep o' nights".'[45]

Hulda Friederichs became 'probably the best known woman interviewer of her day'.[46] The pragmatism and humour that characterizes Friederichs' approach to her profession is captured in an unexpected and somewhat ambiguous panegyric to the power of the presses (as opposed to the mono-lithic Press) at the heart of her Newnes biography. She notes that from the 'dignified façade' of the building that housed Newnes' business on Southampton street in London, where his mass-selling *Tit Bits*, among other papers, was produced, the general passer-by had no sense of 'the marvels of the underground rooms':

where, with rhythmic click and whir, monstrous machines which seem like sentient beings – so marvellous is the work they do, so unlike the usual automatic action of machinery – receive endless rolls of white paper. ... You may watch them scores of times and you may have all the intricacies explained to you by the most matter-of-fact keeper of these giants, but unless yours is the engineering mind, you will never turn away from them without the impression that somewhere about their iron frames they have eyes to see, and brains to understand the tasks they are per-forming, and that in their innermost being, there is an insatiable greed for blank paper, leagues upon leagues of it, which they must swallow and presently disgorge again, all decorated with the tiny hieroglyphics whereby the race of pygmies called mankind is amused.[47]

That same building front 'gives no idea of the hum and buzz of concen-trated energy and activity within on every floor, and in all the labyrinthine passages' above the basement, where journalists like Friederichs and her many forgotten colleagues fed the popular press machines with copy to keep that 'race of pygmies called mankind' amused. Although newspaper pieces are often dismissed as purely mechanical, space-filling dross 'disgorged' for consumption in a perpetual recycling circuit, we are reminded to look for the 'sentient beings' behind the *fin de siècle*'s mass-produced texts, the 'brains' and 'eyes' that help us to find patterns in the hieroglyphics. In these patterns it is possible to find Hulda Friederichs playing a significant role in the production of the phenomenon of the interview. Her strategic negotiations with that revolutionary form testify to an important intervention in the professionalization of women's journalism and, more broadly, to her role in the evolution of the interview in the nineteenth-century British press.

Notes

1. Hulda Friederichs, 'Difficulties and Delights of Interviewing,' *English Illustrated Magazine* (February 1893), 341. The phrase was used by W.T. Stead a year earlier in his advice piece to young women journalists: 'If you want to be a journalist, you must succeed as a journalist – not as a woman or as a man. All that you need, and all that you should ask for, is a fair field and no favour, to prove that you can do the work you ask should be allotted to you. You have a right to ask that your sex should not be regarded as a disqualification; but it is monstrous to erect that accident of your personality into a right to have opportunities denied to your brother.' See [W.T. Stead], 'Young Women in Journalism,' *Review of Reviews* VI (October 1892), 373. Friederichs' own work suggests that she was entirely in agreement with her mentor on these points.
2. Hulda Friederichs, *The Life of Sir George Newnes, Bart.* (London: Hodder and Stoughton, 1911), 229–31. Friederichs' *Life of Sir George Newnes, Bart* included Newnes' autobiographical notes and was written the year after his death. It was republished in 2008 and remains the standard reference work for information about his life. Among her other works are a biography of Gladstone, *In the Evening of his Days. A Study of Mr Gladstone in Retirement* (London: Westminster Gazette, 1896); *The Romance of the Salvation Army* (London: Cassel, 1907); a cowritten biography of the Salvation Army's founder, General Booth (London: Nelson, 1913); and a number of translations of works from Russian and German. See Kate Jackson's *George Newnes and the New Journalism in Britain 1880–1910* (Aldershot: Ashgate, 2001) for a more recent account of Newnes' role in the development of the popular press in late nineteenth-century Britain.
3. Linda Walker, 'Friederichs, Hulda (1856/7–1927),' *Oxford Dictionary of National Biography*, (Oxford University Press, 2004). http://www.oxforddnb.com/view/article/46354 [accessed 8 November 2011].
4. Friederichs is given the title of 'chief interviewer' in Saxon Mill's biography of E.T. Cook, assistant editor of the *PMG* under Stead, and editor from 1890–92. See J. Saxon Mills, *Sir Edward Cook KBE, a Biography* (London: Constable, 1921), 123.
5. Matt Rubery observes that journalists such as William Beatty Kingston, Howard Rusel, and George Augustus Sala all used the interview mode but 'the practice was still uncommon until editor W.T. Stead began to make regular use of interviews during the 1880s,' see *Dictionary of Nineteenth Century Journalism*, general eds, Laurel Brake and Marysa Deemor (London: British Library/Sage, 2008), 325. Similar claims are made in Barbara Garlick and Margaret Harris, eds, *Victorian Journalism: Exotic and Domestic: Essays in Honour of P.D. Edwards* (Queensland: Queensland University Press, 1998), 166, and Harold Herd, *The March of Journalism: the Story of the British Press from 1622 to the Present Day* (London: George Allen & Unwin, 1952), 288, where the development of the interview is included as one of the key technical innovations introduced to the *PMG* by Stead, along with more regular use of illustrations and of crossheads.

6. The lack of acknowledgement of Friederichs' role in the *PMG* is striking: for example, she is not even listed amongst the contributors to the *PMG* in the *Waterloo Directory*; George Eliot is, though she only contributed four articles in 1865. Arguably, this is because George Eliot's pieces are identified through her own journal records. I have yet to source any such records for Friederichs. In this chapter, attribution of articles to Friederichs are made on the basis of her retrospective piece 'Difficulties and Delights of Interviewing', (op. cit) where she claims, unambiguously, a number of *PMG* interviews; as identified by her fellow journalists in other publications, such as Stead's *Review of Reviews*; and occasionally on the basis of style, as inferred from the traits of the interviews that are definitely written by Friederichs. Attributions based on style are indicated by a question mark following Friederichs' name, i.e. [Hulda Friederichs?]

7. Friederichs, 'Difficulties and Delights,' 338.

8. When Henry Yates Thompson sold the *PMG* to William Waldorf Astor in 1892 and the paper became an outlet for Tory interests, many of the old *PMG* staff, including Friederichs, left to join Newnes' liberal *Westminster Gazette*, established in January 1893 to rival Astor's version of the evening daily.

9. Among other leading periodicals, including *Strand Magazine*, Friederichs also wrote for *The Women's Penny Paper*, 'the only paper in the world conducted, written (printed and published) by women,' in 1891; this became the *Woman's Herald* in 1891, where the term 'New Woman' was reputedly invented in an article published on 17 August 1893, 'The Social Standing of the New Woman'. See Michelle Elizabeth Tusan, 'Inventing the New Woman: Print Culture and Identity Politics During the *Fin-de-siècle*,' *Victorian Periodicals Review* 31, no. 2 (Summer 1998), 169–82: 169. Tusan outlines the tension between the representations of the politically committed woman of the new century as the 'New Woman' in the women's press from 1893–97 and the 'counter image of the New Woman as a dystopian vision of society gone wrong' that was promoted in the mainstream news (169).

10. Walker, 'Friederichs, Hulda.'

11. Sally Ledger, *The New Woman: Fiction and Feminism at the Fin de siècle* (Manchester: Manchester University Press, 1997), 2.

12. Ledger, *The New Woman*, 3.

13. By 1893, Friederichs is name-checked in the gossip column of the *London Journal* as a 'sister journalist, who stands almost at the head of our profession,' (15 July 1893, 29).

14. W.T. Stead, 'Future of Journalism,' *Contemporary Review* 50 (Nov. 1886), 663.

15. W.T. Stead's 'The Maiden Tribute of Modern Babylon' appeared in the *PMG* from the 6–10 July 1885 and produced enormous outcry with much criticism directed towards Stead and his paper for the sensational treatment of material, including the use of cross-headings such as 'The Violation of Virgins', and 'Strapping Girls Down'. See R. L. Schultz, *Crusader in Babylon: W. T. Stead and the Pall Mall Gazette* (Lincoln: Nebraska University Press, 1972).

16. [Hulda Friederichs?], 'The Muscovite Musicians: An Interview with Mdme Slavianski,' *PMG* (25 June 1886), 4; [Hulda Friederichs], 'An English Tattooer: An Interview with Mr Sutherland Macdonald,' *PMG* (1 May 1889), 2; [Hulda Friederichs?], 'Birds, Butchers and Beauties: An Interview with a Dealer in Birds' Skins and Feathers,' *PMG* (6 January 1886), 1–2.

17. [Hulda Friederichs?], 'Among the Books at the British Museum: An Interview with Mr R. Garnett,' *PMG* (21 November 1884), 11; [Hulda Friederichs?], 'On the Track of the Daffodil: An Interview with Mr Barr,' *PMG* (9 April 1889), 3.

18. Friederichs, 'Difficulties and Delights,' 342.
19. For instance, she interviewed Princess May and the best-selling author Hesba Stretton for *Young Women* in 1893.
20. Friederichs, *Life of Sir George Newnes*, 112.
21. [Hulda Friederichs], 'Darwinism at the Music Hall: A Chat with "Professor" Petrescu on the Art of Balancing,' *PMG* (3 November 1890), 3. Patricia O'Hara notes that New Women writers are 'mostly silent about the music hall and the women who performed there', while the 'At Home' profiles, through which the general public met the stars of the music hall, had a general purpose to 'gentrify and domesticate' these women. See Patricia O'Hara, 'The Women of Today: The Fin-de-Siècle Women of *The Music Hall and Theatre Review*,' *Victorian Periodicals Review* 30, no. 2 (Summer 1997), 141–56: 143, 147. Friederichs' piece, as I suggest, offers a more complicated intervention into these gendered spheres in her critique of the male impresarios of the music halls, rather than through the domestication of music-hall women.
22. Margaret D. Stetz, 'Publishing Industries and Practices' in *The Cambridge Companion to the Fin de Siècle*, ed. Gail Marshall (Cambridge: Cambridge University Press, 1997), 113–130: 115.
23. See 'Dr Koch at home,' *PMG* (26 November 1890), 1–2 and 'A visit to Dr Koch's Consumption Hospital,' *PMG* (29 November 1890), 1–2.
24. [Hulda Friederichs?] 'The Gun Wanted at Abu Klea,' *PMG* (24 January 1885), 1–2; [Friederichs], 'Darwinism,' 3.
25. Richard Salmon, '"Signs of Intimacy"': the Literary Celebrity in the "Age of Interviewing",' *Victorian Literature and Culture* 25, no. 1 (1997), 159–77: 159.
26. Salmon, '"A Simulacra of Power": Intimacy and Abstraction in the Rhetoric of New Journalism,' *Victorian Periodicals Review* 30, no. 1 (Spring 1997), 41–52: 43.
27. P.D. Edwards, *Dickens's 'Young Men' George Augustus Sala, Edmund Yates and the World of Victorian Journalism* (Aldershot: Ashgate, 1997), 4. Edwards notes that Sala complained of his work for *Household Words* in the early 1850s in particular that the 'need to conform to the Dickensian style of the magazine, and the fact that all of his contributions were anonymous, retarded the growth of his reputation'; the same could be argued of Friederichs' work for the *PMG*, but as Edwards argues of Sala, 'in reality, much of his writing for *Household Words* was widely recognized and admired and it opened the way for him to become, within ten or twelve years, one of the 2 or 3 best known journalists in England' (5).
28. As Edwards notes of Yates' influential personal style pioneered in his 'Lounger at the Clubs' column for the *Illustrated Times* from June 1855, 'Implicitly or explicitly, the immanent "I" of the column is always liable to become its subject as much as its author' (Edwards, *Dickens's Young Men*, 43). Yates' style of course was deliberately flippant and gossipy; Friederichs has a more purposeful undertone to her interview pieces, though she does not eschew the sensational or pathetic to keep her audience entertained and on side.
29. Alexis Easley, *First-Person Anonymous: Women Writers and Victorian Print Media 1830–1870* (Aldershot: Ashgate, 2004), 2.
30. Stephen Koss, *The Rise and Fall of the Political Press in Britain*, vol. 1 (London: Hamish Hamilton, 1981), 343.
31. Friederichs, 'Difficulties and Delights,' 338.
32. Friederichs, 'Difficulties and Delights,' 338.
33. Friederichs, 'Difficulties and Delights,' 342.
34. [Friederichs], 'An English Tattooer,' 2.

35. [Friederichs], 'An English Tattooer,' 2.
36. [Friederichs], 'An English Tattooer,' 2.
37. [Friederichs], 'An English Tattooer,' 2.
38. [Friederichs], 'Darwinism,' 3. Her gender is also noted in 'On the Track of the Daffodil'. For this long interview on the arrival of the most favoured of spring flowers, we are told the *PMG* sends a 'lady representative' of the paper to interview a commercial grower of daffodils, see [Friederichs?], 'On the Track of the Daffodil,' 3.
39. [Friederichs], 'Darwinism,' 3.
40. Friederichs, 'Difficulties and Delights,' 341.
41. On the genesis of this term, 'New Woman,' see note 9.
42. Sally Ledger, 'The New Woman and Feminist Fictions' in *The Cambridge Companion to the Fin de Siècle*, ed. Gail Marshall (Cambridge: Cambridge University Press, 1997), 153–68: 153–4.
43. See 'Should sensible women follow the fashions?' *Temple Magazine* (November 1896) and 'Why do women prefer to remain unwed?' *Temple Magazine* (April 1898). She is also one of five contributors to the extended piece on interviews in the *Idler* in 1896, 'Are Interviewers a Blessing or a Curse,' *Idler* (January 1896), 583–94.
44. See the *Review of Reviews* (April 1903), 373, for this summary of the *Young Man* symposium.
45. The quote is from *Julius Caesar* (Act 1, Sc. 2), spoken by Caesar to Anthony in the context of his anxiety about Cassius' 'lean and hungry look', as signifying a threat to Caesar: it is typical of Friederichs' arch, double-edged humour to invoke the reference in this context. Cited in *Review of Reviews* (April 1903), 373.
46. Barbara Onslow, *Women of the Press in Nineteenth-Century Britain* (London: Macmillan, 2000), 225. A summary of *Westminster Gazette* journalists in the *Bookman* in 1898 points up Friederichs' 'bright and varied work ... especially in the way of interviewing' and notes that 'she has probably penetrated further into the Gladstone circle than any other journalist and is an acknowledged authority on domestic life at Hawarden'; see 'The Journalist: The Staff of the *Westminster Gazette*,' *The Bookman* (January 1898), 124–5, 125.
47. Friederichs, *Life of Sir George Newnes, Bart.*, 82–3.

10

Representing the Professional Woman: The Celebrity Interviewing of Sarah Tooley

Terri Doughty
Vancouver Island University

Sarah Tooley's name is recognized today only, if at all, for her work establishing other women's names, including those of Sarah Grand, Clementina Black, Beatrice Webb, Mary Kingsley, L. T. Meade, and Alice Meynell. Tooley's biography of Florence Nightingale and history of nursing are also still cited in studies of that profession. But from the 1890s throughout the first half of the twentieth century, Tooley enjoyed recognition in her own right in Britain as a prominent and respected journalist. Frances E. Willard quotes a reviewer in the *Sun* of 1 March 1894 praising 'another of Mrs. Tooley's really clever interviews'.[1] Reporting on a talk by W. T. Stead in 1909, the *Times* includes Tooley as one of only five audience members significant enough to be named.[2] At the Golden Anniversary of the Society of Women Journalists in May, 1944, Tooley was honoured with a bouquet of flowers from Clemence Dane, the President of the Society.[3] However, Tooley's celebrity faded, possibly because her work, predominantly interviewing and writing biographical sketches and biographies, has seemed to late twentieth-century readers and scholars less significant than the work of other women writers of the period. Yet as Sally Mitchell has observed, seemingly ephemeral journalism indeed has its uses. Not only does it 'illuminate social history',[4] but in the case of Tooley's celebrity interviewing, it both participates in and allows critical assessment of the production of the female professional. Tooley's interviews with women from a variety of fields of work, both paid and unpaid, steadfastly promote the professional capability of women. Moreover, herself a celebrated journalist and subject of interviews, Sarah Tooley represents a model – though a complex one – of the professional woman as journalist.

Interviews with Tooley, along with an entry in *Who Was Who* and census data, comprise the main sources of biographical information on her. She was born Sarah Anne Southall, daughter of Thomas, at Brierley Hill, Staffordshire, in 1857.[5] Tooley notes in an interview that her parents died when she was young, and after spending time at a boarding-school she lived with relatives in London.[6] Her boarding-school, Greenhill House, in Stourbridge, Worcestershire, run by Miss Hannah Maria Moorehouse,[7] must have stimulated Tooley's interest in literature, as she attended literary classes conducted by Henry Morley at the London University College for two years.[8] Tooley seems also to have pursued literary research, as she is credited in *Who Was Who* with having discovered the birthplace and birth certificate of Elizabeth Gaskell. Her other activities in London while unmarried are largely unknown: the 1881 census lists her living as a boarder in Marylebone, London; whether she was boarding with relatives is unclear. A year later, at age 25, she married George W. Tooley, a minister, at Stourbridge, and moved with him to Dumfries.

In her interview with Arthur Lawrence in 1896, Tooley claims that she had unfulfilled literary ambitions;[9] however, Tooley did not begin seriously to pursue writing as a career until after her marriage. When her husband developed an unspecified spinal complaint which left him unable to work, she responded by seeking literary work. Tooley's first published piece, sometime between 1883 and 1887, was a sketch of Lochmaben, Dumfries, in the *People's Friend*, a weekly penny family paper published in Dundee.[10] Her next endeavour was a collection of biographical sketches, *Lives, Great and Simple*, published by the Walter Scott Publishing Co. of Newcastle-upon-Tyne.[11] Tooley observes wryly that 'the financial result, so far as I was concerned, was not very extraordinary'.[12] Eventually, she and her husband decided to move to London so that she could make contacts to pursue more remunerative literary and journalistic work.

Tooley was not unusual in turning to journalism as a source of income in the late Victorian period. As Barbara Onslow states, 'Money, or rather lack of it, was a major reason why women entered journalism'.[13] Information on pay for journalistic work varies, but aspiring young women could find reports suggesting a starting income from £50 to £100, all the way up to incomes of £600 or £700.[14] There was no shortage of advice, as many of the girls' and women's magazines of the 1880s and the 1890s featured articles on careers in journalism. The advice showed little consistency, however, even within a single article. In *Woman's World* in 1890, Mary Frances Billington asserts both that journalism offers opportunity to women and that 'it is not a woman's profession in the open unreserved sense of the term'.[15] Similarly, in an interview with the celebrated journalist Emily Crawford in the *Young Woman* in 1894, the anonymous interviewer reports that Crawford 'seldom encourages others to engage in the work in which she herself has been so successful'.[16] Perhaps these reservations were due to the perception, reinforced in many articles on journalism as a career for women, that too many women expected it to be an easy route to financial independence, and that the field was becoming too crowded. For instance, W. T. Stead, in the *Young Woman* in 1892, complains of the applications he receives from

> many ladies [who] imagine that, whenever they want money, the most obvious resource is to rush off to the nearest editor to ask him to pay for articles which are utterly worthless.[17]

Whether or not Stead's complaint was valid, the number of women who described themselves as 'author, editor, writer' in the census had more than doubled between 1871 and 1891, to 660.[18] Despite this discouraging context, Sarah Tooley, with her literary background and skill, still aspired to a career in journalism, seeking contacts for an entrée to the profession. The necessity of such contacts for the woman journalist was a widespread perception in the period. As one writer notes, 'If she has any friends on the Press, the young lady will not find any difficulty in getting started'.[19] Similarly, Emily Crawford says in her interview that her own career began when a private letter was shown by a friend to a London editor. This deflects any suggestion that she sought attention or notoriety: her subsequent career came of her being 'discovered'. Tooley also seems to have benefited from certain professional contacts. She notes that her husband knew some of the leaders of the women's rights movement;[20] as she wrote early in her journalistic career a great deal for the *Women's Penny Paper* and its later incarnations, the *Woman's Herald* and the *Woman's Signal*, she may well have benefited from those contacts. Interestingly, however, Tooley later resisted this narrative of her career inception, stating '[i]ntroductions to editors are a snare and a delusion, although the novice is apt to think that they are the key to success'.[21] She contends instead that women journalists succeed based on hard work. Later, Tooley tells Arthur Lawrence that she began her journalism work with 'fictional sketches' for the *Housewife*[22] and other magazines, stressing her initiative in contacting editors with proposals and samples of her writing.[23] In this way, Tooley indicates that a career in journalism, like hers, is the product of professional application and perseverance, not fortunate happenstance.

Tooley's early work suggests her willingness to turn her hand to whatever might meet an editor's needs, as she later advises prospective women journalists to do.[24] For instance, she reports on the first address of a woman to the Baptist Union for the *Women's Penny Paper* (7 December 1889), writes an opinion piece on 'Women in Our Police Courts' for the *Woman's Herald* (25 July 1891), and also in the *Herald* presents a critique of a comment opposing women's suffrage made in the House of Commons by Liberal politician Henry Labouchère (11 July 1891). Tooley's work at this early point was not specialized in any way. Her career-shaping movement into the field of interviewing built on the momentum of the New Journalism, particularly the rise of the interview as a means of modelling and promoting feminist values.[25] The celebrity interview was a popular feature of many periodicals aimed at general readerships. Beginning with the *Women's Penny Paper*, the interview with a leading female figure also became a key feature of many women's papers and magazines. For Tooley, whose earliest literary efforts were biographical, interviewing for periodicals must have looked like a field of opportunity. Indeed, she presents her interviewing work as an outgrowth of her interest in biography: 'People are decidedly my "game"', she tells Frances Willard.[26] Tooley states that at the outset she determined to 'experiment with a foreigner' (presumably because if she could not publish her interview, her failure would not be well-known in the relatively small world of literary London) and gained an interview with Madame Tel Sono, a woman lawyer from Japan, in England to promote a college she hoped to establish. The resulting interview was published in the *Christian Weekly* and was successful enough to merit quotation in the *Pall Mall Gazette*.[27] Tooley describes this as a defining moment in her career, leading to additional interviewing for the *Pall Mall Gazette*, *Daily Chronicle*, and *Westminster Gazette*.[28] By 1894, Tooley was recognized as a specialist in this field of journalism by becoming herself the subject of Willard's interview in the *Woman's Signal*, as a model to aspiring female journalists.

Despite continuing to write for mainstream papers, much of Tooley's most notable work in the 1890s was done for women's papers and magazines. She states that her early well-received interviews (and presumably some of the general writing she had already done for the paper) led to Lady Henry Somerset inviting her to join the staff of the *Woman's Signal*. She even claims that she was offered and declined the editorship of the paper, which subsequently passed in 1895 to Florence Fenwick-Miller (see Michelle Tusan's chapter in this volume).[29] Around the same time, Tooley was commissioned to interview for the *Young Woman* and *Woman at Home*. Her interviews, all signed, would have placed her name before the public on an almost weekly basis.

Tooley's celebrity as an interviewer is, however, complicated. The interview is a form of journalism that in certain ways effaces the interviewer. Although, as Richard Salmon notes, the interview actually positions the person being interviewed as an object under examination and the interviewer as the interrogating subject, the purpose of the interview, and particularly the celebrity interview, is to hold up the interviewee as a subject of interest and possibly admiration.[30] The interviewer, then, ostensibly functions as a mirror permitting the reflection of the interviewee's various talents and achievements. Arguably, Tooley's name has not lasted till today because the passage of time has trained non-contemporary readers' attention on the subjects of her interviews, not the interviewer. However, since all Tooley's known interviews are signed, they served in their day, as Beetham and Boardman observe regarding the interview generally, to make visible a journalistic career for women.[31] Frances Willard prefaces her interview with Tooley by stating that 'women have special gifts for this branch of newspaper work'[32]; she then continues by explicitly making Tooley an exemplar. Thus, Tooley was indeed famous, but her fame was problematic: her name was widely recognized, but it was made so in large part by relationship to the names of her subjects.

The interview was also initially a controversial form of journalism. Eliza Lynn Linton, who later deigned to be interviewed by Tooley for *Woman at Home*, writes in the *Fortnightly Review* in 1890 that '[w]ith the creation of the interviewer, reticence on the one side is destroyed—on the other, honour goes by the board'.[33] Linton's attack on the interview is particularly noteworthy as she genders the interviewer as a young, inexperienced woman, and characterizes her as obnoxiously intrusive. Indeed, one of the first questions Willard asks Tooley in their interview is how she regards the charge that the interview is 'an unwarrantable invasion of ... privacy.' Tooley neatly sidesteps the question by suggesting not only that the critics take interviews too seriously (a rather disingenuous argument, given that many of the interviews she herself published are designed to be inspirational), but also that improved communications make the world a less isolated and insular place, a positive sign for human development. Earlier in the same interview, Tooley outlines the benefits of the interview:

> ours is a busy age, and when we can hear for ourselves, through the phonograph of daily journalism, what experts and specialists in society and the arts, in Church and state, in science and literature are saying, we know that we are getting at the original sources of information and oftentimes of inspiration also.[34]

Far from being prurient, interviewing is presented here as enlightening, serving cultural, educational, and social functions. Furthermore, by means of the metaphor of the phonograph, Tooley suggests that the journalist, and by extension herself, serves as an objective recorder/relayer of content.

Given the workings of the celebrity female interview in journals of the period, Tooley's claims of objectivity for the interview are somewhat deceptive: interviews were in fact highly ideological productions. As Tusan notes, women's newspapers of the period were actively engaged in constructing a New Woman who was not the freakish creation of the mainstream press's parodies, but rather a respectable woman who 'promised to improve and reform English society'. Tusan identifies as one of the most effective tools of the papers the genre of 'heroic narratives of women who acted in very public ways against inequality'.[35] The new female celebrity interview could function in a similar fashion: unlike earlier constructions of female celebrity located in decorativeness, embodied by actresses or aristocratic beauties, this new kind of female celebrity is embodied by professional women, pioneers in first-wave feminism, and women working to address social problems. Interviews gave these women public platforms from which to articulate their values. Rosemary VanArsdel identifies key functions of the personal interview as 'to persuade, exemplify, illustrate, or hold up for emulation or example'.[36] Henrietta Muller, founder and editor of the *Women's Penny Paper*, describes the interview column as 'one of the strongest weapons which the women's party possesses'.[37] Women could refute charges of female incapacity through the models presented by interviewees. Admittedly, the features of the most desirable model could vary between different publications, each promoting the values of its publisher(s) and/or editor(s). Moreover, there is little evidence to tell whether or not interviewers, particularly those contracted to provide series of interviews, as Tooley frequently was, enjoyed the freedom to pick their own subjects. However, in her own interview with Frances Willard, Sarah Tooley states, 'I never attempt to interview anyone with whom I have not some bond of sympathy, and I generally choose my subjects'.[38] Therefore, Tooley's interviews may arguably be read as engaged both in the promotion of the gender values of the periodicals in which they appeared and in the promotion of her own espoused values.

Tooley generally demonstrated feminist sympathies. She was a member of the Women Writers' Suffrage League, formed in 1908 and open to any writer who had received payment for work and who supported female suffrage. Leaders in the organization viewed journalism as

> an element in the propaganda so quiet as to find a way unchallenged into many Anti strongholds, yet so steady as to show its widespread result only in the retrospect.[39]

Certainly Tooley's journalistic work would fit this 'quiet, steady' description. In her interview with Willard, she claims, 'The granting of the suffrage to women need not upset social and domestic life that I can see'.[40] Tooley then goes on to characterize anti-suffragists as 'nervous old gentlemen', neatly positioning her reader, who, if desiring not to be thus defined, must agree with her. Tooley's brand of feminism, nonetheless, was not radical and may appear somewhat problematic to a twenty-first-century reader. She supported women's right to equal pay for equal work, and she supported legislative reform regarding women's rights:

> Every woman who works or who has a spark of individuality about her, desires to breathe freely in the world, and that cannot be done while she is hampered by social and legal restrictions. Give perfect freedom to women as to men, to do whatever they have the faculty for doing.[41]

However, beside this promotion of women's rights, Tooley still supported a number of conventional gendered assumptions about femininity and domesticity. Tellingly, in a pageant staged by the Actresses' Franchise League and the Women Writers' League in 1914 to celebrate famous men and women (most associated either specifically with women's rights or with battles for freedom), Tooley impersonated Elizabeth Fry, the social reformer.[42] Tooley's insistence on women's capabilities often focuses on their capacity to improve social conditions; discussion of their public work is frequently tempered by acknowledgments of women's domestic responsibilities (as a childless woman, she herself was partially exempt from these, although she did care for an invalid husband until his death in 1916). Tooley's maintenance of a domestic feminine ideal must be read in the context of the period, though, as one of the ways women negotiated hostile, antifeminist criticism. In the same interview with Willard, Tooley notes that as a girl she had been intimidated by the idea of 'the Woman's Rights woman according to the accepted notion of that type of female', but she is quick to follow this by stating that 'this objectionable type of the advanced woman is rarely to be found outside the comic journals'.[43]

As Margaret Beetham and others have observed, it was very common for biographical sketches and interviews to stress the 'womanliness' of even the most advanced proponent of women's rights.[44] Indeed, Willard completes her interview with Tooley by describing how 'the bright little woman went her way'.[45] Often, stressing her smallness emphasizes the femininity of an interviewee. Tooley herself uses similar strategies. Even writing for the feminist *Woman's Signal*, she describes Frances Hodgson Burnett as being 'sweet and gracious' and having 'a fairy touch' in her writing.[46] When reporting on a speech by the women's trades' union activist Clementina Black, Tooley notes that Black spoke in 'soft, womanly tones'.[47] Similarly, Tooley draws attention to the 'brightness and comfort', 'the soft harmonious furnishings and pretty arrangements' of the novelist Annie S. Swan's domestic setting.[48] As this piece was published in *Woman at Home*, 'Annie Swan's magazine', a periodical aimed at the moderate New Woman, it is also copiously illustrated with pictures of Swan's charming domestic life. Yet Tooley evidently recognized this convention's strategic import, writing in an interview with the socialist Beatrice Webb:

> One gets almost tired of saying that the women who are making their impress upon the thought of the day are 'womanly'; of course they are, and that is the great secret of their success. I repeat the formula— Mrs. Sidney Webb is very womanly.[49]

Tooley was well aware of the balancing act required to promote women's rights and professional accomplishment on the one hand and to deflect criticism of unwomanliness on the other. Her use of rhetorical strategies demonstrates clear sympathy with her subjects' efforts to establish public professional identities.

As noted above, Tooley claimed never to interview someone with whom she had no sympathy. Her subjects are wide-ranging, but even a cursory list of her interviewees is a who's who of pioneering professional women, suffragettes, and activists for social justice: Black and Webb (already mentioned), Sarah Grand, Beatrice Harraden, Josephine Butler, Charlotte Carmichael Stopes, Alice Meynell, and Lady Henry Somerset, to name a few. Even when interviewing men, Tooley generally focuses on women's issues, interviewing Professor H. C. Shuttleworth on 'The Ethical Basis of Woman's Rights' and

William Morris on 'A Living Wage for Women'. Tooley records Shuttleworth asking what motivated her to seek him out for an interview, and she responds, 'Your recent sermon at St. Edmund's, in which you spoke so sympathetically of the women's movement'.[50] Tooley also promotes a feminist agenda in her non-interview writing: when reporting for the *Ladies' Realm* on the International Council of Women meeting to be held in London 22 June–2 July, 1899, she suggests that the government should build new tiers of seating for women in the galleries of the House of Parliament: 'What will the foreign delegates think if they are committed to the present ladies' cage?'[51]

When interviewing women, Tooley wherever possible foregrounds their professionalism, pointing out their qualifications and work ethic. She notes that Clementina Black is the secretary of the Women's Provident League and is an 'arduous worker'.[52] Similarly, she points out that Isabel Kenward, noted for her work among factory girls in Birmingham, is not only a 'distinguished student of Somerville Hall, Oxford', but also a coach who prepares girls for university examinations and an author and speaker on issues relating to girls' working lives.[53] In her interview with Josephine Butler, Tooley observes that Butler, despite being in mourning for her husband, 'has been busy pushing forward her propaganda in foreign lands, and in editing *The Dawn*, a quarterly sketch of the progress of the work of the "British, Continental, and General Federation for the Abolition of the State Regulation of Vice"'.[54] Tooley also interviews women notable for their endeavours in non-traditional fields, such as the sculptor Amelia (Mrs. D. O.) Hill, Elizabeth Garrett Anderson, M.D., and the astronomer Margaret Lindsay Huggins. When Tooley explores professional fields aligned with more traditional womanly skills, as in her interview with Miss Harris, Head Mistress of the Ben Jonson Street Schools, or with Miss Hoddenott, Matron at Lady Henry Somerset's home for foundling girls at Reigate, Tooley makes certain to report on the discipline and order achieved by the woman manager. In her interview with Harris, she promotes Harris's plea for 'lady managers for the School Board Districts'.[55] Tooley expresses particular scorn for those who object to women's professional development:

> I almost tremble as I write that word 'trained,' because so many people dislike to see it in conjunction with the word 'woman.' So much nicer, don't you know, for a woman to be straggling and promiscuous; it keeps her interesting and adorably harmless.[56]

Tooley's sarcasm underlines her support for women's access to professional training so that they might develop suitable careers.

Some of Tooley's most strongly worded statements come from the interviews she published in the *Woman's Signal*. It could be argued that, as a professional journalist, she is simply writing what her market requires. However, Tooley's commitment to certain principles may be clearly discerned by examining paired interviews she published in the *Woman's Signal*, billed as a 'progressive paper for women'[57] and in the more conservative *Young Woman*, which targeted an explicitly Christian and 'more serious-minded female readership'.[58] Extremely prolific during the 1890s, Tooley seems often to have made double use of interviews. Publishing interviews with Frances Hodgson Burnett in the *Woman's Signal* in April of 1895 and then in the *Young Woman* in May of 1895, Tooley likely based both articles on a single interview. Similarly, she published interviews with Beatrice Webb in the *Woman's Signal* in July of 1894 and in the *Young Woman* in February of 1895. The seven-month gap in this instance could possibly have necessitated two interviews. Nonetheless, the two pairs of interviews provide the opportunity to analyse any differences in tone between Tooley's writing for the two different periodicals. In the case of Burnett, who had a significant professional investment in her image as a feminine, motherly woman, Tooley's two interviews are remarkably similar. In the *Woman's Signal* interview, Tooley quotes Burnett as stating, 'I would not put any limitations upon what women may do, except when they are mothers'.[59] Similarly, in the *Young Woman* interview, Tooley quotes Burnett's assertion 'It was a rule with me that my writing should never come between me and my children'.[60] Tooley in both of the Burnett interviews appears to be colluding with a professional woman particularly famous for writing about children in her construction of herself as a womanly woman.

In the pair of published interviews with Beatrice Webb, Tooley takes a much stronger feminist tone. In the *Woman's Signal*, Tooley prefaces the interview by noting Webb's authority on the topic of women's labour, describing her most recent publication as 'strong, forcible, logical, and we imagine unanswerable'.[61] Tooley is at pains to note Webb's impressive ability to take on the exclusively male Royal Commission on Labour. Although she describes Webb as winsome, Tooley notes that this characteristic is an asset during debate as it 'might put an opponent off his guard'.[62] Likewise, although the interview in the *Young Woman* has the focus characteristic of that magazine on domestic arrangements and home decor, accompanied by photos of the Webbs' drawing room, Tooley also describes Webb's valiant work amongst poor Jewish immigrants, in which Webb is subjected to various coarsenesses unsuitable for a lady. Moreover, when Webb admits herself to be '"shaky" on the suffrage', Tooley presses her hard, not content to accept women's participation in municipal elections as sufficient: 'There can be no doubt, Mrs. Webb, that women's full suffrage will be attained step by step through local government, but there is no harm in regarding the parliamentary as the final goal.'[63] Clearly, the relative consistency of Tooley's views on women's achievements and rights as expressed across these sets of interviews speak to Tooley's own commitment to these values.

Tooley did not stop at simply promoting the professional capabilities of other women, however. In the face of widespread criticism of women journalists in the 1880s and 1890s, Tooley sought to demonstrate her own professionalism.[64] A number of articles and books asserted that women who entered journalism were uneducated, unskilled, unable to stand up to the rigours of the work schedule, and unprepared for the less ladylike elements of the job. W. T. Stead notes that women journalists are unable to take editorial criticism as men do, responding with 'a good cry over the brutality of men in general and their editor in particular'.[65] Likewise, Mary Frances Billington warns that the aspiring female journalist must be prepared for rigorous editing to 'lose her early amateurishness'. Billington observes further that 'no manager wants a contributor whose grammar needs revision, or whose facts are open to question'.[66] Tooley consciously displays her authority in her interviews by providing markers of her reading and familiarity with current social and political issues. For instance, when interviewing William Morris, Tooley not only opens with a light critique of his fantasy of the transformation of Hammersmith in *News from Nowhere*, but she also debates several points with him regarding women's training and work. When he claims that there are no great women artists, she counters with the painters Elizabeth Thompson and Rosa Bonheur.[67] In this way, Tooley shows herself to be culturally knowledgeable and prepared for the interview.

Tooley also stresses her own perseverance in ensuring she gets her interview. When dealing with a reluctant interviewee, Charlotte Carmichael Stopes, Tooley observes that Stopes was trying to distract her, 'with hope, I fear, that my special errand might be lost sight of'.[68] The continuation of the interview for another almost three columns is a sign of Tooley's triumph. Likewise, concluding an interview with the shy wife of a noted Congregationalist preacher, Tooley congratulates herself on leaving their home 'with an inward satisfaction that I had not been put off the interview by Mrs. Parker's diffidence'.[69] Tooley shows no sign here of the prying impertinence of Eliza Lynn Linton's girl interviewer; rather, Tooley presents herself as a professional interviewer who makes sure she does her job. Indeed, while being interviewed by Arthur Lawrence and asked about any of her adventures while interviewing, Tooley chooses to tell a heroic narrative of how she conducted interviews after having fallen and hurt herself quite badly, smashing her nose and blackening both her eyes. She twice repeats that printers were waiting and describes how she therefore went on to keep her appointments with both the suffragette and anti-vice campaigner Eva Maclaren and the Miss Dawson who agitated for the admission of women to the Wesleyan Conference. Tooley emphasizes how she continued with her task despite her hostesses' repeated expressions of concern, because she was determined to meet her professional obligations.

Tooley, an experienced interviewer herself, is poised when being interviewed, skilfully highlighting her opinions on women practicing journalism and using her own experiences to present readers with herself as an exemplar. Tooley notes that women should never attempt to interview upon subjects which they do not understand. Moreover, they should 'avoid feminine fussiness and feminine fidgets. The question of sex should not be introduced into work, nor a demand for special consideration' for women.[70] In the same interview, she stresses the importance of writing on matters of general and topical interest to the public: 'if it is not what the public wants it is useless for journalism'. Her views are similar to those expressed by W. T. Stead, but Tooley does not intend them to be discouraging. Rather, as she says to Lawrence,

> It is not from any egotistic motive, nor is there anything to be vain about ... that I have been induced to tell you my experience rather minutely; but it may be that the summary of my own early experience may prove of value to some other woman, or, at all events, contain some little hint which can be utilized. I feel sure that there are many women in every way fitted for journalistic work....[71]

Tooley presents her story as a guide to establishing oneself as a professional woman, with herself as exemplar.

The interview with Tooley conducted by Lawrence is particularly interesting in terms of the duelling efforts, on the parts of interviewer and subject, to construct the woman professional. Despite Tooley's self-representation as a model whose achievements are accessible to other women, Lawrence begins by insisting on Tooley's exceptionality, describing her as 'well-nigh unique'. The preamble to the interview reflects some anxiety on the part of the interviewer. Lawrence states, 'it was with a keen recollection of the fact that Mrs. Tooley has reduced interviewing to a fine art that I paid her a visit at her husband's handsome flat'.[72] On the one hand, the interviewer places himself in the position of junior approaching a senior practitioner of their shared craft (although the verb 'reduced' suggests that Tooley has somehow diminished the art by mastering it). On the other hand, the interviewer places Tooley in *her* place by describing her home as belonging to her husband, when it is highly likely that Tooley's work paid for it. Fraser, Green, and Johnston have already noted that Lawrence's physical description of Tooley, referencing physiognomy and highlighting her 'keen blue eyes and fine forehead' suggests that her career is 'genetically ordained'.[73] These details resist the notion that Tooley's example may be easily followed by other women.

Tensions between interviewer and subject continue when the subject of methodology arises. Lawrence affects surprise that Tooley neither uses shorthand nor writes out her interviews immediately after her sessions with her subjects. The implication is that her methods are not very professional. However, Tooley argues that recording a conversation in shorthand is distracting to the subject, preventing a more 'fluent and natural' conversation. Moreover, she contends that if the interview 'simmers', she is better able to focus on its 'salient points'.[74] Lawrence claims to be 'rather staggered' by this. His expressions of amazement at 'the marvellous retentiveness of her memory' suggest exactly the opposite, as he draws attention to the volume of interviews she conducts and the diversity of her topics.[75] Her accuracy is something that Tooley addresses in her interview with Frances Willard, two years previous to the interview with Lawrence. Tooley states then that her only factual error to date has been an assumption she made while interviewing a woman writer 'over the teacups in her private sanctum'. On seeing some projects in process, Tooley reported that the woman was interested in needlework, whereas it turned out that the needlework belonged to the writer's cousin. Tooley tells Willard she finds this 'more amusing than serious'.[76] Lawrence, however, gives Tooley no space to address his polite astonishment, nor his subsequent description of her methodology as essentially impressionistic. Nonetheless she does so tangentially, as she asserts that women are inherently better suited to interviewing work than men, in part because of their capacity for sympathetic engagement, which might not have been entirely comfortable for Lawrence to hear. He is left rather lamely to conclude from his own experience that perhaps women are best interviewed by women and men interviewed by men, despite Tooley having given several examples of successful interviews she herself conducted with notable men, including the evolutionary biologist Alfred Russel Wallace, William Morris, and the painter Frederic Leighton.

Tooley's view that women make the best interviewers overall was not unique. Her assertion that women are prepared to be effective interviewers by their social training in receiving visitors, making calls, and making conversation repeats points made by other women journalists such as Emily Crawford and Elizabeth Banks.[77] Tooley adds that '[t]he intuitive and perceptive faculties with which woman is usually credited are also of invaluable service to her in interviewing'.[78] Contrary to Lawrence's conclusion that journalists of each sex should interview members of the same sex, Tooley claims that she finds it more difficult to interview women than men, despite acknowledging that it seems natural for women to interview women (men are too awkward when interviewing women, she contends). Tooley suggests that women are only challenging to interview, however, because they have been socialized to 'dread publicity ... and are very reticent'.[79] Tooley refers to having to coax some of her female subjects, as noted above in her interviews with Charlotte Carmichael Stopes and Mrs. Joseph Parker. Interestingly, Tooley claims that not only are women interviewers best at drawing out reluctant female subjects but that they are best at getting men to speak freely. She observes to Willard that men are more constrained in the presence of other men; however, they become amazingly expansive in 'a woman's soft and kindly presence'. These men see women as pupils, and in their secure sense of superiority they talk more freely, 'even upon personal matters in a way which they never think of doing to a male visitor'. Tooley characterizes the greatest (male) minds as 'singularly childlike' in their need for (feminine) sympathy.[80] Clearly, Tooley sees her 'intuitive and perceptive qualities' as a kind of feminine secret weapon, much as she describes Beatrice Webb's winsomeness as a tool to mislead her male opponents. Tooley's description of interviewing as a feminine talent works within the broader culture's complicated depiction of the womanly woman writer to assert a set of female professional skills.

Tooley's fame as an interviewer, burgeoning in the 1890s, lasted well into the new century. Her career was given a tremendous boost by the success of her biography of Queen Victoria (1896), which was first published as a series of sketches in the *Woman at Home*. Tooley continued to interview, publishing an interview with 'Lady Henry Somerset at Duxhurst' in the *Christian Observer* (1902), a 'Conversation with Octavia Hill' in the *Daily Chronicle* (24 July 1905), and an interview with Sir Arthur and Lady Conan Doyle in the *Woman at Home* (1908), among others. Lawrence describes Tooley in 1896 as 'a contributor to high-class magazines',[81] and this seems accurately to describe her subsequent career up to the First World War. She wrote numerous biographical sketches, and after the success of her biography of the Queen, she wrote increasingly about noble and royal subjects, both people and places such as stately homes. At the same time, Tooley continued to promote women's professional achievements, contributing a number of articles to *Every Woman's Encyclopaedia* in 1912, including a series in the section on 'The World of Women' entitled the 'Triumph of Women'. The introduction promises a survey of the

> steady and irresistible progress of woman throughout the civilized world. Like a triumphant procession in an ancient pageant, there will pass before the reader the distinguished and ever-increasing army of women who have worked and won.[82]

Many of the women discussed in the series had been subjects of Tooley's interviews.

After the First World War, references to Tooley's journalistic work become less frequent; indeed, by this time she was in her 60s. Nonetheless, Tooley appears to have continued very active in the Society of Women Journalists, having first written about it in an interview with Alice Meynell (then President) published in the *Humanitarian* in 1898. *Who Was Who* describes Tooley as having held office as both Vice-Chairman and Vice-President of the Society. When Robert Blackham, writing a book in the 1930s on notable women, wanted information on 'distinguished woman journalists', his contact at the Society of Women Journalists was Council Member Sarah Tooley.[83] Tooley's contributions to the professionalization of women in journalism continued over the course of a very lengthy and productive career.

A survey of Sarah Tooley's career establishes more than an archive of raw data with which to illuminate British women's history. She models fields of possibility to her female readers: embodying the emerging professional woman in the field of journalism, promoting the cause of women's rights, identifying women's professional opportunities and making visible the different types of professional women active at the end of the nineteenth century. In addition, Tooley holds her own with male interview subjects and male interviewers, carving out a career in a male-dominated field and redefining her work as women's work, best done by a woman. Tooley may have lacked the notoriety of a Josephine Butler or a Sarah Grand, but her tenacity in building her career and her commitment to celebrating women's work are noteworthy. In making the names of other women, Sarah Tooley definitely made a name for herself, one which deserves to be known today.

Notes

1. Frances E. Willard, 'Mrs. Sarah Tooley: An Interviewer Interviewed,' *Woman's Signal* (15 March 1894), 170.
2. 'Mr. Stead on Journalists,' *Times* (22 March 1909), 15.
3. Sylvia Kent, *The Woman Writer: The History of the Society of Women Journalists* (Stroud: History Press, 2009), 96.
4. Sally Mitchell, 'Ephemeral Journalism and Its Uses: Lucie Cobbe Heaton Armstrong,' *Victorian Periodicals Review* 42, no. 1 (2009), 81.
5. 'Tooley, Mrs. Sarah A.,' *Who Was Who*, vol. 4 (1952; rev., London: Adam and Charles Black, 1958): 1158. I have not been able to locate Tooley's mother's name. Her birth date is that provided on the 1901 census.
6. Arthur H. Lawrence, '"Interviewing" as Women's Work: A Chat with Mrs. Sarah A. Tooley,' *Young Woman* 5 (1896), 441.
7. Frederick Shirley Dumaresq Carteret Bisson, *Our Schools and Colleges*, vol. 2 (London: Simpkin Marshall, 1884), 670.
8. Lawrence, '"Interviewing",' 441.
9. Lawrence, '"Interviewing",' 441.
10. Lawrence, '"Interviewing",' 442. Tooley does not specify the date of the published sketch, and I have been unable to locate it. Information on the *People's Friend* can be found in the *Dictionary of Nineteenth-Century Journalism in Great Britain and Ireland*, eds Laurel Brake and Marysa DeMoor (Ghent: Academia Press; London: British Library, 2009), 489.
11. This volume may have a more complicated history than Tooley suggests in this interview. The British Library has copies of two editions, one indeed published by Walter Scott in 1887, but the other published three years earlier by Kent & Co. Both editions were published in London. The Walter Scott of the publishing company was no relation to the novelist.
12. Lawrence, '"Interviewing",' 442.
13. Barbara Onslow, *Women of the Press in Nineteenth-Century Britain* (Basingstoke: Macmillan, 2000), 17.
14. David Rubinstein, *Before the Suffragettes: Women's Emancipation in the 1890s* (Brighton: Harvester, 1986), 93 n.79.
15. Mary Frances Billington, 'Journalism as a Profession for Women,' *Woman's World* 3 (1890, rpt., New York: Source Books, 1970), 8.

16. 'A Famous Lady Journalist: A Chat with Mrs. Emily Crawford,' *Young Woman* 2, no.18 (March 1894), 185.
17. W. T. Stead, 'Young Women and Journalism,' *Young Woman* 1, no.1 (October 1892), 14.
18. Sally Mitchell, 'Careers for Girls: Writing Trash,' *Victorian Periodicals Review* 25, no. 3 (1992), 109.
19. Edward John Prior, 'How to Become a Lady Journalist,' *Girl's Own Paper* (18 July 1903), 669.
20. Willard, 'Mrs. Sarah Tooley,' 171.
21. Willard, 'Mrs. Sarah Tooley,' 170.
22. This relatively short-lived magazine, from 1886–1890, is listed in Margaret Beetham and Kay Boardman, eds, *Victorian Women's Magazines: An Anthology* (Manchester: Manchester University Press, 2001), 222.
23. Lawrence, '"Interviewing",' 442.
24. Willard, 'Mrs. Sarah Tooley,' 170.
25. Rosemary VanArsdel, 'Women's Periodicals and the New Journalism: The Personal Interview,' in *Papers for the Millions: The New Journalism in Britain, 1850s–1914*, ed. Joel H. Wiener (New York: Greenwood, 1988), 246. See also Michelle Elizabeth Tusan, *Women Making News: Gender and Journalism in Modern Britain* (Urbana: University of Illinois Press, 2005), 114–115.
26. Willard, 'Mrs. Sarah Tooley,' 170; see also Lawrence, '"Interviewing",' 441.
27. Tooley does not provide a specific date, and I have not yet located the article. It would have to have been published in 1893 to coincide with Madame Tel Sono's visit to London.
28. Lawrence, '"Interviewing",' 443.
29. Lawrence, '"Interviewing",' 443.
30. Richard Salmon, 'Signs of Intimacy: The Literary Celebrity in the "Age of Interviewing,"' *Victorian Literature and Culture* 25, no. 1 (1997), 161, 162.
31. Beetham and Boardman, *Victorian Women's Magazines*, 212.
32. Willard, 'Mrs. Sarah Tooley,' 169.
33. Qtd. in Onslow, *Women of the Press*, 14.
34. Willard, 'Mrs. Sarah Tooley,' 170.
35. Tusan, *Women Making News*, 131, 104.
36. VanArsdel, 'Women's Periodicals and the New Journalism,' 245.
37. Qtd. in Tusan, *Women Making News*, 114.
38. Willard, 'Mrs. Sarah Tooley,' 170.
39. Elizabeth Robins, 1911. Qtd. in Sowon S. Park, 'The First Professional: The Women Writers Suffrage League,' *Modern Language Quarterly* 57, no. 2 (1997), 187.
40. Willard, 'Mrs. Sarah Tooley,' 171.
41. Willard, 'Mrs. Sarah Tooley,' 171.
42. 'Pageant of Famous Men and Women,' *Times* (June 30, 1914), 11.
43. Willard, 'Mrs. Sarah Tooley,' 171.
44. Margaret Beetham, *A Magazine of Her Own? Domesticity and Desire in the Woman's Magazine 1800–1914* (London: Routledge, 1996), 128–129; Onslow, *Women of the Press*, 21. On the masquerade of femininity, see also Hilary Fraser, Stephanie Green, and Judith Johnston, *Gender and the Victorian Periodical* (Cambridge: Cambridge University Press, 2003), 44–45.
45. Willard, 'Mrs. Sarah Tooley,' 171.
46. Sarah A. Tooley, 'Child Life: A Talk with the Author of 'Lord Fauntleroy,'' *Woman's Signal* (11 April 1895), 226.

47. Sarah A. Tooley, 'The Servant Question: An Interview with Miss Clementina Black,' *Woman's Signal* (31 January 1895), 66.
48. Sarah A. Tooley, 'An Interview with Annie S. Swan (Mrs. Swan Burnett),' *Woman at Home* 4 (May 1895), 129.
49. Sarah A. Tooley, 'The Labour Commission: Interview with Mrs. Sidney Webb,' *Woman's Signal* (12 July 1894), 18.
50. Sarah A. Tooley, 'The Ethical Basis of Women's Rights: An Interview with Rev. Prof. Shuttleworth, M.A.,' *Woman's Signal* (10 May 1894), 382.
51. Sarah A. Tooley, 'The Woman's International Conference,' *Lady's Realm* (May 1899), 90–95, rpt. in *Eve's Century: A Sourcebook of Writings on Women and Journalism 1895–1918*, ed. Anne Varty (London: Routledge, 2000), 161.
52. Sarah A. Tooley, 'The Servant Question,' 66.
53. Sarah A. Tooley, 'Life amongst Factory Girls: An Interview with Miss Isabel Kenward,' *Woman's Signal* (18 October 1894), 242.
54. Sarah A. Tooley, 'Interesting Reminiscences: A Talk with Mrs. Josephine Butler,' *Woman's Signal* (13 September 1894), 161.
55. Sarah A. Tooley, 'Women's Work in School Management: An Interview with Miss Harris,' *Woman's Signal* (5 April 1894), 222.
56. Sarah A. Tooley, 'The Horticultural College, Swanley: A Day with the Lady Gardeners,' *Woman's Signal* (26 July 1894), 50.
57. Tusan, *Women Making News*, 125.
58. Fraser, Green, and Johnston, *Gender and the Victorian Periodical*, 227.
59. Tooley, 'Child Life,' 227.
60. Sarah A. Tooley, 'The Author of "Little Lord Fauntleroy" at Home: An Interview with Mrs. Hodgson Burnett,' *Young Woman* 3, no. 32 (May 1895), 257.
61. Tooley, 'The Labour Commission,' 17.
62. Tooley, 'The Labour Commission,' 18.
63. Sarah A. Tooley, 'The Growth of a Socialist: An Interview with Mrs. Sidney Webb,' *Young Woman* 3, no. 29 (September 1895), 151.
64. Rubinstein, *Before the Suffragettes*, 86–87; Onslow, *Women of the Press*, 31–33.
65. Stead, 'Young Women and Journalism,' 13.
66. Billington, 'Journalism as a Profession for Women,' 10.
67. Sarah A. Tooley, 'A Living Wage for Women: A Talk with William Morris,' *Woman's Signal* (19 April 1894), 261.
68. Sarah A. Tooley, 'Flints, Suffrage, and Higher Education: An Interview with Mrs. Charlotte Carmichael Stopes,' *Woman's Signal* (6 June1895), 354.
69. Sarah A. Tooley, 'The Home of a Great Preacher: An Interview with Mrs. Joseph Parker,' *Young Woman* 3, no. 28 (1895), 115.
70. Willard, 'Mrs. Sarah Tooley,' 170.
71. Lawrence, '"Interviewing",' 446.
72. Lawrence, '"Interviewing",' 441.
73. Lawrence, '"Interviewing",' 441; Fraser, Green, and Johnston, *Gender and the Victorian Periodical*, 41.
74. Lawrence, '"Interviewing",' 445.
75. Lawrence, '"Interviewing",' 446.
76. Willard, 'Mrs. Sarah Tooley,' 171.
77. For Tooley's points on women interviewers see Willard, 'Mrs. Sarah Tooley,' 170; Lawrence, '"Interviewing",' 446. Crawford and Banks are quoted in Onslow, *Women of the Press*, 54–55.
78. Willard, 'Mrs. Sarah Tooley,' 170.

79. Willard, 'Mrs. Sarah Tooley,' 170.
80. Willard, 'Mrs. Sarah Tooley,' 170.
81. Lawrence, '"Interviewing",' 441.
82. Sarah A. Tooley, 'The Triumph of Woman,' *Every Woman's Encyclopaedia*, vol. 6 (London: Amalgamated Press, [1912]), 4019.
83. Robert J. Blackham, *Woman: In Honour and Dishonour* (London: Sampson, Low, Marston, & Co., [1936]).

11
Ella Hepworth Dixon: Storming the Bastille, or Taking it by Stealth?

Valerie Fehlbaum
University of Geneva

If the journalist Ella Hepworth Dixon is mentioned today, her name is usually associated with her New Woman novel, *The Story of a Modern Woman*. This novel, however, only represents a very small proportion of its author's overall output. Not only did Dixon publish other works of fiction, including her less well-known *My Flirtations* and countless short stories, but for over 40 years she earned her living by contributing on a regular basis to various periodicals. Moreover, albeit for a very brief spell, Dixon even became that *rara avis*, a woman editor, and on her death in 1932 was considered worthy of an obituary in the *Times*.[1] Journalism, therefore, provided Dixon with a certain amount of fame and fortune, and occasionally material for fiction. A close analysis of her work, both fictional and non-fictional, reveals much about her own attitude to her profession, while at the same time providing deeper insights into the problematics of journalism as a career for British women in general at the end of the nineteenth century.

The Story of a Modern Woman was initially published in 1894 to great acclaim, then confined to the *oubliettes* of literary history for decades, only to be re-discovered towards the end of the twentieth century during the first wave of renewed interest in *fin-de-siècle* women writers. Consequently it was republished by Merlin in 1990 in their Radical Fiction series and then by Broadview in 2004.[2] Described by John Sutherland in *The Longman Companion to Victorian Fiction* as 'one of the finest New Woman novels',[3] it recounts the intertwined destinies of two young women friends, both 'modern' in their individual ways. One, Alison Ives, is an angel out of the house doing good works amongst the poor in the East End of London before her almost inevitable marriage; the other, Mary Erle is orphaned and left to fend not only for herself, but also to take care of her younger brother. 'Wish[ing] to make her way in the world and compete with men',[4] she eventually embarks on a career in journalism.

In *Woman* in September 1896 in a series entitled 'My Faith and My Work',[5] Dixon speaks of her conception of the novel:

> *The Story of a Modern Woman* (which was written by-the-bye in 1892–3, before the rush of 'woman-books' began) was an effort to show how unequal is the struggle between the sexes – a struggle which has never been so bitter in the history of the world before – for the things that are most worth having.[6]

Then and now, however, the novel has been read as largely autobiographical, and, of course, even the initials of the two female protagonists, 'A.I.' and 'M.E.', encourage such interpretations. There are also certain undeniable similarities in particular between the apprentice writer and her creator. Like Mary Erle, Dixon (1857–1932) had originally set out to pursue a career in art, but, on the sudden death of her father in 1879, had had to revise her ambitions and think about ways of earning a living. As the daughter of William Hepworth Dixon, long time editor of *The Athenaum* (1853–1869), Dixon must, again like Mary Erle, have benefited from family connections, especially her father's name, at the start of her career. As one of Mary Erle's editors commented: 'The name, of course ... the name counts for *something*. Your late father's name carries weight with a *certain* section of the public.'[7] Nevertheless, when the novel was published in book form by Heinemann some of the most obviously autobiographical details which had appeared in the serialized version in the *Lady's Pictorial* – such as the whole of the original third chapter, entitled 'Wonderings', which traces the heroine's education in Germany – were removed. These passages, nevertheless, remained in Cassell's American edition which might suggest that in England where she would have been better known, the author was deliberately trying to draw attention away from her own life, and complicate an autobiographical reading.

Moreover, throughout the story Dixon emphasizes the enormous discrepancies between life 'as it is' and artistic representations, or *mis*representations, of life. At the Central London School of Art, where early in the novel Mary Erle spends many dreary months, painting from life is considered a 'kind of frivolous extra'.[8] Later, when she learns of her lover's betrayal the scene takes place in a fashionable theatre where 'the foolish, inane, unreal comedy on stage',[9] 'so adorably *untrue to life*' (emphasis added), is in sharp contrast to 'the hideous comedy going on in the box'[10] where Vincent Hemming is seated with Miss Higgins, the vulgar yet wealthy woman he will marry in order to further his career. Ironically, too, Mary is told by one newspaper editor that her realistic novel would not please the British public which 'doesn't expect [novels] to be like life' and wants 'a thoroughly breezy, healthy tone'[11] with a happy ending. When Mary insists that she 'can't help seeing things as they are' and adds, 'I thought ... that the public would take anything – in a newspaper', she is told 'Not in fiction'.[12] At the same time the narrative is regularly punctuated by 'spesh-shul' editions offering the latest 'revolting details' in a celebrity divorce, and Mary even overhears the editor giving instructions to another contributor to touch up photographs of the co-respondents. The truth might be 'supremely attractive' to the likes of Mary, but readers are left to draw their own conclusions about the integrity of some editors.

In the 'Foreword' to her memoirs, entitled *As I Knew Them: Sketches of People I Have Met Along the Way*, published in 1930, Dixon also relates an incident which should put readers on their guard against drawing hasty conclusions from artistic representations. She tells of a young man being so enamoured of her portrait that he tried to persuade her mother to sell it to him, but he 'promptly fled from the house' when she appeared in person, 'grubby with oil-paint ... dressed in an unbecoming black jersey'.[13] Dixon claims that the anecdote reveals her capacity for laughing at herself, and indeed humour was perennially important to her, a topic to which I shall return. The story additionally testifies to Dixon's conception of the multi-faceted aspects of an individual, and the unreliability of artistic impressions. *The Story of a Modern Woman* is similarly multi-faceted, both revealing and concealing, and it would be reductive to consider it only in simple autobiographical terms.

In fact the novel contains much more than merely the fictionalized memoirs of a novice in Fleet Street. It paints, for instance, a highly critical picture of the artistic world in London, a subject dear to the author and one which she regularly discoursed upon in both her fiction and non-fiction. Furthermore, through the character of Alison Ives, the novel encapsulates in many ways Dixon's fundamental belief in 'a kind of moral and social trades-unionism among women', as summed up in her interview for W.T. Stead's 1894 overview of 'The Novel of the Modern Woman'.[14] Then, most importantly, through Mary Erle, the book reveals Dixon's somewhat ambivalent attitude towards the periodical press which, although it provided her with a livelihood for over four decades, was fraught with difficulties for women who wanted to be taken seriously in the journalistic profession.

From the opening pages of the novel the reader is presented with less than flattering images of newspapermen, intruding on private grief for their various publications:

> There was the brisk, smartly-dressed young gentleman who came to do a leader for a daily paper, who had a wandering, observant eye and a leather notebook, and who proceeded to make a number of notes in shorthand, asking innumerable questions as his omnivorous glance travelled rapidly round the study. Another press-man – a small, apologetic man with greyish hair and a timid cough – asked to see the house for the *Evening Planet*. He begged of Elizabeth on the hall steps to tell him if the

Professor had said anything – anything particular, which would work up as a leader.[15]

Not long afterwards at a fashionable kettledrum hosted by her friend's mother, Mary Erle meets society journalists Bosanquet-Barry, the new editor of the *Comet*, 'pluck(ed) nice and hot from Oxford ... who has none of the old hackneyed Fleet Street ideas',[16] and Beaufort Flower, representatives of 'the new idea in journalism', the two of whom, much to her dismay, engage in 'whispering malicious things of one's host or hostess behind their backs'.[17] Later still, when Mary ventures into Grub Street itself, depicted as a decidedly unsavoury place for a young woman, she encounters more unpleasant representatives of the fourth estate, primarily interested in gossip about 'smart people'.

Dixon's career in journalism

By the time the novel was published, Dixon was in her late 30s and had been earning her living by her pen for several years, so she could speak of journalism from first-hand experience. In her memoirs she writes of her 'singularly happy working life',[18] and describes her early years in the profession as trouble-free and light-hearted: 'These journalistic activities were mixed up with a great deal of dancing and dining out; white tulle skirts and natty little laced up bodices took the place of an evening of inky fingers.'[19] Readers will recall the very different début assigned to Mary Erle who spends long, lonely evenings in a gloomy bedsit, experiencing 'the horror of waiting, waiting, waiting'[20] for her lover to return. This may be another distancing technique to distinguish the fictional representation from the real-life writer, or represent a deliberate attempt to minimize her own early difficulties, for Dixon's comments elsewhere, such as in the above-mentioned *Woman* article, indicate she experienced a rather more turbulent working atmosphere than her memoirs later suggested. As late as 1925, writing in the *Westminster Gazette* on opportunities for women, Dixon maintains: 'One of the last citadels to fall was the newspaper office. Here prejudice reigned supreme.'[21] Fortunately, she could conclude, 'But today the Bastille of Journalism has fallen', although her choice of metaphors is surely indicative of the 'bitter' hostilities which women had to overcome in the profession.

As has been well documented by scholars such as Margaret Beetham, Barbara Onslow, and Margaret Stetz,[22] as more and more women took to writing as a career throughout the last decades of the nineteenth century, debates about the role and status of the woman writer increased in intensity and, sometimes, animosity. Dixon herself was painfully aware of such hostility and in one of her early 'Pensées de Femme' columns in the *Lady's Pictorial* even claimed 'I have always been led to suppose, by a perusal of the so-called humorous papers, that if there was one thing on earth which the average man loathed, it was a female writer'.[23] Whilst it might have been considered acceptable for a lady to produce works of fiction or society articles from the safe confines of her private home, entering the public sphere of newspaper offices was an entirely different matter, and openly deplored. In *The Story of a Modern Woman*, for instance, Mary Erle tells her doctor, 'Aunt Julia ... thinks I am given over to the Evil One since I've become a journalist'.[24] In her memoirs Dixon herself admits that in the 'gay nineties' when she 'spent a winter Season in New York', she: 'was *prudent enough* to conceal the fact that [she] had ever written for any journal. A "newspaper woman", over there, had no social standing whatever.'[25] Within a few years, however, the situation must have changed, for in 1900 Dixon signed at least one article in the *New York Independent*.[26] Significantly, it was Americans such as Nellie Bly and Elizabeth Banks who became notorious for engaging in spectacular sensational journalism in the 1880s and 1890s and cited as examples not to be imitated. The British woman journalist, therefore, found herself in an uncomfortable hinterland, unwelcome in the public domain and somewhat ostracized in the private sphere.

As if to refute the '[u]ngallant suspicions ... so frequently cast upon the social and domestic capacities of the writing-woman',[27] many of the articles about women in journalism were accompanied by attractive photographs and flattering verbal images of their so-called womanly skills away from their desks. For instance, in the *Lady's Pictorial* series on 'Lady Journalists', which began in November 1893, whether describing Mrs. Crawford, Miss Emily Faithful, Mrs. Roy Devereux, Mrs. Meynell, or Ella Hepworth Dixon, much emphasis is placed on their 'womanliness', their 'unvarying kindness and courtesy', 'their unimpeachable taste', and their overall refinement.[28] Dixon similarly took care to emphasize the femininity of her fictional women writers. In 'A Scribbler's Comedy', for example, a short story published in *Pall Mall Magazine* in 1895, Dixon creates such a 'radiant vision' in the character of 'John Bathurst', the *nom de plume* of an older, much more glamorous Mary Erle, who gets the better of her editor, largely because he is so charmed by her appearance. 'He objected, in the first place, to the presence of women in newspaper offices', but she is so unlike his usual impression 'of lady journalists in *pince-nez* and women in waterproofs', she 'seemed to illuminate the dingy newspaper office'.[29]

Interestingly, this is the story which Dixon altered most when it was republished in her 1904 collection of short stories, revealing changes perhaps in her own interests as well as those of her reading public. In the original, 'John Bathurst' wrote a collection of short stories entitled 'Yearnings', 'a study in modern femininity' dealing with the 'New Revolt', possibly reminiscent of notorious New Woman writer George Egerton and her *Keynotes* (1893) and *Discords* (1894), which had caused such a sensation when they openly confronted traditional ideas about women, especially their sexual and emotional desires.[30] 'John Bathurst''s editor, who 'hated these squealing women',[31] ultimately offers her a column on the Woman Question, so much in vogue in the 1890s. In the republished version the protagonist writes not fictional texts, but political essays on Free Trade, and in the end her motivations are discovered to be the forwarding of the political career of her husband, a contingency the 'unimaginative' editor had never considered.

The New Woman phenomenon had been extremely shortlived and by 1904 more women were campaigning for practical political advantages. Never a militant herself, Dixon prided herself on being able to gauge and adjust to prevalent trends which would interest her readers. As she remarked in one of her 'Pensées de Femme',

> Irate masculine critics have sometimes accused me of cultivating too high a standard for my sex. ... It is a real pleasure for me to gossip, week by week, to women in *Lady's Pictorial*. Every now and again I get an agreeable note, I hear an appreciative phrase, which tell me I am in touch with many of my readers. It is a privilege, indeed, not to be lightly regarded, that of being able to catch the ear, to put, as it were, one's finger on the pulse of so large a feminine public. In all that makes for progress, for sanity, for purity, for health, I am with them heart and soul.[32]

Dixon and her editors

In the *Westminster Gazette* article mentioning the 'Bastille' of journalism, Dixon openly criticizes some of the earlier prejudices of editors, in particular the limitations they imposed on women:

> Hardly one was broad-minded enough to 'give woman her head' in their columns. The famous exceptions of Mrs Crawford, the Paris correspondent, and of Flora Shaw and 'The Thunderer' only proved the rule.

Women (unless it was fiction) must only write in the 'Woman's Page' and not intrude into the more serious and sacred parts of the paper. A female person might be the greatest actress of her time, or even a successful dramatist, but never, by any chance, could she be entrusted to criticize a play. As to affairs, foreign or domestic, who wanted her opinion? Pictures? She might paint them, but she must not aspire to point out their qualities or defects.[33]

Dixon nevertheless concedes that editors were 'often delightful persons, full of a sly humour',[34] and in her memoirs she gives the impression that she, rather like 'John Bathurst', came into little direct conflict with them. Dixon begins the chapter entitled 'Some Editors':

> Having been an editor myself, I understand the trials, the unutterable boredom, the delerious excitement, the difficulty of 'suffering fools gladly', the delight of pouncing on the right man or woman for one's purpose, which make up the excitement of such a personage.[35]

Unfortunately, so far no external accounts have come to light of her short-lived period in the 'editorial arm-chair',[36] as she calls it in the above-mentioned *Woman* article on 'My Faith and My Work', nor is there evidence of her working for a woman editor, although she claims in her memoirs, 'A woman editor, like a woman doctor, is usually more stiff and uncompromising'.[37] Dixon's accounts of her dealings with men editors, however, suggest a trouble-free existence. She describes, for instance, being approached by several eminent editors such as the first Lord Burnham:

> One day I received a little letter from him saying he had read everything which I had written, and asking me to contribute regularly to the *Daily Telegraph*. The result was a number of travel articles, which were more popular in the late Victorian era than now.[38]

Dixon also devotes an entire chapter to Lord Northcliffe, and describes how Sir Alfred Harmsworth sent for her when he envisaged setting up the *Daily Mirror* initially intended as a daily paper for women. In the same section she relates 'a thrilling moment' at a dinner party given by William Heinemann when her host called out, 'Have you heard that Alfred Harmsworth is buttonholing everybody he sees to say you are the only journalist who knows how to write?'.[39] Moreover, it would seem that she herself was not restricted to the 'Woman's Page'. For example, she writes,

> From early on, I had the good fortune to be a constant contributor to the *Daily Mail*, where I did articles on general subjects for the middle page. As long as Mr. Thomas Marlowe was in the editorial chair, I had only to 'ring up,' suggest a subject and it was taken.[40]

Are these anecdotes again a case of a selective memory, or more evidence of Dixon's ingenuity in manoeuvring her way diplomatically around Fleet Street? Her overall conclusion in 1930 is 'Who, indeed, can say that Fleet Street is unfriendly?'[41], but, as the slightly earlier *Westminster Gazette* article revealed, friendliness did not necessarily signify respect or equality, and in the 1890s there was rather more antagonism than Dixon cared to recall in her memoirs.

One of the most famous contemporary contributions to the debate about women's place in the *fin-de-siècle* newspaper office was Arnold Bennett's *Journalism for Women*, subtitled *A Practical Guide*, and published in 1898. Ever ready to defend her sex, Dixon understandably took umbrage at some of Arnold Bennett's comments. In chapter II, for instance, he declares

> In Fleet Street, there are not two sexes, but two species – journalists and women-journalists... . And we treat these two species differently. They are not expected to suffer the same discipline, nor are they judged by

the same standards. In Fleet Street femininity is an absolution, not an accident.[42]

In one of her more serious 'Pensées de Femme' columns, Dixon retorts:

It is humiliating for the sex to be told at a public dinner, and by no less an authority than the literary critic of the *Daily Telegraph*, not only that we cannot spell, but that we cannot punctuate our sentences. Then, to make matters worse, the editor of a woman's penny paper has written a little book to tell us how to succeed in journalism – a book in which he duly notes the woman-journalist's unbusiness-like habits, her irresponsibility, and – her tendency to devastating headaches![43]

The literary critic to whom she refers might well be W.L. Courtney and 'the editor of a woman's penny paper' must be Arnold Bennett who edited *Woman* and whose *Guide* had been published earlier that year. Dixon then goes on to enumerate various highly successful women journalists such as Mrs. Beer, Miss Flora Shaw, Mrs. Crawford, and Mrs. Meynell, to discredit the idea that 'any one can seriously contend that women have failed in journalism'.[44]

It could be argued in his defence that Arnold Bennett was primarily trying to discourage amateurism and promote a more disciplined, business-like attitude in women writers which would ideally remove any sexual discrimination within the profession, a worthy aim which Dixon would surely have condoned. Furthermore, it should be remembered that in the Victorian literary world in general journalism was often regarded, even for men, as somewhat suspect. For instance, in J. M. Barrie's *When a Man's Single*, singled out by Arnold Bennett as a 'brilliant novel [which] should be studied by every young journalist',[45] a short exchange between the hero's beloved and her mother is revelatory:

'... he is evidently to be a newspaper man all his life.'
'I wish you would say journalist, mamma ... or literary man. The profession of letters is a noble one.'
'Perhaps it is ... but I can't think it is very respectable.'[46]

In the *Guide*, on the other hand, Arnold Bennett regularly refers to the '*art* of journalism' (emphasis added), and his concluding sentences precisely accentuate his desire for greater respect for the profession from those on the inside as well as the outside:

A vast number of women engaged in journalism, I verily believe regard it as a delightful game. The tremendous seriousness of it they completely miss. ... Therefore, my final words to the outside contributor ... are these: Journalism is not a game, and in journalism there are no excuses.[47]

This sentiment is highly reminiscent of two earlier articles on journalism published in *Woman* in a series entitled 'What Women May Do,' signed 'The Editor', in which the author insists:

> From the first let me say I am not going to encourage every girl and woman who occasionally pens an essay or a short story, with or without the satisfaction of seeing it in print, in the belief that she is a journalist. I have not space to deal with amateur journalism, out of which a large number of women make a very small number of pounds per annum, and from which they appear to have no ambition to soar into the higher flights of the profession.[48]

Dixon in fact worked with Arnold Bennett for several years whilst he was editor of *Woman* and received nothing but glowing praise in the pages of his magazine. For example, in December 1894 her 'two first books' are described as 'among the most successful publications of the past few years',[49] and the article concludes:

> Miss Hepworth Dixon is much sought after by editors because she writes carefully, punctually, and honestly, never 'scamping', and having only one quality of work; and her clear bold handwriting is a thing of joy to printers.[50]

Dixon was clearly not one of the unprofessional women Arnold Bennett was targeting. In her memoirs she describes him as 'a gay and kindly editor',[51] so there can have been no lasting enmity between the two.

Both inside and outside the literary industry, however, heated arguments continued to abound on what was appropriate for women to discuss in what remained largely a male-dominated profession. The literary world seemed to be trying to maintain clearly defined separate spheres according to gender. These efforts were especially intense during the heyday of the New Woman, when some women writers such as Sarah Grand and Mona Caird dared to write on subjects which society deemed unsuitable for their sex. In an early chapter in her memoirs, Dixon relates another occasion on which she preferred to hide her identity. Describing her own professional début, she informs readers, 'One of the first newspapers I wrote for was *The World*. Mr. Edmund Yates, undismayed by my youth and inexperience, printed countless short stories of mine and various articles of travel'.[52] She continues: 'A series of short stories was running in the paper called "Town and Country Tales." They had to be what nurses used to call "owdacious." Mine were terribly "knowing".'[53] Most of these were anonymous or signed merely with initials, as was customary in journals at that time. Dixon then relates dancing with a young man who, by way of polite conversation, asks if she has read the latest 'Town and Country Tale', and immediately corrects himself, not knowing that she herself had actually written 'the obnoxious story', saying, 'I don't think it's quite the kind of story you ought to read'.[54] Dixon's reaction is revelatory: 'For a moment I hesitated, and then, being a young person of discretion, I remained silent. Why spoil my evening?'[55]

On one level this could be interpreted as the typical silencing of the female voice. Dixon's final comment, however, hints rather at a skilful capacity for making the most of a difficult situation and, ultimately, serving her own ends. For, indeed, what was to be gained from speaking out? Self-preservation was surely of primary importance. It was certainly a strategy which Dixon employed regularly and is arguably symptomatic of her entire professional life, revealing her astute ability to circumvent the minefields of prejudice surrounding women, especially writing women. Towards the end of her career, in another of her *Westminster Gazette* articles, Dixon herself admitted 'with humiliation that I have never "burned for my faith" at all', and added, 'which is a shameful thing'.[56] This statement might attract scorn from more engaged activists, but at the same time it could help to explain why, in spite of much continued hostility towards literary women, Dixon managed to remain permanently in work, became a selling point for journals herself, and, as mentioned earlier, was even engaged as editor of a woman's magazine. Moreover, she always showed tremendous respect for those who were politically engaged, while castigating those who actively campaigned against voting rights for women. For example, in one of her *Lady's Pictorial* columns Dixon writes:

> Because excellent Mrs Blank, seated placidly in her mansion at Streatham, with a panting motor at the door waiting to convey her to an Anti-Suffrage meeting, has no political ambitions, it is, I take it, at least unfair that she should in any way try to prevent her more public-spirited sisters from attaining the object for which they have made so many and such heroic sacrifices.[57]

My Flirtations and the uses of anonymity

Anonymity could clearly have advantages. Dixon's *My Flirtations* first appeared anonymously in the *Lady's Pictorial* from January to April, 1892, before being published in book form by Chatto and Windus under the pseudonym of 'Margaret Wynman', a pen-name Dixon then used on several other occasions. In her memoirs Dixon writes that she never owned to the authorship of *My Flirtations*, although when *The Story of a Modern Woman* began in serial form in the *Lady's Pictorial* it was signed 'Ella Hepworth Dixon, ("Margaret Wynman," Author of "My Flirtations")'.[58] Moreover, in the above-mentioned article on 'My Faith and My Work' published in *Woman* in September 1896, Dixon had already 'lifted the black gauze veil of Anonymity'.[59] In the article she describes herself as 'a woman with a literary burden on her conscience', and alleges embarrassment at 'so frivolous a book'. At the same time she also raises an issue which several other women writers such as Alice Meynell would tackle more forcefully: authors, especially women, rarely had any control over the actual packaging and promoting of a literary work.

> This booklet bore the egregious title ... of *My Flirtations*, and had clothed itself, unbeknown to the author, in a cover of violent pink, on which some person who will be for ever hateful to me had designed, with considerable archness, a silver fan. Oh, that title; oh, that cover; oh, that silver fan! What have I not suffered from the very thoughts of you?[60]

It is difficult to gauge the exact veracity of Dixon's claims, and modern readers may even find the original cover rather charming. Nevertheless, when *My Flirtations* appeared in the American edition the cover had become green with a simple gold embossed design, suggesting perhaps that her complaints were sincere and had been addressed.

In spite of Dixon's reservations about its appearance, she reports that the work was nonetheless well-received: 'This tiny collection of lampoons enjoyed its chief vogue among heads of colleges at Oxford and Cambridge, among judges in the High Courts, and other folk of a sedate turn in England and America'.[61] In addition, 'Much to the surprise of the author, the journals which she most dreaded, the *Saturday Review*, the *Speaker*, *Spectator*, *Athenaeum*, and the like, were friendly in their criticisms'.[62] Her conclusion is 'Such, it will be seen, are the advantages of *frivolous* anonymity'.[63] Dixon may be implying that had they known the identity of the author of the 'booklet', as she calls it, such readers would not have been so enthusiastic. The critic in the *Lady's Pictorial*, in fact, suggests an almost wilful desire to confuse or arouse curiosity:

> It is not for me to say whether the owner of the clever pen, and the observant eyes, is not already known to the world under another name. In fact, I have my own strong suspicions as to the sex of the writer, and I should not be at all surprised to learn that the pseudonym hides the identity of a well-known literary man. The secret, of course, remains hidden in the breast of the Editor, but I feel sure that my opinion is not without foundation.[64]

However mysterious the authorial identity, the work was certainly enthusiastically reviewed. Barbara in *Woman's* 'Book Chat', for example, begins, 'A prettily bound and exceptionally clever and amusing little series of sketches is *My Flirtations* ...'[65] and adds, 'This little volume ... is much better worth reading than many more pretentious volumes'. Robert Ross in *The Saturday Review* declares:

> The older humour is not dead after all – at least the announcement was premature – and the lady who writes under the name of Margaret

Wynman has vindicated her sex from the old charge of having no appreciation of humour, old or new. *My Flirtations* is one of the most amusing books we have come across for a long time.[66]

Even the critic in *Punch*, famed for its satirical and often highly misogynistic comments, claims, 'It is a literary portfolio of lively sketches of men and women, "their tricks and their manners," all most amusing and told in a naturally easy and epigrammatic style'.[67]

In her memoirs Dixon asserts of *My Flirtations*, 'As it had a foolish title (suggested for publishing reasons) I never owned to its authorship ...'.[68] Letters exchanged between the author and the publishers, however, reveal no mention at all of any desire to change the title. On the other hand, they continually express concern about 'what name is to be given on the title page'. A day after offering Dixon 35 pounds for the reproduction of her 'social sketches entitled *My Flirtations*' Andrew Chatto (who, rather like Mary Erle's editors, notoriously liked a name) wrote to Dixon's sister, Marion, on the subject:

> I had not noticed that 'My Flirtations' were published anonymously, and was under the impression that your sister would put her own name to a publication of the sketches in book form. I would always advise authors to secure to their own names any popularity that may attract to a success, by always publishing in their own names – most pseudonyms are open secrets – But this is not a point I would press in opposition to your sister's wishes, if on consideration she decides to adopt some other pen name.[69]

Chatto and Windus' desire for Dixon to use her own name might also indicate that Dixon's name had acquired a certain value in its own right, since her famous father had by then been dead for well over ten years. Although her contributions to Edmund Yates' *The World* remained largely anonymous, Dixon's signature had already appeared in full in the *Sunday Times* as early as January 1888 below a short story entitled 'Dr Patmore's Patient'.[70] After that she had contributed several signed 'Chats with Celebrities' to the same paper. Simultaneously, she had worked with Oscar Wilde when he took over the editorship of *The Woman's World*, apparently receiving 'the unstinted praise which is so rare in Editors'[71] from Wilde himself for a signed story entitled 'Murder - or Mercy?'[72] which contains some embryonic elements Dixon would later rework into *The Story of a Modern Woman*. She had also attracted the notice of the anonymous reviewer in the *St. James's Gazette* who noted her appeal to readers of both sexes:

> Mr Oscar Wilde and his enchanting fashion plates combine to make *The Woman's World* attractive; and there is much in the magazine which, primarily intended for feminine delectation, is of quite equal importance to such persons as husbands and brothers. Of such are Miss Hepworth

Dixon's paper about 'Women on Horseback' and Miss Evelyne Moore's brightly written article about Angelica Kaufmann.[73]

And slightly later, Dixon's name was again mentioned in the 'Review of August Magazines':

> *The Woman's World* is a capital magazine for a married man to buy. He tells his wife he got it entirely for her sake; but he may always find some very good reading for himself... . Miss Ella Hepworth Dixon gives a very learned and amusing, plentifully illustrated article on 'Cloaks in Europe' (sic) from the days of Frédégonde, the wife of Chilpéric, down to the time when our mothers were young.[74]

By her own account Dixon also

> contributed a few 'interviews at home' of some personal friends [until] Wilde decided, very wisely, to end the series. 'People,' he wrote, 'are beginning to tire of the silver ink-pots, the Persian rug, the brass paper-weight, the palms in pots... .'[75]

Dixon recognizes: 'He was right. Made attractive at first by Edmund Yates in *The World*, this kind of journalism had become passably absurd.'[76] At the end of the same year, a short story, 'A Winter Idyll'[77] signed in Dixon's own name, appeared in *The Lady's Pictorial Christmas Number*, and thus began Dixon's long collaboration with that magazine, which only ended in March 1921 when it amalgamated with *Eve*.

Within three years Dixon's name had definitely become famous enough to be considered worth mentioning in advertisements. For example, the announcement for *The Special Winter Number of 'Woman'* of 1891 declared, 'Every Story, Article, and Illustration will be the work of a Woman', and specifically drew attention to 'A short story by Ella Hepworth Dixon', the only other named author being Mrs. Edward Kennard. After the success of *My Flirtations*, *The Special Holiday Number of 'Woman'* in 1893 again used Dixon's pen-name in its advertisement as one of its 'special features': "a ROMANTIC STORY by MARGARET WYNMAN, Author of "MY FLIRTATIONS"'. It is interesting to note that in a much later exchange of letters between Dixon and Grant Richards in1904, before the publication of her collection of short stories entitled *One Doubtful Hour and Other Sidelights on the Feminine Temperament*, the publisher expresses reservations about the financial success of a collection of short stories '*even with your name*'.[78]

Why, therefore, would Dixon hesitate to put her name to *My Flirtations*? Perhaps because the sketches skated rather too close to recognizable figures. As the title and her chosen pseudonym suggest, *My Flirtations* ostensibly recounts the narrator's 'adventures in the labyrinth of love', to quote from

The Sketch review, and 'in the form of thirteen masterly little sketches, or skits' details 'her impressions of latter-day Lotharios', to use Robert Ross's words in *The Saturday Review*. It compiled a series of twelve individual sketches originally published in the *Lady's Pictorial* with one new addition, according to *The Sketch* critic 'the most daringly thin disguise of an actual personality'.[79] Similar comments by other critics indicate that much fun must have been had by contemporaries trying to identify if not the author at least the author's real-life models for the sketches, including (it was postulated) Oscar Wilde and Richard Le Gallienne. 'Readers who are "in the know" - which is nineteenth century for that tame and simple expression "behind the scenes" will recognize some of the portraits which Margaret Wynman has described with such *merciless fidelity*' observes 'Blue Stocking' in the *Lady's Pictorial*,[80] an opinion shared by the *Punch* critic:

> Some of the characters are evidently intended for portraits, which anyone living in the London world could easily label – (which by changing 'a' into 'I' would be the probable consequence) – were he not baffled by the art of the skilful writer, and by the equally skilful illustrator – our Mr. Partridge ...[81]

This may explain in part the real reason for Dixon's wish to remain anonymous. *My Flirtations* is certainly an amusing comedy of manners, but under the surface gaiety Dixon offers a perceptive satire of people and institutions. For instance, Peggy Wynman's father is introduced as a Royal Academician and they 'live in a nest of artists',[82] which allows the author to highlight the shams and snobberies in the English Art world. Lacking in filial loyalty, Peggy remarks that her father 'paints shocking bad portraits, but the British Public is quite unaware of the fact'.[83] Moreover, it appears to be the father's celebrity that attracts some of the suitors more than the daughter's charms. Very little escapes Dixon's sharp eye for significant detail, and by means of a pithy phrase or two, she reveals a great deal about her contemporaries, treating traditionally sacrosanct icons including the home, the family, and marriage with much cynicism. The *Punch* critic even posits that 'the one mistake ... the authoress has made is that of getting herself engaged in the last story', and hopes she will rather: 'be "engaged" on another volume. She can be married at the end of volume three, and may give us her experiences as the wife of Mr. Whoever-it-may-be.'[84]

As well as entertaining readers, therefore, Dixon can be seen to be participating in contemporary debates such as the marriage question, a topic to which she would return, most especially in 'Why Women are Ceasing to Marry', an essay published in *The Humanitarian* in June 1899. Whilst some New Woman writers such as Mona Caird vituperated against marriage, Dixon employed more subtle means to raise important questions about the institution. Echoing sentiments expressed in *The Story of a Modern Woman*, where

Alison Ives claimed a sense of humour is 'what women ought to cultivate above all other things',[85] in *The Humanitarian* article Dixon suggests,

> The reason why women are ceasing to marry must rather be attributed to a shifting feminine point of view, to a more critical attitude towards their masculine contemporaries. If, of late, they would seem to have shown a disposition to avoid the joys, cares, and responsibilities of the linen cupboard, it is chiefly, I think, because *their sense of humour is often as keen as it was once supposed to be blunted.*[86]

Dixon even provocatively maintains 'the modern spinster's lot, in many respects, [is] an eminently attractive one'.[87] Her own unmarried state might naturally have made her more indulgent of spinsterhood, whilst her professional accomplishments proved to the outside world that marriage might no longer be the only means by which a woman could lead a fulfilling life.

Elsewhere Dixon demonstrated that humour could be employed to confound similar contemporary anxieties about the fairer sex. For example, when apparently scientific discoveries such as Krafft-Ebing's *Psychopathia Sexualis* (1882–1902), Max Nordau's *Degeneration* (1895), and Cesare Lombroso's *The Female Offender* (1895) seemingly provided reliable evidence for the public's anxieties about the New Woman, so often associated with decadence and degeneration, Dixon's ironical comments in her weekly column in the *Lady's Pictorial* indicate her capacity to refute such claims without attracting venomous attacks in return:

> I have lately risen from the perusal of Lombroso's pseudo-scientific work, 'The Female Offender,' with the pleasing conviction that I contained in my own person all the physical and mental peculiarities of the born female criminal. I forget now whether I possessed more especially the characteristics of an epileptic murderess or merely those of an hysterical and cataleptic pickpocket ... .[88]

Even the serious business, still largely unsolved, of the wage-earning woman, a subject which must have been dear to her own heart (and purse), Dixon manages to discuss with a certain flippancy: 'I have it on no less an authority than that of Mr George Meredith that men will never have any real respect for women until those women can and do earn as much money as a man. To have money is beside the question.'[89] She concludes: 'So adieu to a life of luxurious ease, matrons and maids of the twentieth century; gird your loins for the battle and thank heaven when ... you can earn enough to support a husband in the luxury in which he has been brought up!'[90]

Humour would certainly seem to be one of the dominant features of Dixon's literary output, and yet, on rare occasions, even she would find it difficult to look on the funny side. After the success of *The Story of a Modern*

Woman, which in her memoirs she herself described as 'a somewhat gloomy study of the struggles of a girl alone in the world and earning her own living,'[91] Dixon concentrated most of her energies on her periodical contributions, never attempting to write another novel, restricting herself to the occasional short story and only once, in 1908, venturing into the world of drama with a one-act play entitled *The Toyshop of the Heart*, performed at The Playhouse, but never published.

For the play Dixon drew on elements from earlier short stories, especially from 'The Kidnapping of Phil Altamore',[92] 'One Doubtful Hour',[93] and 'The World's Slow Stain', at times using almost identical dialogue from the latter. Each story accentuates what in the *Woman* article on 'My Faith and My Work' Dixon referred to as the 'unequal ... struggle between the sexes'. At one point in 'The World's Slow Stain' the female protagonist, Adela Buller, claims:

> I imagined that men were ... good, you know, and that the women who were treated unfairly were the exceptions, and that it was their own fault, generally, if they were. I did not know that women were stuffed with idiotic theories from their very childhood, and that all my life I should suffer, suffer, suffer, for what I had been taught then. We are not told ... what life is, what it all means, or how to play the game. We are like children to whom a pack of cards is thrown, and who are set down to play a strange game with men who are confirmed gamblers. The rules are never told us, so that we blunder helplessly along, and unless we cheat outrageously, or mark the cards, there's small chance of our winning.[94]

She then adds: 'And what's so funny, is that most "good" men like us to be like that, ignorant, silly, helpless – even cheats. They think it pretty.'[95] In the play, Dixon's character, now called Rose Rosalba, repeats the tirade practically word for word, and then, lest one should think she limits her criticism to men only, she engages in a diatribe against other women who lack a sense of feminine solidarity, so much favoured by *The Story of a Modern Woman*'s Alison Ives:

> I wonder if a woman like your mother could realize ... the difficulties, the temptations of a career like mine. ... O, the women of her class are very hard! ... What do they know of life - your 'guarded women' of England? ... Everything has been smoothed, oiled, made easy for the guarded women who judge *us*, and who fight for their men like tigresses if one of them strays our way.[96]

When one considers that the play was part of a charity matinée where the audience must principally have consisted of such middle-class women, it is perhaps not so surprising that, in spite of the favourable reviews, it was not performed again. Nor would Dixon attempt to write again for the theatre although, apparently, there had been plans for a joint venture with H.G. Wells. Apart from her memoirs written over two decades later, Dixon concentrated her subsequent efforts on what she was so obviously best at – writing for the pages of periodicals, where she could engage much more directly and spontaneously with contemporary issues.

After her death in 1932, Dixon's obituary in *The Times* described her as being 'born to journalism'. One is tempted to add 'and dying in it', since she was still contributing articles on a wide range of topics to magazines until the last year of her life. Journalism thus provided Dixon with interesting, purposeful, enjoyable work, which enabled her to promote, in theory and in practice, the cause of other women and to remain an independent bachelor woman herself, as well as being a source of valuable background material for some of her fiction. Her long career reflects many significant changes taking place for both men and women in the publishing world, including a preference for shorter articles and titbits. At the same time Dixon seems to emulate the motto for *Woman*: 'Forward, but not too fast'. Whilst she constantly defended other women and tried to put into practice Alison Ives' beliefs in women helping other women, there were limitations to the inroads made. By her own example, however, writing for periodicals of various kinds throughout her life as well as editing a woman's magazine, and even turning her name into a selling-point for journals, Dixon made important contributions to the development of the profession of journalism for women. Whilst she cannot be said to have stormed the Bastille, she certainly entered it by stealth and made a more comfortable place for herself and for the women who followed her.

Notes

1. Obituary, *The Times* (13 January 1932), 14.
2. For the purposes of this essay, I shall generally refer to the more readily available Broadview edition. See also Ella Hepworth Dixon, *The Story of a Modern Woman*, 1894 (London: Merlin, 1990).
3. John Sutherland, *The Longman Companion to Victorian Fiction* (Harlow: Longman, 1988), 606.
4. Ella Hepworth Dixon, *The Story of a Modern Woman*, 1894, (Peterborough: Broadview, 2004), 98.
5. Dixon was fifth in the series after 'Roy Devereux,' Mrs. Andrew Dean, Alicia Ramsay, and Mrs. Meynell.
6. *Woman* (23 September 1896), 8.
7. Dixon, *Story*, 108; emphasis in original.
8. Dixon, *Story*, 85.
9. Dixon, *Story*, 142.
10. Dixon, *Story*, 140.
11. Dixon, *Story*, 182.
12. Dixon, *Story*, 147.

13. Ella Hepworth Dixon, *As I Knew Them: Sketches of People I Have Met Along the Way* (London: Hutchinson and Company, 1930), 7.
14. W. T. Stead, 'The Novel of the Modern Woman,' *The Review of Reviews*, X (1894), 64–74: 71.
15. Dixon, *Story*, 44.
16. Dixon, *Story*, 93.
17. Dixon, *Story*, 95.
18. Dixon, *As I Knew Them*, 7.
19. Dixon, *Story*, 31.
20. Dixon, *Story*, 121.
21. Ella Hepworth Dixon, 'The Modern Way: A Social Causerie,' *Westminster Gazette* (14 January 1925), 6.
22. Margaret Beetham, *A Magazine of Her Own? Domesticity and Desire in the Woman's Magazine 1800–1914* (London: Routledge, 1996); Barbara Onslow, *Women of the Press in Nineteenth-Century Britain* (Basingstoke: Macmillan, 2000); Margaret Stetz, 'New Grub Street and the Woman Writer of the 1890s,' *New Approaches to British Fiction of the 1890s*, eds Nikki Lee Manos and Meri Jane Rochilson (London: Macmillan, 1994), 21–46.
23. Ella Hepworth Dixon, 'Pensées de Femme,' *Lady's Pictorial* (4 July 1896), 33.
24. Dixon, *Story*, 144.
25. Dixon, *As I Knew Them*, 100; emphasis added.
26. Ella Hepworth Dixon, 'London in Khaki,' *New York Independent* (26 July 1900), 1794–1796.
27. Dixon, 'Pensées de Femme,' *Lady's Pictorial* (4 July 1896), 33.
28. 'Lady Journalists,' *Lady's Pictorial* (11 November 1893), 734; (25 November 1893), 823; (9 December 1893), 928–929; (23 December 1893), 1020, and (10 February 1894), 176–177.
29. Ella Hepworth Dixon, 'A Scribbler's Comedy,' *Pall Mall Magazine* (1895), 286–294: 286.
30. George Egerton, (Mary Chavelita Dunne Bright), (1893) *Keynotes* and (1894) *Discords* (Repr. London: Virago, 1983).
31. Dixon, 'A Scribbler's Comedy,' 286.
32. Ella Hepworth Dixon, 'Pensées de Femme,' *Lady's Pictorial* (26 December 1896), 966.
33. Dixon, 'The Modern Way: A Social Causerie,' *Westminster Gazette* (14 January 1925), 6.
34. Dixon, 'The Modern Way,' 6.
35. Dixon, *As I Knew Them*, 161.
36. It is often thought that Dixon remained editor of *The Englishwoman* from its début in March 1895 until its demise in 1900. In 'My Faith and My Work' she typically makes light of the brevity of her editorial experience: 'Owing to circumstances over which I had no control, in half a year *The Englishwoman* had changed publishers; and nowadays ... my wastepaper basket at least contains only such MSS of my own as I find necessary to reject myself.' 'My Faith and My Work,' *Woman* (23 September 1896), 8.
37. Dixon, *As I Knew Them*, 161.
38. Dixon, *As I Knew Them*, 163.
39. Dixon, *As I Knew Them*, 163.
40. Dixon, *As I Knew Them*, 141.
41. Dixon, *As I Knew Them*, 163.
42. Arnold Bennett, *Journalism for Women* (London: John Lane, 1898), 10.

43. Ella Hepworth Dixon, 'Pensées de Femme,' *Lady's Pictorial* (9 April 1898), 520.
44. Dixon, 'Pensées de Femme,' 520.
45. Bennett, *Journalism for Women*, 48, footnote.
46. J. M. Barrie, *When a Man's Single* (London: Hodder and Stoughton, 1923), 188.
47. Bennett, *Journalism for Women*, 98.
48. 'What Women May Do,' *Woman* (23 March 1892), 3.
49. *Woman* (5 December 1894), 5.
50. *Woman* (5 December 1894), 5.
51. Dixon, *As I Knew Them*, 178.
52. Dixon, *As I Knew Them*, 31.
53. Dixon, *As I Knew Them*, 31.
54. Dixon, *As I Knew Them*, 31. One is here reminded of the earlier case of Rhoda Broughton's father famously forbidding her from reading her own *Cometh up as a Flower* ([1867], Repr. London: Macmillan and Company, 1910).
55. Dixon, *As I Knew Them*, 31.
56. Dixon, 'The Modern Way: A Social Causerie,' *Westminster Gazette* (30 June 1926), 8.
57. Ella Hepworth Dixon, 'Pensées de Femme,' *Lady's Pictorial* (10 April 1909), 566.
58. *Lady's Pictorial* (6 January 1894), 6.
59. Dixon, 'My Faith and My Work,' 8.
60. Dixon, 'My Faith,' 8.
61. Dixon, 'My Faith,' 8.
62. Dixon, 'My Faith,' 8.
63. Dixon, 'My Faith,' 8, emphasis added.
64. 'Blue Stocking' (Miss Curtis), *Lady's Pictorial* (15 October 1892), 583.
65. Barbara, 'Book Chat,' *Woman* (30 November 1892), 12.
66. Robert Ross, *The Saturday Review* (8 October 1892), 419.
67. *Punch* (21 January 1893), 12.
68. Dixon, *As I Knew Them*, 35.
69. Letter dated 28 April, Chatto and Windus archives, University of Reading Archives and Manuscripts Department.
70. Ella Hepworth Dixon, 'Dr. Patmore's Patient,' *Sunday Times* (29 January 1888): 8.
71. Dixon, *As I Knew Them*, 35.
72. Ella Hepworth Dixon, 'Murder - or Mercy?' *The Woman's World* (October, 1888), 466–469.
73. 'Review of March Magazines,' *St. James's Gazette* (1 March 1889), 7.
74. 'Review of August Magazines,' *St. James's Gazette* (29 July 1889), 6.
75. Dixon, *As I Knew Them*, 35.
76. Dixon, *As I Knew Them*, 35. Despite Dixon's disclaimers, this is precisely what many other women journalists were still writing and what Mary Erle's editor asks her to do in *The Story of a Modern Woman*.
77. Ella Hepworth Dixon, 'A Winter Idyl,' *The Lady's Pictorial Christmas Number* (1888), 25–27.
78. Letter dated 18 January 1904, Grant Richards Correspondence, 'Rare books and Specialty Collections' Library, University of Illinois, Urbana-Champaign. Emphasis added. Ella Hepworth Dixon, *One Doubtful Hour and Other Sidelights on the Feminine Temperament* (London: Grant Richards, 1904).
79. L.F.A., 'The Book and Its Story: *My Flirtations' The Sketch* (8 February 1893), 90–91.
80. 'Blue Stocking,' 583; emphasis added.
81. *Punch* (21 January 1893), 12.

82. Ella Hepworth Dixon, ('Margaret Wynman'), *My Flirtations*, (London: Chatto and Windus, 1892), 3.
83. Dixon, *My Flirations*, 2.
84. *Punch* (21 January 1893), 12.
85. Dixon, *Story*, 74.
86. Ella Hepworth Dixon, 'Why Women are Ceasing to Marry,' *The Humanitarian* (June 1899), 391. Emphasis added.
87. Dixon, 'Why Women,' 394.
88. Dixon, 'Pensées de Femme,' *Lady's Pictorial* (July 13, 1895), 49.
89. Dixon, 'Pensées de Femme,' *Lady's Pictorial* (June 29, 1895), 969.
90. Dixon, 'Pensées de Femme,' *Lady's Pictorial* (June 29, 1895), 969.
91. Dixon, *As I Knew Them*, 136.
92. Ella Hepworth Dixon, 'The Kidnapping of Phil Altamore,' *Lady's Pictorial* (25 November, 1899), 805–807.
93. Ella Hepworth Dixon, 'One Doubtful Hour,' *The Lady's Pictorial Christmas Number* (1897), 16–21.
94. Ella Hepworth Dixon, 'The World's Slow Stain,' *Christmas Number of the World* (21 November 1895), 59.
95. Dixon, 'The World's Slow Stain,' 59.
96. Ella Hepworth Dixon, *The Toyshop of the Heart*, (one-act play, performed 1908 at The Playhouse, but never published, mss. held at The British Library), 20–21. Emphasis in original.

12

Journalism's Iconoclast: Rosamund Marriott Watson ('Graham R. Tomson')

Linda K. Hughes
Texas Christian University

As a complex network dependent on the communications circuit identified by Robert Darnton and the ever-shifting concentrations of symbolic capital within the field of cultural production,[1] journalism must be approached in relational terms with due attention to outliers as well as exemplars. Such an approach is particularly needed for one strand within *fin-de-siècle* print culture, woman-of-letters journalism. As Linda H. Peterson has demonstrated, the proliferating periodical and newspaper outlets of the nineteenth century played a key material and social role for nineteenth-century women writers. With new opportunities to publish art or literary criticism, column-writing, travel and biographical sketches, and essays, more women than ever before entered the field of journalism, a great many of them earning distinction as women of letters.[2] One exemplar, whom Peterson examines at length, was Alice Meynell. Meynell began as a poet whose aspirations to future achievement were embedded in the title of her debut volume of 1875, *Preludes*. But upon marrying she diverted her energies from poetry to journalism, collaboratively editing a journal with husband Wilfred Meynell and actively writing literary and art criticism, a domestic model pioneered by William and Mary Howitt. And it served Meynell well. Her essays in the *Scots* (later *National*) *Observer* and in the *Pall Mall Gazette*'s 'Wares of Autolycus', according to Peterson, first won critical acclaim for Meynell as a 'classic' writer who memorably summoned wisdom amidst the transient backdrop of journalism. Her secure niche as a woman of letters then enabled her to relaunch her career as a modern poet.[3]

I begin with Meynell because the journalist whose career I explore, the many-named woman who wrote under the surnames Armytage, Tomson, and Watson,[4] was so closely linked to Meynell's journalistic career yet serves as her inverse image. Both were at the first 'Literary Ladies' dinner in 1889; both simultaneously contributed to W. E. Henley's *Scots Observer* and, later, to the *Pall Mall Gazette*'s 'Wares of Autolycus'; a Meynell interview appeared in *Sylvia's Journal* under the editorship of Graham R. Tomson; and Tomson declared the genius of Meynell's poetry in a 21 January 1893

Academy review, neatly reversing the recent pronouncement of Coventry Patmore (who awarded that designation only to Meynell's prose). *Vespertilia*, Rosamund Marriott Watson's first volume of poems, was even dedicated to Meynell 'in sincere admiration and friendship'.[5]

Yet journalism seemed to operate by different principles in their two careers. If Meynell's first publication was a volume of poems, the young Mrs. Armytage launched her public writing career with an essay on fashion in the 1883 *Fortnightly Review* ('Modern Dress'); if journalism helped relaunch the poetic career of Meynell, the reputation as a talented poet gave Graham R. Tomson new entrées to journalism, beginning with art criticism and a fashion column and climaxing in roles more often associated with men of letters: a recurring role as literary critic reviewing notable poets in the *Academy*, and as editor of her own magazine. If Meynell fashioned herself as a woman of exemplary personal and domestic propriety while pursuing a highly unconventional career and championing suffragism, Graham R. Tomson's path to an active career in journalism lay through divorce, elopement, and a radical renaming of herself that left her free to manoeuvre in London literary and journalistic networks and to capitalize upon the strong impact that her beauty, intelligence, and wit customarily exercised upon others. Both Meynell and Tomson (and, later, Rosamund Marriott Watson) wrote as journalist-aesthetes, but Meynell's marked style was notable for its 'classic' concision and depth of insight against the backdrop of fleeting change, whereas the most appealing journalism of Meynell's younger colleague featured a style founded upon transience, mild daring, scepticism about eternal truths, and insouciant wit that could entertain or mock.[6] In the end Meynell was hailed as a genius in prose by Coventry Patmore and George Meredith and remained known as a significant minor poet decades after her death, while Rosamund Marriott Watson (like the identities of Tomson and Armytage before her) rapidly slipped into obscurity and seemed likely to remain unknown, until the 1990s. Meynell thus demonstrated the possibility of merging high art, journalism, and respectability,[7] whereas her many-named younger colleague and sometime-associate remained an outlier from first to last.

Tomson/Watson's iconoclasm, if less successful than Meynell's strategies, nonetheless points to her significance for studies of *fin-de-siècle* women journalists, since her career likewise contests theoretical and historical premises that are central to such scholarship. If Foucault underscores an author's multiple identities produced by texts,[8] hers are linked as closely to her (unruly) body as to textual conditions, since each authorial identity died with her change in sexual partners (though with massive traces of her former identities left standing in preceding books and periodicals). Even today journalism is largely seen as disjunct from the culturally prestigious medium of poetry, a pattern endorsed by the current volume insofar as it focuses on journalism as an important object of study unto itself. Not only is Armytage–Tomson–Watson's journalistic career difficult to comprehend apart from her poetry, but some of her poetry also blurs the line between the two genres, and does so in self-aware terms. Likewise, the usual roles played by anonymity, signature, and style in histories of journalism and women writers bend and metamorphose in her career, usefully reminding us of the notorious difficulty (if also imperative) of theorizing journalism as a medium in the face of journalism's massive scale and its entrepreneurial logic of ever-increasing diversification to fill – and find – every available niche.

Traditional readings of Kant that stress the free play of the mind and Modernist injunctions again rhetoric have long encouraged critics and scholars to distinguish sharply between poetry (as distinct from doggerel or versifying) and journalism. But a number of recent studies of nineteenth-century poetry have begun to interrogate that distinction. Kathryn Ledbetter's examination of Tennyson's war and political poetry demonstrates the close interconnections among newspaper journalism, public debate, and Tennyson's poetry not only in the canonical 'Charge of the Light Brigade' but also in his other political poems; and Natalie Houston and I have both argued for the crucial role played by poetry in daily and weekly newspapers.[9] The blurring of boundaries between poetry and journalism is evident in Graham R. Tomson's 'After the Fire', published in *Longman's Magazine* in October 1887. In a headnote the lyric identifies its source in a newspaper:

> It was a touching sight in Westbourne Grove on Thursday afternoon when a womanly heart did sudden honour to the funeral of the four poor fellows who lost their lives heroically in the fire. Three open hearses carried coffins, each laden with flowers; but the fourth coffin was entirely bare of any kindly human tribute. At the corner of Hereford Road the flower-girl who stands by the Café Royal saw the sad omission, ran forward into the roadway, and, aided by an attendant, threw her flowers over the coffin. It was generously and instinctively done, without show, and without even stopping the hearse; but it greatly touched all who saw it.

Both the lyric and its headnote, moreover, were printed in Andrew Lang's monthly causerie entitled 'At the Sign of the Ship'. What may have begun as a poetic response to journalism thus became filler in a journalistic commodity produced by a prominent Oxford-trained man of letters. The lyric recounts the first three coffins' passing by and the 'last bier' 'black and bare', then concludes,

> In a far-off world and dim,
> Strange if the dead man knew
> That of all the flowers they threw
> There was never a flower for him!

Only a common lass,
    Standing beside the way,
    Bartering day by day
Flowers to all who pass –

Only a common lass,
    Selling for daily bread
    Posies of white and red,
Saw the bare coffin pass.

Silent and swift she stept
    Into the dusty road,
    Scattered her basket's load
Over the bier unwept.

Dust on the flowers for dew,
    Only her eyes were dim,
    This was her gift to him,
Strange, if the dead man knew![10]

The lyric invites a reading as metadiscursive verse, imaging as it does how mere commercial commodities can flower into affective expression and appeal, whether the commodities be flowers, lyrics, or newspaper columns.

'After the Fire' was the fifth of Graham R. Tomson's poems published in 'At the Sign of the Ship' and the third under signature; presumably Tomson's prior relationship with the prominent journalist led to Lang's decision to include a transient poem about a news event in his monthly 'conversation' with his readers. Because the lyric originated in a newspaper anecdote and appeared in a magazine, it was thus doubly marked as both poetry and journalism. In poetic terms the lyric joins a long tradition of occasional verse, yet it also nests within a journalistic commodity – Lang's column – that designates it as 'news'. Insofar as 'After the Fire' functions as journalism, the poem also pays tribute to the affective content of human interest journalism that enables it to fulfil some of the same emotive functions as poetess verse that is founded on mourning or sympathy.[11]

The crossover between journalism and poetry is likewise evident in the manifold memorial poems first published in Victorian periodicals, where poetry shared the journalistic function of obituaries. Examples include Matthew Arnold's 'Haworth Churchyard' in the May 1855 *Fraser's Magazine*, responding to Charlotte Brontë's death, Elizabeth Barrett Barrett's 'Stanzas addressed to Miss Landon and Suggested by her "Stanzas on the Death of Mrs. Hemans"' in *New Monthly Magazine* in September 1835, and Graham R. Tomson's 'Eheu!' on the death of the Duke of Clarence, published in the 23 January 1892 *Illustrated London News*.[12] More interesting, however, is the blurring of poetry and journalism in periodical poems on contemporary paintings. Such work needs to be distinguished from paired paintings and poems created by William Blake or D. G. Rossetti, and from poems appearing on paintings' frames or in exhibition catalogues (though these, too, sometimes found their way into print journalism). Free-standing periodical poems responding to paintings in current exhibitions were particularly useful to poets because they so skilfully negotiated between elevated poetic tradition and journalism associated with the leisure industry. Producing a verbal representation of a visual work of art accorded with the ancient rhetorical figure of ekphrasis dating back to the description of Achilles' shield in the *Iliad*. Yet in a periodical context, ekphrasis functioned analogously to narratives of paintings' subjects in contemporaneous art reviews of current exhibitions. The poet could thus function simultaneously as artist and journalist (and hence be paid), while readers could satisfy their interests or pleasure in poetry while also learning how to think and feel before paintings they might soon see at an exhibition. R. Armytage produced two such poems, both signed, in the *Academy* about two especially popular paintings of 1886: '"The Depths of the Sea," after Burne Jones' and '"Mariage de Convenance.—After!" (Orchardson)'.[13]

Both lyrics identified the paintings' topics and their emotive force or appeal, Armytage's sonnet on *The Depths of the Sea* emphasizing the ironic triumph of a desiring mermaid hugging the drowned sailor she carries to her lair:

> Yea, draw him gently through the strange seaways
>> Down through the dim, green, water whispering.
>> Thy cold lips have not kissed so fair a thing
> As this young mariner for many days.
> So well he sleeps, he will not wake to praise
>> Thy wan bright loveliness, nor feel thee cling
>> Around him, neither smile to hear thee sing,
> Though thou dids't lure him hither with thy lays.
>> The bubbles sigh and sparkle overhead,
> How white thou art! but he is paler still,
>> Pale with despair of young days forfeited.
> Smiling thou bear'st him to thy chill green bed.
> Of brightest, bitterest triumph take thy fill,
>> Thou hast his body, but the soul has fled.

Her three octets on the 1886 sequel to Orchardson's highly popular *Mariage de Convenance* (1884) representing a May–December wedding, emphasizes the desolation succeeding the woman's elopement –

> The spacious room seems bare
> And drear beyond compare,

> A man with sparse grey hair
>   Sits grim and lonely—

but infuses a note of journalistic inquiry by inviting readers (and viewers of the painting) to question 'Which was the most to blame? / He? or she only?' and by treating marital breakdown as an overdetermined outcome of ambition and desire:

> A woman rashly bought,
> Ambition coldly sought,
> Passion and Greed—have wrought
>   This desolation.

It was for other poems in *The Bird-Bride. A Volume of Ballads and Sonnets* (1889), which included none of the journalism-poems noted above, that Graham R. Tomson made a name for herself as a poet. The widening literary and artistic networks into which she then entered opened new journalistic opportunities for her in turn, especially since enhanced public recognition imparted exchange value to her name within a market of journalistic commodities. She received numerous offers of column-writing, reviews, and in the early 1890s an editorship in consequence.[14] In the remainder of this essay I want to look at the interplay of style and signature across three modes (and transatlantically): her women's journalism, often but not exclusively anonymous; her role as a woman of letters empowered to pronounce judgement on distinguished contemporary poets; and her signed and unsigned work after she became Rosamund Marriott Watson. Collectively this work shows a surprisingly uneven relationship between style and signature, suggesting additional factors that must be taken into account in analysing both. In drawing upon representative samples of her journalism I give particular attention to publications not previously discussed in scholarship.

Some of her best journalism on the traditional women's topics of fashion and interior decoration was anonymous. Paradoxically, this writing was her most strongly marked stylistic production, as if to counter the invisibility of signature with a signature style. As both Talia Schaffer and I have argued, in her anonymous fashion and interior decoration columns she wrote as a female aesthete, a designation, Schaffer explains, that allowed numerous *fin-de-siècle* women to write progressively, sometimes daringly, under cover of celebrating art and beauty.[15] In her fashion column for W. E. Henley's *National Observer*, Tomson again blurred poetry and journalism by putting them in dialogue with each other to disrupt their conventionally accepted relations. She simultaneously mocked poetry's importance by showing its ready adaptation to journalism, interrogated fashion's transient modes by setting them against the lasting achievement of verbal art (an achievement validated by the familiar excerpts she recirculated), and nonetheless hinted that the art of poetry and art of fashion were kindred forms. And just as she recounted how various ensembles from the exquisite to the ludicrous were pieced together, so her prose paragraphs were also pieced together with fragments of poems gathered from far and wide.

I quote as an instance the first half of her opening paragraph in her column of 19 December 1891 entitled '"Of Solemn Black"' – an allusion to *Hamlet* I.ii.77–78 – when Hamlet protests to Gertrude that neither his 'inky cloak' nor 'customary suits of solemn black' can express his grief:

> With the dark hours a most sad and sullen humour has taken the Spirit of Dress. It is black, and again black, everywhere; so that the shifting show of the streets is even as a concourse of mourners. Impossible of resistance is the dreariness of this inky influence that has descended upon us like the wolf on the fold or the Amateur upon the novel. In truth, we have clothed ourselves with grief as with a garment. And the worst is that black is as great a leveller as the natural law it symbolizes. Indeed, it is astonishing to observe how much alike in it most women seem. There are brilliant exceptions, of course; one most pleasing suit of sable is built of fine wool and silk, the mode of it just touched with old-worldliness, yet not aggressively picturesque. A slim, gored skirt; a hint of high-waistedness given by broad folds of softest silk; falling ruffles (silk) at the throat; with a broad, mouse-coloured beaver, half-hat, half-bonnet, trimmed with black ribbon velvet to a purpose as coquettishly demure as heart could wish. Such phantoms of delight are few; yet you shall find women whom their blacks invest with a certain distinction. But it vanishes in a crowd; and the Great Agrippa of *Struwelpeter* would seem to have been abroad with his inkpot, blotting out the gay tinctures of last winter's wear.[16]

Tomson's poetic allusions here are astonishing in breadth and scope. Her second and third sentence (cp. 'inky') reinvoke her title's allusion to *Hamlet*; but to protest the tyranny of a fashion she derides, she then links it to the irresistible force of attack in Byron's 'The Destruction of Sennacherib' ('The Assyrian came down like the wolf on the fold,' line 1) – simultaneously glancing toward an opposing colour-scheme for those who knew the poem's next line: 'And his cohorts were gleaming in purple and gold' (line 2). Mockingly laughing at non-aesthetes ('Amateurs') who presume that they, too, can write, she shows how the real thing is done by rapidly performing a witty reversal of Tennyson's lines in *In Memoriam* 'In words, like weeds, I'll wrap me o'er, / Like coarsest clothes against the cold' (Section V, 9–10). Grief – the signified of black clothing but also the result to a connoisseur of fashion when black is too prevalent – is here literalized as the garment in which women enslaved to fashion now wrap themselves. Like the aesthete she is, Tomson lauds the imperative of individuality rather than social conformity, then contradictorily itemizes one ensemble fit for imitation, revealing in the process her association of fashion with seduction ('coquettishly demure'). She caps the passage by aligning these desirable garments with Wordsworth's 'She Was a Phantom of Delight', a lyric in which his future wife appears (like this gown) as a transient decorative effect: 'A lovely Apparition, sent / To be a moment's ornament' ('She Was a Phantom of Delight', lines 3–4). To return to her protest against uniformly black streetwear, she instances the children's tale *Struwelpeter*,[17] in which the magician Agrippa punishes boys' racist derision of a young black boy by dipping the offenders in his giant ink pot. And so as a writer she neatly also rounds off the 'inky' motif with which she began in her title. Her subject matter would lead most readers to assume a woman writer, but her style also suggests a knowledgeable and quick-witted one. Though another woman well-acquainted with poetry could presumably write this column, the sheer speed of successive allusions and their appositeness to the context suggest a poet lurking behind commodified fashion journalism. Anonymity in this case inspires the journalist-aesthete, as Tomson's bravura performance announces to readers a distinctive personality worth recalling despite her veiled identity. Some members of her circle, of course, were well aware of the column's authorship, and for them Tomson's fashion writing consolidated her versatility and powers of invention. With some cause her friend, American journalist Elizabeth Robins Pennell, asserted that Tomson's column running from 12 January 1889 to 12 March 1892 was 'a poem with a stately measure in frocks and hats, a flowing rhythm in every frill and furbelow' – yet more testimony to the blurring of poetry and journalism in Tomson's career.[18]

Pennell also maintained in 1893 that as a poet Tomson was better known in America than Meynell,[19] which fact helps explain Tomson's invitation to write a series of three signed articles appearing from 1890–1893 on British 'Women-Authors of To-Day' for the *Independent*, a Congregationalist paper located in New York to which Tomson had contributed signed poems since 1886. Her second article in the series was even given the place of honour as the issue's leader. Her topic, however, signalled the category of 'women's journalism' since her three authors were all children's writers. The essays on Charlotte Yonge, 'Mrs. Alexander' (Irish-born Annie French Hector), and Julia Horatio Ewing never lose sight of the fact that children's writing is under review but neither do they condescend to or sentimentalize this mode of writing. Instead Tomson approaches children's books as yet another branch of art, and this is one reason, perhaps, that the playful wit, seductive overtones, and occasional daring of her anonymous fashion and interior decoration columns disappear. The altered style also suggests her ambition, her intent to be taken seriously when writing under signature before her public. Her principal standards of judgement – realism, craftsmanship, opposition to sentimentality or cant, and a humane sense of humour – likewise call for a less rococo performance of aesthetic sensibility than the fashion column for Henley, which by contrast looks so much more like a performance or display of the female writing self. Perhaps, too, she dropped the layering of allusion evident in her anonymous work from a sense that this would not suit an American audience or progressive religious periodical.

Assuming a relaxed but unmistakable air of authority, Tomson draws upon her own experience of motherhood to establish the dispositions of childhood readers, namely their disinclination to question or resist, their love of adventure, and their delight in characters who bear recognizable similarities to themselves in realistically rendered settings:

> This, the great, growing tendency of the day, is a natural bent enough, and when a story on such lines is artistically conceived and worked out in a manner calculated to encourage neither sentimentality nor morbid self-consciousness, it is not only a means of enjoyment, but may be a very active influence for good.[20]

But she is loath to admit any good done by the most pious of Charlotte Yonge's stories, especially the highly popular *Heir of Redclyffe*, and recruits humour as well as curt judgement to displace Yonge's authority. Tomson mocks Yonge's tendency to begin each book with one or many deaths, cites one of Rhoda Broughton's 'sprightly heroines who likens Miss Yonge's heroes to old governesses in male attire', and concludes the article by asserting that 'the bulk of Miss Yonge's writings are so obviously merely machines for doctrinal purposes that she must be considered, first, as a propagandist, and only secondarily as a *littérateuse'*.[21] Yet she balances such dismissals with deliberate adjudication of Yonge's strengths, including Yonge's thoroughness, energy, honest earnestness, and, in *The Chaplet of Pearls*, refined technique. Such a manoeuvre enhances her authority as critical judge, suggesting her practice of disinterested Arnoldian criticism rather than polemic or showy attack. With the more congenial Mrs. Alexander Tomson is free to concentrate on the author's craft, and in writing of Julia Ewing, an obvious favourite, Tomson waxes enthusiastic over one 'in whose books no artistic quality is sacrificed to spiritual helpfulness', one who excels in artistic construction, humour, and a winning credibility whether she represents the young, the old, or their pets.[22]

This last essay in the series is especially notable because it reflects another of Tomson's simultaneous journalistic commitments in 1893, her art column for the *Morning Leader* under the pseudonym N. E. Vermind (begun in late May 1892).[23] Deeming Ewing a 'born artist' who 'stands alone as a painter of *genre* pictures', Tomson continues:

> No painter, with actual brushes and pigments, has done quite what she has—for her achievements lie beyond the limitations of pictorial

art: yet everything about her method, her masterly skill in selection, the convincing beauty of her colouring, is more akin to the best drawings of Randolph Caldecott than to other productions of the pen and the printing press—with this difference, however, that where he, by the canons of his art was forced to stop, to go thus far and no further, she, bound by no such restrictions, was able to proceed to the end, and to say the very last word upon every theme she took in hand.[24]

Not only does Tomson here enact (and so confirm) her authority as an art journalist and an aesthete, but she also assertively positions children's writing – an oft-dismissed women's genre – within aestheticism as art that merits serious attention as much as other *genre* studies.[25] If writing about children's literature for an American audience presumably did little to augment Tomson's signature back in Britain, she could use the strong symbolic capital her signature had acquired in America to elevate children's writing and the journalism devoted to it. Signature may function in service to celebrity journalism in this case, but it is also serving as a means to intervene in critical and misogynist standards of judgement.

There is relatively little stylistic variance between Tomson's signed literary criticism on female children's authors in America and her more prestigious signed woman-of-letters reviews of contemporary poets in the *Academy* and *Illustrated London News*, another indication of her underlying purpose in the American series. The principal distinction between the two sets of work lies in the prestige of the works under review and her intensified performance of authority as she forthrightly embraces the right to judge – and criticize – prominent male contemporaries. Her judgements are delivered rather more crisply in this London journalism, and if she generously praises where praise is due she entirely suppresses any tone of enthusiasm. Widely known by this time to be a woman, Graham R. Tomson writes in a relatively more masculine mode that suits her male signature while revealing masculinity as a mask, as shown in her 25 June 1892 *Academy* review of W. E. Henley's *The Song of the Sword, and Other Verses*. The occasion posed temptations to sarcasm on one hand or timidity on the other, since Henley had been unhappy when Tomson resigned from the fashion column in March 1892 and published none of her poems in the prestigious *National Observer* for the rest of the year (she returned to this venue only in January 1893). But Tomson swerved neither into spite nor placation when given the chance to judge Henley's work. Holding his 'Hospital Rhymes' up as his own highest standard of excellence, she judges the recent volume 'not in every instance so uniformly admirable as the first' and states gently but unmistakably her disappointment in the title poem: 'the light of his peculiar genius does not shine its clearest in the title-poem of this volume'. Yet she generously praises his '*Andante con moto*' in the 'London Voluntaries' ('full of imagination.... a picture in which every tone and value is justly balanced, every accent rightly placed') and singles out all the excellences of his 'Rhymes and Rhythms'. Having done so, she reverts to the volume's demerits: 'Honestly speaking, we cannot feel that numbers three ("We are the Choice of the Will"), twenty-five ("England, my England"), twenty-four ("What should the Trees"), and one or two shorter pieces, are altogether worthy of their author... .'[26] Abjuring stylistic pyrotechnics, she instead pursues a dialectic of praise and censure to create a performative rhythm of balanced judgement, a stance that accrues to her standing as a critic while also enabling her to blame Henley diplomatically by judging him according to his own highest standard.

William Watson had quickly risen as an important new poet with the publication of his elegy on the death of Tennyson, '*Lachrymae Musarum*', and Tomson was chosen to review for the *Academy* his 1892 volume that took its title from this work. In the review she demonstrates another characteristic strategy of her woman-of-letters critical assessments, an articulation of general principles of literary excellence as a means of providing a critical and theoretical platform on which to base her judgements – in this case the principle of selection, of holding back in order to create an atmosphere of latent richness that is never fully displayed. She again praises lavishly where she can, citing the first two stanzas of '*Lachrymae Musarum*' and terming the poem '[t]hus far ... a masterpiece.... replete with melody and dignity'. But she immediately pivots to 'wish the following twelve lines away' and to dissent absolutely from the line in which, amidst a catalogue of dead poets greeting Tennyson, 'Bright Keats to touch his raiment doth beseech'. This line, Tomson tartly asserts: 'I distinctly resent. The maker of "The Ode to a Nightingale" and "The Ode on a Grecian Urn" need not, should not, '"beseech" to touch anyone's raiment, even that of a co-deity.'[27] While paying due respect to Watson's gifts (he had, after all, warmly reviewed her own 1891 volume in the 9 January 1892 *Academy*), she elevates her own authority as poet-critic by championing a style and a Romantic poet who were considered 'classic'.

Perhaps the most interesting of Tomson's woman-of-letters reviews is her last, partly for its poignancy and partly for its complex management of tone that bespeaks a journalist's finely honed craft. The review is poignant not only because it is the last but also because it appeared only a day or two before the persona of Graham R. Tomson was slain by its creator when she eloped a second time to become Rosamund Marriott Watson. In this notice, Tomson looks back a last time upon the mentor who did so much to introduce Graham R. Tomson to the public at the outset of her career: Andrew Lang. The review's restrained warmth of tone suggests a departing tribute, and Lang's own refusal to take himself seriously seems to effect a more relaxed stance in her writing, resulting in a greater range of tones and voices in her review of *Ban and Arrière Ban: A Rally of Fugitive Rhymes* than her other notices in this mode. She begins by suggesting that Lang has never been given the recognition due him, 'First and foremost, [because] he has dared to be versatile, to make *vers de société* as well as sonnets; even to construct frivolous sonnets and poke fun at the Muse' rather than following the tacit injunction everywhere enforced 'that a poet shall set up for a poet' and never 'come down from his tripod, or drop, so to speak, into the common vernacular ... .'[28] Lang, iconoclastic himself in this respect, 'really cares not the toss of a half-penny or the value of "nuppence" as to whether his poems are taken seriously or no', giving her the opportunity to point out his range – 'humorous trifles, scholarly and graceful translations, or poems of a deeper inspiration' – and his mastery of technique evident in his 'light, yet sure, touch, the art concealing art... '.[29] In answer to his range, she unbends from a performance of masculine authority to write with greater suppleness, modulating from mockery of poetry's usual tendency to 'thump its lute by the roadside in demonstrative ecstasies of rapture or of pain' to a poetic evocation of Lang's own delicacy:

Mr. Lang's is not the sentiment that may be bawled from the roof-tops: it is the sentiment of old romance, of dim memories, all the more beautiful for their vagueness (as the reflection is often more beautiful than the mirrored object), the sentiment of wet spring woods and birds singing in the early dawn.[30]

This is perhaps as personal as Tomson ever becomes in her woman-of-letters reviews. And her use of signature, viewed retrospectively, also changes in this instance. She writes under signature, to be sure, but writes deconstructively, positing a name and then subjecting it to erasure in the next few days, exposing the contingency of signature and its referentiality.

I have commented at length elsewhere about the impact of this poet-journalist's destruction of one signature and adoption of another that was so euphoniously, visually, and semiotically disjunct from the name that had brought her to prominence.[31] 'Rosamund Marriott Watson' could echo or evoke nothing associated with Graham R. Tomson – no doubt just as the poet-journalist wished in discarding a second husband for a third erotic partner. As that earlier analysis argues, in destroying 'Graham R. Tomson' the poet-journalist also destroyed prior networks (including those surrounding Andrew Lang and Elizabeth Robins Pennell), the symbolic capital accrued by Tomson, and her authorial brand that was a recognizable commodity to readers. Rosamund Marriott Watson could, to be sure, continue to publish, issuing three more volumes of poems, two books of interior decoration and gardening journalism, and serving in the early twentieth century as an *Athenaeum* staff reviewer who specialized in poetry, children's writing, gardens, and furniture.[32] Americans were less skittish about divorce than English editors and critics were (especially after the general shock of Oscar Wilde's trials in 1895), and the American critic E. C. Stedman usefully pointed out the link between her two signatures in the notes to his influential 1895 *Victorian Anthology,* a gesture that American magazine editors occasionally followed.[33] In Britain, however, the connection was never publicly acknowledged when it could have done her most good, and she never again commanded the status of woman of letters in the way she could as Graham R. Tomson. Rosamund Marriott Watson remains significant for a study of women's journalism nonetheless because the inverted roles of signature and anonymity in the rest of her career help lend nuance to scholarly understanding of their significance.

Whereas anonymity was the usual *bête noire* of writers in an era of celebrity journalism, anonymity saved Tomson/Watson's 'Wares of Autolycus' column on interior decoration in the *Pall Mall Gazette* in 1894. After a two month hiatus during which she shed one identity and adopted another along with a new live-in partner, she continued to contribute her witty commentaries on interior decoration and, when they ceased in November 1894, could collect them under the title *The Art of the House* (1897) as an original work by Rosamund Marriott Watson (a book that remains one of this author's best known). Writing journalism under signature as Rosamund Marriott Watson, in contrast, did little to augment her fame or recognition. This was especially the case with her columns on gardening in the *Daily Mail* and *New Liberal Review* in 1901–02. She again wrote as a female aesthete, blurring poetry and journalism – literally insofar as lyrics were embedded in her impressionistic, poetic evocations of an artfully-designed garden amidst the backdrop of changing seasons. But by 1901 the vogue of the female aesthete had waned, and this work generated little notice or excitement, even after she collected the columns into a volume entitled *The Heart of a Garden* (1906) and illustrated it with photographs. This instance suggests that a distinction must always be made between signature and *meaningful* signature: though she could still publish under a 'brand' name and wrote well, the new one never caught hold to build up a self-referring network of associations connected to a talented or intriguing author. This lack in turn barred her from access to woman-of-letters journalism that paid most and imparted greatest prestige.

Watson could, had she been so inclined, have capitalized upon her scandalous past, turning her new signature and herself into a spectacle for public entertainment. But she was clearly unable or unwilling to do this. More and more, she was instead driven to the hack journalism of anonymous book reviewing, work that has not yet and probably never will be fully traced.[34] In her heyday as Graham R. Tomson, anonymous journalism had been an entrepreneurial opportunity that offered her space in which to manoeuvre into a distinctive style, and it along with her poetry in turn led to higher forms of woman-of-letters journalism in art and literary criticism. For Rosamund Marriott Watson, signature offered scant advantages and anonymous journalism led only to a door that slammed shut.

Notes

1. Robert Darnton, *The Kiss of Lamourette: Reflections in Cultural History* (New York: W. W. Norton, 1990), 111–12; Pierre Bourdieu, *The Field of Cultural Production*, ed. Randal Johnson (New York: Columbia Univ. Press, 1993).

2. Linda H. Peterson, *Becoming a Woman of Letters: Myths of Authorship and Facts of the Victorian Market* (Princeton: Princeton University Press, 2009), 4. For the proliferating number of women journalists, see Barbara Onslow, *Women of the Press in Nineteenth-Century Britain* (Houndmills, Basingstoke: Palgrave Macmillan 2000), passim.

3. Peterson, 171, 173–76, 181–82. See also F. Elizabeth Gray's chapter on Meynell in this volume.

4. For a brief overview of her life, see my 'Watson, Rosamund Marriott' in the online *Oxford Dictionary of National Biography* (2004), and for a brief overview of her journalism, my entry entitled 'Watson, Rosamund Marriott' in the *Dictionary of Nineteenth-Century Journalism*, eds Laurel Brake and Marysa Demoor (Ghent: Academia Press in conjunction with the British Library, 2009), 635–36. For a detailed examination of both, see my *Graham R.: Rosamund Marriott Watson, Woman of Letters* (Athens: Ohio University Press, 2005). As in *Graham R.*, which asserts its subject's modulating identities as she changed names, I variously adopt the name under which she wrote or acted rather than retroactively (and anachronistically) assigning one name throughout.

5. See *Graham R.*, p. 233.

6. Her embrace of transience is evident in her first traceable publication: 'An artistic triumph in dress can no more be carried in the memory than an exquisite grouping of forms, or a changing of color' ('Modern Dress,' *Fortnightly Review* [September 1883], 352).

7. Talia Schaffer, *The Forgotten Female Aesthetes: Literary Culture in Late-Victorian England* (Charlottesville, VA: University Press of Virginia, 2000), 162–67; Peterson, 176–80.

8. Michel Foucault, 'What is an Author?' *Language, Memory, Practice: Selected Essays and Interviews*, ed. Donald F. Bouchard, trans. Donald F. Bouchard and Sherry Simon (Ithaca: Cornell Univ. Press, 1977), 130, 137–38.

9. Kathryn Ledbetter, *Tennyson and Victorian Periodicals: Commodities in Context* (Aldershot, Hampshire: Ashgate, 2007), 101–42; Natalie Houston, 'Newspaper Poems: Material Texts in the Public Sphere,' *Victorian Studies* (2008), 233–42; Hughes, 'What the *Wellesley Index* Left Out: Why Poetry Matters to Periodical Studies,' *Victorian Periodicals Review* 40, no. 2 (Summer 2007), 91–125. See also Stefanie Markovits, *The Crimean War in the British Imagination* (Cambridge: Cambridge University Press, 2009), 13–14; and Hughes, *The Cambridge Introduction to Victorian Poetry* (Cambridge: Cambridge University Press, 2010), 113–17 ff.

10. 'At the Sign of the Ship,' *Longman's Magazine* (October 1887), 662–63.

11. The poem, I have suggested elsewhere, in turn helped inspire a detail in Thomas Hardy's story 'An Imaginative Woman,' another link between journalism and literature (Hughes, *Graham R.*, 199–200). For poetess verse and its association with affect (both the poetess's and the reader's), see, e.g., Susan Brown, 'The Victorian Poetess,' *The Cambridge Companion to Victorian Poetry*, ed. Joseph Bristow (Cambridge: Cambridge University Press, 2000), 180–202. Lang referred to the author as 'Mr. Graham R. Tomson' in this causerie, another indication of the complex functioning of signature in late Victorian journalism.

12. A[rnold]., 'Haworth Churchyard,' *Fraser's Magazine* 51 (May 1855), 527–30; Elizabeth Barrett Barrett, *New Monthly Magazine* n.s. 45 (September 1835), 82; Graham R. Tomson, 'Eheu!' *Illustrated London News* (23 January 1892), 102. My publication details for Barrett Barrett are drawn from *Elizabeth Barrett Browning: Selected Poems*, eds Marjorie Stone and Beverly Taylor (Peterborough, Ontario: Broadview Press, 2009), 73 n.2.

13. R. Armytage, '"The Depths of the Sea," after Burne Jones,' *Academy* (22 May 1886), 362, and '"Mariage de Convenance.—After!" (Orchardson),' *Academy* (12 June 1886), 415. E. Nesbit also crafted a poem upon Burne Jones's painting exhibited at the 1886 Royal Academy, 'The Depths of the Sea' first published in *To-Day* (33 [September 1886], 93) and then in Nesbit's volume *Lays and Legends* (London: Longmans, Green, and Co., 1887), 153–54. Nesbit, however, breaks out of the frame of self-sufficing ekphrasis to render the painting into a simile of the persona's erotic relationship. For another example of such ekphrastic journalism in response to Burne Jones, see Emily Pfeiffer, 'Sonnet,' *Fraser's Magazine* (August 1879), 185, which responds to Burne Jones's *Annunciation*.

14. I omit her coediting of *Art Weekly* in 1890 with her husband, New English Art Club painter Arthur Tomson, since this short-lived paper has more biographical significance than importance for an understanding of her journalism – albeit providing her with invaluable editing experience.

15. Schaffer, 5 ff.; Hughes, 'A Female Aesthete at the Helm: *Sylvia's Journal* and "Graham R. Tomson," 1893–1894,' *Victorian Periodicals Review* 29, no. 2 (Summer 1996): 173–92. Most of the 'female aesthete' work we discuss was written by Graham R. Tomson; the concluding installments of her *Pall Mall Gazette* columns on interior decoration, however, appeared after her second elopement, when she became Rosamund Marriott Watson. Schaffer uses the sobriquet Rosamund Marriott Watson throughout *Forgotten Female Aesthetes*. Our differing nomenclature explains my omission of a specific name in this sentence.

16. [Graham R. Tomson], '"Of Solemn Black,"' *National Observer* (19 December 1891), 121.

17. *Struwelpeter* was evidently a well-loved tale from Tomson's childhood, since she also mentions it in a letter. See Hughes, 'Rosamund Marriott Watson,' *Kindred Hands: Letters on Writing by British and American Women Authors, 1865–1935*, eds Jennifer Cognard-Black and Elizabeth MacLeod Walls (Iowa City: University of Iowa Press, 2006), 183.

18. Elizabeth Robins Pennell, *Nights: Rome and Venice in the Aesthetic Eighties, London and Paris in the Fighting Nineties*, 2nd ed. (Philadelphia: J. B. Lippincott, 1916), 158.

19. 'Among the minor poets of England several women are conspicuous, and they have published volumes of verse during the last twelve months: Mrs. Graham R. Tomson, who probably is one of the best known in America; "Violet Fane," who, in her time, has been called the English Sappho; Miss Tynan and Mrs. Alice Meynell, both on the staff of that clever paper, the *National Observer*; and Miss Mathilda Blind, who wrote the "Life of George Eliot" for the Famous Women Series.' See Pennell, 'Woman's World in London,' *The Chautauquan: A Weekly Newsmagazine* (1 March 1893), 725.

20. Graham R. Tomson, 'Women-Authors of To-day. Charlotte M. Yonge,' *Independent* (27 November 1890), 8.

21. Tomson, 'Women-Authors of To-day,' 8.

22. Graham R. Tomson, 'Mrs. Alexander' [leader], *Independent* (9 June 1892), 1; 'Women-Authors of To-day. Mrs. Ewing,' *Independent* (6 July 1893), 5.

23. For additional analysis of her art column, see my *Graham R.*, 149–52, and 'Aestheticism on the Cheap: Decorative Art, Art Criticism, and Cheap Paper in the 1890s,' *The Lure of Illustration in the Nineteenth Century: Picture and Press*, ed. Laurel Brake and Marysa Demoor (Houndmills, Basingstoke: Palgrave Macmillan, 2009), 226–30.

24. 'Mrs. Ewing,' 5.

25. Tomson clinches this aim by comparing Ewing's artful compression to a Plato epigram in the Greek Anthology recently translated by Dr. Richard Garnett, Keeper of Printed Books in the British Library.

26. Graham R. Tomson, rev. of *The Song of the Sword, and other Verses*, by W. E. Henley, *Academy* (25 June 1892), 607. Tomson slightly alters the title of the opening sequence in Henley's *A Book of Verses* (1888), 'In Hospital: Rhymes and Rhythms'.

27. Graham R. Tomson, rev. of *Lachrymae Musarum, and other Poems*, by William Watson, *Academy* (26 November 1892), 476–77.

28. Graham R. Tomson, rev. of *Ban and Arrière Ban: A Rally of Fugitive Rhymes*, by Andrew Lang, *Academy* (2 June 1894), 451.

29. Tomson, rev. of *Ban and Arrière Ban*, 451.

30. Tomson, rev. of *Ban and Arrière Ban*, 451.

31. Hughes, 'A Woman Poet Angling for Notice: Rosamund Marriott Watson,' *Marketing the Author: Authorial Personae, Narrative Selves and Self-Fashioning, 1880–1930*, ed. Marysa Demoor (Houndmills, Basingstoke: Palgrave Macmillan, 2004), 144–51.

32. For an account of her writing for the *Athenaeum*, see Demoor, *Their Fair Share: Women, Power and Criticism in the Athenaeum, from Millicent Garrett Fawcett to Katherine Mansfield, 1870–1920* (Aldershot, Hampshire: Ashgate, 2000), 123–27; see also Hughes, *Graham R.*, 289, 298.

33. E. C. Stedman, ed., *A Victorian Anthology, 1837–1895: Selections Illustrating the Editor's Critical Review of British Poetry in the Reign of Victoria* (Boston: Houghton Mifflin, 1895), 708; see also 'Tares: A Book of Verses,' *Bibelot* (1 January 1898), 159.

34. As she confessed to a correspondent in 1905, she had 'left off reviewing fiction. ... I found the welter of novels too much for me when my health gave way' and she suffered a nervous breakdown; see Hughes, *Graham R.*, 277.

13
Anti/Feminism: Frances Low and the Issue of Women's Work at the *Fin de Siècle*

Alexis Easley
University of St. Thomas

In July of 1907, Constance Smedley published an article in the *Fortnightly Review* titled 'The Hedda Gabler of To-day'. In this essay, Smedley defended Ibsen's heroine, calling her a 'woman with a strong individuality' who was 'goaded to her death by the injustice and falsity of the conventions of her world'.[1] Six months later, Frances Low published an angry rejoinder titled 'The Parlour Woman or the Club Woman?' where she referred to Hedda Gabler as a 'travesty of womanhood' and denounced Smedley for her 'lively flights' of irrational argumentation.[2] Low objected to Smedley's contention that domesticity was an intellectual prison, saying, 'it is tragical to find women belittling and degrading what must ever be their divinest means of "development"'.[3] For Frances Low, a woman's rightful place was commanding the 'little kingdom' of home, fulfilling her duty as wife and mother.[4]

Given this exchange in the pages of the *Fortnightly Review*, it is tempting to disregard Frances Low as a backward antifeminist whose writings are most useful as illustrations of what righteous feminists were arguing against. Yet a closer look at Low's career in journalism reveals that her stance on women's issues was more complex and sophisticated than a cursory reading would suggest. At the same time that Frances Low was making a name for herself as an antifeminist and anti-suffragist, she was working as a cultural critic for the *Strand Magazine*, writing detailed analyses of the domestic habits of women and children. Soon thereafter, she began working as an investigative reporter focused on women's employment issues. She published articles in support of pensions for retired professional women and an organized system of daycare referrals for single mothers. Low also actively promoted women's careers in the male-dominated field of print journalism. In 1904, she published a book titled *Press Work for Women* that aimed to demystify the profession, providing young women with the tools they needed to survive in a harshly competitive field. The fact that Low was a founder of the Women's National Anti-Suffrage League and a spokesperson for the movement makes it difficult to place her within the ranks of feminist pioneers, yet Low had an important contribution to make in the discourse on women's work at the *fin de siècle*. Throughout her career, she was devoted to the cause of poor working women and drew attention to the middle-class bias inherent in first-wave feminism. Although Low did not support women's enfranchisement, she nevertheless played a significant role in advancing women's interests in the public realm.

In this chapter, I not only explore Frances Low's life-long commitment to women's employment issues but also her dedication to the anti-suffragist cause. Low's contradictory stance on women's roles in the public realm makes her career an ideal case study for investigating the complex ways that women journalists negotiated shifting definitions of feminism at the *fin de siècle*. As Tamara Wagner has recently pointed out, writers identified as antifeminists often held decidedly 'ambiguous, even contending, views' on women's issues.[5] The concept of feminism was under formation in the closing years of the nineteenth century, emerging from a diverse array of initiatives and debates focused on women's legal and employment rights.[6] Consequently, most *fin-de-siècle* women writers located themselves somewhere on the continuum between what today we might call feminist and antifeminist positions. Indeed, as Barbara Caine notes, we must be attentive to the 'tensions' inherent in women activists' careers and the 'extent to which they were opposed to, inspired by, and constrained by the prevailing discourse on gender, sexuality, and sexual relations'.[7] Rather than viewing women's viewpoints on suffrage as a test of whether they are worthy objects of feminist analysis, we must, as Bush suggests, closely examine their texts with attention to the diversity of their viewpoints and the 'full range of their public work'.[8] An investigation of the career of Frances Low enables us to explore the ways women journalists were able to work both inside and outside conventional notions of domestic ideology as they advanced the cause of women and established themselves in a male-dominated field.

Cultural Criticism

Frances Low (1862–1939) was born in Blackheath, London, the daughter of Jewish immigrants Maximilian Loewe and Therese Schacherl.[9] The family enjoyed sufficient prosperity to provide the 11 Low children with excellent academic training. Sidney, the most famous member of the family, was Oxford educated, and Frances could read in three languages.[10] The early years of Frances Low's career are shrouded in mystery, but it is clear that she formed a beneficial alliance with Walter Besant that led to her appointment in September 1887 as a librarian at the People's Palace, a leisure and educational institution for working men in the East End (built 1886–88).[11] Constance Black, co-librarian at the People's Palace, later described Low as a 'rather fickle and capricious young woman, not at all easy to work with'.[12] The two women nevertheless worked side by side at the library during a period of unprecedented social turmoil in the East End spurred by the

Bloody Sunday riot of 1887 and the Whitechapel murders of 1888. Low worked in this turbulent atmosphere until October of 1888 when she made the decision to devote herself to journalism full-time.[13] Low's ambitiousness as a writer was in part the product of necessity, since after her father's business failed in 1879, she was forced to support her mother and siblings.[14] Novelist Lucy Clifford would later describe her as a 'handsome girl with a beautiful complexion and an ugly mouth', who worked exhaustively to support 'crowds of poor relations'.[15]

Frances Low began writing fiction for middle-class domestic periodicals in 1890, publishing 'An Incident in Mr. Lanford's Life' in *Argosy Magazine* and 'His Little Comedy' in *Murray's Magazine*. During the same year, she published a collection of stories for children titled *The Air Child: and Other New Fairy Tales*.[16] Writing for and about children fitted within the conventional definition of appropriate subject matter for women, so it was an excellent niche market for a young writer.[17] Low's interest in this subject, however, was anything but incidental. Indeed, her writings on women and children during the 1890s reveal a deep interest in the ethnography of domestic life. While Low's brothers, Sidney and Maurice, established themselves as well-known political journalists,[18] Low proved herself to be an insightful chronicler of the everyday lives of women and children. Her most significant studies of domestic culture were published in the *Strand Magazine*[19] between 1891 and 1894: 'The Street Games of Children', 'Queen Victoria's Dolls', 'Boy Soldiers and Sailors', 'Distinguished Women and Their Dolls',[20] and 'Favourite Books of Childhood'. Taken together, these articles demonstrate Low's versatility and attentiveness as a cultural historian and critic. In addition, they reveal her intriguingly complex stance on women's roles as leaders and workers in the public realm.

The first in the series, 'The Street Games of Children' (1891), provides detailed descriptions of several children's games, including 'buck and gobs', 'buttons', and 'London'. Low presents herself as an ethnographer who travels through the 'small back streets' of the city, observing children at play and interviewing bystanders.[21] She is a 'student of child character' who imagines the day when a 'Philosophy of Street Games' will be written.[22] Indeed, she depicts herself as a solitary woman writer at large in the city who is not afraid to spend time in rough neighbourhoods observing and note-taking. 'To get a lucid explanation of the playing is by no means easy business', she remarks, 'partly because, no matter how retired a spot one chooses for the demonstration, a huge crowd of errand boys, bonnetless women, and loafing men is sure to collect round within a few minutes'.[23] After one elderly onlooker tells her that the children's games are the same as those he played as a child, Low concludes that they are a cultural practice that has been handed down through generations. She also discovers that games are played seasonally and that some games are played exclusively by girls or boys while others are inclusive of both sexes.

What is most remarkable about the description of games that follows is not only the level of observed detail she includes but also the complex gender relations she describes. When discussing 'buck and gobs', for example, she notes that the game is 'invariably played best by the girls' even if they are a 'long way behind the other sex in anything involving exact aiming'.[24] Their skill makes them 'formidable rivals' to the boys, 'if not actually better players'.[25] By depicting street games as competition between the sexes, Low evokes broader debates about women's competitiveness in the public sphere. While she stops short of claiming a superior position for women, she nevertheless emphasizes their skilfulness and thus undermines the notion of women's passivity and physical inferiority. Indeed, throughout her description of mixed-gender games, she often uses female pronouns generically when describing players' behaviours, perhaps as a way of reinforcing girls' equal agency as participants. Even when describing female-only games, Low emphasizes girls' authority. She refers to a 'certain Mabel', for example, who is a 'born general' with 'some dozen children under her command every evening'.[26] Likewise, when describing boys-only games such as 'buttons', she draws attention to the ways male players defy gender expectations. She reports that boys rip the buttons off their garments in order to play the game and then sew them back on again before returning home. 'Tain't only them girls can sew!' one boy exclaims.[27] Low presents herself as an observer who simply describes what she sees, yet her observations certainly would have resonated with heated discussions of 'natural' sex characteristics in the popular press.[28] Her characterization of herself as a confident single woman, a 'student' of culture, would seem to undermine notions of women's natural diffidence and domestic virtues. Likewise, by depicting the relationship between the sexes as a nearly egalitarian competition, she undermines the concept of female inferiority.

In 'Queen Victoria's Dolls', published a year later in the *Strand Magazine*, Low continues her minute exploration of children's culture. Her discussion of Queen Victoria's childhood passion for dolls, like her exploration of street games, indirectly addresses the question of whether women are naturally suited for domestic life. As in the street games article, she presents herself as a keen observer whose detailed descriptions are just as exquisite as the dolls themselves. Through these descriptions, she re-imagines the monarch as a 'little being, as yet unweighted with a crown', and in that sense, she comfortably locates the young Victoria within the sphere of middle-class domestic life. Victoria's 132 dolls, modelled after court ladies and performers, are dressed in costumes created by the princess herself. Low writes, 'I hope I have given sufficiently exact details to give my readers some notion of the ingenuity and taste and thought and artistic skill that have been expended upon their costumes'.[29]

As much as the article seems intent on fashioning young Victoria into a domestic paragon, it simultaneously reminds readers of her later status as a powerful ruler. Even if the princess is a 'little being, as yet unweighted with a crown', she is nevertheless 'set apart and shadowed by sovereignty'.[30] Low continues,

> We remember the duties and responsibilities awaiting her, the momentous yea and nay that will some day have to be pronounced by those soft young lips; and then is it any wonder that we turn and watch her among her Lilliputian subjects, stitching, devising, cutting, and measuring infinitesimal garments, with a feeling that is something deeper than what is usually aroused by a child's play?[31]

In this passage, conventionally female pursuits – stitching, devising, cutting, and measuring – are reimagined as metaphors for leading a nation. Playing with dolls can be seen as practice for managing and guiding real people, who, like dolls, benefit from a woman's care, imagination, orderliness, and close attention to detail. Even the male dolls fall under her command. 'M. Albert', a doll modelled after a ballet master at the King's Theatre, is described as being a 'member of the "superior sex"'.[32] Low's use of scare quotes suggests her questioning of sex hierarchies; as a woman, Victoria is 'superior' to all in her domain.

Early on in the essay, Low makes it clear that her project was endorsed by the queen, who took a 'warm interest' in its subject matter.[33] Indeed, Victoria reviewed the article before it was published and added her own annotations. Rather than simply revising her article based on the queen's corrections, Low includes them as footnotes. This has the effect of emphasizing the impressiveness of Low's achievement as a journalist.[34] Queen Victoria is, after all, not the usual sort of celebrity correspondent featured in the *Strand*.[35] Low situates Victoria within conventional roles and stereotypes, yet she simultaneously provides clear justification for her later role as head of state. 'A glimpse of the charming playthings', Low concludes, provides evidence that Victoria is a 'good wife, a good mother, and a wise and exemplary ruler'.[36] Making reference to Queen Victoria's status as wife, mother, *and* ruler enabled Low to argue for women's 'natural' domestic roles while at the same time demonstrating the compatibility of women's domestic and professional responsibilities.

The article clearly resonated with the general public. Shortly after its publication, Low worked with illustrator Alan Wright on a gift book, *Queen Victoria's Dolls*, which was published in three editions between 1892 and 1895.[37] In her introduction to the book, Low writes, 'We see also in these childish achievements the same qualities of self-control, patience, steadiness of purpose, and womanliness, which have been consistently exercised by Queen Victoria in the prominent part played by her on the theatre of life'.[38] 'Womanliness' is shown to be compatible with public visibility and professional competence. Low's use of theatrical metaphor is appropriate given the fact that many of the dolls were modelled after actresses and opera singers, but it also suggests that the theatres of home and public life are just as much sites of performance as the stage. Victoria assumes a 'prominent part' in the public realm, just as Low herself assumes the role of high-profile cultural commentator. Victoria is just as skilled at sewing as she is at ruling, and Low is equally at home on the streets as in the queen's apartments. Low's study of Queen Victoria's dolls, like her investigation of children's street games, emphasizes that the analysis of domestic and leisure habits is key to understanding the character of individuals and the performance of gender. By interpreting the symbols associated with children's dolls and games, she finds that women can assume the parts of generals, monarchs, and female reporters.

Gendered Investigations

In the late 1890s, Frances Low began focusing on a new branch of journalism: art criticism.[39] In 1896, she published an interview with John Everett Millais in the *Strand*, and in 1899, she published a review of a Rembrandt exhibition in the *Pall Mall Magazine* and an article titled 'Women Artists of the Day' in *Windsor Magazine*. In the latter article, Low argues that there has been 'real development of artistic faculties amongst women, but also the birth of artistic powers of which no sign has been given at an earlier period of history'.[40] While she is quick to point out that there has not yet 'been born into the world a feminine Raphael or Titian', she nevertheless provides examples of five contemporary women artists whose work shows a 'high degree of excellence'.[41] Following on the heels of her investigations of domestic life in the *Strand Magazine*, this article reinforces Low's status as a supportive, insightful critic of women's culture and professional life.

During the same time period that Low was writing art criticism, she was also making a name for herself as an investigative reporter. In these pieces, she re-employs the keen eye of the cultural historian and art critic as she describes scenes of poverty and privation. In her first essay in this genre, 'The Receiving Room of the London Hospital', published in the *English Illustrated Magazine* in 1896, Low refers to herself as an 'ethnologist' and 'fastidious spectator', who spends several days in a London charity hospital observing the 'ever-moving play of life'.[42] She describes the drunkards, poor mothers, and youthful physicians from an artist's perspective:

> What contradictions, too, and arresting contrasts! Side by side with a man, from whose shocking brute-beast countenance all human qualities have been obliterated, there sits a young work-girl, whose thin chin, delicately moulded cheek, and soft pensive blue eyes, recall the picture of some medieval painter, and diffuse something of spiritual beauty around her.[43]

Low offers no remedy for the misery and pain she sees and instead provides a heart-wrenching portrait intended to promote readerly interest and sympathy.[44]

In 1897, Low directed her investigative journalism specifically toward exposing the injustices faced by working women. With the publication of 'How Poor Ladies Live' in the *Nineteenth Century*, Low began a campaign to assist impoverished gentlewomen in the metropolis. In this article, Low includes excerpts from interviews with several retired teachers in order to expose the 'difficulty for middle-aged ladies to obtain any occupation by which they can maintain themselves'.[45] In the process, Low attacks school employers who provide insufficient wages, and, even more controversially, middle-class women, who have entered the workforce out of desire rather than necessity, thus 'causing the supply of trained labour to be out of all proportion to the demand'.[46] She offers four solutions to the problem: (1) creating a bureau for middle-class women's work, which would serve as a clearing house of information about women's employment trends and opportunities; (2) discouraging middle-class women from pursuing paid work unless they must earn wages out of necessity; (3) establishing a pension system for women teachers; and (4) constructing a greater number of old age homes for retired gentlewomen.

In this way, Low begins to chart out her own complex stance on the issue of professions for women. She makes it clear that she does not object to women's work; in fact, she praises the retired teachers she interviews, extolling their 'silent heroism'.[47] However, she believes that women should not seek employment outside the home unless they are forced to do so out of necessity. In the meantime, well-to-do women could devote themselves to 'unpaid labour' helping their sisters in need.[48] In a postscript to a follow-up article, 'How Poor Ladies Live: A Rejoinder', published in the *Nineteenth Century* in July 1897, Low offers to put women readers in contact with any one of the 'patient dumb sufferers' she features in her article so that they may provide charitable relief.[49] Indeed, her efforts soon bore fruit. In a 1900 article published in *Leisure Hour*, 'Where Poor Ladies Can Live in London', Low reports that her previous essays on the subject have resulted in 30 women being offered pensions by wealthy donors.[50] And once again she criticizes 'well-to-do ladies who, to relieve the tedium of their lives, enter the labour market to-day, making the struggle more severe and bitter for the genuine bread-winners'.[51]

Meanwhile, Low began to take interest in the plight of poor women with dependent children. In an 1898 article published in the *Fortnightly Review*, 'A Remedy for Baby-Farming', she draws attention to the lack of safe day-care available to single working women and calls for the establishment of a bureau for licensing and inspecting the homes of childcare providers. Low suggests this bureau would be run by a central committee of ladies who would employ a 'paid secretary and two lady inspectors'.[52] Here, as in the

'How Poor Ladies Live' series, Low offers practical solutions to real economic problems faced by working women. By imagining the creation of new institutions to monitor the treatment of elderly women and single mothers, she simultaneously envisions new fields of work for women in the public realm as inspectors and philanthropists. Low's investigative journalism would thus seem to be feminist in the sense that it promotes the interests of women as workers in a harshly competitive economic marketplace and offers concrete proposals for how women can band together and provide mutual support. Of course, her criticism of women who enter the paid workforce for any reason other than necessity seems distinctly antifeminist. Yet Low's passionate advocacy of the interests of poor women and her keen awareness of the intersection between class and gender make her a decidedly complex figure – one who defies a simple binary distinction between feminist and antifeminist activism.

Press Work for Women

Early on in her career, Frances Low was dedicated to fostering self-help among women journalists. In 1892, she co-founded the Writer's Club at Hastings House on the Strand, an institution devoted to providing social and working space for women writers.[53] And from 1902 to 1903, she published a series of articles titled 'Journalism for Girls' in the *Girl's Realm*. The success of this series led Low to publish a book-length handbook, *Press Work for Women*, which appeared in 1904. As recent critics have noted, this handbook is rather pessimistic in its outlook.[54] Indeed, Low asserts that 'women's journalism, as conducted at present ... is not worthy of the powers, knowledge, and training of the *highly cultivated* woman'.[55] It is instead best pursued by 'moderately intelligent' young women who excel at hack writing for newspapers and popular magazines.[56] Echoing her earlier critique of upper-class women in the workforce, Low argues that this decline is in part due to the fact that the profession is overstocked with women who write for 'vanity' rather than necessity, thus driving down wages for the 'genuine bread-winner, who lives by her earnings'.[57] Low calls for the creation of a trades union that would serve the 'legitimate woman journalist, who finds herself cruelly handicapped to-day by the selfishness of her well-to-do sisters'.[58] Low had very good reason to be pessimistic. Even though she was one of the more successful of these 'legitimate' women journalists, she nevertheless struggled to support herself by her writing. Due to poor health, she was forced to appeal to the Royal Literary Fund in 1900 and 1913.[59] And the 1901 census found Low and her sister Florence living in a household without servants.[60] Indeed, Low seems to be referring to herself in *Press Work for Women* when she describes the cultivated women writer who 'find herself in middle age doomed to hack work and a poverty very close to destitution'.[61]

While Low's handbook is undeniably pessimistic – and perhaps appropriately so given the working conditions most women journalists faced at the *fin de siècle* – it is also a decidedly progressive text that aims to demystify the profession for single women. 'It is essential', Low emphasizes, 'that the journalistic novice should embark on her career clear-eyed, with a knowledge of the conditions prevailing in the market'.[62] Toward this end, Low provides a wealth of practical information, including publishers' addresses, rates of remuneration, proofreading guidelines, self-marketing strategies, and a list of literary societies. Such an approach might be called 'practical feminism' in the sense that it is aimed at providing women with the tools to become savvy and self-sufficient freelance writers in the professional marketplace. While her reference to women's journalism throughout as 'wares' or 'goods' might seem harshly realistic, it nevertheless served the purpose of de-romanticizing the profession, forcing women to understand their roles as workers in a fiercely competitive industry.

Like many women writers of the *fin de siècle*, Low often referred to women's capabilities in an essentialist way. In *Press Work for Women*, she refers to women's 'instinctive gift for taking in the details of dress at a swift glance'.[63] However, the book as a whole emphasizes the contingency of the writing self. Rather than encouraging women to express an authentic voice or an essential femininity in their work, she advises them to cut their 'literary coat' according to the needs of specific audiences and editors who are paying for their services.[64] She encourages the woman journalist 'to dispose of her wares to advantage' rather than take up any great mission or passionate personal interest.[65] Taking a pragmatic approach, she highlights the necessity of assuming whatever poses are necessary for survival. 'Take up one or more expert subjects', she remarks, 'Dress, employments, complexion, what you will (so long as it is *in demand*), and make your name known as an authority thereon; but, at the same time, *refuse nothing* which you can do without dishonour'.[66] Such reflections on the journalist's craft would seem to call into question the presumed earnestness of Low's own work as a reporter. Did she write about the domestic lives of women and children only because such subject matter was 'in demand'? Did she investigate the conditions faced by poor women simply because this would enable her to make her 'name known as an authority thereon'?

These are, of course, unanswerable questions. But it is important to note that Low's harsh realism in *Press Work for Women* is balanced by an underlying idealism about the journalist's mission. She concludes the volume with a statement of her belief in the future of women's contributions to the field, writing,

> No one who has any observation can doubt that women's journalism is capable of fulfilling a great modern mission – nothing less than that of giving the vast majority of middle-class women all the education

they receive after leaving school, and of influencing them, whether consciously or not, in the direction of simplicity, good taste, good sense, moderation, and duty.[67]

Here Low defines the journalist's role as popular educator – a stance that seems consistent with most of her other writing from the 1890s to the 1920s. But throughout Low's writing there is nevertheless a persistent tendency toward self-contradiction. She asserts that there are essential differences between men and women, yet simultaneously throws such distinctions into question. She attacks women who enter the workforce for anything other than dire necessity, yet envisions new social institutions staffed by middle-class women supervisors and inspectors. She extols the virtues of domestic, unpaid labour, yet provides women with the tools they need to succeed in a male-dominated publishing industry.

Low's contradictory views on women's work were a product not only of her belief in genteel, cultivated womanhood but also of her circumstances as an independent single woman struggling for survival. Wagner reminds us that we must be attentive to women's 'careful negotiation of art, work, the domestic, and the public, including the pressures generated by the mass market'.[68] Part of this negotiation for Low was establishing a market-able name for herself, which was at least in part a product of necessity, rather than choice. In *Press Work for Women*, Low notes that the journalist's 'work increases in value as her name gets known'.[69] Indeed, by the end of the nineteenth century, the name 'Frances Low' often appeared in print. Even though Low struggled financially, she managed to keep her name in circulation by speaking out against what she saw as the excesses of the women's employment movement. In her article, 'A Woman's Criticism of the Women's Congress', published in the *Nineteenth Century* in 1899, Low sharply criticizes the congress, calling it a 'lamentable waste of energy and a painful exhibition of ignorance and folly'.[70] Although she admits that there were 'many useful and even admirable contributions to the programme', she nevertheless finds it 'meaningless and mischievous because it was not representative and impartial'.[71] This was because the 'experiences of suc-cessful women only were given: the life of the average journalist or actress, with its struggles, its sordid anxieties, its overwork and underpay, was never referred to, there being a universal conspiracy to represent woman's wage-earning work as wholly desirable and beneficial'.[72] The perspectives of actual working men and women, she argues, were largely ignored.

Earlier in the essay, Low attempts to de-romanticize the notion of inde-pendent wage-earning, calling it 'permission ... to struggle and starve like men, to spend our best years in an unavailing effort to provide for old age and sickness'.[73] Meanwhile, those women who chose to be homemakers are deemed a 'disgrace to mankind'.[74] Certainly, as Bush has argued, Low was in some sense pleading her own 'bitter resentment of a life of enforced wage labour, which she juxtaposed with frivolous suffragist aspirations towards a life beyond domestic confines'.[75] However, Low was also articulating critiques of middle-class feminism that would be raised by other women activists at the *fin de siècle*, including Beatrice Webb and Barbara Hutchins. As Barbara Caine has noted, first-wave feminism to a large extent 'lacked any analysis of class or the importance of class in determining the actual nature of women's oppression'.[76] Low thus provided a much-needed critique of the middle-class bias inherent in feminist debates over professional employment. Even though Low maintained an anti-suffrage stance, she nevertheless played an instrumental role in illuminating the barriers faced by single women in a harshly competitive world of work, where every field was 'overcrowded with well-equipped applicants'.[77]

Anti-Suffragette

By 1906, Frances Low's opposition to middle-class feminism was channelled specifically into the anti-suffrage campaigns. In a 1906 letter to the editor of the *Times*, Low writes, 'We oppose woman suffrage (not selfishly we hope) because on any conceivable basis of woman suffrage the entire political balance would be affected, altered, and ultimately decisively adjusted'.[78] On 11 January Beatrice Duff wrote a letter in support of Low's position, calling the suffragists a 'small band of narrow-minded women' and recommending the circulation of an anti-suffragist petition.[79] Indeed, as Bush has pointed out, Low's letter 'paved the way for the largest anti-suffrage women's petition since the famous 1889 Appeal and Protest'.[80] A year later, Low wrote a follow-up series of letters to the *Spectator* calling for a more formal organizational structure that would support anti-feminist efforts – the soon to be established Women's National Anti-Suffrage League (WNASL).

Like many other anti-suffragists, Low distrusted democratization and believed that most women were too frivolous to participate meaningfully in the franchise. 'The mass of women', she writes in her 1906 letter to the *Times*, 'will not represent our truest, highest interests'.[81] Instead of seeking the vote, women should advance their cause through the 'agency and force' associated with the 'Press, public opinion, society, and above all and more than all, the home'.[82] Low mentions the press as a proper outlet for women's influence, thus echoing her earlier arguments in *Press Work for Women*, yet she contradicts herself by asserting that the field of journalism should be open to a select few. If women were allowed to vote, she argues,

> We expect confidently to see in politics what we now see in journalism – viz., the interests and tastes and sentiments of the thoughtful, cultivated, intellectual women swamped by the tastes, sentiments, and interests of the mass of ill-educated, uncultured, trivial-minded women whose most absorbing interests are dress and society gossip.[83]

Low's contradictory stance on women's employment is particularly apparent in a series of columns on the domestic arts published in the *Daily Chronicle* in 1907. In a column titled 'Household Service and the National Life', she argues that the 'greatest service' women can provide to their nation is the 'maintenance of homes at their highest possible perfection – in other words, the creation of the environment in which the growing generation is trained in its earliest and most responsive years'.[84] Yet Low exempts women of genius from this righteous domestic servitude when she refers to domestic work as the 'highest and greatest service that women in general (I leave women of genius out of consideration altogether; they may safely be regarded as abnormal) can render to any civilized State'.[85] She no doubt includes herself in the category of 'abnormal' women who have the right to influence the 'civilized state' in more direct ways – in other words, by writing for the press. Such women of genius, she believed, were constantly under threat by the greater mass of women who neglected their domestic responsibilities to pursue journalistic careers. As Low pointed out in *Press Work for Women*, democratization in the popular media had drowned out the voices of exceptional, cultivated women, who were unappreciated in the 'modern newspaper world'.[86]

However, Low's views on democratization, like her views on women's employment, were decidedly contradictory. After all, by writing *Press Work for Women*, she had made a significant contribution to the democratization of the profession. Likewise, she professed to believe that women's most proper realm of influence was the home, yet she criticized women of leisure for their insularity – their inability to understand the struggles faced by the larger mass of working women. The indeterminacies inherent in Low's position on women's work were addressed in a 1907 *Punch* poem, 'Domestic Dignity', which satirized her views on household management. *Punch* was specifically responding to her contention in the *Daily Chronicle* that 'any woman of intelligence worth her salt would unconsciously manage to teach her subordinates and imbue them with the sense of her own respect for exquisite, immaculate cleanliness'.[87] These 'subordinates' include her family members, who should be responsible for making their own beds, a task 'each ought to perform for himself and herself'.[88] To suggest that men should share in this household duty of course undermines Low's thesis that domestic work is women's responsibility. Instead, she becomes a commander of subordinates, including her husband.

'Domestic Dignity' depicts Low as a despotic 'Christabel' who commands her husband to clean his room: 'It is wrong, she explains, / That our poor Mary Janes / Should be set making beds for a man.'[89] He complains, 'I must prepare the bed to air, / And dust with care each bedroom chair; / The quilt I must arrange / With light and loving hand, / And tuck the sheet so smooth and neat / At Christabel's command.'[90] This amusing response to Low's article reminds us that behind Low's seeming conservatism was a radical redefinition of the gender politics of home. If the virtuous woman could best serve her country by managing her household, such management could be interpreted as 'command' which threatened the very hierarchies it was intended to preserve. The use of the name 'Christabel' in the poem is most likely an allusion to Christabel Pankhurst, who had become famous in 1905 for interrupting a Liberal political meeting with suffragist demands. That the views of Low and Pankhurst would be conflated in the minds of popular readers is fascinating considering how divided the two women were on the subject of votes for women. *Punch* viewed her stance on domestic politics as being just as radical as Pankhurst's outspoken feminism. Even if suffragists and anti-suffragists carefully demarcated their positions, such distinctions could be lost on general readers, who might classify all outspoken women as female radicals.

Indeed, for some, Frances Low was a champion of women's rights, regardless of her anti-suffragist stance. In 1907, *Canadian Magazine* quotes one woman as saying: 'There is a very large, a very considerable body of women workers who do use their fullest capacities in the furtherance of public work, such as Mrs. Scarlieb, Mrs. Fawcett, Mrs. Creighton, Miss Frances Low, Miss Cobden, and others with brilliant records, who have helped forward the great movements of modern times towards the emancipation of women.'[91] And later, in Low's obituary, she is remembered as a 'pioneer figure among women journalists' who was 'probably the real originator of newspaper articles on careers for women'.[92] The interpretation of Low as an activist dedicated to the advancement of women is in many ways unfathomable to modern readers. Following the binary logic which has characterized our understanding of late Victorian feminism, Frances Low would seem to fit squarely in the antifeminist camp with Millicent Garrett Fawcett as her righteous opponent.[93] Clearly, twenty-first-century understanding of 'feminist' and 'anti-feminist' positions does not always agree with the way late Victorians perceived such categories.

Endings

By the early twentieth century, Low had certainly made a name for herself as an anti-feminist journalist. However, after 1927, she virtually disappears from literary history. Her obituary, published in the *Times* in 1939, reports that she was 'forced to abandon her writing career' due to 'serious illness'.[94] Nothing else is known of the silent decade between her final publications and death. Did Low, like the women she interviewed in 'How Poor Ladies Live', end up in a state of 'want and distress and destitution'?[95] Did she realize her greatest fear of becoming one of those elderly women 'who have neither pensions nor relatives, and are wholly dependent upon their own precarious earnings and the intermittent aid of strangers'?[96] Indeed, as Low wrote, it was a fate 'almost too painful for the mind to contemplate', yet it was a necessary counter-image to the idealized portrayals of women's working lives so often circulated at the *fin de siècle*.[97] The narrative of the march towards women's emancipation must always be haunted by the image of those women who struggled, and ultimately failed, to achieve what Low sarcastically called 'glorious "independence"'.[98]

By bringing the plight of the genteel woman worker to the attention of the general public and offering women practical advice for entering the field of journalism, Low expressed convictions similar to those held by the Victorian activists we call feminists.[99] Likewise, as a cultural critic, she studied the lives of women and children in a complex way, subtly challenging notions of essential feminine identity. As an investigative reporter, she highlighted the struggles of single mothers and retired professional women, proposing, and to some degree realizing, social change that benefited women in practical ways. She also de-mystified the journalistic profession, providing practical strategies women could use to survive in a harsh professional marketplace. Just as importantly, she drew attention to the middle-class bias inherent in the women's movement at the *fin de siècle*, reminding readers of the suffering multitude of single women workers, who cared less about self-fulfilment than survival. Even if she believed that marriage and family should be the focus of most women's lives, she nevertheless championed the interests of 'redundant' women who were forced to work for a living. Although Low never diverged from her anti-suffrage stance, she made an important contribution to literary history and the women's movement.

Notes

1. Constance Smedley, 'The Hedda Gabler of To-day,' *Fortnightly Review* 82 (July 1907): 79, 83.
2. Frances Low, 'The Parlour Woman or the Club Woman?' *Fortnightly Review* 83 (January 1908): 116, 113.
3. Low, 'The Parlour Woman,' 124.
4. Low, 'The Parlour Woman,' 121.
5. Tamara Wagner, *Antifeminism and the Victorian Novel* (New York: Cambria, 2009), 5.
6. For discussion of the problem of defining late Victorian feminism and antifeminism, see Valerie Sanders, *Eve's Renegades: Victorian Antifeminist Women Novelists* (New York: St. Martin's, 1996), 1–9, and Barbara Caine, *Victorian Feminists* (Oxford: Oxford University Press, 1992), 4–5.
7. Caine, *Victorian Feminists*, 4.
8. Julia Bush, *Women Against the Vote: Female Anti-Suffragism in Britain* (Oxford: Oxford University Press, 2007), 9.
9. Early on, the family converted to the Theistic faith of Reverend Charles Annesley Voysey. See Desmond Chapman-Huston, *The Lost Historian: A Memoir of Sidney Low* (London: Murray, 1936), 22–23.
10. In a letter to Frederick Macmillan, novelist Lucy Clifford refers to Frances as 'hard working – cultured, educated – sane in her views, anti-suffrage – well read in

three languages'. Quoted in Marysa Demoor, *Their Fair Share: Women, Power and Criticism in the* Athenaeum, *from Millicent Garrett Fawcett to Katherine Mansfield, 1870–1920* (Aldershot: Ashgate, 2000), 29. According to Chapman-Huston, Frances and her sister Florence were educated 'at an old-fashioned Dames' School at Bexley'. Chapman-Huston, *The Lost Historian*, 20.

11. The People's Palace building was later absorbed into the University of London complex. See Richard Garnett, *Constance Garnett: A Heroic Life* (London: Sinclair-Stevenson, 1991), 64. For more information on the construction and administration of the building, see [James, Miss. M. S. R.], 'The Peoples' Palace Library,' *The Library* 2 (1890), 341–51.

12. Quoted in Garnett, *Constance Garnett*, 57. Low and Black each received £80 per year for their work. Constance Black, sister to feminist Clementina Black, married William Garnett in 1889 and went on to become a translator of Russian literature.

13. According to her obituary, Low began publishing her work at age 18 (ca. 1880). It is difficult to identify these early pieces, but in *Press Work for Women* she refers to an early article on 'Old School Books' published in the *Evening Standard* and an article on the 'Care and Education of Feeble-minded Children' in the *Times*. Frances Low, *Press Work for Women* (London: Upcott Gill, 1904), 33, 51. The latter article is probably 'Report of the Royal Commission on the Blind, & c: III. Idiots, Imbeciles, and Feeble-Minded Children,' *Times* (July 27, 1889): A4. In addition to the articles I have cited in this chapter, Low published a large body of work in periodicals and newspapers, including the *Athenaeum, Hearth and Home*, and the *Girl's Realm*. See Demoor, *Their Fair Share*, 30; 'Notes and News,' *The Author* 7–8 (1897): 193; and Sally Mitchell, 'Careers for Girls: Writing Trash,' *Victorian Periodicals Review* 25, no. 3 (1992): 113.

14. See Chapman-Huston's *The Lost Historian* for a discussion of the Lows' early family life. Sidney, as the eldest child, was forced to take on a lead role in supporting the family, but Frances seems to have contributed as well.

15. Quoted in Demoor, *Their Fair Share*, 29.

16. Later, she published a second collection, *Little Men in Scarlet: and Other Fairy Tales* (London: Jerrold, 1896).

17. In *Press Work for Women*, Low writes, 'Even more suitable for women than reporting is the field offered by feminine subjects, such as household economy, practical dressmaking, advice on dress, cookery, house furnishing, and women's employments, in all of which the woman journalist has an immense advantage over her male rival', 20–21.

18. Sidney was editor of the *St. James Gazette* (1888–97) as well as author of *Governance of England* (1904), *Vision of India* (1906), *Egypt in Transition* (1914), and other works. After emigrating to the United States in 1875, Maurice became a correspondent for the *Boston Globe* and published *Some Light on the Canadian Enigma* (1899), *An Unwritten Chapter on American Diplomacy* (1900), *Protection in the United States* (1901), and other works. Sidney and Maurice were knighted in 1918 and 1922, respectively.

19. The *Strand Magazine* was an illustrated middle-class monthly founded by George Newnes in 1891. For further details on its audience and publication history, see Reginald Pound, *Mirror of the Century*: The Strand Magazine, *1891–1950* (New York: A. S. Barnes, 1967). In *Press Work for Women*, Low recommended the *Strand Magazine* to beginning writers due to its policy of 'payment on acceptance' and its openness to publishing the 'new-comer', 20.

20. This article provides an especially fascinating exploration of gender roles and the New Woman. I have not analysed it here since it receives extensive treatment in Chapter 6 of my forthcoming book, *Literary Celebrity, Gender, and Victorian Authorship, 1850–1914* (Newark: University of Delaware Press, 2011).
21. Frances Low, 'The Street Games of Children,' *Strand Magazine* 2 (November 1891): 513.
22. Low, 'Street Games,' 516, 513.
23. Low, 'Street Games,' 513.
24. Low, 'Street Games,' 514.
25. Low, 'Street Games,' 514.
26. Low, 'Street Games,' 517.
27. Low, 'Street Games,' 514.
28. See Caine, *Victorian Feminists*, 248–59, and Bush, *Women Against the Vote*, 13–15.
29. Frances Low, 'Queen Victoria's Dolls,' *Strand Magazine* 4 (September 1892): 236.
30. Low, 'Queen Victoria's Dolls,' 223.
31. Low, 'Queen Victoria's Dolls,' 223.
32. Low, 'Queen Victoria's Dolls,' 230.
33. Low, 'Queen Victoria's Dolls,' 223.
34. For a discussion of Queen Victoria's patronage of the *Strand Magazine*, see Pound, *Mirror of the Century*, 8–9.
35. See chapter 6 of my forthcoming book, *Literary Celebrity, Gender, and Victorian Authorship*, where I discuss the incorporation of celebrity news in the *Strand Magazine* and other periodicals at the *fin de siècle*.
36. Low, 'Queen Victoria's Dolls,' 238.
37. In her introduction to the book, Low refers to the 'astonishing amount of attention and interest' her article garnered. Frances Low, *Queen Victoria's Dolls* (London: Newnes, 1894), 1. The book was published by George Newnes, general editor of the *Strand Magazine*.
38. Low, *Queen Victoria's Dolls*, 5.
39. In *Press Work for Women*, Low notes that she was in the habit of making weekly visits to the National Portrait Gallery, 34. And an 1899 report in the *Journal of Education* notes that Low gave an address on 'How to make the National Gallery a pleasurable place to Children' at the 'Hastings and St. Leonard's Branch of the Parents' Education Union'. The notice also makes reference to Low's 'forthcoming book on the National Gallery for children', which apparently was never published. 'Jottings,' *Journal of Education* 21 (February 1899): 110.
40. Frances Low, 'Women Artists of the Day,' *Windsor Magazine* 9 (February 1899): 283.
41. Low, 'Women Artists', 283. The artists are Maud Earl, Louise Jopling-Rowe, Blanche Jenkins, Margaret Dicksee, and Lucy Kemp-Welch.
42. Frances Low, 'The Receiving Room of the London Hospital,' *English Illustrated Magazine* 152 (May 1896): 175.
43. Low, 'The Receiving Room,' 175.
44. Of particular interest is Low's attention to the unjust prejudice experienced by poor Jewish families. This is the only reference to the family's Jewish heritage I have been able to uncover in Low's oeuvre. This may have been due to the family's conversion to Theism (see note 9 above).
45. Frances Low, 'How Poor Ladies Live,' *Nineteenth Century* 41 (March 1897): 405.
46. Low, 'How Poor Ladies Live,' 405. This article spurred three spirited rejoinders by Eliza Orme, Edith Shaw, and William Bousfield, which were published in the *Nineteenth Century* in April 1897, 613–19.

47. Low, 'How Poor Ladies Live,' 408.
48. Low, 'How Poor Ladies Live,' 416.
49. Frances Low, 'How Poor Ladies Live: A Rejoinder and a "Jubilee" Suggestion,' *Nineteenth Century* 42 (July 1897): 168.
50. Frances Low, 'Where Poor Ladies Can Live in London,' *Leisure Hour* (October 1900): 1071.
51. Low, 'Where Poor Ladies,' 1074.
52. Frances Low, 'A Remedy for Baby-Farming,' *Fortnightly Review* 63 (February 1898): 286.
53. For background on the club, see David Rubinstein, *Before the Suffragettes: Women's Emancipation in the 1890s* (New York: St. Martin's, 1986), 224; and Elizabeth Crawford, *The Women's Suffrage Movement: A Reference Guide, 1866–1928* (London: University College London Press, 1999), 129–30.
54. See Demoor, *Their Fair Share*, 19–21; and Hilary Fraser, Stephanie Green, and Judith Johnston, *Gender and the Victorian Periodical* (Cambridge: Cambridge University Press, 2003), 40. For a discussion of the broader discourse on journalistic careers for girls at the *fin de siècle*, see Mitchell, 'Careers for Girls.'
55. Low, *Press Work for Women*, 2–3. Her emphasis.
56. Low, *Press Work for Women*, 4.
57. Low, *Press Work for Women*, 39.
58. Low, *Press Work for Women*, 39.
59. Demoor, *Their Fair Share*, 30.
60. Bush, *Women Against the Vote*, 169.
61. Low, *Press Work for Women*, 3.
62. Low, *Press Work for Women*, 5.
63. Low, *Press Work for Women*, 10.
64. Low, *Press Work for Women*, 18.
65. Low, *Press Work for Women*, 40.
66. Low, *Press Work for Women*, 6. Emphasis in the original.
67. Low, *Press Work for Women*, 92.
68. Wagner, *Antifeminism and the Victorian Novel*, 7.
69. Low, *Press Work for Women*, 8.
70. Frances Low, 'A Woman's Criticism of the Women's Congress,' *Nineteenth Century* 46 (August 1899): 201.
71. Low, 'A Woman's Criticism,' 201.
72. Low, 'A Woman's Criticism,' 201–2.
73. Low, 'A Woman's Criticism,' 198.
74. Low, 'A Woman's Criticism,' 199.
75. Bush, *Women Against the Vote*, 169.
76. Caine, *Victorian Feminists*, 247.
77. Low, 'A Woman's Criticism,' 200.
78. Frances Low, 'An Unnoticed Aspect of Woman Suffrage,' *Times* (27 December, 1906): 9B.
79. Beatrice Duff, 'Unnoticed Aspects of Woman Suffrage,' *Times* (11 January, 1907): 6C.
80. Bush, *Women Against the Vote*, 169. An anti-suffrage petition, 'An Appeal against Female Suffrage', appeared in the *Nineteenth Century* in June 1889, and Millicent Garrett Fawcett's rejoinder appeared a month later in the same journal. See Bush for a discussion of the importance of this exchange in the debate over suffrage at the *fin de siècle*, 141–62.
81. Low, 'An Unnoticed Aspect,' 9B.

82. Low, 'An Unnoticed Aspect,' 9B.
83. Low, 'An Unnoticed Aspect,' 9B.
84. Frances Low, 'Household Service and the National Life,' *Daily Chronicle* (23 October 1907): 4.
85. Low, 'Household Service,' 4.
86. Low, *Press Work for Women*, 3.
87. Frances Low, 'Women and the Arts of Home,' *Daily Chronicle* (30 October 1907): 6.
88. Low, 'Women and the Arts,' 6.
89. 'Domestic Dignity,' *Punch* 133 (13 November 1907): 352, ll.21–23.
90. 'Domestic Dignity,' ll.31–36.
91. 'Are Women Unbusinesslike?,' *Canadian Magazine* 28 (1907): 402.
92. 'Obituary: Miss Frances Low,' *Times* (10 April 1939): 13G.
93. Indeed, Low and Fawcett sparred in the pages of the *Daily Chronicle*. See Frances Low, 'True Sphere of Woman: A Reply to Mrs. Fawcett,' *Daily Chronicle* (4 November 1907): 3.
94. 'Obituary: Miss Frances Low,' 13G.
95. Low, 'How Poor Ladies Live,' 415.
96. Low, 'How Poor Ladies Live,' 415.
97. Low, 'How Poor Ladies Live,' 415.
98. Low, 'A Woman's Criticism,' 198.
99. As Bush points out in *Women Against the Vote*, 'Differences of judgment and emphasis, rather than of principle, divided many of the more conservative suffragists from the more progressive anti-suffragists', 54. In fact, the Writer's Club co-founded by Frances Low in 1892 attracted many suffragists, including Constance Smedley and Flora Annie Steel, which suggests that there must have been significant social interaction between women on both sides of the suffrage debate (Crawford, *The Women's Suffrage Movement*, 129). Smedley's decision to leave the Writer's Club and found the rival Lyceum Club for women in 1904 might have been cause for some of the vitriol in the Low–Smedley exchange in the *Fortnightly Review* alluded to in my introduction to this chapter.

Complete Bibliography

Adams, Jad. *Hideous Absinthe: A History of the Devil in a Bottle* (Madison, Wisconsin: The University of Wisconsin Press, 2004).

Anderson, Nancy Fix. 'Autobiographical Fantasies of a Female Anti-Feminist: Eliza Lynn Linton as Christopher Kirkland and Theodora Desanges,' *Dickens Studies Annual: Essays on Victorian Fiction* 14 (1985), 287–301.

——. *Woman Against Women in Victorian England: A Life of Eliza Lynn Linton* (Bloomington: Indiana University Press, 1987).

'Are Women Unbusinesslike?' *Canadian Magazine* 28 (1907), 402.

'Armenians at Hawarden: Mr Gladstone and the Refugees,' *Woman's Signal* (25 April 1895), 264–265.

'Armenian Atrocities,' *Woman's Signal* (9 May 1895), 302.

Armytage, R. '"The Depths of the Sea," after Burne Jones,' *Academy* (22 May 1886), 362.

——. '"Mariage de Convenance.—After!" (Orchardson),' *Academy* (12 June 1886), 415.

——. 'Modern Dress,' *Fortnightly Review* (September 1883), 352.

Arnold, Matthew. 'Haworth Churchyard,' *Fraser's Magazine* 51 (May 1855), 527–530.

——. 'Up to Easter,' *Nineteenth Century* 123 (May 1887), 629–643.

Ashwell, Frances. 'One Phase of Journalism,' *Woman's Signal* (12 September 1895), 171–172.

'At the Sign of the Ship,' *Longman's Magazine* (October 1887), 662–663.

A.U. [Elizabeth Robins Pennell]. 'Art and Artists,' *Star* (4 July 1892), 4.

——. 'Art and Artists,' *Star* (13 February 1893), 3.

——. 'Art and Artists,' *Star* (28 February 1905), 4.

——. 'Authoresses,' *Saturday Review* 16 (10 October 1863), 483–484.

——. 'A Few February Shows,' *Star* (14 February 1893), 4.

——. 'The Grafton Gallery,' *Star* (23 February 1893), 4.

——. 'Minor Art Exhibitions,' *Star* (11 February 1892), 4.

Badeni, June. *The Slender Tree: A Life of Alice Meynell* (Padstow, Cornwall: Tabb House, 1981).

Barbara. 'Book Chat,' *Woman* (30 November 1892), 12.

Barrett, Elizabeth Barrett. 'Stanzas Addressed to Miss Landon and Suggested by her "Stanzas on the Death of Mrs Hemans",' *New Monthly Magazine* n.s. 45 (September 1835), 82.

Barrie, J.M. *When a Man's Single* (1888); reprinted (London: Hodder and Stoughton, 1923).

Beer, Gillian. 'Knowing a Life: Edith Simcox—Sat est vixisse?' *Knowing the Past: Victorian Literature and Culture*, ed. Suzy Anger (Ithaca: Cornell University Press, 2001), 252–266.

Beerbohm, Max. 'Mrs. Meynell's Cowslip Wine,' *Tomorrow* (September 1896), 162.

Beetham, Margaret. *A Magazine of Her Own? Domesticity and Desire in the Woman's Magazine, 1800–1914* (Routledge: London, 1996).

——. 'Periodicals and the New Media: Women and Imagined Communities,' *Women's Studies International Forum* 29 (June 2006), 231–240.

Beetham, Margaret and Kay Boardman, eds. *Victorian Women's Magazines: An Anthology* (Manchester: Manchester University Press, 2001).

Bell, E. Moberly. *Flora Shaw (Lady Lugard D.B.E.)* (London: Constable, 1947).

———. Correspondence: Manager's Letter Book, *The Times* Record Office, London.

Bell, E.H.C. Moberly. *The Life & Letters of C.F. Moberly Bell* (London: The Richards Press, 1927).

Bennett, E. Arnold. *Journalism for Women: A Practical Guide* (London and New York: John Lane, 1898).

Billington, Mary Frances. 'Journalism as a Profession for Women,' *Woman's World* 3 (1890); reprinted (New York: Source Books, 1970), 8–10.

Bisson, Frederick Shirley Dumaresq de Carteret. *Our Schools and Colleges*, vol. 2 (London: Simpkin Marshall, 1884).

Black, Helen C. *Notable Women Authors of the Day* (1893); reprinted (Freeport, NY: Books for Libraries Press, 1972).

Blackham, Robert J. *Woman: In Honour and Dishonour* (London: Sampson, Low, Marston, & Co., 1936).

de Blowitz, Henri. 'Journalism as a Profession,' *Contemporary Review* 63 (January 1893), 37–46.

'Blue Stocking' [Miss Curtis]. 'Review of *My Flirtations*,' *Lady's Pictorial* (15 October 1892), 583.

Bodenheimer, Rosemarie. 'Autobiography in Fragments: The Elusive Life of Edith Simcox,' *Victorian Studies* 44, no. 3 (Spring 2002), 399–433.

———. *The Real Life of Mary Ann Evans: George Eliot, Her Letters and Fiction* (Ithaca: Cornell University Press, 1994).

'Books Worth Reading. The Life of Frances Power Cobbe,' *Woman's Signal* 2, no. 46 (15 November 1894), 317.

'Books Worth Reading: The Life of Frances Power Cobbe. Part II,' *Woman's Signal* 2, no. 47 (22 November 1894), 333.

'Books Worth Reading: The Life of Frances Power Cobbe. Part III,' *Woman's Signal* 2, no. 48 (29 November 1894), 349.

Boumelha, Penny. 'The Woman of Genius and the Woman of Grub Street: Figures of the Female Writer in British *Fin-de-siècle* Fiction,' *English Literature in Transition* 40, no. 2 (1997), 164–180.

Bourdieu, Pierre. *The Field of Cultural Production*, ed. Randal Johnson (New York: Columbia University Press, 1993).

Bradshaw, A. 'Deserted Armenia,' *Our Sisters*, 2, no. 14 (1897), 52.

Brake, Laurel. 'The Old Journalism and the New: Forms of Cultural Production in London in the 1880s,' *Papers for the Millions: The New Journalism in Britain, 1850s to 1914*, ed. Joel H. Wiener (New York: Greenwood Press, 1988), 1–24.

———. *Subjugated Knowledges: Journalism, Gender and Literature in the Nineteenth Century* (New York: New York University Press, 1994).

———. 'Writing Women's History: "The Sex" Debates of 1889,' *New Woman Hybridities: Femininity, Feminism, and International Consumer Culture, 1880–1930*, eds Ann Heilmann and Margaret Beetham (London: Routledge, 2004), 51–73.

Brake, Laurel and Julie Codell, eds *Encounters in the Victorian Press: Editors, Authors, Readers* (Houndmills, Basingstoke: Palgrave Macmillan, 2005).

Brake, Laurel and Marysa Demoor, general eds. *Dictionary of Nineteenth Century Journalism* (London: British Library/Sage, 2008).

Brass, Tom. 'Contextualizing Sugar Production in Nineteenth-Century Queensland,' *Slavery and Abolition* 15, no. 1 (April 1994), 100–117.

Broomfield, Andrea. 'Eliza Lynn Linton, Sarah Grand and the Spectacle of the Victorian Woman Question,' *English Literature in Transition* 37, no. 4 (2004), 251–272.

——. 'Much More than an Antifeminist: Eliza Lynn Linton's Contribution to the Rise of Victorian Popular Journalism,' *Victorian Literature and Culture* 29, no. 2 (2001), 267–283.

Broomfield, Andrea and Sally Mitchell, eds. *Prose by Victorian Women: An Anthology* (New York and London: Garland, 1996).

Broughton, Rhoda. *Cometh up as a Flower* (1867); reprinted (London: Macmillan and Company, 1910).

Brown, Daniel, and Hilary Fraser, eds. *English Prose of the Nineteenth Century* (London: Longman, 1997).

Brown, Lucy. *Victorian News and Newspapers* (Oxford: Clarendon, 1985).

Brown, Susan. 'The Victorian Poetess,' *The Cambridge Companion to Victorian Poetry*, ed. Joseph Bristow (Cambridge: Cambridge University Press, 2000), 180–202.

Browning, Elizabeth Barrett. *Elizabeth Barrett Browning: Selected Poems*, eds. Marjorie Stone and Beverly Taylor (Peterborough, Ontario: Broadview Press, 2009).

Bush, Julia. *Women Against the Vote: Female Anti-Suffragism in Britain* (Oxford: Oxford University Press, 2007).

Caine, Barbara. *Victorian Feminists* (Oxford: Oxford University Press, 1993).

Campbell, Kate. 'W. E. Gladstone, W. T. Stead, Matthew Arnold and a New Journalism: Cultural Politics in the 1880s,' *Victorian Periodicals Review* 36 (Spring 2003), 20–40.

Chambers, Deborah, Linda Steiner and Carole Fleming. *Women and Journalism* (London and New York: Routledge, 2004).

Chambers, Edmund K. 'Mrs. Meynell,' *The Bookman* 3, no. 6 (August 1896), 516–519.

'Change in Ownership of the "Herald,"' *Women's Penny Paper* (30 April 1892), 1.

Chapman-Huston, Desmond. *The Lost Historian: A Memoir of Sidney Low* (London: Murray, 1936).

'Character Sketch,' *Woman's Signal* 5, no. 110 (6 February 1896), 81–84.

'The Christmas Magazines,' *Times* (23 December 1897), 10.

Clarke, Meaghan. *Critical Voices: Women and Art Criticism in Britain* (Aldershot: Ashgate, 2005).

Cobbe, Frances Power. *The Duties of Women: A Course of Lectures* (London: Williams and Norgate, 1881).

——. 'Journalism as a Profession for Women,' *Women's Penny Paper* (3 November 1888), 5.

——. *The Life of Frances Power Cobbe, by Herself*, 2 vols. (London: Richard Bentley, 1894).

——. *Our Policy: An Address to Women Concerning the Suffrage* (London: London National Society for Women's Suffrage, 1870).

Colby, Vineta. *The Singular Anomaly: Women Novelists of the Nineteenth Century* (New York: New York University Press, 1970).

Conboy, Martin. *Journalism in Britain: A Historical Introduction* (London: Sage, 2011).

'The Condition of Armenian Women,' *Women's Penny Paper* (15 November 1890), 57.

Crawford, Elizabeth. *The Women's Suffrage Movement: A Reference Guide, 1866–1928* (London: University College London Press, 1999).

Crawford, Emily. 'Journalism as a Profession for Women,' *Contemporary Review* 64 (1893), 362–371.

Darnton, Robert. *The Kiss of Lamourette: Reflections in Cultural History* (New York: W.W. Norton, 1990).

'Death of Miss Cobbe,' *Echo* (6 April 1904).

Demoor, Marysa, ed. *Marketing the Author: Authorial Personae, Narrative Selves and Self-Fashioning, 1880–1930* (Houndmills, Basingstoke: Palgrave Macmillan, 2004).

——. *Their Fair Share: Women, Power and Criticism in the* Athenaeum, *from Millicent Garrett Fawcett to Katherine Mansfield, 1870–1920* (Aldershot: Ashgate, 2000).

Dillane, Fionnuala. 'Re-Reading George Eliot's "Natural History": Marian Evans, "the People," and the Periodical,' *Victorian Periodicals Review* 42, no. 3 (2009), 244–266.

Dixon, Ella Hepworth. *As I Knew Them: Sketches of People I Have Met Along the Way* (London: Hutchinson and Company, 1930).

———. Correspondence between Grant Richards and Ella Hepworth Dixon, Rarebooks and Special Collections, University of Illinois Library, Urbana-Champaign.

———. 'Dr. Patmore's Patient,' *Sunday Times* (29 January 1888), 8.

———. 'The Kidnapping of Phil Altamore,' *Lady's Pictorial* (25 November 1899), 805–807.

———. 'Like to Like,' *Woman Holiday Number* (1893), 3–10.

———. 'London in Khaki,' *New York Independent* (26 July 1900), 1794–1796.

———. 'The Modern Way: A Social Causerie,' *Westminster Gazette* (14 January 1925), 6; (30 June 1926), 8.

———. 'Murder - or Mercy?' *The Woman's World* (October 1888), 466–469.

———. 'My Faith and My Work,' *Woman* (September 1896), 8.

———. ['Margaret Wynman']. *My Flirtations* (London: Chatto and Windus, 1892).

———. 'One Doubtful Hour,' *The Lady's Pictorial Christmas Number* (1897), 16–21.

———. *One Doubtful Hour and Other Sidelights on the Feminine Temperament* (London: Grant Richards, 1904).

———. 'Pensées de Femme,' *Lady's Pictorial* (29 June 1895), 969; (13 July 1895), 49; (4 July 1896), 33; (26 December 1896), 966; (9 April 1898), 520; (10 April 1909), 566.

———. 'A Scribbler's Comedy,' *Pall Mall Magazine* V (1895), 286–294.

———. (1894). *The Story of a Modern Woman* (London: Merlin, 1990).

———. (1894). *The Story of a Modern Woman* (Peterborough: Broadview, 2004).

———. *The Toyshop of the Heart*, one-act play, performed 1908 at The Playhouse, but never published, mss. held at The British Library.

———. 'An Unconventional Girl,' *London Society Holiday Number* (June 1888), 90–100.

———. 'Why Women are Ceasing to Marry,' *The Humanitarian* (June 1899), 391–396.

———. 'A Winter Idyl,' *The Lady's Pictorial Christmas Number* (1888), 25–27.

———. 'The World's Slow Stain,' *Christmas Number of the World* (21 November 1895), 59–61.

'Domestic Dignity,' *Punch* 133 (13 November 1907), 352.

D.S.M. [D.S. MacColl]. 'The Grafton Gallery,' *Spectator* (23 February 1893), 256.

———. 'The Standard of the Philistine,' *Spectator* (18 March 1893), 357.

Duff, Beatrice, 'Unnoticed Aspects of Woman Suffrage,' *Times* (11 January 1907), 6C.

Easley, Alexis. 'Authorship, Gender and Power in Victorian Culture: Harriet Martineau and the Periodical Press,' *Nineteenth-Century Media and the Construction of Identities*, eds Laurel Brake, Bill Bell and David Finkelstein (Houndmills, Basingstoke: Palgrave, 2000), 137–177.

———. *First-Person Anonymous: Women Writers and Victorian Print Media, 1830–1870* (Aldershot: Ashgate, 2004).

———. *Literary Celebrity, Gender, and Victorian Authorship, 1850–1914* (Newark, DE: University of Delaware Press, 2011).

'Eastern Question Conference,' *Illustrated London News* (16 December 1876), 577.

Eccles, Charlotte O'Conor. 'The Experiences of a Woman Journalist,' *Blackwood's Edinburgh Magazine* 153 (June 1893), 830–838; reprinted in *Victorian Print Media: A Reader*, eds Andrew King and John Plunkett (Oxford: Oxford University Press, 2006), 330–334.

An Editor. *How to Write for the Press: A Practical Handbook for Beginners in Journalism* (London: Horace Cox, 1899).

The Editor [Fitzroy Gardner]. 'What Women May Do. –I,' *Woman* (23 March 1892), 3.
———. 'What Women May Do. – II,' *Woman* (30 March 1892), 4.
Edwards, P.D. *Dickens's 'Young Men': George Augustus Sala, Edmund Yates and the World of Victorian Journalism* (Aldershot: Ashgate, 1997).
Egerton, George [Mary Chavelita Dunne Bright]. *Keynotes and* (1894) *Discords* (1893); reprinted (London: Virago, 1983).
Eliot, George. *The George Eliot Letters*, ed. Gordon S. Haight, 9 vols. (New Haven: Yale University Press, 1954–55).
'A Famous Lady Journalist: A Chat with Mrs. Emily Crawford,' *Young Woman* 2, no. 18 (March 1894), 183–185.
Fenwick-Miller, Florence. *Harriet Martineau* (London: W. H. Allen, 1884).
Flint, John. *Cecil Rhodes* (Boston and Toronto: Little Brown & Company, 1974).
Flint, Kate. *The Victorians and the Visual Imagination* (Cambridge: Cambridge University Press, 2000).
Foucault, Michel. 'What is an Author?' *Language, Memory, Practice: Selected Essays and Interviews*, ed. Donald F. Bouchard, trans. Donald F. Bouchard and Sherry Simon (Ithaca: Cornell Univ. Press, 1977), 113–138.
'Frances Power Cobbe,' *Woman's Journal* 1, no. 13 (2 April 1870), 97.
'Frances Power Cobbe,' *Woman's Journal* 11, no. 10 (6 March 1880), 76.
'Frances Power Cobbe Dead,' *New York Times* (6 April 1904).
'Frances Power Cobbe and the Woman Question,' *Woman's Journal* 26, no. 11 (16 March 1895), 87.
Frank, Katherine. *A Voyager Out: The Life of Mary Kingsley* (Boston: Houghton Mifflin Company, 1986).
Fraser, Hilary, Stephanie Green and Judith Johnston. *Gender and the Victorian Periodical* (Cambridge: Cambridge University Press, 2003).
Friederichs, Hulda. [?], 'Among the Books at the British Museum: An Interview with Mr R. Garnett,' *Pall Mall Gazette* (21 November 1884), 11.
———. 'Are Interviewers a Blessing or a Curse?' *Idler* (January 1896), 583–594.
———. [?] 'Birds, Butchers and Beauties: An Interview with a Dealer in Birds' Skins and Feathers,' *Pall Mall Gazette* (6 January 1886), 1–2.
———. 'Darwinism at the Music Hall: A Chat with "Professor" Petrescu on the Art of Balancing,' *Pall Mall Gazette* (3 November 1890), 3.
———. 'Difficulties and Delights of Interviewing,' *English Illustrated Magazine* (February 1893), 341.
———. 'Dr Koch at Home,' *Pall Mall Gazette* (26 November 1890), 1–2.
———. 'An English Tattooer: An Interview with Mr Sutherland Macdonald,' *Pall Mall Gazette* (1 May 1889), 2.
———. [?] 'The Gun Wanted at Abu Klea,' *Pall Mall Gazette* (24 January 1885), 1–2.
———. *In the Evening of his Days. A Study of Mr Gladstone in Retirement* (London: Westminster Gazette, 1896).
———. 'The Journalist: The Staff of the *Westminster Gazette*,' *The Bookman* (January 1898), 124–125.
———. *The Life of Sir George Newnes, Bart* (London: Hodder and Stoughton, 1911).
———. [?] 'The Muscovite Musicians: An Interview with Mdme Slavianski,' *Pall Mall Gazette* (25 June 1886), 4.
———. [?] 'On the Track of the Daffodil: An Interview with Mr Barr,' *Pall Mall Gazette* (9 April 1889), 3.
———. *The Romance of the Salvation Army* (London: Cassel, 1907).
———. 'Should Sensible Women Follow the Fashions?' *Temple Magazine* (November 1896).

——. 'A Visit to Dr Koch's Consumption Hospital,' *Pall Mall Gazette* (29 November 1890), 1–2.

——. 'Why Do Women Prefer to Remain Unwed?' *Temple Magazine* (April 1898).

Fryckstedt, Monica. 'Geraldine Jewsbury's *Athenaeum* Reviews: A Mirror of Mid-Victorian Attitudes to Fiction,' *Victorian Periodicals Review* 23, no. 1 (1990), 13–25.

Fulmer, Constance. 'Edith Simcox (1844–1901),' *Nineteenth-Century British Women Writers: A Bio-Bibliographical Critical Sourcebook*, ed. Abigail Burnham Bloom, (Westport, CT: Greenwood Press, 2000), 367–369.

——. 'Edith Simcox: Feminist Critic and Reformer,' *Victorian Review* 31, no. 1 (Spring 1998), 105–121.

——. 'A Nineteenth-Century "Womanist" on Gender Issues: Edith Simcox in Her *Autobiography of a Shirtmaker*,' *Nineteenth-Century Prose* 26, no. 2 (Fall 1999), 110–126.

Fulmer, Constance, and Margaret E. Barfield. *Edith Jemima Simcox: Victorian Scholar and Reformer: 1844–1901* (Web 7 June 2001).

Garlick, Barbara and Margaret Harris, eds, *Victorian Journalism: Exotic and Domestic: Essays in Honour of P.D. Edwards* (Queensland: Queensland University Press, 1998).

Garnett, Richard. *Constance Garnett: A Heroic Life* (London: Sinclair-Stevenson, 1991).

Good, Howard. 'The Journalist in Fiction, 1890–1930,' *Journalism Quarterly* (Summer 1985), 187–214.

Goodbody, John. '"The Star": Its Role in the New Journalism,' *Victorian Periodicals Review* 20 (Winter 1987), 141–150.

Gosse, Edmund. 'George Eliot,' *Aspects and Impressions* (London: Cassell, 1922).

Graves, Adrian. *Cane and Labour: The Political Economy of the Queensland Sugar Industry, 1862–190* (Edinburgh: Edinburgh University Press, 1993).

Greg, William Rathbone. 'Why Are Women Redundant?' 1862 (London: Trübner, 1869).

Hamilton, Susan. 'Marketing Antifeminism: Eliza Lynn Linton's "Wild Women" Series and the Possibilities of Periodical Signature,' *Antifeminism and the Victorian Novel: Rereading Nineteenth-Century Women Writers*, ed. Tamara S. Wagner (Amherst, NY: Cambria, 2009), 37–55.

Hampton, Mark. 'Defining Journalists in Late Nineteenth-Century Britain,' *Critical Studies in Media Communication* 22, no. 2 (2005), 138–155.

——. *Visions of the Press in Britain, 1850–1950* (Urbana and Chicago: University of Illinois Press, 2004).

Harraden, Beatrice. 'Mrs. Lynn Linton,' *The Bookman: A Review of Books and Life* 8 (September 1898), 16–17.

——. 'My Fatal Visit to an Editor,' *Belgravia* 64 (February 1888), 82–91.

Helsinger, Elizabeth K., Robin Lauterbach Sheets and William Veeder. *The Woman Question: Defining Voices, 1837–1883*, vol. 1 of *The Woman Question: Society and Literature in Britain and America, 1837–1883* (New York: Garland, 1983).

Herd, Harold. *The March of Journalism: The Story of the British Press from 1622 to the Present Day* (London: George Allen & Unwin, 1952).

Hinkson, Katharine Tynan. *The Middle Years* (London: Constable & Co., 1916).

The History of The Times: *The Twentieth Century Test, 1884–1912* (New York: The Macmillan Company, 1947).

Hogarth, Janet E. 'The Monstrous Regiment of Women,' *Fortnightly Review* 68 (1897), 926–36.

Hopkins, Tighe. 'Anonymity? II,' *The New Review* 2 (March 1890), 265–76.

Horrocks, Jamie. 'Camping in the Kitchen: Locating Culinary Authority in Elizabeth Robins Pennell's *Delights of Delicate Eating*,' *Nineteenth-Century Gender Studies*

(Summer 2007), http://ncgsjournal.com/issue32/horrocks.htm [accessed 10 November 2011].

Houston, Natalie. 'Newspaper Poems: Material Texts in the Public Sphere,' *Victorian Studies* (2008), 233–42.

Hughes, Kathryn. *George Eliot: The Last Victorian* (New York: Cooper Square Press, 2001).

Hughes, Linda K. 'Aestheticism on the Cheap: Decorative Art, Art Criticism, and Cheap Paper in the 1890s,' *The Lure of Illustration in the Nineteenth Century: Picture and Press*, eds Laurel Brake and Marysa Demoor (Houndmills, Basingstoke: Palgrave Macmillan, 2009), 226–30.

——. *The Cambridge Introduction to Victorian Poetry* (Cambridge: Cambridge University Press, 2010).

——. 'A Female Aesthete at the Helm: *Sylvia's Journal* and "Graham R. Tomson," 1893–1894,' *Victorian Periodicals Review* 29, no. 2 (Summer 1996), 173–92.

——. *Graham R.: Rosamund Marriott Watson, Woman of Letters* (Athens, OH: Ohio University Press, 2005).

——. 'Rosamund Marriott Watson,' *Kindred Hands: Letters on Writing by British and American Women Authors, 1865–1935*, eds. Jennifer Cognard-Black and Elizabeth MacLeod Walls (Iowa City: University of Iowa Press, 2006), 183.

——. 'Watson, Rosamund Marriott,' *Dictionary of Nineteenth-Century Journalism*, eds. Laurel Brake and Marysa Demoor (Ghent: Academia Press in conjunction with the British Library, 2009), 635–636.

——. 'Watson, Rosamund Marriott,' in the online *Oxford Dictionary of National Biography* (2004).

——. 'What the *Wellesley Index* Left Out: Why Poetry Matters to Periodical Studies,' *Victorian Periodicals Review* 40, no. 2 (Summer 2007), 91–125.

——. 'A Woman Poet Angling for Notice: Rosamund Marriott Watson,' *Marketing the Author: Authorial Personae, Narrative Selves and Self-Fashioning, 1880–1930*, ed. Marysa Demoor (Houndmills, Basingstoke: Palgrave Macmillan, 2004), 144–151.

'Ibsen's Plays,' *Saturday Review* 69 (4 January 1890), 15–16.

Israel, Kali. *Names and Stories: Emilia Dilke and Victorian Culture* (Oxford: Oxford University Press, 2002).

Jackson, Kate. *George Newnes and the New Journalism in Britain 1880–1910* (Aldershot: Ashgate, 2001).

James, Heather. 'The Geography of the Cult of St David: A Study of Dedication Patterns in the Medieval Diocese,' *St David of Wales: Cult, Church and Nation*, eds. J. Wyn Evans and Jonathan M. Wooding (Suffolk: Boydell P, 2007), 41–83.

James, Miss. [M. S. R.] 'The People's Palace Library,' *The Library* 2 (1890), 341–351.

Jones, Aled. *Powers of the Press* (Hants, UK: Scolar, 1996).

Jones, Kimberly Morse. 'The "Philistine" and the New Art Critic: A New Perspective on the *L'Absinthe* Debate of 1893,' *British Art Journal* 11 (Fall 2008), 50–61.

Joseph and Elizabeth R. Pennell Papers. Elizabeth R. Pennell Diaries. Harry Ransom Center, University of Texas at Austin.

'Jottings,' *Journal of Education* 21 (February 1899), 109–110.

Kent, Sylvia. *The Woman Writer: The History of the Society of Women Journalists* (Stroud: History Press, 2009).

Koss, Stephen. *The Rise and Fall of the Political Press in Britain*, vol. 1 (London: Hamish Hamilton, 1981).

'Lady Henry Somerset's Efforts for the Armenian Refugees,' *Woman's Signal* (15 October 1896), 246.

'Lady Henry Somerset's Letter of Thanks,' *Woman's Signal* (18 March 1897), 172.

'Lady Journalists,' *Lady's Pictorial* (11 November 1893), 734; (25 November 1893), 823; (9 December 1893), 928–929; (23 December 1893), 1020; (10 February 1894), 176–177.

Lady's Pictorial: A Newspaper for the Home (18 March 1902), 316.

Langenau, Baroness. 'What a Woman Did: A True Story,' *Woman's Signal* (27 May 1897), 5.

Lawrence, Arthur H. '"Interviewing" as Women's Work: A Chat with Mrs. Sarah A. Tooley,' *Young Woman* 5 (1896), 441–447.

Lawrenny, H. 'Custom and Sex,' *Fortnightly Review* 17 (63; New Series) (1 March 1872), 310–322.

———. [Response to a review of 'Custom and Sex'], *Examiner* 3349 (6 April 1872), 351.

———. Rev. of *Ahmed le Fellah* by Edmond About, *Academy* 1 (9 October 1869), 6–7.

———. Rev. of *Madame Recamier et les Amis de sa Jeunesse* by Michel Lévy, *Academy* 4, no. 67 (1 March 1873), 81–82.

———. Rev. of *Middlemarch* by George Eliot, *Academy* 4.63 (1 January 1873), 1–4.

———. Rev. of *Théâtre Complet de Beaumarchais* by G. D'Heylli and F. de Marescot, *Academy* 9 (11 June 1870), 223–4.

Layard, George Somes. *Mrs. Lynn Linton: Her Life, Letters, and Opinions* (London: Methuen & Co., 1901).

———. 'Mrs. Lynn Linton and the Girl of the Period,' *Saturday Review* 91 (June 1901), 771.

Ledbetter, Kathryn. *Tennyson and Victorian Periodicals: Commodities in Context* (Aldershot: Ashgate, 2007), 101–142.

Ledger, Sally. 'The New Woman and Feminist Fictions,' *The Cambridge Companion to the Fin de Siècle*, ed. Gail Marshall (Cambridge: Cambridge University Press, 1997), 153–168.

———. *The New Woman: Fiction and Feminism at the Fin de siècle* (Manchester: Manchester University Press, 1997).

Lee, Alan J. *The Origins of the Popular Press in Britain 1855–1914* (London: Croom Helm, 1976).

Leppington, Blanche. 'Review of *Amiel's Journal*,' *Contemporary Review* 47, no. 279 (March 1885), 334–352.

'A Letter from Frances Power Cobbe,' *Woman's Journal* 11, no. 14 (3 April 1880), 104.

'Letters to the Editor,' *Woman's Signal* (27 February 1896), 189.

Lewsen, Phyllis. *Selections from the Correspondence of John X. Merriman*, vol. 2 (Cape Town: Van Riebeck Society, 1963).

L.F.A. 'The Book and Its Story: *My Flirtations*,' *The Sketch* (8 February 1893), 90–91.

Liddle, Dallas. *The Dynamics of Genre: Journalism and the Practice of Literature in Mid-Victorian Britain* (Charlottesville and London: University of Virginia Press, 2009).

Linton, Eliza Lynn. *The Autobiography of Christopher Kirkland* (London: Richard Bentley and Son, 1885).

———. 'A Counter-Blast,' *English Illustrated Magazine* 121 (October 1893), 85–89.

———. 'Literature Then and Now,' *Fortnightly Review* 53 (April 1890), 517–531.

———. 'Mrs. Grundy's Kingdom,' *Forum* 8 (February. 1890), 697–704.

———. 'A Retrospect,' *Fortnightly Review* 45 (1886), 614–29.

'Literary Notices,' *Woman's Journal* 25, no. 44 (3 November 1894), 346.

'Literature Reviews,' *Athenæum* 3013 (25 July 1885), 105.

Low, Frances. *The Air Child: and Other New Fairy Tales* (London: Griffith, Farran, Okedeen, and Welsh, 1890).

———. 'Boy Soldiers and Sailors,' *Strand Magazine* 4 (August 1892), 145–53.

———. 'Distinguished Women and Their Dolls,' *Strand Magazine* 8 (September 1894), 250–257.

——. 'Favourite Books of Childhood,' *Strand Magazine* 8 (August 1894), 128–136.

——. 'His Little Comedy,' *Murray's Magazine* 8 (November 1890), 638–648.

——. 'Household Service and the National Life,' *Daily Chronicle* (23 October 1907), 4.

——. 'How Poor Ladies Live,' *Nineteenth Century* 41 (March 1897), 405–417.

——. 'How Poor Ladies Live: A Rejoinder and a "Jubilee" Suggestion,' *Nineteenth Century* 42 (July 1897), 161–168.

——. 'Impressions of the Rembrandt Exhibition in Amsterdam,' *Pall Mall Magazine* 17 (January 1899), 87–95.

——. 'An Incident in Mr. Lanford's Life: A Sketch,' *Argosy Magazine* 49 (May 1890), 429–439.

——. *Little Men in Scarlet: and Other Fairy Tales* (London: Jerrold, 1896).

——. 'The Parlour Woman or the Club Woman?' *Fortnightly Review* 83 (January 1908), 113–124.

——. *Press Work for Women: A Text Book for the Young Woman Journalist* (London: Upcott Gill, 1904).

——. *Queen Victoria's Dolls* (London: Newnes, 1894).

——. 'Queen Victoria's Dolls,' *Strand Magazine* 4 (September 1892), 223–38.

——. 'The Receiving Room of the London Hospital,' *English Illustrated Magazine* 152 (May 1896), 175–82.

——. 'A Remedy for Baby-Farming,' *Fortnightly Review* 63 (February 1898), 280–286.

[——.] 'Report of the Royal Commission on the Blind, &c: III. Idiots, Imbeciles, and Feeble-minded Children,' *Times* (27 July 1889), A4.

——. 'Some Early Recollections of Sir John Everett Millais,' *Strand Magazine* 11 (June 1896), 603–611.

——. 'The Street Games of Children,' *Strand Magazine* 2 (November 1891), 513–520.

——. 'True Sphere of Woman: A Reply to Mrs. Fawcett,' *Daily Chronicle* (4 November 1907), 3.

——. 'An Unnoticed Aspect of Woman Suffrage,' *Times* (27 December 1906), 9B.

——. 'Where Poor Ladies Can Live in London,' *Leisure Hour* (October 1900), 1071–1074.

——. 'A Woman's Criticism of the Women's Congress,' *Nineteenth Century* 46 (August 1899), 192–202.

——. 'Women and the Arts of Home,' *Daily Chronicle* (30 October 1907), 6.

——. 'Women Artists of the Day,' *Windsor Magazine* 9 (February 1899), 283–291.

Markovits, Stefanie. *The Crimean War in the British Imagination* (Cambridge: Cambridge University Press, 2009).

Mansfield, Elizabeth. 'Articulating Authority: Emilia Dilke's Early Essays and Reviews,' *Victorian Periodicals Review* 31, no. 1 (1998), 75–86.

Maynard, Mary, 'Privilege and Patriarchy: Feminist Thought in the Nineteenth Century,' *Sexuality & Subordination: Interdisciplinary Studies of Gender in the Nineteenth Century*, eds Susan Mendus and Jane Rendall (London and New York: Routledge, 1989), 222–46.

M.B.W. 'The Oldest New Woman,' *Woman's Signal* (7 February 1895), 85.

McKenzie, Keith A. *Edith Simcox and George Eliot* (Oxford: Oxford University Press, 1961).

Meem, Deborah T. 'Eliza Lynn Linton and the Rise of Lesbian Consciousness,' *Journal of the History of Sexuality* 7, no. 4 (1997), 537–560.

Mercer, Patricia. *White Australia Defied: Pacific Islander Settlement in Northern Queensland* (Townsville: History Department, James Cook University, 1995).

Meredith, George. *The Letters of George Meredith*, ed. C.L. Cline, 3 vols. (Oxford: Clarendon Press, 1970).

———. *The Letters of George Meredith to Alice Meynell: With Annotations Thereto, 1896–1907* (London: Nonesuch Press, 1923).

———. 'Mrs. Meynell's Two Books of Essays,' *The National Review* 27, no. 162 (August 1896), 762–770.

Meyer, Peter G., ed. *Brushes with History: Writing on Art from* The Nation (New York: Thunder's Mouth Press/Nation Books, 2001).

Meynell, Alice. 'Alexander Smith,' *Pall Mall Gazette* (12 January, 1898); reprinted in *The Wares of Autolycus: Selected Literary Essays of Alice Meynell*, chosen and introduced by P. M. Fraser (London, New York, and Toronto: Oxford University Press, 1965), 78–81.

———. 'Charlotte and Emily Brontë,' *Dublin Review*, (July–September 1911); reprinted in *Hearts of Controversy*, (London: Burns & Oates, 1917), 77–99.

———. *The Children* (London and New York: John Lane, 1896).

———. 'Children in Burlesque,' *The Children* (London and New York: John Lane, 1896), 69–71.

———. 'The Classic Novelist,' *Pall Mall Gazette* (16 February 1894); reprinted in *The Second Person Singular* (Oxford: Oxford University Press, 1921), 62–67.

———. *The Colour of Life, and Other Essays on Things Seen and Heard* (London: John Lane, 1896).

———. 'A Corrupt Following,' *Pall Mall Gazette* (January 10, 1900); reprinted in *Prose and Poetry* (London: Jonathan Cape, 1947), 176–180.

———. 'Elegy Written in a Country Churchyard,' *Pall Mall Gazette* (21 April 1897); reprinted in *The Wares of Autolycus: Selected Literary Essays of Alice Meynell*, chosen and introduced by P. M. Fraser (London, New York, and Toronto: Oxford University Press, 1965), 28–31.

———. 'The English Women-Humorists,' *North American Review*, (June 1905), 857–872; reprinted in *The Wares of Autolycus: Selected Literary Essays of Alice Meynell*, chosen and introduced by P. M. Fraser (London, New York, and Toronto: Oxford University Press, 1965), 111–126.

———. *The Flower of the Mind: A Choice Among the Best Poems* (London: Grant Richards, 1897).

———. *Hearts of Controversy* (London: Burns & Oates, 1917).

———. 'The Honours of Mortality,' *Pall Mall Gazette* (29 September 1893); reprinted in *The Colour of Life* (London: John Lane, 1896), 30–31.

———. 'In Memoriam,' Introduction to *In Memoriam* (Red Letter Library, Blackie & Co., 1904); reprinted in *The Wares of Autolycus: Selected Literary Essays of Alice Meynell*, chosen and introduced by P. M. Fraser (London, New York, and Toronto: Oxford University Press, 1965), 150–154.

———. *John Ruskin* (Edinburgh and London: Blackwood, 1900).

———. 'Miss Mitford,' *Pall Mall Gazette* (23 February 1898); reprinted in *Wares of Autolycus: Selected Literary Essays of Alice Meynell*, chosen and introduced by P. M. Fraser (London, New York, and Toronto: Oxford University Press, 1965), 82–85.

———. 'Mr. Coventry Patmore's Odes,' *National Observer* (25 July 1891); reprinted in *The Rhythm of Life* (London: John Lane, 1896), 89–96.

———. 'Oblivion,' *Pall Mall Gazette* (16 August 1895); reprinted in *The Wares of Autolycus: Selected Literary Essays of Alice Meynell*, chosen and introduced by P. M. Fraser (London, New York, and Toronto: Oxford University Press, 1965), 5–8.

———. 'Poetesses,' *Merry England* 2:11 (March 1884), 290–302.

———. *Prose and Poetry*. With biography and critical introduction by Vita Sackville-West (London: Jonathan Cape, 1947).

——. 'Some Thoughts of a Reader of Tennyson,' *Dublin Review* (January–March 1910); reprinted in *Hearts of Controversy* (London: Burns & Oates, 1917), 1–22.

——. *The Wares of Autolycus: Selected Literary Essays of Alice Meynell*. Chosen and Introduced by P. M. Fraser (London, New York, and Toronto: Oxford University Press, 1965).

——. 'A Woman of Masculine Understanding,' *Pall Mall Gazette* (11 October 1895); reprinted in *Wares of Autolycus: Selected Literary Essays of Alice Meynell*. Chosen and Introduced by P. M. Fraser (London, New York, and Toronto: Oxford University Press, 1965), 8–12.

Meynell, Viola. *Alice Meynell: A Memoir* (London: Jonathan Cape, 1929).

Mill, John Stuart. *The Subjection of Women* (London: Longman's, 1869).

Mills, Saxon. *Sir Edward Cook KBE, a Biography* (London: Constable, 1921).

'Miss Frances Power Cobbe,' *Womanhood* 9, no. 51 (1903), 192.

Mitchell, Sally. 'Careers for Girls: Writing Trash,' *Victorian Periodicals Review* 25, no. 3 (1992), 109–113.

——. 'Ephemeral Journalism and its Uses: Lucie Cobbe Heaton Armstrong 1851–1907,' *Victorian Periodicals Review* 42, no. 1 (2009), 81–92.

——. 'Victorian Journalism in Plenty,' *Victorian Literature and Culture* 37 (2009), 311–321.

'Miss Flora Shaw,' *Pall Mall Gazette* (4 July 1889), 7a.

Moore, Clive, Jacqueline Leckie and Douglas Munro, eds. *Labour in the South Pacific* (Townsville: James Cook University of Queensland, 1990).

'Mr. Stead on Journalists,' *Times* (22 March 1909), 15.

Nesbit, E. 'The Depths of the Sea,' *To-Day* 33 (September 1886), 93.

——. *Lays and Legends* (London: Longmans, Green, and Co., 1887).

Nicoll, W. Robertson. 'George Augustus Simcox,' *A Bookman's Letters*, 4th edn (London: Hodder & Stoughton, 1908), 105–113.

Niessen, Olwen Claire. *Aristocracy, Temperance and Social Reform* (Online: Tauris Academic Studies, 2007).

'Notes and News,' *The Author* 7–8 (1897), 193.

'Obituary: Lord Henry Somerset,' *Times* (11 October 1932), 16.

'Obituary: Miss Ella Hepworth Dixon,' *Times* (13 January 1932), 14.

'Obituary: Miss Frances Low,' *Times* (10 April 1939), 13G.

O'Hara, Patricia. 'The Women of Today: The Fin-de-Siècle Women of *The Music Hall and Theatre Review*,' *Victorian Periodicals Review* 30, no. 2 (Summer 1997), 141–156.

Onslow, Barbara. *Women of the Press in Nineteenth-Century Britain* (London: Macmillan, 2000).

Owen, George. *The Description of Penbrokshire*. 1603, ed. and notes Henry Owen. 1892 (London: Bedford Press, 1897). Issue 1, Part 2.

Owen, Henry. *Old Pembroke Families in the Ancient County Palatine of Pembroke* (London: Charles J. Clark, 1902).

Owen, Roger. *Lord Cromer: Victorian Imperialist, Edwardian Proconsul* (Oxford: Oxford University Press, 2004).

'Pageant of Famous Men and Women,' *Times* (30 June 1914), 11.

Park, Sowon S. 'The First Professional: The Women Writers' Suffrage League,' *Modern Language Quarterly* 57, no. 2 (1997), 185–200.

Patmore, Coventry. 'Mrs. Meynell, Poet and Essayist,' *The Fortnightly Review* 58 (1 December 1892), 761–766.

Pater, Walter. *The Renaissance: Studies in Art and Poetry* (London: MacMillan and Co. Limited, 1904).

Pennell, Elizabeth Robins. 'In the World of Art,' *Woman* (15 June 1892), 8.

——. *Nights: Rome, Venice, in the Aesthetic Eighties: London, Paris, in the Fighting Nineties* (Philadelphia and London: J.B. Lippincott Company, 1916).

——. *Over the Alps on a Bicycle* (London: T. Fisher Unwin, 1898).

——. 'A Protest and What it Suggests,' Sidney Woodward Papers, Archives of American Art, Smithsonian Institution, Washington D.C.

——. *The Whistler Journal* (Philadelphia: J.B. Lippincott, 1921).

——. 'Woman's World in London,' *The Chautauquan: A Weekly Newsmagazine* (1 March 1893), 725.

Pennell, Joseph. 'The Triumph of Whistler,' *Bookman* 36 (1913), 158–164.

Pennell-Whistler Collection, Special Collections, Library of Congress, Washington D.C.

Perkin, Harold. *The Rise of Professional Society: England since 1880* (London and New York: Routledge, 1989).

Peterson, Linda. *Becoming a Woman of Letters: Myths of Authorship and Facts of the Victorian Market* (Princeton: Princeton University Press, 2009).

Pfeiffer, Emily. 'Sonnet,' *Fraser's Magazine* (August 1879), 185.

The Philistine [John Alfred Spender]. 'The New Art Criticism – A Philistine's Remonstrance,' *Westminster Gazette* 1 (9 March 1893), 1–2.

Phillips, Evelyn March. 'The New Journalism,' *The New Review* (13 August 1895), 182–89.

Pound, Reginald. *Mirror of the Century: The Strand Magazine, 1891–1950* (New York: A. S. Barnes, 1967).

'Preferences of an Eclectic,' *Pall Mall Gazette* (12 November 1897), 4.

Prettejohn, Elizabeth. 'Aesthetic Value and the Professionalization of Victorian Art Criticism, 1837–78,' *Journal of Victorian Culture* 2 (Spring 1997), 71–94.

Prior, Edward John. 'How to Become a Lady Journalist,' *Girl's Own Paper* 24, no. 1229 (18 July 1903), 668–669.

Prochaska, F.K. *Women and Philanthropy in Nineteenth-Century England* (Oxford: Clarendon Press, 1980).

Psomiades, Kathy. *Beauty's Body: Femininity and Representation in British Aestheticism* (Stanford: Stanford University Press, 1997).

'Record of Events: The Institute of Journalists,' *Englishwoman's Review* (15 October 1894), 244–51.

Redinger, Ruby. *George Eliot: The Emergent Self* (New York: Knopf, 1975).

'Report of Women's National Liberal Association Meeting,' *Woman's Signal* (21 May 1896), 331.

Repplier, Agnes. *Our Convent Days* (Boston and New York: Houghton Mifflin Company, 1905).

'Review of August Magazines,' *St. James's Gazette* (29 July 1889), 6.

'Review of March Magazines,' *St. James's Gazette* (1 March 1889), 7.

'Review of *My Flirtations*,' *Punch* (21 January 1893), 12.

'Review of *The Works of the Late Right Honourable Henry St. John, Lord Viscount Bolingbroke* by David Mallet,' *Quarterly Review* 149 (January–April 1880), 2–47.

'Reviews,' *Englishwoman's Review* 26, no. 224 (15 January 1895), 59–62.

Roberts, Helene. 'Exhibition and Review: The Periodical Press and the Victorian Art Exhibition System,' *The Victorian Periodical Press: Samplings and Soundings*, eds Joanne Shattock and Michael Wolff (Leicester: Leicester University Press, 1982), 79–107.

Roberts, Lewis C. '"The Production of a Female Hand": Professional Writing and the Career of Geraldine Jewsbury,' *Women's Writing* 12, no. 3 (2005), 399–418.

Robins, Anna Gruetzner, ed *Walter Sickert: The Complete Writings on Art* (Oxford: Oxford University Press, 2000).

Robinson, Charles J. 'Rev. of *Episodes in the Lives of Men, Women, and Lovers,'* *Academy* 521 (28 April 1882), 296–7.

Romanes, George J. 'The Mental Differences Between Men and Women,' *Nineteenth Century* (May 1887), 654–672.

Ross, Robert. 'Review of *My Flirtations,'* *The Saturday Review* (8 October 1892), 419.

Rubinstein, David. *Before the Suffragettes: Women's Emancipation in the 1890s* (New York: St. Martin's, 1986).

Ruskin, John. *Fors Clavigera: Letters to the Workmen and Labourers of Great Britain,* new edn, 4 vols. (London: George Allen, 1896).

———. 'Of Queen's Gardens,' *Sesame and Lilies: Two Lectures Delivered at Manchester in 1864* (London: Smith, Elder & Co., 1865).

———. *Selections from the Writings of John Ruskin* (London: Smith, Elder and Co., 1863).

Sackville-West, Vita. Introduction. *Prose and Poetry* (London: Jonathan Cape, 1947), 7–26.

Salmon, Richard. 'Signs of Intimacy: The Literary Celebrity in the "Age of Interviewing."' *Victorian Literature and Culture* 25, no. 1 (1997), 159–177.

———. '"A Simulacra of Power": Intimacy and Abstraction in the Rhetoric of New Journalism,' *Victorian Periodicals Review* 30, no. 1 (Spring 1997), 41–52.

Sanders, Valerie. 'Eliza Lynn Linton and the Canon,' *Rebel of the Family,* ed. Deborah T. Meem (Orchard Park, NY: Broadview, 2002), 457–487.

———. *Eve's Renegades: Victorian Antifeminist Women Novelists* (New York: St. Martin's, 1996).

Sandon, John. 'Certain Critics: An Estimate,' *Artist and Journal of Home Culture* 15 (1 March 1894), 77–78.

Schaffer, Talia. *The Forgotten Female Aesthetes: Literary Culture in Late-Victorian England* (Charlottesville, VA: University Press of Virginia, 2000).

———. 'The Importance of Being Greedy: Connoisseurship and Domesticity in the Writings of Elizabeth Robins Pennell,' *The Recipe Reader: Narratives, Contexts, Traditions,* eds. Janet Floyd and Laurel Foster (Aldershot: Ashgate, 2003), 105–126.

Schultz, R. L. *Crusader in Babylon: W. T. Stead and the Pall Mall Gazette* (Lincoln: Nebraska University Press, 1972).

Scott, Joan W. 'The Evidence of Experience,' *Critical Inquiry* 17, no. 4 (Summer 1991).

Sebba, Anne. *Battling for News: The Rise of the Woman Reporter* (London: Hodder & Stoughton, 1994).

Seeley, Tracey. 'Alice Meynell, Essayist: Taking Life "Greatly to Heart,"' *Women's Studies* 27 (1998), 105–130.

Shannon, Richard. *Gladstone and the Bulgarian Agitation* (London: Thomas Nelson, 1963).

Shaw, Flora L. 'The Australian Outlook,' *Royal Colonial Institute* 25 (1893–94), 138–165.

———. 'The British South Africa Company,' *Fortnightly Review,* 46 n.s. (November 1889), 662–668.

———. *Colonel Cheswick's Campaign,* 3 vols. (London: Longmans, Green, and Co., 1886).

———. 'Consular Protection in Morocco,' *Pall Mall Gazette* (17 October 1887), 5; (25 October 1887), 2–3; (27 October 1887), 2–3; (31 October 1887), 2–3; (9 November 1887), 2; (1 December 1887), 2–3.

———. Correspondence: Fawcett, M.G. to Shaw, Shaw Papers, Rhodes House Library, Oxford University.

——. Correspondence: Lugard, Flora to Frederick Lugard, Margery Perham Papers, Rhodes House Library, Oxford University, MP 309/1, ff. 24–25.

——. Correspondence: Shaw, Louise (Lulu) to Flora Shaw, Shaw Papers, Rhodes House Library, Oxford University.

——. Correspondence: Shaw to Charles Eliot Norton, Gibraltar, Papers of Charles Eliot Norton, Houghton Library, Harvard University.

——. Correspondence: Shaw to Colonel Charles Brackenbury, Shaw Papers, Rhodes House Library, Oxford University.

——. Correspondence: Shaw to Francis Wingate, Cairo, Wingate Papers, Sudan Archive, University of Durham.

——. Correspondence: Shaw to Lugard, Shaw Papers, Rhodes House Library, Oxford University.

——. Correspondence: Shaw to William T. Stead. Stead Papers, Churchill College, University of Cambridge.

——. 'Dry-Nursing in the Colonies,' *Fortnightly Review* 46 n.s. (September 1889), 373.

——. 'An Episode, A Story,' *New Princeton Review* 2 (1887), 106–129.

——. 'The Future of Australia,' *The Queen: The Lady's Newspaper & Court Chronicle* (Saturday, 20 January 1894), 82; *The Gentlewoman* (20 January 1894), 76.

——. 'The Future of Morocco,' Letter to the Editor, the *Morning Post* (8 November 1889), 2.

——. 'George Meredith,' *New Princeton Review* 3 (1887–1888), 220–229.

——. 'Gibraltar,' *Sunday Magazine* (July 1887), 453–459.

——. *Hector: A Story for Young People* (London: George Bell & Sons, 1882).

——. 'Letters from Australia, II. The Sugar Industry in Queensland,' *The Times* (7 January 1893).

——. 'Majorca, I,' *Sunday Magazine* 19 (May 1890), 302–308.

——. 'Majorca, II,' *Sunday Magazine* 19 (June 1890), 407–415.

——. *Phyllis Browne* (Boston: Little, Brown and Company, 1883).

——. 'Rose of Blackboy Alley – An East End Story,' *Sunday Magazine* (September–October 1883), 564–570, 597–603.

——. *A Sea Change* (London: George Routledge and Sons, 1885).

——. 'The Story of Zebehr Pasha, as told by himself, Parts I, II, and III,' *Contemporary Review* 52 (September, October, and November 1887), 333–349, 568–585, 658–682.

——. 'Under the Peak,' [Tenerife] *Good Words* 30, no. 47 (October 1889), 665–670; (November 1889), 742–747.

Shaw, Gerald. *The Garrett Papers* (Cape Town: Van Riebeeck Society, 1984).

Shelley, Lorna. 'Female Journalists and Journalism in Fin-de-siecle Magazine Stories,' *Nineteenth Century Gender Studies* 5, no. 2 (Summer 2009) http://ncgsjournal.com/issue52/shelley.htm [accessed 16 November 2011].

Showalter, Elaine. *A Literature of Their Own: British Women Novelists from Brontë to Lessing* (Princeton: Princeton University Press, 1977).

——. *Sexual Anarchy: Gender and Culture at the Fin de Siècle* (London: Bloomsbury, 1991).

Simcox, Edith. 'At Anchor,' *Fraser's Magazine* 623 (November 1881), 624–629.

——. 'Autobiographies,' *North British Review* 51 (January 1870), 383–414.

——. *Autobiography of a Shirtmaker. A Monument to the Memory of George Eliot*, eds. Constance M. Fulmer and Margaret Barfield (New York: Garland, 1998).

——. 'The Capacity of Women,' *Nineteenth Century* 127 (September 1887), 391–403.

——. 'Contemporary Literature,' *North British Review* 51, no. 101 (October 1869), 196–304.

——. 'A Diptych,' *Fraser's Magazine* 619 (July 1881), 42–56.

——. 'Eight Years of Co-Operative Shirtmaking,' *Nineteenth Century* 15 (June 1884), 1037–1054.

——. *Episodes in the Lives of Men, Women, and Lovers* (London: Trübner, 1882) and (Boston: Osgood, 1882).

——. 'Ideals of Feminine Usefulness,' *Fortnightly Review* 27, no. 161 (May 1880), 656–671.

——. 'Love and Friendship,' *Fraser's Magazine* 622 (October 1881), 448–461.

——. 'Midsummer Moon,' *Fraser's Magazine* 620 (August 1881), 204–211.

——. 'The Native Australian Family,' *Nineteenth Century* 45, no. 269 (July 1899), 41–65.

——. *Natural Law: An Essay in Ethics* (London: Trübner, 1877).

——. 'New Books,' *Fortnightly Review* 15, no. 85 (January 1874), 109–120.

——. 'On the Influence of John Stuart Mill's Writings,' *Contemporary Review* 22 (June 1873), 297–318.

——. *Primitive Civilizations, or Outline of the History of Ownership in Archaic Communities* (London: Swan Sonnenschein, 1894).

——. Rev. of *A Comtist Lover, and Other Studies* by Elizabeth Rachel Chapman, *Academy* 760 (27 November 1886), 357–359.

——. Rev. of *A Thousand Years of the Tartar* by E. H. Parker, *Academy* 1221 (28 September 1895), 239–240.

——. 'Rural Roads,' *Macmillan's Magazine* 52, no. 3 (11 September 1885), 371–393.

——. ['The Editor'] 'Women's Work and Women's Wages,' *London Times* 13, no. 11 (November 1885), 539–547.

Smedley, Constance. 'The Hedda Gabler of To-day,' *Fortnightly Review* 82 (July 1907), 77–90.

Somerset, Lady Henry. 'Annual Address,' *Woman's Signal* (25 June 1896), 405.

——. 'At the Back of the Hills,' *North American Review* 201 (January/June 1915), 727–729.

——. Correspondence: Somerset to Francis Power Cobbe, Huntington Library CB 745.

——. 'A Cry from Armenia,' Response to a Letter from Armenian Women of Constantinople to Lady Henry Somerset, *Shafts* 3, no. 9 (1895), 132.

——. 'The Darker Side,' *North American Review* 154, no. 1 (January 1892), 64–68.

——. 'Editorial,' *Woman's Herald* (10 August 1893), 392.

——. 'Foreign Troubles,' *Woman's Signal* (10 October 1895), 232.

——. 'Frances Elizabeth Willard,' *North American Review* 166:4 (April 1898), 429–436.

——. 'Introduction,' *The Life of Frances E. Willard*, Anna Adams Gordon (Evanston, Illinois: National Woman's Christian Temperance Union, 1914), ix–xii.

——. 'Introduction,' *Frances E. Willard: My Happy Half-Century*, Frances E. Willard (London: Ward, Lock, and Bowden, 1894), xiii–xvi.

——. 'Lead Editorial,' *Woman's Signal* (29 August 1895), 487.

——. 'Nagging Women: A Reply to Dr. Edson,' *North American Review* 160 (January/June 1895), 311–312.

——. 'Our Policy,' *Woman's Herald* (3 February 1893), 1.

——. *Our Village Life* (London: Sampson Low and Co), 1884.

——. 'A Personal Word From Lady Henry Somerset,' *Lend a Hand* 9, no. 4 (October 1892), 264–266.

——. 'Practical Temperance Legislation,' *Contemporary Review* 76 (October 1899), 512–527.

——. 'The Renaissance of Women,' *North American Review* 159 (July/December 1894), 490–497.

——. 'Ring out the Old,' *Woman's Herald* (21 December 1893), 2.

——. 'The Story of Our Farm,' *North American Review* 175, no. 5 (November 1902), 691–700.

——. 'Editorial,' *Woman's Signal* (22 April 1895), 121.

Spielmann, Marion H. 'Press-Day and Critics II,' *Magazine of Art* (1892), 222–228.

Stead, W.T. 'Future of Journalism,' *Contemporary Review* 50 (November 1886), 663.

——. 'The Novel of the Modern Woman,' *The Review of Reviews*, X, (1894), 64–74.

——. 'Young Women and Journalism,' *Young Woman* 1, no. 1 (October 1892), 12–14.

——. 'Young Women in Journalism,' *Review of Reviews* VI (October 1892), 373.

Stedman, E.C., ed., *A Victorian Anthology, 1837–1895: Selections Illustrating the Editor's Critical Review of British Poetry in the Reign of Victoria* (Boston: Houghton Mifflin, 1895).

Stern, Kimberly Jo. *The Victorian Sibyl: Women Reviewers and the Reinvention of Critical Tradition*. Unpublished PhD dissertation, Princeton, 2005.

Stetz, Margaret. 'New Grub Street and the Woman Writer of the 1890s,' *New Approaches to British Fiction of the 1890s*, eds Nikki Lee Manos and Meri Jane Rochilson (London: Macmillan, 1994), 21–46.

——. 'Publishing Industries and Practices,' *The Cambridge Companion to the Fin de Siècle*, ed. Gail Marshall (Cambridge: Cambridge University Press, 1997), 113–130.

Stokes, John. *In the Nineties* (New York: Harvest Wheatsheaf, 1989).

Sutherland, John. '*The Academy*,' *The Stanford Companion to Victorian Fiction* (Stanford: University of Stanford Press, 1989).

——. *The Longman Companion to Victorian Fiction* (Harlow: Longman, 1988).

Taunton, Matthew. 'People's Friend,' *Dictionary of Nineteenth-Century Journalism in Great Britain and Ireland*, eds Laurel Brake and Marysa Demoor (Ghent: Academia Press; London: British Library, 2009), 489.

'Testimony of Frances Power Cobbe: Municipal Woman Suffrage in England,' *Woman's Journal* 10, no. 11 (15 March 1879), 81.

Thring, G.H. 'History of the Society of Authors,' British Library Mss. Add. 56868–56869, f. 47.

Thornton, Alfred. *Diary of an Art Student in the 1890s* (London: Sir Isaac Pitman & Sons, Ltd., 1938).

Thoumaian, Lucy. 'Letter to the Editor,' *Woman's Signal* (6 June 1895), 416–417.

Tilley, Elizabeth. 'Trading in Knowledge: *The Irish Builder* and Nineteenth-Century Journalism,' *Revue LISA/LISA e-journal* [Online], 3, no. 1 (2005) [accessed 20 December 2011].

Tinker, Edward Larocque. *The Pennells* (London: n.p., 1951).

Tomson, Graham R. 'Eheu!' *Illustrated London News* (23 January 1892), 102.

——. '"Of Solemn Black,"' *National Observer* (19 December 1891), 121.

——. 'Mrs. Alexander,' *Independent* (9 June 1892), 1.

——. Rev. of *Ban and Arrière Ban: A Rally of Fugitive Rhymes*, by Andrew Lang, *Academy* (2 June 1894), 451.

——. Rev. of *Lachrymae Musarum, and other Poems*, by William Watson, *Academy* (26 November 1892), 476–477.

——. Rev. of *The Song of the Sword, and other Verses*, by W. E. Henley, *Academy* (25 June 1892), 607.

——. 'Women-Authors of To-day. Charlotte M. Yonge,' *Independent* (27 November 1890), 8.

——. 'Women-Authors of To-day. Mrs. Ewing,' *Independent* (6 July 1893), 5.

'Tooley, Mrs. Sarah A.,' *Who Was Who*, vol. 4 1941–1950 (1952) (London: Adam and Charles Black, 1958), 1158–1159.

Tooley, Sarah. 'The Author of "Little Lord Fauntleroy" at Home: An Interview with Mrs. Hodgson Burnett,' *Young Woman* 3, no. 32 (May 1895), 253–260.

——. 'Child Life: A Talk with the Author of "Lord Fauntleroy,"' *Woman's Signal* (11 April 1895), 226–227.

——. 'The Ethical Basis of Woman's Rights: An Interview with the Rev. Prof. Shuttleworth, M.A.,' *Woman's Signal* (10 May 1894), 382–383.

——. 'Flints, Suffrage, and Higher Education: An Interview with Mrs. Charlotte Carmichael Stopes,' *Woman's Signal* (6 June 1895), 354–355.

——. 'The Growth of a Socialist: An Interview with Mrs. Sidney Webb,' *Young Woman* 3, no. 29 (September 1895), 145–151.

——. 'The Home of a Great Preacher: An Interview with Mrs. Joseph Parker,' *Young Woman* 3, no. 28 (January 1895), 109–115.

——. 'The Horticultural College, Swanley: A Day with the Lady Gardeners,' *Woman's Signal* (26 July 1894), 49–51.

——. 'Interesting Reminiscences: A Talk with Mrs. Josephine Butler,' *Woman's Signal* (13 September 1894), 161–163.

——. 'An Interview with Annie S. Swan (Mrs. Burnett Smith),' *Woman at Home* (4 May 1895), 127–136.

——. 'The Labour Commission: Interview with Mrs. Sidney Webb,' *Woman's Signal* (12 July 1894), 17–18.

——. 'Liberal Women and the Suffrage,' *Woman's Herald* (11 July 1891), 601.

——. 'Life amongst Factory Girls: An Interview with Miss Isabel Kenward,' *Woman's Signal* (18 October 1894), 242–243.

——. 'A Living Wage for Women: A Talk with William Morris,' *Woman's Signal* (19 April 1894), 261.

——. 'The Servant Question: An Interview with Miss Clementina Black,' *Woman's Signal* (31 January 1895), 66–67.

——. 'The Triumph of Woman,' *Every Woman's Encyclopaedia*, vol. 6 (London: Amalgamated Press, 1912), 4019.

——. 'The Woman's International Conference,' *Lady's Realm* (May 1899), 90–95; reprinted *Eve's Century: A Sourcebook of Writings on Women and Journalism 1895–1918*, ed. Anne Varty (London: Routledge, 2000), 159–161.

——. 'Women at the Baptist Union,' *Women's Penny Paper* (7 December 1889), 75.

——. 'Women in our Police Courts,' *Woman's Herald* (25 July 1891), 635.

——. 'Women's Work in School Management: An Interview with Miss Harris,' *Woman's Signal* (5 April 1894), 221–223.

'Traits and Travesties, Social and Political,' [Rev. of *Episodes* by Edith Simcox]. *Athenaeum* 2850 (10 June 1882), 725–726.

'Tree of Knowledge,' *New Review* 10 (June 1894), 675–690.

Tuell, Anne Kimball. *Mrs. Meynell and her Literary Generation* (New York: E. P. Dutton, 1925).

Tusan, Michelle. 'The Business of Relief Work: A Victorian Quaker in Constantinople and her Circle,' *Victorian Studies* 51, no. 4 (Summer 2009), 633–661.

——. 'Inventing the New Woman: Print Culture and Identity Politics during the *Fin-de-Siècle*,' *Victorian Periodicals Review*, 31, no. 2 (Summer 1998), 169–182.

——. *Women Making News: Gender and Journalism in Modern Britain* (Urbana: University of Illinois Press, 2005).

Tweedie, Ethel Brilliana. 'A Chat with Mrs. Lynn Linton,' *Temple Bar* 102 (July 1894), 355–364.

Tyrrell, Ian. 'Lady Isabella Caroline Somerset,' *Dictionary of National Biography* (Oxford: Oxford University Press, 2004).

Valtin, Alison. 'Clementina Black,' *Prose by Victorian Women: An Anthology*, eds Andrea Broomfield and Sally Mitchell (New York and London: Garland, 1996).

VanArsdel, Rosemary. *Florence Fenwick-Miller* (Aldershot, UK: Ashgate, 2001).

——. 'Mrs. Florence Fenwick-Miller and *The Woman's Signal*, 1895–1899,' *Victorian Periodicals Review* (Fall 1982), 107–118.

——. 'Women's Periodicals and the New Journalism: The Personal Interview,' *Papers for the Millions: The New Journalism in Britain, 1850s to 1914*, ed. Joel H. Wiener (New York: Greenwood, 1988), 243–256.

Vicinus, Martha. *Intimate Friends: Women Who Loved Women, 1778–1928* (Chicago: University of Chicago Press, 2004).

Wagner, Tamara. *Antifeminism and the Victorian Novel* (New York: Cambria, 2009).

Walker, Linda. 'Friederichs, Hulda (1856/7–1927),' *Oxford Dictionary of National Biography* (Oxford University Press, 2004).

Waller, Philip. *Writers, Readers, and Reputations: Literary Life in Britain 1870–1918* (Oxford: Oxford University Press, 2006).

Waltman, John Lawrence. *The Early London Journals of Elizabeth Robins Pennell*. University of Texas at Austin, unpublished PhD dissertation, 1976.

Watson, Rosamund Marriott. 'Tares: A Book of Verses,' *Bibelot* (1 January 1898), 159.

'What Women May Do,' *Woman* (23 and 30 March 1892), 3–4.

Wilkes, Joanne. *Women Reviewing Women in Nineteenth-Century Britain* (Aldershot: Ashgate, 2010).

Willard, Frances E. 'Mrs. Sarah Tooley: An Interviewer Interviewed,' *Woman's Signal* (15 March 1894), 169–171.

'Woman Suffrage Leaflets,' *Woman's Journal* 25, no. 3 (15 September 1894), 295.

Woolf, Virginia. *The Diary of Virginia Woolf*, vol. 2 (1920–1924), ed. Anne Olivier Bell (London: Hogarth Press, 1978).

Zierer, Laurie. 'Edith Jemima Simcox,' *Prose by Victorian Women: An Anthology*, eds Andrea Broomfield and Sally Mitchell (New York and London: Garland, 1996), 523–525.

Index